# Dark Forces at Work

# LEXINGTON BOOKS HORROR STUDIES

Series Editor:
Carl Sederholm, Brigham Young University

Lexington Books Horror Studies is looking for original and interdisciplinary monographs or edited volumes that expand our understanding of horror as an important cultural phenomenon. We are particularly interested in critical approaches to horror that explore why horror is such a common part of culture, why it resonates with audiences so much, and what its popularity reveals about human cultures generally. To that end, the series will cover a wide range of periods, movements, and cultures that are pertinent to horror studies. We will gladly consider work on individual key figures (e.g., directors, authors, show runners, etc.), but the larger aim is to publish work that engages with the place of horror within cultures. Given this broad scope, we are interested in work that addresses a wide range of media, including film, literature, television, comics, pulp magazines, video games, or music. We are also interested in work that engages with the history of horror, including the history of horror-related scholarship.

**Titles in the Series**
*Dark Forces at Work: Essays on Social Dynamics and Cinematic Horrors*, edited by Cynthia J. Miller and A. Bowdoin Van Riper

# Dark Forces at Work

## Essays on Social Dynamics and Cinematic Horrors

Edited by Cynthia J. Miller
and A. Bowdoin Van Riper

LEXINGTON BOOKS
*Lanham • Boulder • New York •London*

Published by Lexington Books
An imprint of The Rowman & Littlefield Publishing Group, Inc.
4501 Forbes Blvd., Ste. 200, Lanham, MD 20706
www.rowman.com

6 Tinworth Street, London SE11 5AL, United Kingdom

Copyright © 2020 The Rowman & Littlefield Publishing Group, Inc.

*All rights reserved.* No part of this book may be reproduced in any form or by any electronic or mechanical means, including information storage and retrieval systems, without written permission from the publisher, except by a reviewer who may quote passages in a review.

British Library Cataloguing in Publication Information Available

**Library of Congress Cataloging-in-Publication Data available**

Names: Miller, Cynthia J., 1958- editor. | Van Riper, A. Bowdoin, editor.
Title: Dark Forces at work : essays on social dynamics and cinematic horrors / edited by Cynthia J. Miller, A. Bowdoin Van Riper.
Description: Lanham : Lexington Books, 2019. | Series: Lexington Books horror studies | Includes bibliographical references and index.
Identifiers: LCCN 2019040467 (print) | LCCN 2019040468 (ebook) | ISBN 9781498588553 (cloth) | ISBN 9781498588560 (epub) | ISBN 9781498588577 (pbk)
Subjects: LCSH: Horror films—History and criticism. | Monsters in motion pictures. | Motion pictures—Social aspects.
Classification: LCC PN1995.9.H6 D255 2019 (print) | LCC PN1995.9.H6 (ebook) | DDC 791.436164—dc23
LC record available at https://lccn.loc.gov/2019040467
LC ebook record available at https://lccn.lco.gov.2019040468

For everyone who, in a world beset by dark forces, still believes in the "better angels of our nature"

# Contents

Acknowledgments — x

Introduction — 1

## PART I. NATIONAL IDENTITY: HAUNTING THE HOMELAND

1. Ringing Home, Missed Calls, and Unbroken Land-Lines: Domestication of, and Miscommunication in, K- and J- Horror — 15
   *Rea Amit*

2. Redefining the *Heimat*: Austrian Horror Cinema and the "Home" in a Global Age — 33
   *Michael Fuchs*

3. Korean National Trauma and the Myth of Hypermasculinity in *The Wailing* (2016) — 53
   *Luisa Hyojin Koo*

4. The Witch, the Wolf, and the Monster: Monstrous Bodies and Empire in *Penny Dreadful* — 63
   *Allyson Marino*

## PART II. MARKET FORCES AND THEIR MONSTERS

5. Recession Horror: The Haunted Housing Crisis in Contemporary Fiction — 79
   *Lindsey Michael Banco*

6  Classism and Horror in the 1970s: The Rural Dweller as a Monster 99
*Erika Tiburcio Moreno*

7  All against All: Dystopia, Dark Forces, and Hobbesian Anarchy in the *Purge* Films 115
*A. Bowdoin Van Riper*

8  Motor City Gothic: White Youth and Economic Anxiety in *It Follows* and *Don't Breathe* 131
*Russell Meeuf and Benjamin James*

## PART III. IDEOLOGY: YOU JUST HAVE TO BELIEVE

9  Gothic Neoliberalism in 1980s British Horror Cinema 147
*Fernando Gabriel Pagnoni Berns, Juan Juvé, and Emiliano Aguilar*

10  Infringing on Cycles of Oppression: Artisanal Bricolage and Synthesis in Mumblegore 163
*Brandon Niezgoda*

11  Faith as Confinement: Alejandro Amenábar's *The Others* (2004) 181
*Maria Gil Poisa*

## PART IV. HISTORY NEVER DIES

12  The Pursuit of Certainty: Legends and Local Knowledge in *Candyman* 195
*Cynthia J. Miller*

13  "Nothing Is What It Seems": Montage and Misread Histories in Nicolas Roeg's *Don't Look Now* (1973) 211
*Thomas Prasch*

14  "Tens of Thousands of Men Died Here": Desire, Revenge, and Memories of War in Edgar G. Ulmer's *The Black Cat* 227
*James J. Ward*

15  Peril, Imprisonment, and the Power of Place in Jordan Peele's *Get Out* 247
*Michael C. Reiff*

# PART V. THE HORRORS OF PLACE

16  The Hovel Condemned: The Environmental Psychology of Place in Horror  267
    *Jacqueline Morrill*

17  Coming Home to Horror: Stephen King's Derry and Castle Rock  279
    *Alissa Burger*

18  *It Follows* and the Uncertainties of the Middle Class  293
    *Katherine Lizza*

19  "We're All in Our Private Traps": Reconfiguring Suburbia's Protective Borders in *Psycho* (1960)  305
    *Kevin Thomas McKenna*

Index  323

About the Editors  331

About the Contributors  333

# Acknowledgments

Our deepest thanks to all of the wonderful colleagues who have contributed their time, energy, and creativity to this project, shining their lights in the darkened corners where our fears and anxieties dwell. As with any scholarly work, this collection also owes its existence to all those scholars, in and out of the horror genre, who have been thinking and writing about cinematic grapplings with the forces that shape our personal and social worlds, and we would like to thank them, as well. Of course, our thanks to Judith Lakamper and the rest of the team at Lexington for their support of this project, from start to finish.

# Introduction

## Cynthia J. Miller and A. Bowdoin Van Riper

From childhood onward, we are all accustomed to tales of the monstrous—things that go "bump" in the night and threaten our fragile sense of safety at home; the terrors of strangers and strange places; the horrifying costs of tempting fate and venturing into the unknown. As we grow older, we recognize the social and psychological urges that set these cautionary tales in motion, yet their power never completely fades. Instead, they shift, just a bit—adjusting their tone to the adults that we have become—but they continue to whisper warning. Creaking floorboards no longer signal the awakening of the monster under the bed, but rather, the possibility of an intruder invading our home; mysterious strangers are no longer manifestations of the supernatural, but rather, agents of foreign or domestic terror; the decrepit house at the end of the road no longer speaks to our fascination with the unknown, but rather, to our deep-seated fears of poverty and isolation. We have grown up, and our fears have grown with us, like a suit of clothes that somehow always seems to fit.

It's often said that every era gets the monster it needs, and in many ways, it seems that our need has become great. Nationalism, religion, race, gender, and political economy are all widely acknowledged sources from which our notions about the monstrous rise up and manifest in films across genres. In his seminal 1996 article "Monster Culture: Seven Theses," Jeffrey Cohen points to these social forces, and the fears they engender, as the root of our understandings of monsters and the monstrous, as does Timothy Beal in "Our Monsters, Ourselves" (2001).[1] However, there has been little sustained work to date that grounds its analysis in the films, rather than the theories, in order to explore the ways in which institutions, identities, and ideologies work in the horror genre. This collection brings new scholarly work to that conversation, focusing on the social forces and ideologies that play a key role in constructing and framing fear, monsters, and the monstrous in horror films. Of particular interest here is the ways in which our lives are increasingly shaped by our fears, leading us to embrace surveillance, grasp for control and certainty, shore up the barriers between ourselves and others, and punish difference. The forces that move, and move through, our personal and social worlds have, indeed, become dark.

## HIDDEN HANDS AND UNSEEN CURRENTS

"I am the master of my fate," Victorian poet William Ernest Henley stoutly declared in 1875. "I am the captain of my soul." Born into the most privileged class of what was then the most powerful nation on Earth, he had the luxury—as the citizens of Britain's far-flung empire or the working-class residents of his native Gloucester did not—of believing it was true. That he *did* believe it (or profess to believe it) says, ironically, less about the contours of his own thoughts than about the web of social and cultural influences within which those thoughts were formed. The ability of individuals to transcend their circumstances through work and will, the transformative power of self-improvement, and the certainty that the unfettered market would reward the virtuous and hard-working while punishing the wicked and idle, were commonplaces of the Victorian elite.

Henley's celebration of individual autonomy remains popular—an internet search for "master of my fate" in conjunction with "captain of my soul" yields half-a-million results—but the foundations of our belief in it have steadily eroded. Evicted from the center of the cosmos in the late seventeenth century, and ousted from the center of the natural world in the mid-nineteenth century, humans found their dominion over their own thoughts and actions challenged in the first decades of the twentieth century.[2] The pioneering works of Sigmund Freud in psychology, Franz Boas in cultural anthropology, and Thorstein Veblen in economics (among many others) suggested that humans move through life like rowers who, though seemingly able to choose their direction and speed at will, are simultaneously borne to their ultimate destination by powerful currents of which they are barely aware.[3] The political, economic, and social upheavals of the new century reinforced a worldview that emphasized abstract forces, rather than the acts of "great men," as the driver of historical change.[4] Particularly in the years after 1945, works in the burgeoning genres of popular psychology and sociology promised to reveal the ways in which such forces shape the lives of individuals, neighborhoods, and communities.[5]

Stephen Pinker, among others, has argued that these unseen forces need not be deleterious.[6] Even sociocultural and economic forces that are capable of fostering great good in the societies on which they act can, in the end, be a double-edged sword. The staggering efficiency of industrial capitalism raises standards of living and broadens the distribution of wealth, but drives its beneficiaries to irrational patterns of consumption and traps its victims in a downward spiral of loss and despair. Nationalism can be a source of shared pride and a bulwark of resistance to conquest and tyranny, but also a breeding ground for xenophobia, prejudice, and violence against those deemed "other." The motivating power of ideology—shared belief in a transcendent idea—can bring about, in years or even months, changes that the slow-turning wheels of practical politics might take a generation to accomplish. Once unleashed and hurtling forward, however, that power is always at risk of escaping the control of those who set it in motion—a result played out so often in the modern era that historian Eric Hobsbawm dubbed the twentieth century "the Age of Extremes."[7]

Geography and history modulate those forces—ideologies, nationalisms, and markets are all shaped by the specific places and times in which they arise—but also exert their own, independent influence. More than just a reiteration of national or regional cultural differences in other terms, geography is also about communities. The social dynamics specific to tiny rural villages, sprawling bedroom suburbs, or dying industrial cities create habits, and leave mental scars, that residents of those places—even if their homes are separated from one another by thousands of miles—readily recognize in one another. The impact of history is even more pervasive and even more profound. "The past is never dead," William Faulkner wrote. "It's not even past."[8] A son of the early-twentieth-century American South, who watched memories of an older world cast dark shadows over the newer one being built around him, he had reason to know.

The hidden forces that shape our lives—little glimpsed, less understood—need not be feared, but those that drive the films considered in this volume are "dark" in their effect, as well as their covert nature. Like the personified monsters of our childhoods, we know *just* enough about them to be fearful, but not enough to combat them until it is, perhaps, too late.

## MAKING MONSTERS

Fear, as David Scruton observes, "is a social act which occurs within a cultural matrix," and thus serves as the connective tissue linking the individual, society, and horror.[9] It is, as H. P. Lovecraft contended, "the oldest and strongest emotion of mankind," and "the oldest and strongest kind of fear is fear of the unknown."[10] Terror, after all, he notes, appears in the earliest folklore, sacred writings, and chronicles as human beings sought to exert control over their increasingly complex relationships with their natural and social environments.[11] This is as true in the contemporary moment—when history, individuality, subjectivity and culture are all "composed of a multitude of fragments"—as it was at the time of Lovecraft's writing.[12] Difference, change, risk, the perception of scarcity, the striving for power—all challenge our mastery of our worlds and are capable of evoking that ancient emotion. As Cohen posits,

> The monster is born at [a] metaphoric crossroads, as an embodiment of a certain cultural moment—of a time, a feeling, and a place . . . [incorporating] fear, desire anxiety, and fantasy, giving them life, and an uncanny independence.[13]

The horror genre, with its tales of the supernatural, the morbidly perverse, the gruesome and the grotesque, offers a ready vehicle for addressing that fear. Our real-world "monsters" shift into fantastic guises that loosen them from their social moorings, allowing us to reimagine our relationship with them and safely experience their presence in our lives. Our monsters, after all, are us.[14]

Motion pictures, in particular, allow us to give shape and form to our anxieties and imagine the outcomes of our moral struggles. The world of the cinema is liminal space: We cross the threshold and enter into darkness, where time is seemingly held in suspension, and experience the drama on the screen, no longer existing in the world outside the theater, yet not part of the world of the narrative. Our external lives are unchanged—we have not, in fact, battled the undead, been possessed by demons, faced attacks by aliens, or been held captive by cannibalistic hillbillies—yet our inner worlds have, at least temporarily, transformed.

Horror movies have, from the genre's very beginnings, engaged with social issues, institutions, and ideologies. They are, as Andrew Tudor describes, an "embedded feature of our social lives"—neither a proximal cause nor a direct reflection of our attitudes and behaviors, but part of the process of producing and reproducing culture.[15] As such, the genre defines and portrays the fearful as well as "providing the building blocks out of which people construct the experience of fear itself."[16] Plastic and responsive, as the social context shifts and changes, horror films shift and change, in tandem. Countless examples may be drawn from horror staples: Vampire films that critique diseased aristocracy in one era address fears of homosexuality and contagion in another, and economic anxieties in still another.[17] Similarly, in over eighty years of horror films, zombies have been mobilized to address anxieties surrounding racism, communism, contagion, and atomic destruction, as well as to critique consumerism, greed, and political entropy.[18] Monsters plague our consciousness as we strive for a future free of constraints, only to fall back in fear.

Religion, science, the proliferation of technology, fears of aging, globalization, violence, and political unrest have all received significant attention in horror cinema—all united by overarching themes of loss of control and the struggle against disorder, or what Jeffrey Cohen has termed "category crisis."[19] In the world of horror cinema, as in the real world, the struggle to keep doubt and chaos at bay is ongoing, particularly as the foundations of social legitimacy continue to erode. Fear of social change, anxiety surrounding contradiction, terror over impotence all inform our horror narratives, along with the confusion that follows in their wake. As Tudor suggests:

> No longer sheltered by the unquestioned values of traditional social order, we find ourselves faced with the fearful prospect of unpredictable social relations in a world now open to the possibility of escalating chaos.[20]

Change, however, is inevitable. Dark forces are at work. Let the horror begin.

## DARK FORCES

Divided into five sections, *Dark Forces* begins with one entitled "National Identity: Haunting the Homeland." The opening essay of the section and the book, Rea Amit's "Ringing Home, Missed Calls, and Unbroken Land-Lines: Domestication of, and Miscommunication in, K- and J- Horror," uses modern telecommunication technology as a lens through which to examine the fraught relationship between Korea and Japan. A century of conquest, colonization, exploitation, and halting rapprochement between the two countries has, in recent decades, given way to freer exchanges of cultural products, including nationally branded horror films. Despite this, Amit argues, the substance of the films reflects not only unresolved tensions between the two countries, but between their citizens and the social pressures of the modern world. The next essay, Michael Fuchs's "Redefining the *Heimat*: Austrian Horror Cinema and the 'Home' in a Global Age," shows how the *Heimat* film—a silent-era subgenre specific to German-language cinema—has been fused with American horror conventions to create *Dead in 3 Days*, *Dead in 3 Days 2*, and *Blood Glacier*. Traditional *Heimat* films used sweeping landscape vistas as a way to reinforce Austrian national identity. The new *Heimat*-horror hybrids, Fuchs argues, retain that focus but, mindful of the growing transnational threats such as global warming, transform "home" from a national identity to a global one.

The figure of the powerful patriarch, Luisa Hyojin Koo argues, is central not just to Korean film, but to Korean national identity. The patriarch—capable of taking charge of, and resolving, any situation—embodies Korean masculinity and national strength, and films committed to the "rejuvenation" of the patriarch-figure (and thus the nation) have become common in recent years. In "Korean National Trauma and the Myth of Hypermasculinity in *The Wailing* (2016)," however, Koo examines a popular Korean horror film that deliberately subverts these associations. *The Wailing,* she argues, features a patriarch-hero who defies Korean ideas about masculinity and presents women and Japanese nationals not (as in traditional films) as its enemies, but as its innocent victims. The first section concludes with Allyson Marino's "The Witch, the Wolf, and the Monster: Monstrous Bodies and Empire in *Penny Dreadful*," which reads the literary monsters featured in the Showtime television series as symbols of Britain's struggle to define a new identity for itself amid the cultural cross-currents created by industrialization and imperialism. The principal characters definition of "self" is, Marino contends, complicated throughout the series not only by their outsider status—as literal monsters or, in protagonist Vanessa Ives's case, as a woman in society defined by its violent misogyny—but by Britain's uncertainty over the identity of its (national) self.

The second section, "Market Forces and Their Monsters," considers tales that use economics as the wellspring of their horror. Lindsey Michael Banco begins by connecting the cycle of haunted-house films that began with *The Amityville Horror* with a slightly older, and far broader, cycle of haunted-house novels that established many of the subgenre's central tropes and themes. His essay "Recession Horror: The Haunted Housing Crisis in Contemporary Fiction" shows that social issues such as gentrification, urban flight, and the pursuit of upward mobility in economically precarious times are as central to the horror in such tales as traditional ghosts and monsters, allowing them to articulate deeper, more broadly resonant fears. Homes also figure prominently in the next essay, Erika Tiburcio Moreno's "Classism and Horror in the 1970s: The Rural Dweller as a Monster." A close reading of two films from the redneck-horror subgenre inaugurated in the 1970s, it shows how the killers' cluttered, bizarrely decorated homes function as a reflection not only of their disordered minds, but—by flouting the very norms of "good taste" that society expects them to emulate—of their irredeemably lower-class status. Classism lies at the core of such films, Moreno concludes, turning nominally human individuals into monstrous Others.

Class divisions are also evident in "All against All: Dystopia, Dark Forces, and Hobbesian Anarchy in the *Purge* Films," A. Bowdoin Van Riper's study of a trilogy of films that combine the conventions of traditional horror and science-fiction dystopia. Van Riper explores how the violent acts portrayed in the films—committed on the single night each year when all crime is legal—paint a terrifying picture of human nature. Rather than freeing the criminal dregs of society to kill one another and encouraging the strong to exterminate the weak, as the architects of the Purge intend, the annual night of anarchy instead reveals the razor-thin line that divides ordinary people from monsters. Tales of empty streets, crumbling buildings, and desperate circumstances, the films that Russell Meeuf and Benjamin James explore in the final essay of the section also have a dystopian feel. They take place, however, not in a science-fictional future, but in the once thriving industrial downtown and middle-class neighborhoods of present-day Detroit, now left desolate by the Great Recession of 2007. In "Motor City Gothic: White Youth and Economic Anxiety in *It Follows* and *Don't Breathe*," the authors examine the films' use of traditional horror tropes to explore the fears of young, white, middle-class Detroiters that the economic collapse has left them with no home, no way to make a living, and no future.

The third section—"Ideology: You Just Have to Believe"—begins with an essay, "Gothic Neoliberalism in 1980s British Horror Cinema," that situates films such as *Hellraiser, Scream for Help,* and *Dream Demon* amid the Conservative Party ascendancy led by Margaret Thatcher. Authors Fernando Gabriel Pagnoni Berns, Juan Juvé, and Emiliano Aguilar argue that the films' modernization of Gothic horror tropes such as family decay, oppression of women, and an atmosphere of brooding menace and fear serve as a commentary on the ultraconservative ideology of Thatcher and her followers and its transformative impact on British society. It is followed by Brandon Niezgoda's essay, "Infringing on Cycles of Oppression: Artisanal Bricolage and Synthesis in Mumblegore," which traces the efforts of a group of young filmmakers to create an alternative model of film production, disrupting the Hollywood power structures that have facilitated sexual harassment in the film industry. "Mumblegore" films apply the collective, independent spirit of the "Mumblecore" movement to the horror genre, while using horror elements to comment on the treatment of women on traditional Hollywood sets.

In the section's final essay, "Faith as Confinement: Alejandro Amenábar's *The Others* (2004)," Maria Gil Poisa examines an unexpected narrative that combines the Gothic tradition with critical—particularly Spanish—commentary on the Catholic faith. The film, a ghostly home invasion story, focuses on a devout and overprotective mother who suffers, along with her children, from photosensitivity. As she keeps her family safely shuttered in their home, isolated from the world around them, the film's narrative examines the real and metaphorical darkness created by her blind faith. Gil Poisa explores the ways in which the family's home, which should be a site of safety, becomes a prison that obscures the truth.

The volume's fourth section, "History Never Dies," features a series of essays examining films that make manifest the horrors of the past, reminding us that they continue to lurk just below the surface of our daily lives. In "The Pursuit of Certainty: Legends and Local Knowledge in *Candyman*," Cynthia J. Miller looks at competing claims to knowledge and truth in Bernard Rose's classic tale of grisly murders in the Cabrini-Green housing project of Chicago. Miller argues that issues of race, class, and gender all play a role in truth-claims about horrors that pit the certainties of privileged white academics and authorities against those of the marginalized black residents of the projects. Thomas Prasch's essay, "'Nothing Is What It Seems': Montage and Misread Histories in Nicolas Roeg's *Don't Look Now* (1973)" continues this thread of uncertainty, but follows a very different path. Here, Prasch examines Roeg's use of montage in the film to create a complex—and conflicted—narrative that illustrates, on numerous levels, that nothing is what it seems. This premise, Prasch argues, can be applied to emotions, relationships, ideologies, time, and even fate itself. Roeg's jarring style, he notes, blurs past, present, and future for both the characters and the film's audiences, with sometimes horrifying consequences.

In the essay that follows, James J. Ward explores the ways in which real-world history and horror are merged—and conflated—in "Tens of Thousands of Men Died Here": Desire, Revenge, and Memories of War in Edgar G. Ulmer's *The Black Cat*." Here, Ward unpacks the film's monstrous imagery to examine the role played by both Ulmer's exposure to the horrors of war growing up in Vienna and the shared historical consciousness of those residing in "the bloodlands" of eastern and central Europe. Ward then illustrates how these two historically generated elements fueled the director's creation of a cinematic geography of evil that had no rival. The section closes with a look at a more contemporary film that brings us back to the merging of race, class, economics, and ideological horrors in Michael C. Reiff's essay, "Peril, Imprisonment and the Power of Place in Jordan Peele's *Get Out*." Here, Reiff examines the ways in which Peele uses the racialized horrors of *Get Out* to consider the wider ramifications of what the United States—a home to diverse peoples with disparate and often contradictory histories—stands for in the twenty-first century. Reiff's essay also situates Peele's voice as a director in the field of other current thinkers on race, location, and home in current discourse on American national identity.

The volume's final section explores "The Horrors of Place." Here, however, place serves as much more than just a setting for horror; rather, it is a locus for identity, affect, and affiliation. In "The Hovel Condemned: The

Environmental Psychology of Place in Horror," Jacqueline Morrill looks at several generations of damaged families who dwell within damaged homes and then go on to ultimately damage other people—specifically, those who judge and invade what they cannot understand. Through films such as *Texas Chainsaw Massacre* (1974), *Scream* (1996), *House of 1000 Corpses* (2003) and its sequel *The Devil's Rejects* (2005), and *Halloween* (2007), Morrill examines the intimate connection between home and horror.

In the section's next essay, "Coming Home to Horror: Stephen King's Derry and Castle Rock," Alissa Burger explores the contrast, in both Tommy Lee Wallace's 1990 miniseries and Andrés Muschetti's 2017 big-screen blockbuster, between home as a small-town ideal and the dark realities of the characters' individual houses, as well as the ways in which horror is inextricable from the idea of home. Burger frames her discussion within a contrast of the ideal imagined versus the horrific reality that Derry presents, in order to interrogate the connections between the past and the present, the home and the horrific. In "*It Follows* and the Uncertainties of the Middle Class," Katherine Lizza continues the section's critical inquiry into place, as she examines the ways in which the 2014 film exploits the vulnerabilities of a population concerned with maintaining working-class whiteness. Lizza argues that *It Follows* is, at its heart, a narrative about the fears of the middle-class, and in particular, anxieties surrounding financial stability. Its horrors increase as it blurs the distinctions between affluence and poverty in the characters' movements through Detroit and its neighboring suburbs.

The section and the volume close with a look at one of horror's classic homes, in Kevin McKenna's essay, "'We're All in Our Private Traps': Reconfiguring Suburbia's Protective Borders in *Psycho.*" Here, McKenna offers an examination of Alfred Hitchcock's *Psycho* (1960), which explores Marion's and Norman's homes as emblematic of suburbanization's desires, failures, and contradictions as a politically sanctioned ideal during the late 1950s. McKenna argues that both characters violate legal, geographical, and domestic boundaries and as a result open up to ambiguous identifications of monster and victim in the liminal setting of the Bates Motel, yet on a deeper level both share a desire for suburbanization's promises of clear boundaries between urban from suburban and protective privacy from the threatening public sphere.

## NOTES

1. Cohen, "Monster Theory: Seven Theses;" Beal, "Our Monsters, Ourselves."
2. Cohen, *Birth of a New Physics;* Dennett, *Darwin's Dangerous Idea*; Van Riper, *Men among the Mammoths*, 144–183.
3. Porter and Ross, eds., *History of the Modern Social Sciences.*

4. For example, Frederick Jackson Turner's "Frontier Thesis" in the 1890s and Charles Beard's interpretation of the Constitution as a product of economic, rather than idealistic, influences in the 1910s.

5. See, for example: Wylie, *Generation of Vipers;* Packard, *Hidden Persuaders*; Friedan, *Feminine Mystique*; Underhill, *Why We Buy,* and Turkle, *Alone Together.*

6. Pinker, *Better Angels of Our Nature.*

7. Hobsbawm, *Age of Extremes.*

8. Faulkner, *Requiem for a Nun*, act 1, scene 3.

9. Scruton, *Anthropology of Fear*, 10.

10. Lovecraft "Supernatural Horror in Literature."

11. Ibid.

12. Cohen, "Monster Culture," 3.

13. Ibid, 4.

14. Beal, "Our Monsters, Ourselves."

15. Tudor, *Monsters and Mad Scientists*, 212.

16. Ibid., 212–213.

17. For example, compare *Dracula* (1931), *Fearless Vampire Killers* (1967), and *Near Dark* (1987).

18. For example, see *White Zombie* (1932), *Creature with the Atom Brain* (1955), *Night of the Living Dead* (1968), *Dawn of the Dead* (1978), *28 Days Later* (2002), and *Fido* (2006).

19. Cohen, "Monster Culture," 6–7.

20. Tudor, *Monsters and Mad Scientists*, 223.

## BIBLIOGRAPHY

Beal, Timothy K. "Our Monsters, Ourselves." *Chronicle of Higher Education* 48, no. 11 (2001): B18.

Cohen, I. Bernard. *The Birth of a New Physics*, revised and updated edition. New York: Norton, 1985.

Cohen, Jeffrey Jerome. "Monster Culture: Seven Theses." In *Monster Theory: Reading Culture*, 3–25. Minneapolis: University of Minnesota Press, 1996.

Dennett, Daniel C. *Darwin's Dangerous Idea: Evolution and the Meaning of Life.* New York: Simon and Schuster, 1995.

Faulkner, William. *Requiem for a Nun.* New York: Vintage, 1951.

Friedan, *The Feminine Mystique.* New York: Norton, 1963.

Hobsbawm, Eric J. *The Age of Extremes: A History of the World, 1914–1991.* New York: Vintage, 1996.

Lovecraft, H. P. "Supernatural Horror in Literature." 1927, rev. 1933–1934. *The H. P. Lovecraft Archive.* http://www.hplovecraft.com/writings/texts/essays/shil.aspx

Packard, Vance. *The Hidden Persuaders.* New York: McKay, 1957.

Pinker, Steven. *The Better Angels of Our Nature: Why Violence Has Declined.* New York: Viking, 2011.

Porter, Theodore, and Dorothy Ross, eds. *History of the Modern Social Sciences.* [Cambridge History of Science, vol. 7]. Cambridge: Cambridge University Press, 2003.

Scruton, David, ed. *Sociophobics: The Anthropology of Fear.* Boulder, CO: Westview Press, 1986.

Tudor, Andrew. *Monsters and Mad Scientists: A Cultural History of the Horror Movie.* London: Blackwell, 1989.

Turkle, Sherry. *Alone Together: Why We Expect More of Technology and Less of Ourselves.* New York: Basic Books, 2011.

Underhill, Paco. *Why We Buy: The Science of Shopping.* New York: Simon and Schuster, 1999.

Van Riper, A. Bowdoin. *Men among the Mammoths: Victorian Science and the Discovery of Human Prehistory.* Chicago: University of Chicago Press, 1993.

Wylie, Philip. *Generation of Vipers.* 1942. New York: Rinehart, 1955.

*Part I*

# NATIONAL IDENTITY: HAUNTING THE HOMELAND

*Chapter One*

# Ringing Home, Missed Calls, and Unbroken Land-Lines

## Domestication of, and Miscommunication in, K- and J-Horror

Rea Amit

This essay explores representations of misconnections between the domestic and public spheres in adaptations and remakes of South Korean and Japanese horror films. These depictions of failed forms of communication are emblematic of technophobia, as well as threats to the notion of national identity at the end of the twentieth and the beginning of the twenty-first century.

Relationships between the Japanese and Korean peoples are overshadowed by a history of horrific colonization. Although Japan played an important role in establishing the Korean film industry,[1] Japanese cultural products, including films, were banned on the Korean peninsula for many years after World War II.[2] During the 1990s and early 2000s, despite minor geopolitical and other disputes, the countries seemed to the outside world to have come to terms with their problematic shared past.[3] This is partially thanks to international global flows. For example, since the 1990s, Hollywood has remade many Japanese and South Korean films, which circulate throughout the world as international or transnational cultural products. This internationalization of culture has led nationally branded products such as K- and J-pop, television dramas, and horror films, to be equally well received on both sides of the Daehan/Tsushima Strait.

Despite globalization and geographic proximity, as well as linguistic and cultural similarities, however, there is still more that separates the two countries than connects them. Resentment toward Koreans in Japan and toward Japanese in South Korea is widespread on social media, where nationalistic, xenophobic, and jingoistic sentiments loom large. Just as globalization has failed to overcome traditional cultural divides, new forms of communication have failed to foster new relationships between the two societies.

The antagonism between South Korea and Japan is evident in the two countries' branded K- and J-horror films. This essay explores four: *Ringu*

(1998), *The Ring Virus* (1999), *Phone* (2002), and *One Missed Call* (2003). As remakes (or, in the case of *One Missed Call,* alleged remakes), these four films might suggest a renewed connection between the countries, as well as—given the centrality of mobile phones in these films—new possibilities for social interactions. However, given what was gained and lost through the adaptation processes, and the tensions between individuals and society in the films, the films ultimately depict claustrophobic closed spaces that are part of larger domestic spheres. Although landline phones do appear in these films, cellular phones play a more significant role, remapping spaces between the home and the outside by drawing lines of spatial insularity. These are vivid lines on the land that emphasize the threat posed by an outside invader to the domestic sphere, which is simultaneously private and emblematic of a shared national identity.

## FEAR OF PHONES

Wes Craven's 1996 film *Scream* represents a milestone in the history of cellular phones in horror cinema. In one scene, an anonymous caller on a cell phone tells a woman speaking on a landline that he is just outside the house, ready to break in. Cell phones thus allow greater mobility and means with which to terrorize victims. As Allison Whitney explains:

> These fears are enhanced by the cell phone's close connection to the body of its user, rather than the fixed location of a land line. The cell phone also facilitates the further breakdown of public and private distinctions, but now in an opposite direction, where the private realm comes to intrude upon the public sphere.[4]

In other words, from the intruder's perspective, the victim's private space can now be anywhere, because devices for distant (tele)communication became mobile and processes of dislocation and relocation shifted with the physical space an individual occupied. The integrity of one's space in the public sphere can now be easily penetrated by the simple dialing of a code that is usually not secret.

There is nothing culturally specific about the fact that cell phones can incite fear in new ways. However, notions of public and private spaces are not the same in different societies. Indeed, East Asian countries might have slightly different ways to mark such territories. These different social and cultural norms influence the way audiences respond to various depictions in films. In Japan, for example, interiority and exteriority are normally marked not only by the position of individuals within a given space, but also by the way they talk. The Japanese terms *uchi/soto* (inside/outside) establish the way interpersonal interactions are conducted and how spaces are divided. Although every language has similar terms, as linguist Charles J. Quinn points out, in Japanese: "[t]he social domain is particularly rich in *uchi* and *soto* expressions, which place another person 'inside' or 'outside' the same bounded area as oneself."[5]

An early scene in *Ringu* demonstrates these notions. Two teenage girls, alone at one of their homes, discuss a trip one of them took with three schoolmates the week before: the group watched a video, and when it was over, the phone rang. The person who answered received a warning that she had one week left to live. While the two girls talk, the landline phone rings. Tacitly, they make a highly unusual decision: the visiting friend answers the phone. Technically, the visitor is "outside," confronting an exterior speaker on the same platform. In contrast, if the host had answered, she would have been "inside," speaking with, in a sense, a possible intruder to her domestic sphere. Fear mounts during the moments before she answers.

The host has her back to the camera, looking at her friend, who hesitates before answering the phone. Yet the visiting friend does not expect to be the person targeted. Her language is familiar, "hello" (*moshi moshi*), and not the way one would normally greet a person on the phone at one's own home. Following the conventions of the genre, fear is alleviated—it turns out that the call is from the host's mother.

*Tensions mount at the ringing of a phone in* Ringu.

## *RINGU* IN THE NEW TRANSMEDIA, TRANSNATIONAL CIRCUIT

Most scholars considering the role of media in *Ringu* have focused on VHS tapes, largely ignoring phones. This focus is understandable, because copying videocassettes is the cause of the horror. For example, Julian Stringer extrapolates from the notion of copying tapes in the film a larger statement on the relationship between media, or what she calls "media recycling," by emphasizing on the fact that the film originates from a novel, its various adaptations, and influences throughout the globe in different media formats.[6]

Mitsuyo Wada-Marciano goes further, seeing in *Ringu* a new form of transmedia commodity. Although she acknowledges the use of phones, she ultimately places much greater importance on the notion of transmission, and how the film itself is distributed worldwide through digital media, mainly on DVDs.[7] She convincingly argues that, despite a few elements in the film that require geographical knowledge about Japan, the film became, through the advances of new media, a cornerstone of Japanese horror cinema, now known as J-horror.

A later study of the film also examines its inter-medial and transnational aspects, but not by referring to videotapes, literature, or the transition to digital filmmaking. Rather, Carlos Rojas highlights the film's use of a distorted photo. He refers to Jacques Derrida's discussion of the term "parergon" in the context of painting, which allows a broader analysis of a work as a continuous process beyond the boundaries of its frames. Rojas contends that all the films influenced by *Ringu* should be considered J-horror, whether they were produced in Japan or not. He argues that the blurred photo in *Ringu* is emblematic of the blurred framework of J-horror, of what is inside this nationally framed media phenomenon (its intertext) and what is outside it (its paratexts) by virtue of its continuous copying, replays, remakes, and reframing.[8]

None of these analyses deny the culturally specific aspects of *Ringu* or the films that followed it, but they do, albeit not explicitly and perhaps unintentionally, associate the film's title and the notion of circularity. Aaron Gerow makes this point most explicitly: "'[r]ing' itself can thus refer to the endless process of making copies of copies, of images repeating images—and thus to the logic of simulacrum."[9] That is, from a global prospective, or an "outside" view, the word ring could signify a circular, or perhaps a spiral, movement that circles Japan equally along with other countries. From an "inside" perspective, however, the meaning is different. In the Japanese language, the word *ringu* does not mean circular shape, but only the sound of ringing. Scholars have largely ignored this fact and its centrality in the film's narrative, but from the film's earliest scenes, ringing and telecommunication play a crucial role. In the American adaptation of the film, *The Ring*, this significance is lost, although the film otherwise tends to closely follow the Japanese version.

## PARALLEL RINGS, DIFFERENT MEANINGS

In the opening of *The Ring*, as in that of *Ringu*, two teenage girls are at home, discussing events from the week before. Unlike the Japanese version, however, when the landline telephone rings in the American adaption, the visiting girl mentions her disbelief in the story about the cursed tape when she decides to pick up the phone. Even more significantly, she answers by announcing that it is the residence of her hosting friend, and giving their family name rather than her own. Although this practice is not unheard of in the United States, and is common in Japan, it is nonetheless a deviation from the Japanese version.

Peijen Beth Tsai points out that, in order to allow new audiences to appreciate the film, the American adaptation had to adjust conventions from the Japanese version, to match Western ones.[10] Tsai asserts that although any adaptation of a film from one language to another must do more than simply translate words, it is particularly important in horror cinema to alter certain visual codes that may work differently in Japan and in the United States. The evidence of the Japanese origins of *The Ring* lies, therefore, not in the plot, but rather in what she calls a "Japan cameo," which includes certain references to Japan and to the East Asian look of the ghost.

Similarly, Thy Phu largely ignores minute stylistic differences between the two versions and avoids criticizing cultural appropriation. Instead, she identifies both versions as J-horror, which for her is not a marker of national identity. Rather, following Chika Kinoshia, she argues: "The use of 'J' instead of 'Japanese' suggests that the prefix functions as a floating signifier [and is] aptly capturing the relative fluidity with which these films circulate," and, she adds, "J-Horror is in this sense not, if it is at all, an exclusively national cinema."[11] In other words, Phu sees in the film not as "inside" nor "outside," but rather much as other scholars writing about J-horror do: containing a mere layer of Japanese qualities, which are significant, perhaps, but only insofar as they are constantly negotiating with later films.

In sharp contrast, James Weirzbicki suggests an "inside" approach to J-horror by referring to Japanese musical traditions. For him, rather than a new subgenre, recent Japanese horror films are a continuation of what he calls "kaidan films." According to Weirzbicki, what is lost in American adaptations of Japanese horror films is a unique background sound that originates from a premodern, traditional use of horrific sounds in Japanese performance traditions. Weirzbicki situates J-horror within the broader history of Japanese horror tales and associates diegetic sounds in recent films with premodern performing arts such as the kabuki theater.

Weirzbicki is not alone in seeing connections between contemporary Japanese horror films and premodern literary traditions. Valerie Wee argues that *Ringu* is largely based on what she calls "traditional Japanese aesthetics," while *The Ring* is rooted in "Western traditions and practices."[12] Such sweeping categorizations are complicated, however, since it is difficult, for example, to see direct connections between modern and ancient Japan. Moreover, as Noriko T. Reider mentions, *kaidan*—a type of tale that became popular during the Edo Period (1603–1868)—did not all belong to the horror genre. Most revolved around mysterious (though not necessarily horrific) narratives, from which the name of the category emerged.[13]

There are, therefore, two opposing trends in the scholarship on *Ringu* and the J-horror phenomenon to which it gave rise: One tries to globalize it, while the other tries to essentialize it. Although the former is more prominent and consistent with other trends in recent transnational discourses, and although the latter is reminiscent of early writings on non-Western cultures, neither adequately captures the intricate communicative dynamics that *Ringu*, and J-horror in general, showcase.

## FROM *KAIDAN* TO K-HORROR

Although adaptation and franchising of Asian films on a large scale in the West is relatively new, Rayna Davinson has shown that the practice has a long and complex history in South Korea.[14] The Korean peninsula is the part of the Asian mainland closest to the Japanese archipelago, and the two regions are also similar in terms of culture and language; not surprisingly, therefore, there are cinematic connections between the two countries. These connections stem, however, not from the proximity of the regions but rather from the fact that Japan occupied the Korean peninsula when cinema arrived in Asia, and Korean filmmakers worked, from the earliest days of Korean cinema, under the supervision of the Japanese colonial government.[15]

The rebranding of Korean cinema after World War II was thus a matter of resistance to Japanese colonizers, and the newly installed independent Korean government banned Japanese cultural products for several decades.[16] The Korean authorities limited the showing of Japanese films in South Korea mainly to those that gained international acclaim. *Ringu* was not unique in this respect: distributers released it to South Korean theaters only after the film won an award at the Brussels International Festival of Fantasy Film.

In contrast, the Korean adaptation of the film that marked the beginning of K-horror, *The Ring Virus*, was unique in that it was "co-financed by Japanese and Korean production companies," and indicated "that the cultural embargo between the two nations was beginning to soften."[17] Although the Korean film industry by this time had produced a few domestically successful horror films, it was perhaps the Japanese adaptation that sparked the K-horror phenomenon.

*The Ring Virus* is noticeably more distinct from *Ringu* than *The Ring* is, and the difference is clear from the opening scene. Unlike the Japanese and American versions, the first ring sound in the South Korean adaptation is made by an alarm clock. This beginning is similar to that of the original book by Koji Suzuki. In *The Ring Virus*, as in the book, a single girl is in her room, studying for an exam while her parents are away. However, in contrast to both the book and other film adaptations, the girl encounters the horror while speaking on the phone with her boyfriend, who simultaneously dies.

James Byrne, explaining the discrepancies between the Japanese and Korean versions and focusing particularly on the opening, argues that the Korean version is "more involved in melodrama" than the Japanese one.[18] He contends that Japanese horror filmmakers work more to arouse fear, while their Korean counterparts invest more in the characters' general emotional states. Although this argument might be consistent with both films, it is less accurate in the opening sequences. Byrne points out the shorter, less affective opening of *The Ring Virus*. Yet, such effect might be true not just in terms of fear but also in the melodramatic aspects. Be that as it may, the entire Korean version is more faithful to the novel than the Japanese adaptation. Thus, unlike the American version, which is clearly an adaptation of the Japanese film, the Korean film, perhaps as an act of defiance, is not a remake but a new adaptation. Nonetheless, the two films communicate with each other in a manner that exposes their cultural leanings by the ways they diverge from the novel. The use of phones is telling in this respect.

Depictions of ringing and phone calls in the films are emblematic of the relationship between the films, the national film cultures from which they emerged, and the counterbranding of K- and J-horror. That is, even if the international branding of the films allows them to coexist independently, it is through indirect or broken communication between the two that they most clearly manifest themselves.

## CALLING SPHERES

The opening pages of the novel are unlike the opening of any of the films in that no phones appear. It is only in the second scene that a phone (specifically, a phone booth) is mentioned. Public phones, although indeed located outside of the domestic sphere, are still closed spaces within the public sphere and allow some degree of isolation from the outside world.

The novel takes place in 1990, before the advent of the cell phones which are prominent in the films. However, as Steve Jones points out, feelings of disconnection and alienation between individuals are common tropes in the novel.[19] Social anxiety plays out in similar ways in both the Korean and Japanese film versions, and this anxiety intensifies through the use of phones that break down the boundaries between otherwise well-defined spaces. For example, in another early scene in *Ringu* a phone rings in the home of the first victim. The viewer, however, may not be aware that it is the same location already shown. The film's main character, TV journalist Reiko Asakawa, and her son, Yōichi, are visiting relatives who have just lost their daughter to "a strange disease." The previous scene shows Reiko investigating what seems to be an unrelated case of mysterious deaths. When her cell phone rings, she is in a semidomestic sphere, but the phone call transforms the space, because the caller is her coworker. The call is not just a metaphor: the coworker tells Reiko the name of the school attended by victims in the case she is investigating. Reiko appears concerned, perhaps even frightened, by the news, but the reason for her fear is not obvious to the viewer. In effect, her public/work sphere has collapsed into her private/domestic sphere. She now knows that her relative died in a way similar to the victims of disease in her investigation, and that they all attended the same school.

In contrast, in *The Ring Virus*, a landline phone rings after the funeral in the victim's house. The caller is not looking for the film's main protagonist, Sun-ju, and the viewer neither sees nor hears the caller. Rather, the call is an interference with the postfuneral ceremonial atmosphere at the house.

In his study on cognitive socialization, Hiroshi Azuma writes that while the notions of inside/outside (*uchi* and *soto*) may have originated in Confucian ethics and govern the way Japanese social groups interact with one another, in Korea, Confucianism dictates even "intrafamilial relationships."[20] Commentators on Korean horror films, too, have pointed to possible connections between Confucian social order, or the lack thereof, as the source of horror in Korean films. This connection is particularly significant for the roles, in such films, of women—mothers, but also young girls[21]—who defy Confucian principles.

Many scholars have examined gender issues in Asian horror film in general, and Japanese and Korean horror in particular. For example, identifying the ubiquity of female ghosts in Asian horror films, Hunju Lee mentions the "era of women" in the background during the 1990s— around the time when the branding of J- and K-horror began.[22] Gender is especially pertinent to *Ringu* and its Korean counterpart, because both films present strong female protagonists who are ambitious career women and single mothers. Both films thus suggest the theme of female liberation and overall progressiveness. Although Elise Tipton dates the use of the slogan "era of women" in Japan to the early 1990s,[23] Barbara Holthus argues that mass media outlets had already started to use the term in the 1980s as a commercial scheme to sell more products to female consumers.[24] The Japanese media industry thus depicted liberated women as appealing and modern, probably before similar capitalistic strategies reached South Korea.[25]

The depiction of strong women is therefore a sign of modernization and Westernization, much like images of cutting-edge technological advances. In many respects, the cell phones in *Ringu* and *The Ring Virus* allow their protagonists to remain both resilient and feminine (at least in their roles as mothers). For example, Reiko frequently calls her son on her cell phone when she is at work. One sequence in *The Ring Virus* is especially telling with respect to the mobile phone's role in the service of new feminine agency. The first time a character uses a cell phone in the film is when Sun-ju meets a doctor to ask him about the causes of the mysterious deaths. The doctor is reluctant to answer her questions and is largely dismissive of her. He is lying down when Sun-ju first enters the room and gets up only after she takes the phone from her bag. She does not use the phone, however, just holds it until she leaves the room at the end of the scene.

In addition to epitomizing female command over technology and the role of feminine agency in creating a modern, Western atmosphere, *The Ring Virus* sends a message of defiance to *Ringu* by depicting a strong, technologically savvy female protagonist who asserts her agency within modern Korean society.

## SPIRALING FAILED FORMS OF COMMUNICATION

Japan's occupation of the Korean Peninsula continues to be a source of postwar friction between South Korea and Japan. During the 1990s, two interrelated issues fueled much of the bad blood between the only two democracies in East Asia. The first was what South Korea and other nations considered Japan's weak acknowledgment of the responsibility of its army for the atrocities committed during the war. Japan's heads of government and Emperor spoke only ambiguously about Japan's crimes during the war. South Koreans demanded a stronger apology, while Japanese wanted a softer one.[26] The other issue was Japan's efforts to present a distorted history of the war. As a result, a heated contention erupted over Japan's introduction of new history textbooks.[27] Both issues are problems of communication.

Beyond this intricate relationship, both societies were changing rapidly during the last decade of the twentieth century and into the beginning of the new century. In South Korea this change stemmed largely from the country's developing democracy, whereas in Japan the 1990s were marked by the collapse of the bubble economy, leading to what economists called a "lost decade."[28] In both countries, however, new media significantly altered daily life for the majority of the population. No single device is more significant in this regard than the cell phone.

Although technology usually aids people in their daily lives, at times a new device introduces various degrees of social angst, as mobile phones did in East Asia. For example, in his study on young mobile phone users in South Korea between 1997 and 2002, Kyong Yoon identified an extensive anxiety problem.[29] Even if such social problems are a common and temporary side effect of the "Shock of the New" symptom,[30] Larissa Hjorth showed that mobile phones introduced South Korea to a new reality while fostering the creation of new haptic and aural spaces.[31]

Japanese sociologist Hidenori Tomita echoed some of Kyong Yoon's concerns with regard to mobile phone use among youth in Japan and anticipated the new sense of reality that such devices usher in.[32] Hidenari opens his discussion by referring to the release in Japan of the South Korean film *Phone*, which he argued was emblematic of the fears the new communication

*A killer answers the ringing phone of his victim in* Phone.

medium introduced to Japanese society. The film showcases not just the calling function cell phones but their texting function, which allows characters to witness past conversations between individuals, even deceased individuals. Mysterious phone calls still play a horrific role in the film, both in terms of the narrative, and, perhaps even more importantly, in terms of film style, as seen in the image of an attacker holding a knife in one hand, answering the ringing phone of his victim during a snowstorm.

Texting plays an even more crucial part in the film. When the protagonist accesses the phone of the film's main villain (and original victim), she reads her past exchanges with her lover and discovers why she has become what Hyun-suk Seo calls a "virgin ghost" (*heonyeo-gwisin*).[33] The naming of this type of supernatural being in Korean horror films is ironic, or even cynical. In *Phone*, for example, the ghost is not really a girl with no sexual experience, but one who has been treated unfairly by her married lover and his wife. Her repressed memories cause her to come back as a ghost to unleash her revenge. The exchanges the virgin ghost in *Phone* had with her lover before being killed are left on the phone, and the protagonist reads them in what Daniel Martin calls "'repressed memories' as a method of communication."[34]

*One Missed Call* is not a legitimate remake of *Phone*. Rather, it is based on a Japanese novel. However, Mark Schilling, a prominent Japanese cinema critic, has suggested that *One Missed Call* is a remake of an unnamed Korean film.[35] Regardless, *Phone* surely influenced Japanese novelist Yasushi Akimoto and the producers of the film version of *One Missed Call*. Not only are narrative aspects (especially the centrality of the cell phone) similar, the films share stylistic elements—most notably the grotesque nature of the ghost, which did not exist in *Ringu* and *The Ring Virus*.

While the film is supposedly based on a novel, the novelist, Akimoto, achieved more acclaim in the Japanese music industry known as J-pop. The novel itself, like *Ringu*, is part of an ongoing series of books, and although the film adaptation largely falls into the J-horror category, the film also undermines that genre. The film continually refers to other media, mainly television, and takes the genre to its limits by overplaying plot twists.

One character in *Phone* mentions Japan at one point, but there seems to be no direct, deep connections between the film and Japan, or with *One Missed Call*, Korea, or *Phone*. Any dialogue between these two films as reflections of their respective countries takes place only on a metadiscursive level. In several respects, *One Missed Call* is already a metahorror film, so it is relatively easy to put it in the context of any film or genre, including one centering on the use of mobile phones. Moreover, *One Missed Call* subsumes previous landmarks in the history of J- and K-horror, doubling-down ad absurdum on

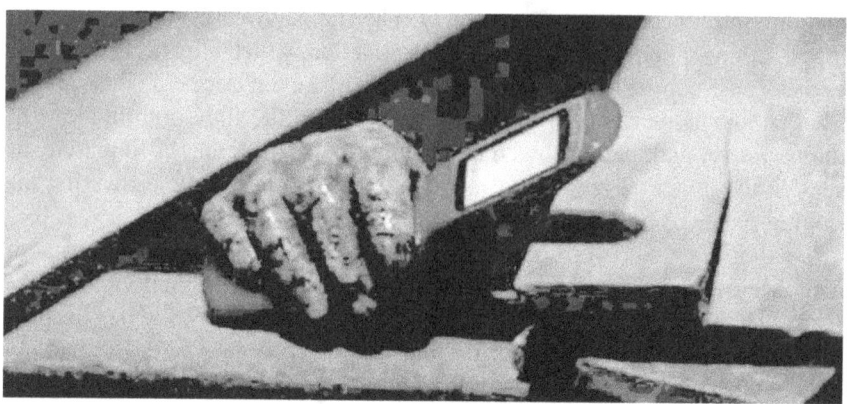

*Texts from the grave in* One Missed Call.

the notion of copying that begun with *Ringu*. The ghost in the film, like those in the other films, is also a victim who calls from her grave. Unlike the other films, however, her curse sends a message to her victims from the future, informing them about their upcoming deaths, and she herself calls and texts victims with similar messages.

*One Missed Call* has become a media phenomenon, and in 2005, the Japanese television network TV Asahi released a TV series adaptation. By this time, several Japanese channels regularly showed Korean dramas, following the unprecedented success of *Winter Sonata* in 2004 that sparked a Korean wave (*Hallyu* in Korean, *Kanryū* in Japanese) of interest in Korean media products in Japan. However, the wave also awoke in Japanese society the dormant demons of xenophobia and anti-Korean sentiment that had existed in the country for decades or even centuries.[36]

## CALL FROM THE PAST ABOUT A FEARFUL FUTURE

In the four films discussed here, female victims return to haunt the living. They use new communication technologies, asking for contrition and for closure that never comes. Even when the dead body is found, the curse continues, either within the narrative of the film, or through the larger system of copying, reproduction, and transnational distribution. Such (meta)narratives are not unique to K- and J-horror, nor does the use of new media in promoting the films (or those represented in them) render the subject matter exceptional. However, transnational discourses are not confined to a specific medium, and even if neither audiences nor producers are aware of it, there is an overarching media ecology within which narratives are reframed.

Remarkably, the issue looming largest over the Korean-Japanese relationship today surrounds female victims: the Korean "comfort women" (*ianfu* in Japanese) who were forced into sexual slavery by invading Japanese forces. Surviving comfort women have called for retribution for what happened to them during the war. Filmmakers did not necessarily intend to link their characters with those real stories. Rather, in contextualizing these films within the transnational discourse of K- and J-horror, it is important to consider the fluidity of such narratives, not just within the framework of the genre, but also within the global context. In both the Korean and Japanese media environments within which filmmakers, producers, distributors, and consumers interact, real narratives about the comfort women continue to stir tensions and animosity. Although mobile phones are emblematic of the miscommunication and social anxiety that persists between individuals as well as between the two nations, other more traditional media outlets also contribute to the rising tensions. Television is one such medium, but another, as Hyeong-Jun Pak shows, is the newspaper. Pak's study reveals that *Ringu* was released in South Korean during a short-lived period when major newspapers in South Korea and Japan gave favorable coverage to the relationship between the countries. However, a few years later, newspapers' tones changed and began to cover the relationship combatively.[37]

Ji Young Kim calls such waves of positive attitudes that turned combative and vice versa a vicious cycle that is driven by patterns of symbolic politics. By this term Kim argues that, rather than calculated diplomatic disputes, the Japanese-South Korean conflict changes according to political leaders' and the public's emotions. Politicians construct a narrative of the relationship that reflects their own emotions, or those to which they feel the public is receptive.[38] History itself, and the issues in dispute, thus become secondary.

The women's call for contrition is real, and it keeps the ghosts of the past alive. These ghosts were once suppressed memories, but they resurface sporadically through indirect forms of expression. Cinema as cultural, and for some, national, commodity, reflects social undercurrents. Although the "J" in J-horror may have initially been a floating signifier, given the appearance of K-horror, the national signification became a real border-mark on the geopolitical area known as East Asia. In this context, calls by victims in films branded as J- or K-horror ring with an unsettling truth.

## NOTES

1. Chung and Diffrient, *Movie Migrations*, 22–23.
2. Huat, "Conceptualizing an East Asian Popular Culture," 207.

3. The most significant source of friction remains the colonial past, despite other issues around small islets in the Sea of Japan, whose naming, too, is in dispute. Although South Korea continues to protest Japan's weak acknowledgment of its colonial past, the relationship between the two countries is strengthening; in 2002 they even cohosted the FIFA World Cup.
4. Whitney "Can You Fear Me Now?," 129.
5. Quinn, "The Terms *uchi* and *soto* as Windows on a World," 42.
6. Stringer, "The Original and the Copy," 304–305.
7. Wada-Marciano, "J-Horror," 20–21.
8. Rojas, "Viral Contagion in the *Ringu* Intertext," 424–429.
9. Gerow, "The Empty Return," 22.
10. Tsai, "Adapting Japanese Horror," 272–289.
11. Phu, "Horrifying Adaptations," 55.
12. Wee, *Japanese Horror Films and Their American Remakes*, 97–98.
13. Reider, "The Emergence of Kaidan-shū," 80–81.
14. Denison, "Japanese and Korean Film Franchising and Adaptation," 105–117.
15. Taylor-Jones, *Rising Sun, Divided Land*, 22–23.
16. In fact, likely because of the geographical proximity, smugglers were able to distribute Japanese VHS tapes and CDs to Korea despite the ban, and Korean TV networks dubbed Japanese anime into Korean, changed the names of characters and places and broadcast these as Korean. See Doobo, "Globalization and Cinema Regionalization in East Asia," 247–248.
17. Byrne, "Wigs and Rings," 186.
18. Ibid., 188.
19. Jones, "Video Nasty," 219–220.
20. Azuma, "Two Modes of Cognitive Socialization," 275.
21. Peirse, "Tracing Tradition in Korean Horror Film," 37–38; Ng, "Women as Cultural Wound," 128–129.
22. Lee, "Transformations of the Monstrous Feminine," 102.
23. Tipton, "Being Women in Japan, 1970–2000," 208.
24. Holthus, "Sexuality, Body Images and Social Change," 144.
25. During most of the 1980s, South Korean dictator General Chun Doo-hwan suppressed democratic progress in the country.
26. See Yamazaki, "Crafting the Apology," 156–173.
27. See, for instance, Nozaki, "Japanese Politics and the History Textbook Controversy, 1982–2001," 603–622.
28. See Hayashi and Prescott, "The 1990s in Japan," 206–235.
29. Yoon, "Making of Neo-Confucian Cyberkids," 753–771.
30. See Hughes, *Shock of the New*, 1990.
31. Hjorth, "Being Real in the Mobile Reel," 91–104.
32. Hidenori, "Kētai de kodomo no ningennkankei ga Kawatta," 130–135.
33. Seo, "That Unobscure Object of Desire and Horror," 166.
34. Martin, "Between the Local and the Global," 149–150.
35. http://japanesemovies.homestead.com/productiontrends.html
36. See Hayashi and Lee, "Potential of Fandom," 207–208.

37. Pak, "News Reporting on Comfort Women," 1007–1008.
38. Kim, "Escaping the Vicious Cycle," 31–60.

## BIBLIOGRAPHY

Azuma, Hiroshi. "Two Modes of Cognitive Socialization in Japan and in the United States." In *Cross-Cultural Roots of Minority Child Development*, Volume 3, edited by Patricia M. Greenfield and Rodney R. Cocking, 275–284. New York: Psychology Press, 1994.

Byrne, James. "Wigs and Rings: Cross-Cultural Exchange in the South Korean and Japanese Horror Film." *Journal of Japanese and Korean Cinema* 6, no. 2 (2014): 184–201.

Chung, Hye Seung, and David Scott Diffrient. *Movie Migrations: Transnational Genre Flows and South Korean Cinema*. New Brunswick, NJ: Rutgers University Press, 2015.

Denison, Rayna. "Japanese and Korean Film Franchising and Adaptation." *Journal of Japanese and Korean Cinema* 6, no. 2 (2014): 105–117.

Doobo, Shim. "Globalization and Cinema Regionalization in East Asia." *Korea Journal* (Winter 2005): 233–260.

Gerow, Aaron. "The Empty Return: Circularity and Repetition in Recent Japanese Horror Films." *Minikomi* 64 (2002): 19–24.

Hayashi, Fumio, and Edward C. Prescott. "The 1990s in Japan: A Lost Decade." *Review of Economic Dynamics* 5, no. 1 (2002): 206–235.

Hayashi, Kaori, and Eun-Jeung Lee. "The Potential of Fandom and the Limits of Soft Power: Media Representations on the Popularity of a Korean Melodrama in Japan." *Social Science Japan Journal* 10, no. 2 (2007): 197–216.

Hidenori, Tomita. "Kētai de kodomo no ningennkankei ga Kawatta: 'Sekai' to jōji setsuzoku suru kodomotachi." *Kansai Daigaku Gakujutsu Ripojitori* 57, no. 14 (2003): 130–135.

Hjorth, Larissa. "Being Real in the Mobile Reel: A Case Study on Convergent Mobile Media as Domesticated New Media in Seoul, South Korea." *The International Journal of Research into New Media Technologies* 14, no. 1 (2008): 91–104.

Holthus, Barbara. "Sexuality, Body Images and Social Change in Japanese Women's Magazines In the 1970s and 1980s." In *International Research Center for Japanese Studies* No. 3, edited by Ulrike Wohr, Barbara Hamill Sato, and Sadami Suzuki, 137–162. Kyoto: Kokusai Nihon bunkakenkyū sentā, 2000.

Huat, Chua Beng. "Conceptualizing an East Asian Popular Culture." *Inter-Asia Cultural Studies* 5, no. 2 (2004): 207.

Hughes, Robert. *The Shock of the New: Art and the Century of Change*. New York: McGraw-Hill, 1990.

Jones, Steve. "Video Nasty: The Moral Apocalypse in Koji Suzuki's Ring." *Literature Interpretation Theory* (2012): 212–225.

Kim, Ji Young. "Escaping the Vicious Cycle: Symbolic Politics and History Disputes between South Korea and Japan." *Asian Perspective* 38, no. 1 (2014): 31–60.

Lee, Hunju. "Transformations of the Monstrous Feminine in the New Asian Female Ghost Films." *Diogenes* 62, no. 1 (2018): 100–114.

Martin, Daniel. "Between the Local and the Global: 'Asian Horror' in Ahn Byung-ki's *Phone* and *Bunshinsaba*." In *Korean Horror Cinema*, edited by Alison Peirse, and Daniel Martin, 145–157. Edinburgh: Edinburgh University Press, 2013.

Ng, Andrew Hock Soon. "Women as Cultural Wound: Korean Horror Cinema and the Imperative of Han." In *The Ghostly and the Ghosted in Literature and Film: Spectral Identities*, edited by Lisa Kroger and Melanie R. Anderson, 119–135. Newark: University of Delaware Press, 2013.

Nozaki, Yoshiko. "Japanese Politics and the History Textbook Controversy, 1982–2001." *International Journal of Educational Research* 37 (2002): 603–622.

Pak, Hyeong-Jun. "News Reporting on Comfort Women: Framing, Frame Difference, and Frame Changing in Four South Korean and Japanese Newspapers, 1998–2013." *Journalism & Mass Communication Quarterly* 93, no. 4 (2016): 1006–1025.

Peirse, Alison. "Tracing Tradition in Korean Horror Film." *Asian Cinema* (Spring/Summer 2011): 31–44.

Phu, Thy. "Horrifying Adaptations: *Ringu*, The Ring, and the Cultural Contexts of Copying." *Journal of Adaptations in Film and Performance* 3, no. 1 (2010): 43–58.

Quinn, Charles J. "The Terms *uchi* and *soto* as Windows on a World." In *Situated Meaning: Inside and Outside in Japanese Self, Society, and Language*, edited by Jane M. Bachnik and Charles Quinn, 38–72. Princeton, NJ: Princeton University Press, 1994.

Reider, Noriko T. "The Emergence of Kaidan-shū: The Collection of Tales of the Strange and Mysterious in the Edo Period." *Asian Folklore Studies* 60, no. 1 (2001): 79–99.

Rojas, Carlos. "Viral Contagion in the *Ringu* Intertext." In *The Oxford Handbook of Japanese Cinema*, edited by Daisuke Miyao, 424–429. New York: Oxford University Press, 2014.

Seo, Hyun-Suk. "That Unobscure Object of Desire and Horror: On Some Uncanny Things in Recent Korean Horror Films." In *Horror to the Extreme: Changing Boundaries in Asian Cinema*, edited by Jinhee Choi and Mitsuyo Wada-Marciano, 163–178. Hong Kong: Hong Kong University Press, 2009.

Stringer, Julian. "The Original and the Copy." In *Japanese Cinema Texts and Contexts*, edited by Alastair Phillips and Julian Stringer, 296–307. New York: Routledge, 2007.

Taylor-Jones, Kate E. *Rising Sun, Divided Land: Japanese and South Korean Filmmakers*. New York: Columbia University Press, 2013.

Tipton, Elise K. "Being Women in Japan, 1970–2000." In *Women in Asia: Tradition, Modernity, and Globalisation*, edited by Louise P. Edwards and Mina Roces, 208–245. Crows Nest, NSW: Allen & Unwin, 2000.

Tsai, Peijen Beth. "Adapting Japanese Horror: *The Ring*." *Asian Cinema* 20 (2009): 272–289.

Wada-Marciano, Mitsuyo. "J-Horror: New Media's Impact on Contemporary Japanese Horror Cinema." In *Horror to the Extreme: Changing Boundaries in Asian*

*Cinema*, edited by Jinhee Choi and Mitsuyo Wada-Marciano, 15–38. Hong Kong: Hong Kong University Press, 2009.

Wee, Valerie. *Japanese Horror Films and Their American Remakes.* New York: Routledge, 2013.

Whitney, Allison. "Can You Fear Me Now? Cell Phones and the American Horror Film." In *The Cell Phone Reader: Essays in Social Transformation*, edited by Anandam Kavoori and Noah Arceneaux, 125–138. New York: Peter Lang, 2006.

Yamazaki, Jane W. "Crafting the Apology: Japanese Apologies to South Korea in 1990." *Asian Journal of Communication* 14, no 2 (2004): 156–173.

Yoon, Kyong. "The Making of Neo-Confucian Cyberkids: Representations of Young Mobile Phone Users in South Korea." *New Media & Society* 8, no. 5 (2006): 753–771.

*Chapter Two*

# Redefining the *Heimat*

## Austrian Horror Cinema and the "Home" in a Global Age

Michael Fuchs

The Austrian national anthem begins with a catalog of places and occupations characteristic of the country. Mountains, rivers, fields, and cathedrals define the landscape connecting the imagined community to (and through) shared traditions and a shared past while also hinting at natural resources whose potential has yet to be exploited. Industry comes up next, bearing promises for the nation's future. The fourth verse proudly proclaims that Austria is the home of well-known and (culturally, socially, and/or politically) significant "sons and daughters." In German, the line (in its current form) reads, "Heimat großer Töchter und Söhne."[1] While I silently translated *Heimat* as "home" just a few lines above, the word, which "shuns unequivocal clearness and [which] is inherently ambiguous,"[2] does not simply equate with "home," as it refers to the home, the homeland, the country of origin, the nation-state, specific regions, specific villages, cities, or towns, and the birthplace (among other things), not to mention the varied affects and emotions related to these ideas. In addition, "home" and "homeland" do not carry the ideological baggage of "Heimat."

The concept of *Heimat* only emerged in the late eighteenth century, becoming a core component (alongside Christianity) of the national identities in the German-speaking countries. In the course of the nineteenth century, the *Heimat* became an increasingly important motif in the arts, helping anchor the national identity in a world rapidly changing due to modernization and individuals' concomitant feelings of alienation from their roots.[3] After World War I and the dissolution of the Austro-Hungarian Empire, the Austrian *Heimat* discourse became infused with sentimentality and nostalgia, as it became inseparable from loss—a feeling which has persisted to this day. The concept's nationalist undercurrents were exploited first by the Austro-fascists of the 1930s and then by the Nazis. In the aftermath of World War

II, the concept became key to Austrian self-definition. The 1960s and 1970s witnessed a more critical stance to the idea before *Heimat* came to be re-associated with nationalist groups in the 1980s, followed by a mainstream reappropriation of the concept in its traditionally "innocent" meaning in more recent years.

Paradoxically, as Peter Blickle has pointed out, "some people thought during the National Socialist period . . . that the supposedly apolitical *Heimat* celebrations were and are a bulwark against fascism."[4] The error in reasoning should become particularly evident when considering that the *Heimatfilm* surged in the wake of World War II, as the genre offered "a way to disavow the cultural rupture of 1933–45" by evoking a particular "state of mind" and "actual places, suggesting nation while being specific to the region."[5] Accordingly, this genre defined by "Agfa-colored images of . . . forests, landscapes, and customs, of happiness and security" is anything but apolitical.[6] Similar to the ways in which the western allowed Americans to cling to the idea of the frontier as a defining element of the American national identity, the Austrian *Heimatfilm* helped define the Austrian national identity in the years after World War II and anchor the national identity in a simultaneously trans- and ahistorical utopia. Interestingly, when Austrian cinema went global in the late twentieth century, Austrian films rediscovered and recovered past cinematic styles and genres.[7] In particular, *Heimatfilm* imagery returned, as spectacular vistas of Austria's idyllic landscapes began to pop up in films and genres seemingly unrelated to the purportedly innocent genre.

As a genre which idealizes the nation, however, the *Heimatfilm* simultaneously exposes "all that our civilization represses or oppresses," to adopt a phrase Robin Wood used to define the American horror movie.[8] This chapter will discuss three recent Austrian horror movies which draw on the visual grammar of the *Heimatfilm*: *In 3 Tagen bist du tot* (*Dead in 3 Days*, 2006), *Blutgletscher* (*Blood Glacier*, 2013), and *Angriff der Lederhosenzombies* (*Attack of the Lederhosen Zombies*, 2016). By infusing horror films with images evoking *Heimatfilme* (or reimagining them as horror movies, depending on one's perspective), these films negotiate the meanings of both *Heimat* and *Heimatfilme* by exposing the uncanny undercurrents always latently present in the concept of "Heimat." After all, *Heimat* is "an intoxicant" which "makes people feel giddy and spirits them to . . . an uncontaminated space, a realm of innocence."[9] Horror, on the other hand, may possibly be the most political of genres, as "it serves an important function as a progressive and sometimes radical genre, in the face of increasingly reactionary stances."[10] As such, horror often (but definitely not always) challenges "the official ideology."[11]

The three movies explored here simultaneously distance the diegetic events from their Austrian contexts by acknowledging transnational as well as intertextual flows and further entrench their texts in Austrian cultural practice through their use of visual icons typically associated with Austria and Austrian cinema. In this way, the films not only epose the significance of everything that is not *Heimat* to the definition of *Heimat*, but also recognize the interdependencies between the local and the global in our contemporary age.

## INTERTEXTUALITY AND TRANSNATIONAL CINEMAS

Since the meaning of *Heimat* only emerges from the various interplays between the concept of *Heimat* and the meanings of other signifiers within a network of signs, *Heimat* only exists in difference (or *différance*, according to Jacques Derrida). As with any other sign, its meaning is always-already liminal, as meaning potentials are actualized through performative acts. In addition, any sign only means something in relation to other signs; that is, in the liminal spaces between (and partly overlapping with) other signs and their meanings. When slightly scaling up these ideas from individual signifiers to entire texts, one quickly arrives at the concept of intertextuality. Structuralists conceive of intertextuality as "a relationship of copresence between two [or more] texts" and the "presence of one text within another."[12] This somewhat "restrictive sense," as leading narratologist Gérard Genette himself put it,[13] tends to downgrade intertextuality to little more than "the *intentional allusion* (overt or covert) to, citation or quotation of previous texts."[14] However, similar to the production of meaning as such, intertextuality only comes into existence through the performative act of "reading" a text. As a result, "a text is not a line of words releasing a single 'theological' meaning . . . but a multidimensional space in which a variety of writings, none of them original, blend and clash."[15] Intertextuality thus collapses the very notion of an original, as "the origin" becomes "indiscernible."[16]

These core ideas in intertextuality studies connect well with discourses about transnational cinemas and help explain a major shift that scholarship on global cinemas has undergone in recent years. In 2003, Kim Newman still claimed that "the dominant strains of any given genre . . . are American." "Only the martial arts movie," he continued, "grew up away from Hollywood, a non-American alternative to the western." However, the "mainstream of the horror film," in particular, "is American."[17] Newman's thinking draws on unidirectional theories of globalization which diagnose an "asymmetry in the transfer of culture," which epitomizes "cultural or media imperialism."[18] While the United States has had a lasting impact on the Western world since World War II, the main tool of expanding and cementing its power has been neither economic nor military, but US-American popular culture, which has been perpetuating US-American myths and viewpoints across the Western world (if not the entire globe). As Joseph Nye has explained, popular culture allows America not only "to get what [it] want[s] through attraction rather than coercion or payments," but also "to shape the preferences of others."[19] This influence on "the preferences of others" is a key element in Nye's concept of "soft power," for it does not simply operate in a unidirectional manner. Soft power is relational and requires a certain kind of cooperation from the "receiving" end. Nye argues, for example, that "what the target thinks is particularly important, and the targets matters as much as the agents."[20]

Until the early 2000s, the sheer omnipresence of American horror in the global domain and the ways in which horror seems to speak to universal human fears as much as to specific cultural contexts at particular historical moments turned American horror movies (with British films a distant second) into the go-to texts for scholars exploring the "dark arts." In their introduction to the seminal volume *Horror International* (2005), Steven Jay Schneider and Tony Williams acknowledge this point, noting that the "dominance of American film production and the ready availability of US films . . . have gone a long way toward engendering the disproportionate critical focus on [American] cinematic horror."[21] However, from the earliest days of horror scholarship, this nearly exclusive focus on American productions has been accompanied by at least the latent acknowledgment of the inter- and transnational influences which effectively "made" American horror, from the narrative blueprints the British Gothic provided and the horror icons British Gothic novels of the nineteenth century established to the influences of German Expressionism on the aesthetics of US horror films of the 1930s and 1940s. Indeed, as Sophia Siddique and Raphael Raphael remark in their introduction to *Transnational Horror Cinema* (2016): "From its origins, what would eventually be called 'the horror genre' has been deeply transnational, both in contexts of production and reception. The first works of horror stitch together the flesh of various national and generic texts."[22]

To be sure, it would be misleading (if not delusive) to claim that US-American horror has not had an impact on horror film traditions around the globe in the last eighty years. In an essay on the relationships between Hollywood and Latin American cinema, Ana López suggests that "Hollywood's international presence has had acute effects not only on Hollywood itself . . . but on all other filmmaking nations."[23] The same argument may be made about US-American horror films, which (in part due to their global dominance) influence local horror traditions while at the same time drawing on material from across the globe. Accordingly, despite the dominance of American horror films on the global market, "the influence of US horror filmmaking practices, formulas, and (sub)generic conventions has by no means been unidirectional," as horror films from around the world "are engaged in a dynamic process of cross-cultural exchange with American mainstream, independent, and underground horror alike."[24] In this transnational exchange of meanings made possible by the commercial flows of entertainment products across the globe, the divisions between source texts and target texts, originals and adaptations or appropriations, blur (if not disintegrate altogether) and become replaced by constant (re-)negotiations, as a unidirectional process is replaced by a dialogic relationship. This is why Iain Robert Smith has diagnosed "the deeply interconnected histories of Hollywood and world cinema," which become particularly manifest in "cross-cultural borrowings and syncretism."[25]

## SERIAL MURDER IN THE SALZKAMMERGUT

*In 3 Tagen bist du tot* merges the innocence evoked by *Heimatfilm* imagery with fears and anxieties engendered by American slasher-film templates to produce a nearly paranoid worldview in which the boy-next-door serial killer may haunt not only American suburbs, but also Austrian small towns. The opening of *In 3 Tagen* resembles that of a detective story, as the narrative begins with a man hanging himself, followed by a young woman named Mona, drenched in blood, begging an unknown person to rescue someone called Nina. Layer by layer, the movie then begins to unravel not only the significance of the suicide, but also who Nina is and how Mona ended up limping along a road in the woods seriously injured.

*In 3 Tagen* centers on a clique who have just passed their *Matura* exams, replacing the typically American high school graduation ceremony with a distinctly Austrian element. On the way home from school, the tomboyish Nina, who is established early on as the Final Girl, receives a text message predicting her death in the next three days. Of course, she believes the message to be a prank, but when the clique goes to a concert the same evening where her boyfriend Martin does not return from the restroom and she finds the message "You'll be dead in 3 days" on his phone, she begins to believe that something has happened to him.[26] Unsurprisingly, all members of the clique have received the same text message. The police are unwilling to help, telling the group that people have to be missing for twenty-four hours in order to start an official investigation, in particular when considering that Martin was drunk and "may have found a girl and is enjoying himself somewhere," as Kogler, the policeman on duty and coincidentally also Martin's cousin, remarks.[27] The next morning, Nina discovers Martin floating in the local lake, chained to a parasol stand (a dose of Austrian local color). Martin's death kicks off a series of grisly murders, with all victims but one (a boy who rescues Nina when the killer is about to kill her) being members of Nina's clique.

Although images indebted to the *Heimatfilm* appear repeatedly in the course of the movie, the scene of Nina discovering Martin makes explicit the discord between the beautiful setting and the horrors taking place in the small town of less than eight thousand people. The lake—Traunsee, to be more precise—plays a key role here. Symbolically, water is evocative of the psyche, as the surface (and what is directly beneath it) is visible, while its actual depths are always hard to guess. As Bruce Kawin has explained, "There is room in the water for things to grow to great size or great numbers without being detected. . . . The water is a natural cover, a hiding place and a source for the monster. . . . [W]ater radiates danger and concealed horror."[28] The film's director, Andreas Prochaska, has echoed these ideas, remarking that "the Traunsee has an uncanny quality, not the least because at up to 197 meters deep, it is one of the deepest lakes in Austria."[29] In other words, much may literally be hidden beneath the beautiful lake's surface as the town's inhabitants carry on their lives in blissful ignorance.

In *In 3 Tagen*, the water functions as a symbolic vehicle to repress the memory of the death of young Fabian about ten years before the diegetic present. Fabian knew Nina and her clique. One day, they played hockey on the frozen lake, and when the puck ended up on a thinner part of the ice the group asked Fabian to retrieve it. He hesitated at first, then agreed, but as he slid toward the puck the ice broke beneath him, and he drowned in the cold water. In typical slasher-film manner, the killer (Fabian's mother) is

*Nina sitting by the Traunsee, a few minutes before discovering Martin's body a couple of feet from the shore, in* In 3 Tagen bist du tot.

*Redefining the* Heimat

out to avenge this past wrong. In a telling scene, Nina reminds her friends of Fabian's death. Judging by their reactions, all of them had forgotten about the incident. Clemens protests: "It was an accident and could have happened to anyone of us." "Yes, sure. But it didn't," responds Nina, noting: "We were all incredibly stupid."[30] From a psychoanalytical perspective, Fabian's mother, who tries to take revenge for this past mistake and becomes the film's monster, represents the return of this repressed memory.

On another level, this return of the repressed becomes magnified in the form of an Austrian "national uncanny," to adapt the term Renée Bergland uses for the spectral role of Native Americans in the American imagination.[31] Ebensee, the film's setting, harbored a concentration camp during the Nazi regime. While Ebensee was "only" a subcamp in the Mauthausen network (Mauthausen was the larger of the two main camps in Austria) and opened rather late in World War II, 8,500 to 11,000 people died there between November 1943 and May 1945. Like many other former concentration camp sites, Ebensee participates in what Norman Finkelstein has called "the Holocaust industry,"[32] thereby literally capitalizing on past aberrations. More importantly within the present context, however, the traces of the atrocities committed by the Nazi regime are at odds with Ebensee's outward beauty and apparent innocence. The Nazi reign may be past, but it is part of Austrian

*The gate of the former concentration camp Ebensee is a jarring reminder of past atrocities, signposting the tension between outward beauty of the surroundings of the Traunsee and the specters haunting the region.*

history and has left its marks on the national psyche, no matter the attempts to downplay or outright ignore its influences on the present moment. *In 3 Tagen* draws on this tension to expose the contradictions inherent in the concept of *Heimat*. The traditional notion of the *Heimat* necessitates the rigid exclusion of that which contradicts or questions, let alone subverts, the idea of the *Heimat*. Crucially, the *Heimat* is an idealized conception produced by an imagined community still rooted in a past golden age which never was, but which the community still clings to and nostalgically yearns for.

The film's allusiveness similarly questions the *Heimat* by disconnecting the film's setting—which is clearly anchored in Austrian culture—from its Austrian roots through its submersion in intertextuality. Indeed, some reviewers even pointed out that "the film includes so many typical elements of the horror genre that it appears as if the filmmakers tried to work off a list."[33] To be sure, *In 3 Tagen* primarily responds to the slick and stylish neoslashers produced in the United States in the decade preceding the release of Prochaska's movie. The Austrian film's narrative premise recalls that of *I Know What You Did Last Summer* (1997), as the central group of characters accidentally kills someone but then decides not to report the incident. In fact, *Last Summer*'s accident following, and resulting from, a night of partying and drinking is mirrored in an early scene in *In 3 Tagen*, in which the clique runs over a deer. The anonymous killer who is identified by a raincoat is, likewise, indebted to *Last Summer*, while the twist concerning the gender of the killer echoes *Urban Legends* (1998). When Clemens stresses, "This is not a movie; this is really happening,"[34] the line tips its proverbial hat to the self-consciousness characteristic of the neoslashers of the 1990s and early noughties. Similar to most of these films, *In 3 Tagen* does not try to establish a hyperreal world in which nothing is real, but rather uses this metatextual comment to support its realist illusion. The scene toward the end of the film in which Fabian's mother throws Nina into the lake moves farther back in slasher history, as it evokes the conclusion of *Friday the 13th* (1980).

While *In 3 Tagen* would offer many more connections to American slashers (and European arthouse films), chasing down the spectral intertexts haunting the text of *In 3 Tagen* is not the point here. Rather, the textual fragments coming from various sources, stitched together and enriched by specifically Austrian elements, create a new cultural artifact whose origin and sociohistorical location is hard to define. Yes, *In 3 Tagen* emphasizes its setting in an Austrian small town, but its reliance on numerous other texts which are clearly of foreign origin destabilizes its Austrian character as much as it anchors its narrative in specifically national and local contexts. This dualism points at the interconnectedness between the local and the global in the twenty-first century; they are not so much binaries as ideas entangled in a larger network in which the *Heimat* loses its meaning as a point of origin, but becomes all the more meaningful as a marker of a shared identity.

## CONTEMPORARY CAPITALISM'S NECROTIC EXOSTOSES

*Angriff der Lederhosenzombies* picks up on the interrelatedness between global processes and their local effects early on. In the opening scene, a man is driving through a snow-covered wood on a snowmobile to the tune of Ennio Morricone's iconic *The Thing* (1982) theme. The music triggers associations of isolation in a snowed-in place and the appearance of a monster—and *Lederhosenzombies* delivers on both of these promises. Just a minute into the film, viewers see a zombie deer gnawing at a human forearm. After the opening credits have introduced a man engaging in some shady and dubious scientific experiments, another man (named Knaup) is shown talking to a potential Russian investor named Chekov, trying to convince the businessman to invest in the region: "Next year we gonna get a new lift with a heating for the butt—a cable car."[35] The shady man from the credits, Franz, walks up to them, hugs Chekov, and "welcome[s]" him "to the future," since he believes he has a solution for the "fucking climate change."[36] Franz has created a "miracle," which allows his company to "make [their] own snow with the push of a button."[37] While snow cannons were invented more than fifty years ago, Franz's machine is new, utilizing "Solanum +10." The film never explains what this Solanum +10 is, but what soon becomes clear is that exposure to it turns humans into zombies. Chekov comes too close to the machine and starts vomiting green goo within a few seconds. When Knaup wants to transfer him to the next hospital, Franz protests, stating that he will not allow the Russian to leave before he has agreed to invest some money.

Whereas Franz and Knaup's dependence on foreign investments hints at transnational flows of capital, the zombie figure supports the idea of transnational interconnections. After all, the zombie is a transnational creation, emerging from "the violent encounter between Europe and its colonial possessions."[38] As Agnieszka Soltysik Monnet has explained, the zombie myth "descended from African religious beliefs," but only truly developed "in the New World and is thus inextricably linked to the traumatic experience of Africans brought to the Caribbean to be worked to death."[39] In Haiti, the zombie was a "powerful symbol of . . . misery and doom,"[40] which lent itself well to Western appropriation in the wake of the US occupation of the island, as the zombie quickly morphed into a metaphor for the "modern industrial practice of occupation culture."[41] While the zombie may signify anything from conformity to slavery,[42] the symbol's connection to exploitation has stood the test of time. Indeed, a Marxist understanding of the zombie figure in late capitalism suggests that it is a "mythic symbol of alienation: of a spiritual as well as physical alienation; of the dispossession of the self through the reduction of the self to a mere source of labour."[43]

Crucially, in *Lederhosenzombies*, the first character to turn into a zombie is the embodiment of transnational capitalism, Chekov. Indeed, since Chekov spreads the zombie virus primarily by infecting locals, he personifies the necrotic drive undergirding the capitalist venture. As Justin McBrien has argued, the "history of capitalism's expansion" is defined by "the process of *becoming extinction*," explaining that "[t]his *becoming extinction* is not simply the biological process of species extinction," but also

> the extinguishing of cultures and languages, either through force or assimilation; it is the extermination of peoples, either through labor or deliberate murder; it is the extinction of the earth in the depletion [of] fossil fuels, rare earth minerals, even the chemical element helium; it is ocean acidification and eutrophication, deforestation and desertification, melting ice sheets and rising sea levels; the great Pacific garbage patch and nuclear waste entombment; McDonalds and Monsanto.

Capitalism, McBrien continues, "reproduc[es] the means of production by its destruction."[44] Since it feeds on humans who subsequently become undead, the zombie figure represents par excellence the process McBrien describes. Since Chekov is a businessman before turning into a zombie, the death drive (not in the Freudian sense) of capitalism becomes all the more evident—Chekov produces death, which only generates more death. Significantly, by eradicating practically everyone in the ski resort, Chekov ultimately creates negative value, pointing at the unsustainability of capitalist processes from the perspective of the world ecology. While, in *Lederhosenzombies*, a small resort in the Alps suffers from capitalist exploitation, one can only speculate about the large-scale implications. For example, if Chekov had been in the upper management of some bigger corporation, its stock value might have plummeted after his death, leading to ever more short-term negative value—not to mention the long-term negative value for the planet, seldom taken into account.

In addition, by linking the development of Solanum +10 to attempts at finding a solution to inconveniences caused by climate change, *Lederhosenzombies* addresses two more important points (admittedly in exaggerated ways). First, apparently, Franz does not even try to find a sustainable solution for the region's (let alone the world's) ecological problems, but rather tries to earn quick profits without considering the long-term implications of his actions. His search for a means of counteracting the negative (commercial) effects of climate change is driven by greed rather than any considerations for the nonhuman and rest of the human world. Second, the film raises the question of "how . . . a planetary transformation" such as climate change "might affect particular places and individuals."[45] As *Lederhosenzombies* demonstrates, the effects of the global phenomenon of climate change are primarily felt and experienced on the local level. *Lederhosenzombies* establishes a connection between this local level and the *Heimat*, for the area attacked by the zombies is a kitschy village surrounded by snow-covered mountains—a visual signifier of the *Heimat* in the Austrian imagination. However, this place becomes irreversibly transformed by its global interrelations. The isolated village is no longer cut off from the rest of the world, but rather part of this vast network of flows characteristic of the contemporary age, thereby raising the question whether the *Heimat* may still be the *Heimat*.

## ZOMBIE BACTERIA IN THE ANTHROPOCENE

*Blutgletscher* explores, in greater detail, the ecological critique *Lederhosenzombies* hints at. The film opens with an insert, stating, "In 2014, the last skeptics fall silent. The climate disaster is worse than ever imagined. Antarctica's ice will be gone within a decade. The Alpine glaciers will disappear. The consequences are unclear but we know one thing. Life on Earth will change forever. We will change."[46] This paratext suggests that the film (released in 2013) imagines a near-future "what if" scenario which "envision[s] a kind of change that has not occurred before," but which is, in fact, taking place right now.[47]

The film's story centers on a team of three Austrian scientists and a technician working at a remote climate research station in the borderland between Tyrol and South Tyrol (filmed in the Ortler Alps in the border region between Switzerland and Italy). The day before an Austrian government minister visits the facility, Janek, the technician, and Falk, a mineralogist, discover the titular blood glacier and take a sample of the red substance.[48] When investigating the sample, the scientists conclude that single-celled organisms have surfaced due to snowmelt. As bizarre creatures—ranging from a "fox [which has] mandibles, like a beetle" and an about four-inch-long mosquito to "a hybrid of a woodlouse and a fox" and a vulture-insect hybrid—begin to appear, the scientists discover that the microorganism liberated from permafrost uses the host's body to combine the genetic information of various species in an attempt to create new species ready for survival in a world affected by climate change. Once the scientists and Janek understand what type of threat they are facing, *Blutgletscher* morphs into a siege movie, as

*Janek and Falk discover the blood glacier in* Blutgletscher.

the hybrids begin to attack the research station. Janek, his former partner Dr. Tanja Monstatt (a climatologist herself), Minister Bodicek, and their guide Bert survive the attacks, but the film concludes on a somewhat downbeat note, as it not only confronts viewers with the genetic and evolutionary alterations that climate change will entail for human beings, but moreover suggests that these transformations and mutations are, at this point, virtual certainties.

Upon seeing the movie (then still under the English title *The Station*) at the Toronto Film Festival in the fall of 2013, *The Hollywood Reporter*'s Borys Kit concluded that the film "is Austria's answer to *The Thing*."[49] Indeed, even though *Blutgletscher* may be considered "the latest unofficial *The Thing* rip-off,"[50] the "material, historical and political conditions which surround and penetrate the moment of production and subsequent moment(s) of reception" produce a unique cultural artifact whose significance—at least in part—lies in its differences from the Carpenter movie.[51] Of course, genre cinema is always "dependent on traces of other stories, familiar images and narrative structures, [and] intertextual allusions."[52] The attendant reliance on genre conventions, Yvonne Leffler has argued, creates a "determinist pattern . . . so intense that the fictional world . . . contain[s] nothing that is unique."[53] *Blutgletscher* instrumentalizes this "pan-determinism," as Matt Hills has referred to the generic pressures on specific genre texts,[54] to mirror life in the Anthropocene, which is characterized by the constant oscillation between power and powerlessness. After all, in the age of the human, humankind has become both *"perpetrator and victim,"* as it has caused unintended changes across the planet and suffers from the unexpected outcomes of anthropogenic actions (such as hurricanes and tsunamis).[55] The species "rival[s] the great forces of Nature," as Will Steffen, Paul J. Crutzen, and John R. McNeill have argued,[56] but simultaneously becomes increasingly aware of its constant state of "out-of-controllness."[57]

While the plot and basic premise of *Blutgletscher* are indebted to *The Thing*, the relocation from Antarctica to the Alps highlights the interrelations between the local and global in the early twenty-first century. The story's setting in the Eastern Alps acknowledges that "we are all, as human beings, embodied and physically located."[58] As a result, "[t]he paradigmatic experience of global modernity for most people . . . is that of staying in one place but experiencing the 'dis-placement' that global modernity *brings to them*."[59] Communication studies scholar Susanne Moser has suggested that the effects of climate change become most apparent in remote and uninhabitable places (e.g., the polar regions and open seas), which "have to compete for attention with immediately felt physical needs, professional demands, economic necessities, or social obligations."[60] However, the Alps have truly become icons of climate change in Europe, not least because they are key to the local tourism industries (particularly winter tourism). Accordingly, the setting in the barely inhabited (by humans) high mountains enhances the critique of human-caused climate change, as even these "innocent" places witness and experience its effects in astounding ways.

While the scientists mention climate change repeatedly in the opening exchanges, the topic of global warming becomes particularly prevalent in a scene in which the minister's team is hiking up the mountains. While walking up the mountains, Dr. Tanja Monstatt acknowledges (real) glaciologists' conclusions when she remarks that "the glacier is retreating much faster than we expected—at an exponential rate!"[61] A few minutes later, Bert, the senior alpinist guiding Minister Bodicek and her entourage to the research facility, starts stressing how different the mountains looked only a few decades back. As he gazes at a barren part of a mountain, he reminisces, "It is hard to believe, but when I was a kid, we used to sled over there." As he points to the right, he continues, "The glacier ended over there. Everything's gone."[62]

The verbal highlighting of the shrinking glacier emphasizes the deviation from *Heimatfilm* imagery. Up to this point, the minister's entourage journeyed through landscapes that seemed to have been taken from a photo book, eating Austrian *Brettljause* (a type of snack consisting of hearty and savory sausages, and sometimes also such fare as pork chops, cheese, and dark bread) against the backdrop of green pastures and snow-covered mountain peaks. In addition, the scene spotlighting the shrinking glacier exposes the dualism of mountain images used in the first half of the film, because the scientists and Janek work in a barren landscape high above the timberline. Thanks to their twenty-first-century technology, they do not necessarily fight for survival, but are nonetheless confronted with an environment hostile to life. Bodicek's group, on the other hand, traverses picturesque hiking trails—nature civilized and commercially developed by culture. As the minister and Bert look at the nearly vanished glacier, they look at a world transformed by climate change, and into a future defined by a radically altered environment.

In this way, the global process of climate change impacts the conception of the *Heimat*. Whereas the *Heimatfilm* imagined a fantastic, ahistorical space that was often simultaneously located in the past and projected into the future, *Blutgletscher* diagnoses the incompatibility of these ideals with the realities of life in the early twenty-first century. The dystopian signifiers of pebble and dust have replaced the utopian signifier of green pastures, as the *Heimat* has become entangled with global flows, unable to remain innocent and isolated from the rest of the world.

## *HEIMAT* IN A GLOBAL WORLD

The *Heimat* is an idealized space located simultaneously in the past and present, which paradoxically also holds promises for the future. As Bernd Hüppauf has argued, while *Heimat* is always multiple (as it is a highly individual affect space), any given community has a shared *Heimat*, which defines norms, sets values, shapes ideas, and unites the imagined community.[63] This *Heimat* is limited in its geographical expanse; it is small, contained, and not highly complex. The *Heimat* is linked to childhood, both on the personal and communal level—the *Heimat* conveys ideas of a more innocent age, which is frozen in time.

Reflecting these notions, the *Heimatfilm* is "set in a timeless, unchanging landscape, a location somehow outside any historical matrix."[64] However, the three horror films discussed here demonstrate that the *Heimat* cannot extract itself from global processes and phenomena. From climate change to global capitalism, these symptoms of globalization threaten the very idea of "die Heimat." As the *Heimat* becomes entangled in transnational flows, it can no longer maintain the demarcation lines seemingly necessary for its very definition, thereby irrevocably changing it, if not dismantling it altogether. While the three films emphasize the local effects of globalization, they do not mourn the possible loss of the *Heimat*. *In 3 Tagen bist du tot*, in particular, highlights the dark specters haunting the concept since its inception, but in even more pronounced ways in the post–World War II era. By acknowledging the exclusionary practices required for the very construction of the *Heimat*, *In 3 Tagen* exposes the artificial character of the *Heimat*. Since cultures constantly renegotiate the concepts they have created, the idea of the *Heimat* will adapt to the changing world of the twenty-first century—even if the snow-covered mountain peaks of the Alps have become a fantasy anchored in a past which actually once was.

## NOTES

1. Until 2011, the line read "Heimat bist du großer Söhne" (home of "great" sons), but it was legally adapted to acknowledge the significance of female Austrians, as well.
2. Hüppauf, "Heimat," 110; my translation.
3. Boa and Palfreyman, *Heimat—A German Dream*, 1–3.
4. Blickle, *Heimat*, 138.
5. Reimer, "Picture-Perfect War," 320.
6. Kaes, *From Hitler to Heimat*, 15.
7. von Dassanowsky and Speck, "New Austrian Film," 3–8.
8. Wood, *Hollywood from Vietnam to Reagan*, 68.
9. Rentschler, "No Place Like Home," 37.
10. Wells, *The Horror Genre*, 24.
11. Hawkins, *Art Horror*, 61.
12. Genette, *Palimpsests*, 1–2.
13. Ibid., 1.
14. Allen, "Intertextuality"; italics in original.
15. Barthes, "Death of the Author," 146.
16. Barthes, *S/Z*, 164.
17. Newman, "Preface," 7.
18. Wagnleitner, *Coca-Colonization*, 2.
19. Nye, *Soft Power*, x, 5.
20. Nye, *Future of Power*, 84.
21. Schneider and Williams, "Introduction," 2.
22. Siddique and Raphael, "Introduction," 2.
23. López, "Facing Up to Hollywood," 419.
24. Schneider and Williams, "Introduction," 2.
25. Smith, *Hollywood Meme*, 2.
26. *In 3 Tagen bist du tot*; my translation.
27. Ibid.; my translation.
28. Kawin, *Horror and the Horror Film*, 79.
29. Quoted in Pühringer and Schaner, "Mit hiesigen Mitteln"; my translation.
30. *In 3 Tagen bist du tot*; my translation.
31. Bergland, *The National Uncanny*.
32. Finkelstein, *Holocaust Industry*; see also Cole, *Selling the Holocaust*; Reynolds, *Postcards from Auschwitz*.
33. Schiffauer, "Tatort Traunsee," 40.
34. *In 3 Tagen bist du tot*; my translation.
35. *Angriff der Lederhosenzombies*. I quote from the international ("English") audio track, which, in fact, mixes several languages. When Austrians talk to other Austrians, they use German; when they talk to internationals, they usually use (broken) English.
36. Ibid.
37. Ibid.

38. Monnet, "Transnational Zombie," 144.
39. Ibid.
40. Russell, *Book of the Dead*, 11.
41. Fay, "Dead Subjectivity," 90.
42. Bishop, *American Zombie Gothic*.
43. Laroche, "The Myth of the Zombi," 56.
44. McBrien, "Accumulating Extinction," 116–17; italics in original.
45. Heise, *Sense of Place*, 206.
46. *Blutgletscher*. Quotations from the film are taken from the dubbed version available through Netflix US.
47. Heise, *Sense of Place*, 206.
48. There is an actual "Blood Glacier" in Antarctica. At the toe of Taylor Glacier is a small waterfall carrying sanguine water. Similar to the film, scientists originally believed that red algae were the source of the water's reddish color, but over the years, scientists discovered that the water streaming down the Blood Falls was not meltwater, but actually coming from a saltwater lake hidden beneath the glacier (Badgeley et al.).
49. Kit, "Toronto: *The Station* Is Austria's Answer to *The Thing*."
50. Taylor, "*Blood Glacier* Is Campy and Limp."
51. Mazdon, *Encore Hollywood*, 26.
52. Spooner, *Contemporary Gothic*, 10.
53. Leffler, *Horror as Pleasure*, 191.
54. Hills, *Pleasures of Horror*, 65.
55. Beck, *Risk Society*, 38; italics in original.
56. Steffen, Crutzen, and McNeill, "The Anthropocene," 614.
57. Clark, "Panic Ecology," 88.
58. Tomlinson, *Globalization and Culture*, 149.
59. Ibid., 9; italics in original.
60. Moser, "Communicating Climate Change," 34.
61. *Blutgletscher*.
62. Ibid.
63. Hüppauf, "Heimat," 112–13.
64. King, "Placing *Green Is the Heath*," 133.

## BIBLIOGRAPHY

Allen, Graham. "Intertextuality." *The Literary Encyclopedia*. January 24, 2005. https://www.litencyc.com/php/stopics.php?rec=true&UID=1229

*Angriff der Lederhosenzombies*. Directed by Dominik Hartl. 2016. Ahrensfelde: Capelight Pictures, 2017. Blu-ray.

Badgeley, Jessica A., et al. "An Englacial Hydrologic System of Brine within a Cold Glacier: Blood Falls, McMurdo Dry Valleys, Antarctica." *Journal of Glaciology* 63, no. 239 (2017): 387–400.

Barthes, Roland. "The Death of the Author." In *Image—Music—Text*, edited and translated by Stephen Heath, 155–64. New York: Hill & Wang, 1978.
———. *S/Z: An Essay*. Translated by Richard Miller. New York: Hill & Wang, 1974.
Beck, Ulrich. *Risk Society: Towards a New Modernity*. Translated by Mark Ritter. Thousand Oaks, CA: Sage, 1992.
Bergland, Renée L. *The National Uncanny: Indian Ghosts and American Subjects*. Hanover, NH: University Press of New England, 2000.
Bishop, Kyle. *American Zombie Gothic: The Rise and Fall (and Rise) of the Walking Dead in Popular Culture*. Jefferson, NC: McFarland, 2010.
Blickle, Peter. *Heimat: A Critical Theory of the German Idea of Homeland*. Rochester, NY: Camden House, 2002.
*Blutgletscher*. Directed by Marvin Kren. 2012. Planegg: Koch Media, 2014. Blu-ray.
Boa, Elizabeth, and Rachel Palfreyman. *Heimat—A German Dream: Regional Loyalties and National Identity in German Culture, 1890–1990*. Oxford: Oxford University Press, 2000.
Clark, Nigel. "Panic Ecology: Nature in the Age of Superconductivity." *Theory, Culture & Society* 14, no. 1 (1997): 77–96.
Cole, Tim. *Selling the Holocaust from Auschwitz to Schindler: How History Is Bought, Packaged, and Sold*. New York: Routledge, 2000.
Fay, Jennifer. "Dead Subjectivity: *White Zombie*, Black Baghdad." *CR: The New Centennial Review* 8, no. 1 (2008): 81–101.
Finkelstein, Norman G. *The Holocaust Industry: Reflections on the Exploitation of Jewish Suffering*. London: Verso Books, 2000.
Genette, Gérard. *Palimpsests: Literature in the Second Degree*. Translated by Channa Newman and Claude Doubinsky. Lincoln: University of Nebraska Press, 1997.
Hawkins, Joan. *Cutting Edge: Art-Horror and the Horrific Avant-Garde*. Minneapolis: University of Minnesota Press, 2000.
Heise, Ursula K. *Sense of Place and Sense of Planet: The Environmental Imagination of the Global*. New York: Oxford University Press, 2008.
Hills, Matt. *The Pleasures of Horror*. London: Continuum, 2005.
Hüppauf, Bernd. "Heimat – die Wiederkehr eines verpönten Wortes: Ein Populärmythos im Zeitalter der Globalisierung." In *Heimat: Konturen und Konjunkturen eines umstrittenen Konzepts*, edited by Gunther Gebhard, Oliver Geisler, and Steffen Schröter, 109–40. Bielefeld: transcript Verlag, 2007.
*In 3 Tagen bist du tot*. Directed by Andreas Prochaska. 2006. Vienna: HOANZL, 2010. Blu-ray.
Kaes, Anton. *From Hitler to Heimat: The Return of History as Film*. Cambridge, MA: Harvard University Press, 1992.
Kawin, Bruce F. *Horror and the Horror Film*. London: Anthem Press, 2012.
King, Alasdair. "Placing *Green Is the Heath* (1951): Spatial Politics and Emergent Western German Identity." In *Light Motives: German Popular Film in Perspective*, edited by Randall Halle and Margaret McCarthy, 130–47. Detroit, MI: Wayne State University Press, 2003.

Kit, Borys. "Toronto: *The Station* Is Austria's Answer to *The Thing.*" *The Hollywood Reporter.* September 7, 2013. https://www.hollywoodreporter.com/heat-vision/toronto-station-is-austrias-answer-623648

Laroche, Maximilien. "The Myth of the Zombi." In *Exile and Tradition: Studies in African and Caribbean Literature,* edited by Rowland Smith, 44–61. New York: Dalhousie University Press, 1976.

Leffler, Yvonne. *Horror as Pleasure: The Aesthetics of Horror Fiction.* Translated by Sara Death. Stockholm: Almqvist & Wiksell, 2000.

López, Ana M. "Facing Up to Hollywood." In *Reinventing Film Studies,* edited by Christine Gledhill and Linda Williams, 419–37. London: Arnold Publishing, 2000.

Mazdon, Lucy. *Encore Hollywood: Remaking French Cinema.* London: BFI, 2000.

McBrien, Justin. "Accumulating Extinction: Planetary Catastrophism in the Necrocene." In *Anthropocene or Capitalocene? Nature, History, and the Crisis of Capitalism,* edited by Jason W. Moore, 116–37. Oakland, CA: PM Press, 2016.

Monnet, Agnieszka Soltysik. "The Transnational Zombie: Postcolonial Memory and Rage in Recent European Horror Film." In *Transnational Mediations: Negotiating Popular Culture between Europe and the United States,* edited by Christof Decker and Astrid Böger, 143–59. Heidelberg: Universitätsverlag Winter, 2015.

Moser, Susanne C. "Communicating Climate Change: History, Challenges, Process and Future Directions." *WIREs Climate Change* 1, no. 1 (2010): 31–53.

Newman, Kim. "Preface." In *Fear without Frontiers: Horror Cinema across the Globe,* edited by Steven Jay Schneider, 7–10. London: FAB Press, 2003.

Nye, Joseph S. *The Future of Power: Its Changing Nature and Use in the Twenty-First Century.* New York: Public Affairs, 2011.

———. *Soft Power: The Means to Success in World Politics.* New York: Public Affairs, 2004.

Pühringer, Julia, and Petra Schaner. "Mit hiesigen Mitteln eine spannende Geschichte." *Alles Film.* October 13, 2006. http://www.allesfilm.com/show_article.php?id=22766

Reimer, Robert C. "Picture-Perfect War: An Analysis of Joseph Vilsmaier's *Stalingrad* (1993)." In *Light Motives: German Popular Film in Perspective,* edited by Randall Halle and Margaret McCarthy, 304–25. Detroit, MI: Wayne State University Press, 2003.

Rentschler, Eric. "There's No Place Like Home: Luis Trenker's *The Prodigal Son* (1934)." *New German Critique* 60 (1993): 33–56.

Reynolds, Daniel P. *Postcards from Auschwitz: Holocaust Tourism and the Meaning of Remembrance.* New York: New York University Press, 2018.

Russell, Jamie. *Book of the Dead: The Complete History of Zombie Cinema.* Rev. Ed. London: Titan Books, 2014.

Schiffauer, Jörg. "Tatort Traunsee." *Ray Filmmagazin* 9 (2006): 38–40.

Schneider, Steven Jay, and Tony Williams. "Introduction." In *Horror International,* edited by Steven Jay Schneider and Tony Williams, 1–12. Detroit, MI: Wayne State University Press, 2005.

Siddique, Sophia, and Raphael Raphael. "Introduction." In *Transnational Horror Cinema: Bodies of Excess and the Global Grotesque*, edited by Sophia Siddique and Raphael Raphael, 1–15. New York: Palgrave Macmillan, 2016.

Smith, Iain Robert. *The Hollywood Meme: Transnational Adaptations in World Cinema*. Edinburgh: Edinburgh University Press, 2016.

Spooner, Catherine. *Contemporary Gothic*. London: Reaktion Books, 2006.

Steffen, Will, Paul J. Crutzen, and John R. McNeill. "The Anthropocene: Are Humans Overwhelming the Great Forces of Nature?" *Ambio* 36, no. 8 (2007): 614–21.

Taylor, Drew. "Review: Low Budget Austrian Horror Movie *Blood Glacier* Is Campy and Limp." *IndieWire*. May 1, 2014. https://www.indiewire.com/2014/05/review-low-budget-austrian-horror-movie-blood-glacier-is-campy-and-limp-86462/

Tomlinson, John. *Globalization and Culture*. Cambridge: Polity Press, 1999.

von Dassanowsky, Robert, and Oliver C. Speck. "New Austrian Film: The Non-Exceptional Exception." In *New Austrian Film*, edited by Robert von Dassanowsky and Oliver C. Speck, 1–17. New York: Berghahn Books, 2011.

Wagnleitner, Reinhold. *Coca-Colonization and the Cold War. The Cultural Mission of the United States in Austria after the Second World War*. Translated by Diana M. Wolf. Chapel Hill: University of North Carolina Press, 1994.

Wells, Paul. *The Horror Genre: From Beelzebub to* Blair Witch. London. Wallflower Press, 2000.

Wood, Robin. *Hollywood from Vietnam to Reagan . . . and Beyond*. Rev. and Exp. Edn. New York: Columbia University Press, 2003.

*Chapter Three*

# Korean National Trauma and the Myth of Hypermasculinity in *The Wailing* (2016)

Luisa Hyojin Koo

In May 2016, my father went to the theater to watch the most popular domestic film of the week in Korea: *The Wailing*. He did not enjoy the film. When asked why not, he could not pinpoint a single factor. Instead, he said, "It leaves a bad taste." The main character in *The Wailing* is a policeman and the father of a young daughter (who happens to share my Korean name). His social status and gender should provide him with authority and power in a traditional setting. The world, however, has changed. The protective, hypermasculine patriarch is ineffective in the face of growing female subjectivity. Upon examining the film, I conjecture that the film's critique of hypermasculinity left my father, an aging patriarch who recently quit his thirty-year career, with a bad taste. "It's okay, my baby. You know daddy's a policeman. I'll take care of everything. Daddy will," the main character whispers as he dies at the hands of his ghost-possessed daughter. Perhaps my father saw here an example of the failures of patriarchy. *The Wailing* questions Korea's national myth of hypermasculinity that results from national trauma of domination.

*The Wailing*, directed by Na Hong-jin and released in 2016, is set in the small county of Gokseong, where sudden deaths occur soon after a mysterious Japanese man moves to town. Victims develop rashes, then go on to kill themselves and their entire families in their homes. At one of the earlier crime scenes the hero, Jong-gu, meets a young woman in white who tells him that the Japanese man is a ghost wreaking havoc on the townspeople. In the beginning of the film, it is unclear whether the Japanese man is the monster or not. As the film progresses, however, it is revealed that the young woman herself is the evil ghost, but Jong-gu is unable to comprehend that a young woman can possess such depravity and power. Instead, he fixates on the Japanese man. When Jong-gu's daughter Hyo-jin develops a rash and starts acting violently, Jong-gu heads to the Japanese man's house and breaks his furniture, issuing a warning to stay away from his family and town. At the same time, Jong-gu's mother-in-law senses that Hyo-jin's illness is related to a ghost, not the Japanese man, and calls on a male shaman to perform a ritual. Jong-gu stops the ritual before it is completed when Hyo-jin screams that it hurts, and instead returns to the Japanese man's house, armed and with others, to kill the man. In the next scene the Japanese man is thrown in front of the truck Jong-gu is driving. Jong-gu confirms that the man is dead, and, feeling relieved, he throws the body off the side of the road. In the background the young woman in white, who had presumably pushed the Japanese man to his death, watches from afar as Jong-gu dumps the body. When the strange murders do not stop with the Japanese man's death, the shaman then realizes that the ghost is not the Japanese man but the young woman in white. He calls Jong-gu, but even as the shaman explains how dangerous the young woman is, Jong-gu refuses to change his assumptions, asking: "Then who's the Japanese man?" Hanging up the phone, Jong-gu runs into the young woman. She tries to convince him one last time that the Japanese man is the real threat. Instead of running home as the shaman tells him, however, Jong-gu hesitates when the woman tells him that if he goes home now his entire family will die. Persuaded by her words, Jong-gu arrives home too late, to find that his daughter has killed both his wife and his mother-in-law. As Hyo-jin walks toward him with a knife in her hand, Jong-gu claims that he will take care of everything.

## NATIONALITY AND HYPERMASCULINITY

*The Wailing* is a Korean film that reveals a unifying national myth rooted in both history and national trauma. National trauma, or historical trauma, is a tragic event from the past that "bleeds through conventional confines of time and space."[1] The trauma of the historical event transcends time and space and becomes integral to the formation of national identity. Embedded in *The Wailing* are legacies of the historical domination of Korea by the Japanese and the resulting creation of the national myth of hypermasculinity. Hypermasculinity in the film *The Wailing* results in ethnic and gender prejudice in the main character Jong-gu, who cannot perceive of a threat that is not external.

Hypermasculinity refers, here, to the exaggerated performance of masculinity, often by a father figure in a film, with the intention of legitimizing male violence within the film narrative. The term is derived from research conducted by psychologists Donald L. Mosher and Silvan S. Tomkins, who in 1988 conducted a study to observe how masculine behavior is ranked superior to feminine behavior within all-male groups.[2] As Mosher and Tomkins note, "macho ideology honors the 'superior, masculine' affects and humiliates the displayer of 'inferior, feminine' affects. [...] Not just a male, and not just masculine, the macho must be hypermasculine in ideology and action."[3] First used as a description of machismo, hypermasculinity is based on the assumption of male subjectivity. While machismo emphasizes both violence among men and sexualization of women, hypermasculinity emphasizes male subjectivity and subsequent behavior. Although the study was conducted in the United States, the researchers observed gendered behavior across different racial groups. As implied in the original research, the term hypermasculinity is not limited to a certain racial group or Americans. I will use the term in this chapter to explore the hegemonic masculinity that reinforces gender and social hierarchy in contemporary Korean portrayals of male-identified post-trauma narratives.

In *The Wailing* the main character, Jong-gu, tries to protect his family and town by confronting the Japanese man. He ultimately fails because his fear of (male) infiltration prevents him from seeing the (female) danger that already lurks within. The hypermasculine subject can see the female only as an extension of itself, not as an independent subject with the potential to act as a threat, so the hypermasculine subject must direct aggression instead toward the male extranational Other, while protecting intranational female objects. In other words, historical trauma results in the incorrect expectation of an Other in *The Wailing* as necessarily both male and national (Japanese).

The earliest concept of the nation is based on Otherization. Political theorist Benedict Anderson defines nation as "an imagined community" that is both limited and sovereign.[4] A nation is imagined because the members within a nation assume a unifying identity that is neither tangible nor substantive. People of a nation cannot know all the individual members, but can imagine a binding identity through the concept of nationality. The nation is limited in the sense that there exists an Other juxtaposed against the self. The national borders define and limit the nation as a separate unit, which stands as sovereign. Film theorist Susan Hayward engages with the close relationship between sociopolitical culture and nationness in French national cinema. Hayward claims that the use of "nation" is a political and cultural mode of asserting national identity, as culture creates a meaning in order to maintain a sense of unity as a nation. Nation is therefore a political construct, a necessarily perpetuated myth that legitimizes institutions and customs within the nation. Hayward also recognizes a tautological relationship between cinema and the nation: because cinema is a political cultural product, it "affirms what it reflects, and is affirmed by what it reflects."[5] Thus, national cinema cannot be considered separate from the nation and the national myth, and the nation forms in the context of political and cultural history.

Postcolonial film theorist Wimal Dissanayake argues that national cinema plays a crucial role in perpetuating a unifying national myth that marks a nation as unique and whole.[6] National identity and legitimacy derives from the national myth that reinforces the unity of the nation and validates its institutions. In this way, national cinema perpetuates national myths, and through this process of perpetuation, myth becomes a part of self-identity of the nation. Deriving from a national trauma, national myth reinvents the nation as a unified whole, while disregarding fragments and marginalized groups. National myth presents a singular narrative that serves as the binding self-image of the nation. National trauma scholar Linnie Blake argues that such singular narratives of national myth serve to constantly repress national trauma in an attempt to maintain a cohesive identity. Korea's national trauma is primarily located in the period of Japanese colonialism, which lasted from 1910 to 1945. The Japanese domination is traumatic because it is more than a moment of tragedy in history. E. Ann Kaplan explains that traumas "can never be 'healed' in the sense of a return to how things were before a catastrophe took place."[7] Korea is no longer dominated by Japan, yet the experience of colonialism is relevant and impactful even today.

## COLONIALISM AND CULTURE

Japanese colonialism has had a lasting impact on Korean national identity because it focused on cultural assimilation, thereby repressing an inherently "Korean" spirit. Korean schools under Japanese rule were forbidden to teach the Korean language, and many people were forced to adapt Japanese-style names. Like other colonial powers before them, the Japanese sought to eradicate the distinctive cultures of their conquered territories and make them part of Japanese territory culturally, as well as politically. During and after colonialism, Korean cultural products, including films, attempted to preserve and publicize an authentic Korean culture in opposition to the imposed Japanese culture. With the Eulsa Treaty in 1905, Korea was officially declared a protected state under Japanese imperialism. The treaty, however, was actually intended to advance the domination of Korea by the Japanese, opening up channels through which many Japanese entered Korean lands, and prompting an influx of Japanese and Hollywood films to Korea as entertainment. There are records of Korean schools showing educational films, but though motion picture projectors were brought from Japan as early as 1905, it was not until 1912 that theaters were set up for the masses.[8] Films screened in Korea during the early 1910s were predominantly Hollywood productions.[9] It was not until 1922 that Koreans produced feature-length films, starting with *Chunhyangjeon*. By 1924, the Korean film production company Chosun Kinema was set up in Busan, often colliding with the emerging cultural rule under imperial Japan. Policies on Korean films restricted depictions of traditional culture and patriotic themes, and filmmakers struggled to find ways, despite the regulations, to express an identifiable, "authentic" Koreanness and preserve their unique Korean heritage.

Korea's national cinema was thus formed in opposition to the dominance of the Japanese colonizers, who were necessarily and perpetually depicted as the Other. Korean cinema began with a narrow definition of what constitutes a good Korean film. Early Korean films were *minjok* films, or as Tae-geun An defines them, films that contain sensibilities that communicate only to Koreans.[10] A *minjok* film not only tells the story of the Koreans but is also produced by Koreans. An argues that early films in Korea started out as a direct response to oppressive Japanese colonial rule, which influenced the way artforms were perceived as cultural rather than commercial products. Cultural expression became a way to rebel against assimilation, functioning as a repository for the oppressed Korean spirit. As Japanese colonialism ended and the Korean market expanded, insular *minjok* films were replaced by more commercialized films that often mirrored Hollywood blockbusters and genre films. Nevertheless, even as Korean films expanded to cater to international audiences as well as domestic ones, opposition to Japanese colonialism remained a defining force that played a key role in distinguishing a uniquely Korean sensibility. Particularly, the trauma of domination as seen from the male subject's perspective is tragic because his possessions, family, and nation were taken away by an outsider. The hypermasculine self in contrast aggressively protects its belongings and its objects. Nancy Abelmann addresses the explicit focus on masculine sufferings when discussing Korean national trauma. She outlines how loss or displacement of male subjectivity has been the mode of expressing colonialism.[11] In other words, the national trauma has been rendered as the sufferings of male Koreans. Even though *The Wailing* is set in modern-day Korea that is no longer dominated by the Japanese, the film nevertheless relates back to the historical trauma and hypermasculinity in response to the national trauma.

## INTERROGATING HYPERMASCULINITY

*The Wailing* is unique in its critique of the hypermasculinity that Jong-gu assumes in response to a supposed threat to his home. As with other national films that accentuate the necessity of hypermasculinity when faced with danger, *The Wailing* first depicts Jong-gu as a patriarch living in a society of changing values and gender roles. Jong-gu's home, as well as other homes in the neighborhood, are modified versions of the traditional Korean-style *hanok* house. Inside the house, however, the family dynamic is nontraditional. A traditional family dynamic prescribes that the newly married couple live with the husband's family. The woman becomes a *part* of his family in perpetuity, as an old Korean saying states, "A daughter-in-law should become the ghost of the house into which she marries." Instead, Jong-gu lives with his wife, daughter, and mother-in-law, and his home therefore shows shifting gender dynamics as his mother-in-law assumes the role of the matriarch. Jong-gu is seen as lacking authority compared to his stronger female family members. For example, the mother-in-law forces Jong-gu to eat breakfast, which he throws up at the gruesome crime scene while his fellow police officers stare in pity. Another example is when Jong-gu's wife initiates sex, and as they engage in intercourse in the confines of their car (the only private place in the house) Hyo-jin catches them. Jong-gu runs away in embarrassment as his daughter and wife stare at him.

While the film depicts Jong-gu as a patriarch lacking in power at the beginning of the film, the presence of an outsider, a Japanese man, legitimizes Jong-gu's transition to a hypermasculine role. The Japanese man, recently having moved to Gokseong, instills a sense of mystery, hatred, and fear in the townspeople, who believe that the strange murders started after he arrived. He is the outsider, and Japanese colonial history marks him as a former oppressor. Before Jong-gu meets the Japanese man, he hears two rumors about him: one is that the man is raping a local woman, and the other, which Jong-gu hears from a young woman in white, is that he is a blood-drinking monster. The rumor of rape is a direct reference to "comfort women," numerous young Korean women who were tricked or forced into servicing Japanese soldiers sexually during World War II. The surviving comfort women voice the trauma of the experience even today.

Just as the Japanese man is portrayed as a rapist, the young woman, in contrast, appears as a strange but powerless victim. She wears a white shirt and skirt that resembles traditional Korean mourning clothes (*sobok*) and tells Jong-gu that the Japanese man is a monster: "If you keep seeing him around, it's because he's stalking you. To suck your blood dry." The rumors fortified with past historical trauma are enough for Jong-gu to envision the foreigner as nonhuman and dangerous.

Hyo-jin's illness instigates Jong-gu's aggression toward the Japanese man because Jong-gu can only see his daughter as needing his protection. Hyo-jin wakes up from a nightmare with rashes developing on her legs. She cries, "Do something, Daddy. Someone keeps banging the door trying to get in. A strange man. He's trying to get in." Hyo-jin's words directly allude to an image of infiltration, a dangerous and unknown male Other trying to enter through the door to Jong-gu's home by way of Hyo-jin. Sensing a direct threat against his home and his family, Jong-gu assumes the role of the hypermasculine by locating the Japanese man as the perpetrator and ransacking his house and possessions, reversing the roles of oppressor and victim.

The Japanese man's house resembles a traditional Korean house from the outside. However, inside it is filled with things Jong-gu calls "perverted" and strange: Japanese Noh masks, Shunga (Japanese erotic art), and a Shinto shrine with animal sacrifices. The markedly Japanese items in the house further highlight the outsider status of the Japanese man while providing a reason for Jong-gu to identify the man as dangerous *because* he is Japanese. Reversing the historical invasion, Jong-gu trespasses in the Japanese man's house to break his things. He yells: "What the fuck are you doing in my town? Do you know whose daughter you're messing with?" The Japanese man's presence triggers a visceral reaction from Jong-gu as a father, a policeman, and a Korean. With bravado, Jong-gu claims that "this is Gokseong, my turf." Subverting the historical destruction of Korean culture by Japanese colonialism, Jong-gu tries to reclaim hypermasculine authority for himself. He claims protection over his family, town, and country from the dangerous Other.

Unlike many other national films, however, *The Wailing* involves conflicts that are not dissolved by Jong-gu's assumption of a hypermasculine role. The outside threat that Jong-gu fights via his hypermasculine identity is misplaced due to his prejudices: first, that the threat of the male Other can only be subdued by hypermasculinity and second, that no female can be an Other or a threat. To that end, Jong-gu is unable to doubt the young woman in white. Unlike the Japanese man who appears frequently in his dreams as the monster, the young woman does not scare Jong-gu. She appears strange but harmless. Part of her unthreatening demeanor derives from her gender and age. She appears innocent and weak, incapable of harming others. Jong-gu is unable to sense the danger she poses because of his prejudice—extranational prejudice stemming from the historical trauma of Japanese domination as well as intranational prejudice rooted in the hypermasculine myth that sees women as needing protection.

The female ghost reveals Jong-gu's prejudice against women, as well as an existing cultural image of female ghosts in the horror genre. The role of the female ghost in this film diverges from that of the traditional Korean horror genre. Folklore and ghost stories have long influenced Korean horror films, especially until the 1970s.[12] A female ghost is a common theme in earlier horror films that depict women's subordinate social status and resulting sufferings. Typically, the female ghost is a young woman who had been hurt or murdered by a man or an older woman of higher social status. The young woman becomes an avenging ghost to haunt those who have wronged her. These female ghosts derive power from their grief, and target only their oppressors.[13] The feminine power of revenge in traditional Korean tales is specific and poignant, never indiscriminate and evil.

Traditional Korean horror is strongly influenced by melodrama working in tandem with hypermasculinity to reinforce male-centric viewpoints and expectations. The female ghosts in early Korean horror genre were more pitied than feared, representing one of the several ways that Korean horror has been influenced by melodramatic narrative. As Alison Peirse and Daniel Martin states, "The strong streak of melodrama in Korean horror is one of the defining characteristics of the genre."[14] The origin of melodramatic narrative in early Korean cinema derives in part from a theatrical style called *Shinpa* in Japanese films. *Shinpa* focused on melodramatic plots and social critique of class structure, with an emphasis on feminine sufferings. As Peirse and Martin argues, "*Shinpa* connotes tragic tales of romance and female suffering, defeatist narratives with inevitably sad endings, designed as quintessential 'tear jerkers.' So influential is the melodramatic mode in Korean cinema that its narrative qualities frequently emerge in horror."[15] As a precursor to melodrama, *Shinpa* films were distributed throughout Korea where consumers preferred the particular melodramatic narrative it used. Seo In-sook argues that the exhibition of *Shinpa* films contributed to both political and ideological control over Korea as well as served to establish Korea as a marketplace for Japanese products.[16] Although traditional Korean tales were featured in *Shinpa*-style films, they were directed and produced by the Japanese. By the mid-1930s there were twelve million viewers in theaters on average, while the population was twenty-three million, but most were Hollywood imports and Japanese *Shinpa* style films.[17]

The melodramatic notion of the binary between good and evil exists in ghost films throughout 1970s and 1980s in Korea. By the late 1980s, Peirse and Martin observe that practitioners of horror began to experiment, yet the genre still predominantly portrayed Confucian traditional family dynamics.[18] Unable to deviate far from the family dynamics and patriarchal structure, traditional Korean horror reinforced the binary division between good and evil. On the contrary, *The Wailing* shows the very discrepancy between the traditional binaries of good and evil as well as male and female. *The Wailing* is singular in providing a subtle critique of the hypermasculine myth that prevents Jong-gu from acknowledging a young woman, not an ethnic Other male subjectivity, as a source of danger. Unable to conceive of the young woman as capable of indiscriminate evil, Jong-gu asks, "Why my daughter?" While he was quick to accept the Japanese man as being evil, he cannot see the seemingly harmless young woman as embodying such evil for no apparent reason. The absence of a reason for the female ghost's atrocities is significant because it reverts Jong-gu's male-centered understanding of the source and form of feminine power. The female ghost forces Jong-gu to observe female subjectivity as, not a part of, but separate from male subjectivity.

## CONCLUSION

The reading of *The Wailing* through the lens of national trauma and its subsequent myth of hypermasculinity allows the audience to consider the groups excluded from this unified national identity, or what Dissanayake calls a countermemory.[19] Countermemory provides a more multileveled image of the nation while interrogating the single privileged myth. *The Wailing* works as a countermemory by subverting gender expectations in Korean horror films. Historically, Korean horror developed to be focused on the repressed victim (often a young female) that had been wronged by the abusive villain (often male) due to melodramatic narrative's influence. The ghost that haunts people is not the villain but the victim. The true evil of traditional Korean horror genre lies with the villain that oppressed and victimized the ghost in its past life that led to its death.

By providing a female ghost with no visible oppressor, the film questions the efficacy of the national myth of hypermasculinity that categorizes women as powerless objects requiring protection. As a lingering historical trauma, Korea's history of Japanese colonialism triggers the national myth of hypermasculinity that celebrates aggressive protection of property. The deprivation of power and material resources of the past affects Jong-gu's response in the film as he doggedly chases the wrong source of fear. *The Wailing* shows how repeating historical trauma and its subsequent myths are insufficient to address gender dynamics in modern-day Korea.

## NOTES

1. Lowenstein, *Shocking Representation*, 1.
2. Mosher and Tomkins, "Scripting the Macho Man."
3. Ibid., 64.
4. Anderson, *Imagined Communities*, 6.
5. Hayward, *French National Cinema*, x.
6. Dissanayake, *Colonialism and Nationalism*, xii–xiv.
7. Kaplan, *Trauma Culture*, 19.
8. Cho, "Film Policy during Japanese Colonialism," 50.
9. Ibid., 51.

10. An, *100 Years of Korean Film History*, 26.
11. Abelmann, *The Melodrama of Mobility*, 187–88.
12. Peirse and Martin, *Korean Horror Cinema*, 2.
13. Ibid., 2.
14. Ibid., 5.
15. Ibid.
16. Seo, *Postcolonialism in Korean Films*, 118.
17. Cho, "Film Policy during Japanese Colonialism," 66–67.
18. Peirse and Martin, *Korean Horror Cinema*, 8.
19. Dissanayake, *Colonialism and Nationalism*, xxiii.

## BIBLIOGRAPHY

Abelmann, Nancy. *The Melodrama of Mobility: Women, Talk, and Class in Contemporary South Korea*. Honolulu: University of Hawaii Press, 2003.

An, Tae-geun. *100 Years of Korean Film History*. Book Story, 2013.

Anderson, Benedict. *Imagined Communities: Reflections on the Origin and Spread of Nationalism*, 3rd ed. London: Verso, 2006.

Blake, Linnie. *The Wounds of Nations: Horror Cinema, Historical Trauma and National Identity*. Manchester, UK: Manchester University Press, 2008.

Cho, Jun-hyung. "Film Policy during Japanese Colonialism: 1903–1945." In *A History of Korean Film Policy*, edited by Dong-ho Kim, 45–106. Paju: Nanam Publishing House, 2005.

Dissanayake, Wimal, editor. *Colonialism & Nationalism in Asian Cinema*. Bloomington: Indiana University Press, 1994.

Hayward, Susan. *French National Cinema*, 2nd ed. London: Routledge, 2005.

Kaplan, Ann E. *Trauma Culture: The Politics of Terror and Loss in Media and Literature*. New Brunswick, NJ: Rutgers University Press, 2005.

Lowenstein, Adam. *Shocking Representation: Historical Trauma, National Cinema, and the Modern Horror Film*. New York: Columbia University Press, 2005.

Mosher, Donald L., and Silvan S. Tomkins. "Scripting the Macho Man: Hypermasculine Socialization and Enculturation." *Journal of Sex Research* 25, no. 1 (February 1988), 60–84.

Peirse, Alison, and Daniel Martin, editors. *Korean Horror Cinema*. Edinburgh: Edinburgh University Press, 2013.

Seo, In-sook. *Postcolonialism in Korean Films: A Discussion of Han and Shinpa*. Seoul: Geulnurim Publishing Company, 2012.

*The Wailing*. Directed by Na Hong-jin. Seoul: 20th Century Fox, 2016.

*Chapter Four*

# The Witch, the Wolf, and the Monster

## *Monstrous Bodies and Empire in* Penny Dreadful

Allyson Marino

Originally referred to as Penny Bloods because of the violence and gore they contained, Penny Dreadfuls were weekly serial papers published in nineteenth-century England and sold for a penny each. They were marketed toward London's working-class and undereducated populations, and the stories, which depicted violence, crime, murder, and sexual indecorum, were widely criticized as contributing to moral degradation. The early versions of the serial publications were influenced by the frightening features of eighteenth-century Gothic literature such as crumbling castles, superstition and omens, and the supernatural.[1] Although the popularity of Penny Dreadfuls continued to soar during the nineteenth century as literacy rates increased, their poor reputation points to a national identity crisis in Victorian England due to socioeconomic shifts that occurred during the eighteenth and nineteenth centuries in Britain. During the eighteenth century, literacy rates among the working class increased along with the rise of access to education and continued industrialization. Both processes changed who had access to wealth. Additionally, nationalism and discussions of national identity continued to hold space in the late nineteenth century as England worked to reinforce its position as a colonial power. Restrictions on proper moral behavior for British citizens evolved in response to these societal changes. Because the social elite worried about the stories' corrupting influence on England's youth and working class, they accused Penny Dreadfuls of infecting the nation with immorality and impropriety at a time when England was defending its colonial power and struggling to maintain a national identity amid social and economic instability.

*Penny Dreadful*, a British-American television series that debuted on Showtime in early 2014 and ran for three seasons, shares the Gothic influences and tensions of its namesake. The story line takes place against the backdrop of a colonial nation striving to define itself at home and abroad. Fittingly, the show confronts this national identity crisis through the lenses of horror and the monstrous. Set in 1890s Victorian England, *Penny Dreadful* features familiar characters from nineteenth-century horror and colonial fiction including Victor Frankenstein, Dorian Gray, and Mina Murray. Vampires, werewolves, witches, demons, and reanimated corpses populate this world—characters drawn from texts as varied as Alan Moore's *League of Extraordinary Gentleman* and Kim Newman's *Anno Dracula* series to the novels of steampunk writers such as K. W. Jeter and Tim Powers. The central protagonist, Vanessa Ives, navigates the polluted, foggy streets of London, lined by crumbling estates and newly constructed factories, as she battles a cast of monstrous beings at night and in shadowed spaces. Vanessa sees herself as engaging in a battle of good against evil and, as she eventually acknowledges, two conflicting parts of herself: one, a proper upper-class Victorian woman and the other a powerful and defiant supernatural being. On the surface, the show's narrative unfolds as an homage to Gothic and Victorian horror stories. Campy at times, but still closely echoing the original stories, the series comments on the shifting definitions of class, gender, and nation during the latter period of Great Britain's colonial empire in the late nineteenth century, when concepts of self and home were disrupted, contested, and defined. While the complicated processes of colonialism and the formation of a national identity took place over centuries and in the various time periods during which the original stories were produced, England's long history and identity crisis at the end of the nineteenth century serve as important backdrops for the series. Each of the main characters struggles with concepts of the Self and the Other while England's shifting national identity looms in the background. These monstrous protagonists and antagonists are ultimately homeless because they exist in the liminal spaces of society. They are at home neither in nation nor self.

The first season of the series introduces the familiar main conflict. Vanessa's closest childhood friend, Mina Murray, has been abducted by a Dracula-type figure. Mina's wealthy explorer father, Sir Malcom Murray, enlists Vanessa's help in rescuing his daughter from the monster. He has already lost one child to infection while traveling together on the African continent. Now Vanessa and Sir Malcom both blame themselves for Mina's abduction and are desperate for redemption. Transgressing the boundaries of Victorian sexual morality, both have engaged in affairs and each blames their own boundary-crossing for Mina's susceptibility to the monster. To aid in Mina's rescue, they collect a group of characters, each monstrous in his own way—American cowboy and sharpshooter Ethan Chandler, later revealed as a werewolf; Victor Frankenstein, still the curious scientist; and Dorian

Gray—all of whom enact their own side stories along the way. Other characters with important stories of *their* own interact with the central monster-hunting team. The image of the witch, represented by Vanessa and several other characters throughout the series; the shape-shifting werewolf figure of Ethan Chandler; and the monstrous Frankenstein-created creature, Caliban all function as symbols of unstable gender, class, and race definitions as colonial England interacts with both its colonies and working class in a relationship of monstrous motherhood. In the series, we can read often-discussed ideas about horror, monstrosity, and monstrous femininity specifically through the lens of colonial anxiety.

## THE VICTORIAN GOTHIC

While we usually understand Victorian fiction as engaging with constructions of gender and sexuality during its time period, we can examine Victorian Gothic fiction—and the earlier novels that influenced it—as challenging patriarchal representations of power and sexuality against the backdrop of rising industrialization. Even the original Penny Dreadfuls were full of tales of monsters, depraved women, and marginal figures the public could easily identify as existing outside the boundaries of acceptable Victorian (British) moral behavior. Monsters in both the Penny Dreadfuls and Victorian horror fiction represent the Other—that is, the identity situated against the default, whether national or gendered. In horror writing and films, monsters are described as unknowable figures, or as Noel Carroll explains, "categorically transgressive," and this uncomfortable ambiguity is what creates their monstrosity.[2] Carroll explains that "monsters are not only physically threatening; they are cognitively threatening," and hence they can be read as "challenges to the foundations of a culture's way of knowing."[3] In addition to representing the Other or the unknowable, monstrous figures in *Penny Dreadful* act as a sign of defiance and resistance to the rigid definitions that frame them. Here, monsters are sympathetic characters. They are heroes even in their monstrosity, and they acknowledge and embrace their differences as possibility and power.

Monstrous women in particular are defined and shaped by those in more powerful positions, who, in the end, turn out to be the real monsters. Patriarchy and colonialism are revealed, in the series, as monstrous ideologies. With this commentary, *Penny Dreadful* turns a twenty-first century lens onto the familiar grand narratives of Victorian England, bringing new attention to the intersection of colonial expansion and patriarchy. Cultural and literary critics such as Julian Wolfreys, David J. Skal, and Stephen T. Asma have argued that monsters can be understood as representations of societal or personal anxiety—a challenge to identity. When considered through the lens of colonialism and colonial history, monsters, here, stand as representations of national anxiety due to the era's economic and cultural instability that arose as destructive colonial ideology was challenged and exposed. Monstrosity, in this case, is the manifestation of fear over the loss of economic and social power.

In *The Victorian Gothic*, Julian Wolfreys explains that "the gothic becomes truly haunting in that it can never be pinned down as a single identity, while it returns through various apparitions and manifestations, seemingly everywhere."[4] Alexandra Warwick notes that the Victorian Gothic focuses on two settings in particular: the domestic space and the urban space.[5] *Penny Dreadful* moves between both spaces: the margins of the city—underground tunnels, the docks, overcrowded working class slums—and the beautiful, yet even more terrifying, interiors of opulent houses and ancestral estates. Likewise, Kate Ferguson Ellis argues that, in the eighteenth and nineteenth centuries, domestic spaces were defined in opposition to public spaces and framed by larger culture as safe spaces or havens.[6] For women in particular, home is the space of reproduction, where their main charge is to reproduce for the nation—to make more citizens. The ideology of the "angel in the house" reinforced this cultural placement. A short poem of the same title, written by Coventry Patmore in 1854, was very popular in its time period and into the early twentieth century. The poem presents an ideal male-female relationship and their expected gender roles, idealizing women as angels in the home, devoting themselves to their husbands. Women were expected to be the moral guardians of the nation, and to instruct new citizens—future colonial soldiers—in the ways of the nation. In the mid-1700s, before the rigid hierarchies of the Victorian period developed, the rise of the Gothic novel with its "crumbling castles as sites of terror" pointed to fear over shifting roles for women and the upper classes. As industrialization took root in the latter part of the century, the "crumbling castles" of Gothic novels signaled the decay of the landed upper classes as new economic structures shook the foundations of traditional class-based society.

While the physical and metaphorical domestic spaces of the landed classes were depicted as disintegrating and unstable in eighteenth- and nineteenth-century Gothic literature, public spaces were also deemed troubling, especially for women. The public realm was accessible only to men and the upper classes, while home spaces were safe, private, and protected—feminine spaces. The Victorian Gothic engages with the concept of binary, segregated spaces but imagines the house to be just as rife with ambiguities and danger as public spaces, particularly for women of both the upper and working classes, for whom homes are sites of servitude and entrapment. *Penny Dreadful*, with its colonial tensions, presents the idea of the home as unsafe as public spaces and extends the critique further. In this binary hierarchy, the nation is home (the domestic space) and the colonized spaces on the outskirts are also unsafe, full of the unknown and populated by the Other. These public spaces bring home fear, which invades and infects the home nation. Boundaries that are ideologically constructed as rigid—us/them, domestic/public, male/female, human/monster—become permeable and ambiguous. The ambiguity—the inability to define and neatly categorize—becomes monstrous, as represented by some of the characters and their fight against what they define as evil. In the series, everyone is sick or infected in some way. No one is pure or immune. The characters are repellent and feel repelled at the same time. The idea that everything exists in an interstitial space—that there is no either/or, only both—extends to conceptions of national identity as well. As boundaries are revealed as ideological constructions, so, too, are borders between nations and national identities.

## PATRIARCHY AND IMPERIALISM

*Penny Dreadful*'s characters echo this sense of un-homing. Vanessa is safe nowhere. Her hauntings and possessions occur no matter the location, and, in many cases, public spaces are safer for her than her own home. Her scariest experiences happen in the enclosed spaces of her bedroom; in the country house of her mentor and adviser, the Cut-Wife; and in the prison rooms of the asylum where she is locked away. For Frankenstein's creature—John Clare, also known as Caliban—home is a shifting concept: a site of refuge only when it is located in shadowed spaces or underground. In his life before his recreation as Frankenstein's creature, his home is shown as an infected space, crowded and filthy, where his dying son lies helpless in his bed as Caliban struggles to earn enough money to keep his family alive. Another important character, Irish immigrant Brona Croft, who is later murdered, reanimated, and renamed Lily by Frankenstein, is always unhomed. She begins and ends as a liminal figure, first as a sex worker in London, poor and suffering from tuberculosis, and then as another of Frankenstein's creatures, existing between life and death. Likewise, Sir Malcom Murray has returned from his colonial endeavors abroad but finds himself unable to truly return home. In the final season, after burying his friend and confidant, Sembene, he explains, "What romance I saw in Africa is done for me.... The land is tainted now beyond repair, and I want to be quit of the filthy place. What then? Are there no fresh wonders left? No worlds yet to conquer?"[7] Although he voices this sentiment in the final season, it pervades the entire series.

Ethan Chandler is driven from his home due to colonial violence and is never able to recapture what home once meant for him. He is introduced on the show as a sharpshooting cowboy from the Wild West—a symbol of American frontier spirit and westward expansion—whose background involves great crimes against indigenous populations, and whose past is inseparable from the history of colonialism. Ethan first appears in the story as a stereotypical American cowboy figure, even wearing a costume and playing up an accent. The audience learns, however, that this is just a role—a construction—and not an authentic identity. Like the United States itself, Ethan hides many dark and violent incidents in his past. His story line as a werewolf is eventually revealed to be tied to that past: he was a soldier in the Indian Wars and slaughtered a family of indigenous Apache. His own monstrous identity is linked not only to crimes against humanity committed in the name of imperialism, but to Native American ideas on shape-shifting, or "skinwalking." Ethan's struggle with his two selves—or as he says, "the monsters inside us"—has now become an inseparable part of his identity.[8] The violence that he commits while in his werewolf form symbolizes the violence that will always be a part of him because of his murderous actions as a colonizer. He explains: "There are such sins at my back, it would kill me to turn around."[9] He cannot run away from his past, nor from the colonial past of his nation. Ethan's journey offers one of the more direct examples of shifting identities in the series. He has fled his home at the start of the narrative and is repeatedly called, and finally dragged, back to confront his own personal history as well as the larger history of colonialism.

Perhaps most important in the colonial story line is Victor Frankenstein's famous creature, reinterpreted and, in the show, named "Caliban" by his creator. His namesake recalls the monstrous depiction of a defiant indigenous savage in Shakespeare's last play, *The Tempest*. After escaping from Frankenstein, Caliban renames himself, choosing John Clare after the Romantic peasant poet who valorized the natural world. He finds truth in this name rather than in the Enlightenment's embrace of scientific inquiry and reasoning. As John Clare, he recites Romantic poetry from memory and resides in the underground and marginal spaces on the outskirts of society, preferring to hide his monstrous self in the shadows. As in Mary Shelley's original novel, this story line critiques the new world of scientific inquiry, advancing human technology and even, it can be argued, patriarchal power. The name Caliban, however, is also important, since it implicates the history of British colonialism in the creation of a monstrous new society. Britain's ideology of expansion and conquest, in all its forms, is revealed to be the true original monster—the mother of all monsters.

Published in 1611, *The Tempest* is situated during a time of European exploration of the new world, between the ideals of the Renaissance and the forward-looking, utopian concerns of the Enlightenment. In a nod to colonial explorations that began over a hundred years prior, Shakespeare's play begins with a shipwreck on an island inhabited by the exiled Duke of Milan, now called Prospero; his pure and virginal daughter, Miranda; an island spirit called Ariel; and the monstrous Caliban. Caliban lived on the island with his mother, Sycorax, before Prospero landed there himself. After killing Sycorax, Prospero takes on Caliban as his slave. Caliban, though, does not accept his slavery without resistance. He reminds Prospero that he has rights to the island. He calls out Prospero on his colonial project by refusing the proto-Enlightenment principles that ushered in colonialism and slavery. Caliban resists the new order, reminding Prospero that "You taught me language, and my profit on't/Is, I know how to curse. The red plague ride you/For learning me your language."[10]

There are several important ideas here that work to situate the colonial anxieties confronted in *Penny Dreadful*. In the series, Caliban's naming suggests that the roots of the anxieties and instability in Victorian England were deeply entrenched. Colonial expansion was just taking root in 1611, driven by the need to not only collect resources, make fortunes, and control trade and military routes, but also to fulfill ideas of a utopian new world, fueled by Renaissance desires to leave behind the plagues and corruption of Europe and to look for an overseas Eden in which to begin anew. This utopian vision—deeply discussed in *The Tempest* as characters bide their shipwrecked time on the island—was generally only for the wealthy. Laboring classes in the home nations and abroad, as well as the indigenous peoples in colonized spaces, were marginalized, disenfranchised, or enslaved. On the island, Caliban is enslaved and dehumanized. He is monstrous. The Caliban of *Penny Dreadful* is a different kind of monster but still disenfranchised and enslaved—a science experiment—who, like is namesake in Shakespeare and his literary representation in Shelley's novel, steadfastly displays his anger and resentment over his position.

Finally, there is the symbol of Sycorax. Though she is mentioned only briefly in the play, she is still Caliban's powerful mother—a witch. She is the first one to be destroyed as the colonizers impose their new order on the island. The figure of the witch, whether the 1660s European and early US colonies' versions or in the shape of a midwife, healer, or hysterical woman in later centuries, reappears again and again in colonial history, both in Europe and the New World, and is important for understanding Vanessa's character and her link to Caliban. By naming the creature Caliban, the series suggests a monstrous lineage from early colonialism and the Enlightenment ideals that led to industrialization, the subjugation of women, and ideas about what constitutes a monster.

## WOMEN AND WITCHES

Vanessa considers herself a spiritualist but can be considered a witch figure, especially in light of her training with Joan Clayton, known as the Cut-Wife and revealed, in the second-season episode "The Nightcomers," as another important monstrous and rebellious figure. The Cut-Wife's cottage is located in a rural, isolated landscape, away from the smog and pollution of industrialized London—Wordsworth country. Here, physically set apart from civilized society, she teaches Vanessa traditional women's knowledge and warns her that there is a price to pay: "So it is always for those who do for women."[11] The Cut-Wife keeps her hair short, is old, lives alone, is a healer, and provides contraception and abortion. The locals come to her, yet are terrified of her. She is a strong and powerful figure in the series, and even though people in her community spit on her and degrade her, she remains philosophical: "Why people in this world hate what is not them, why they fear all they don't know, why they hate themselves most of all—for being weak, for being old, for being everything all together that is not godlike. Which of us can be that? Monsters all, are we not?"[12]

While much has been written about the figure of the witch in literature and film in history, more recently there has been a return to the witch figure in texts and film engaging with themes of colonialism and imperialism, including the portrayal of Vanessa. There is a gap, however, in scholarship that connects the two. In her important text *Caliban and the Witch: Women, the Body, and Primitive Accumulation*, scholar Silvia Federici offers one such consideration of the figure of the witch. She sees the witch hunts that took place in the sixteenth and seventeenth centuries as forces for constructing and maintaining gender identity, which were integral to the development of colonialism and capitalism. She further contends that the rebel figures of witches and monsters, continue to resonate even five hundred years later. Federici argues that Marx's idea of primitive accumulation was integral to the very development of capitalism. By looking at this historical development, we can better understand negotiations of gendered and economic power today. To demonstrate her case, Federici dissects the witch hunts, describing them as essential to the development of colonialism and capitalism, and arguing that violence, particularly violence against women, is inherent in all stages of capitalist globalization from our colonial past to our contemporary industrialized and transnational world. Federici explains:

> The witch-hunt occurred simultaneously with the colonization and extermination of the populations of the New World, the English [land] enclosures, the beginning of the slave trade, the enactment of the "bloody laws" against vagabonds and beggars, and it climaxed…between the end of feudalism and the capitalist "take off" when the peasantry in Europe reached the peak of its power but, in time, also consummated its historic defeat.[13]

She argues that the witch hunt led to further divisions between genders and an increased distrust of women, reorganizing and reducing women's bodies into "machine[s] for the production of new workers."[14] In this paradigm, it is women's bodies that are exploited and resisted, appropriated and subordinated. This idea is compelling when thinking about *Penny Dreadful*, as the changing economy of England is almost a character itself in the background. The city is decaying and people are hungry, searching for work. While wealthy landowners, such as Sir Malcom, live in comfort, Caliban/John's original family struggles to put food on the table. England's colonial history (and, by the 1890s, its history of industrialization and an established middle class) affects each of the characters, and, as the central protagonist, Vanessa's very body is caught in a war between these forces.

The monstrous figure of the witch is closely tied to the struggle for control over women's reproductive bodies and the role of these bodies in gendered divisions of labor. In historical witch hunts, the accused were often older, conventionally unattractive single women. Likewise, the stereotypes abounded in literary representations until recently. Those accused of being witches in the witch hunts of the sixteenth and seventeenth centuries were often healers and midwives. The persecution of women for maternal and medical knowledge continued in the eighteenth and nineteenth centuries—up to the time period of *Penny Dreadful*—which saw the establishment of industrialization, the embrace of the scientific method, and rise of a male-dominated medical profession. The rise of scientific inquiry, industrialization, and colonial expansion mirrored and reinforced the now thoroughly entrenched gendered division of labor.

Women's labor was increasingly restricted to the reproductive, especially for upper-class women, such as Vanessa. Anne Barstow explains that "having a female body was the factor most likely to render one vulnerable to being called a witch."[15] These gendered reproductive bodies reflected a form of difference, and, as Barry Keith Grant has argued, "the experience of horror in cinema is almost always grounded in the visual representation of bodily difference."[16] Not just for Vanessa but for all the monstrous bodies in the series the audience is reminded of this difference. Historically, women's bodies that did not conform to stereotypical rigid gender roles linked to biological essentialism were defined as monstrous—as witches. Likewise, under colonialism, bodily difference was used as justification for colonization. As Barstow also points out, in the early days of colonialism, many believed that indigenous people were not even human and their bodies were considered "dirty" and "unclean."[17]

*Penny Dreadful*'s opening scene is important in framing Vanessa's struggle as a woman in her society as well as in the linking of patriarchy and colonialism in the overall construction of the monstrous. The opening scene features a rosy-cheeked and flushed child sleeping next to her mother in bed. The mother leaves the safety of the bed to use the bathroom and is brutally yet mysteriously killed. The child rises to find her mother and is also killed. These brutal murders continue to terrorize the city as the murderer remains on the loose and takes other victims. The first images of the show are of motherhood, abruptly and monstrously destroyed. In true Neo-Victorian style, the series does not shy away from confronting the physical body—blood, sex, excrement, body parts—and all the taboo and hidden aspects of bodily experience remain on full display.

This brutal scene abruptly shifts to Vanessa, on her knees in front of a crucifix, fiercely praying, seemingly possessed. Throughout most of the series, she is a devout Catholic and wishes for a redemption that she feels unentitled to claim. The rest of the first episode continues to introduce themes that repeat throughout the three seasons. Almost immediately, Vanessa, Ethan, and Sir Malcom descend to the subterranean passages beneath London, crowded with vampires and their human prey and researchers studying corpses. Motherhood returns again and again in the forms of crying infants and the blood-covered corpses of a mother and infant found by Vanessa while she searches for Mina. These opening scenes are the first of many references to violence against women's bodies and to the idea of women's bodies as sites of reproduction, with an emphasis on motherhood.

Vanessa's journey of self-discovery, her own monstrous *bildungsroman*, requires her to reconcile the primal and powerful parts of herself with the demands and dictates of the larger society. The plot involving Mina's abduction is set into motion by Vanessa's transgression of seducing her best friend Mina's fiancé, which disrupts Mina's entry into marriage and reproduction—the prescribed roles for women of their status. *Penny Dreadful* is set in the late nineteenth century, as England undergoes a national identity crisis, social boundaries tighten in the face of shifting economics, and rigid gender roles are reinforced. Federici's understanding of the historical process of the creation and reinforcement of the gendered division of labor is useful here. She argues, "It was only in the 19th century . . . that the 'modern family' centered on the full-time housewife's unpaid reproductive labor was generalized in the working class, in England first and then later in the United States."[18] In the upper classes, rigid gender roles still protected the transference of property, while the division was necessary within the working class for production. Women bore the burden of domestic work inside the home as well as paid labor outside the home. This long process has been dubbed "housewifization" by scholar Maria Mies, who traces its roots to the transition from feudalism to capitalism in Western Europe.

Mies also indicts the centuries-long history of Western European colonialism in her argument.[19] As England came in contact with other nations through colonization, she argues, it tightened its own symbolic borders and paid increased attention to national identity at home. As keepers of the home, women were considered responsible for passing on moral and national identity to their children. As the devaluation of women's work increased, prostitution increased as well. As prostitution was criminalized, so were other forms of women's control over their own bodies by church and state institutions. Federici explains that in the sixteenth and seventeenth centuries women "who dared to work out of the home, in a public space and for the market, were portrayed as sexually aggressive shrews or even as 'whores' and 'witches'" and appeared regularly as figures in literature of the time period.[20] The figure of the witch stands as powerful contrast to the "passive, obedient, thrifty, of few words . . . chaste" image of woman encouraged at the time. When Vanessa is sent to the asylum, a disciplining institution, she tells her attendant, "It's meant to make me *normal* . . . Like all the other women you know. Compliant. Obedient. A cog in an intricate social machine . . . and no more."[21] No matter which path Vanessa chooses, she can never be "normal."

The series does not resolve any of these issues. Instead, it problematizes and complicates them. In an article titled, "Why *Penny Dreadful* Was One of the Best Shows of the Modern Era," Eric Diaz writes, "In one of the many strokes of genius John Logan had when conceptualizing the series, the true horror in *Penny Dreadful*, it turns out, was misogyny."[22] This perspective directly contrasts the traditional horror genre's idea of the monstrous feminine. In *Penny Dreadful*, it is misogyny that is to be feared—not women and their bodies, not the monstrous figure of the witch. The abrupt ending of the show seems to confirm this position. Ultimately, no matter what a woman does or what she chooses, she will be unhappy. There is a price to pay. This neo-Victorian show, like most Victorian novels, offers women a choice of three outcomes: marriage, convent, or death. Vanessa chooses death.

## CONCLUSION

While Vanessa meets a devastating end in the series finale, Lily's story shows a type of resistance, albeit a violent one. In another nod to England's colonial history, Dr. Jekyll appears in the final season as another hybrid or liminal character, half-Indian and half-British, arriving to aid Victor in "taming" his latest creation: Lily Frankenstein, formerly Brona Croft. Lily is "born" aware of her past life as a sex worker, a marginal character existing on the edges of society, before she is re-created as a male fantasy in her new life, a definition she forcefully resists. Dr. Jekyll suggests that this resistance can be curtailed, asking Victor: "What if I could tame her? Domesticate her?"[23] Her character points to an overt critique of patriarchy and its intersection with colonial/economic power structures. As women's bodies can be created and domesticated as natural resources, so too can land be sought and restructured for colonial gains.

Lily, however, sees the men who paid for sex with her—along with Victor, who re-created her—as the true monsters. She summons an army of "fallen" women to enact revenge, urging them to bring her the severed hands of bad men, perhaps in an act of metaphoric castration. Lily explains, "We are not women who crawl. We are not women who kneel. And for this we will be branded radicals; revolutionists. Women who are strong and refuse to be degraded and chose to protect themselves are called monsters."[24] Lily's anger toward the larger society she inhabits, and the men who define and use her physical body, transforms to furious misandry as the show progresses. Her powerful speeches throughout the series point directly to misogyny as a shaping force, and she works to reclaim her body through her defiant acts. Her rage transcends her monstrous resurrected body and stems from her gendered experience. In this way, she reclaims power from those establishing the hierarchy. Read alongside John Clare/Caliban's story line and the other narratives of colonialism in the series, colonialism and patriarchy are aligned, and indicted as part of the same monstrous ideology.

These liminal characters come to stand as monstrous Others, crossing or engaging with artificial dichotomies created by Western culture. As the second-season title reminds the audience, "the devil is in all of us." The main characters in the series reflect—and at times resist—overarching colonial narratives. For Vanessa and Lily in particular, *gender* is intrinsically linked with the colonial project, but the site of their original monstrosity is their femaleness. As a witch and a prostitute, both defy social constructions of appropriate gender performance in addition to occupying their supernatural roles. Lily's anger toward the larger society and men who define and use her physical body transforms to furious misandry as the show progresses. Their bodies are resisting bodies, rebelling bodies. They refused to be disciplined by every institution that has tried to do so, particularly in Vanessa's case, the church and the nation. Ultimately, the colonial nation reveals itself to be the true monster in *Penny Dreadful*.

## NOTES

1. Springhall, *Youth, Popular Culture and Moral Panic*, 71–97.
2. Carroll, *Philosophy of Horror*, 33.
3. Ibid., 34.
4. Wolfreys, "I Could a Tale Unfold," xv.
5. Warwick, "Victorian Gothic," 34.
6. Ellis, *The Contested Castle*, 6.
7. *Penny Dreadful*, "The Day Tennyson Died," directed by Damon Thomas, written by John Logan. Showtime, May 1, 2016.
8. "Little Scorpion," directed by Brian Kirk, written by John Logan. Showtime, June 14, 2015.
9. "Demimonde," directed by Dearbhla Walsh, written by John Logan. Showtime, June 1, 2014.
10. *The Tempest,* Act I, scene 2, line 437.
11. "The Nightcomers," directed by Brian Kirk, written by John Logan. Showtime, May 17, 2015.
12. Ibid.
13. Federici, *Caliban and the Witch*, 165.
14. Ibid., 12.
15. Barstow, *Witchcraze*, 16.
16. Grant, *Dread of Difference*, 6.
17. Barstow, *Witchcraze*, 127.
18. Federici, *Caliban and the Witch*, 98.
19. Mies, *Patriarchy and Accumulation*, 100.
20. Federici, *Caliban and the Witch*, 96.
21. "Blade of Grass," directed by Toa Fraser, written by John Logan. Showtime, May 21, 2016.
22. Diaz, "Why Penny Dreadful Was One of the Best Shows of the Modern Era."
23. "Predators Near and Far," directed by Damon Thomas, written by John Logan. Showtime, May 8, 2016.
24. "No Beast So Fierce," directed by Paco Cabezas, written by John Logan. Showtime, June 5, 2016.

## BIBLIOGRAPHY

Asma, Stephen T. *On Monsters: An Unnatural History of Our Worst Fears*. Oxford: Oxford University Press, 2009.

Barstow, Anne Llewellyn. *Witchcraze: A New History of the European Witch Hunts*. San Francisco: Pandora, 1994.

Carroll, Noel. *Philosophy of Horror: Or, Paradoxes of the Heart*. New York: Routledge, 1990.

Diaz, Eric. "Why Penny Dreadful Was One of the Best Shows of the Modern Era." Nerdist.com, June 22, 2016. https://nerdist.com/why-penny-dreadful-was-one-of-the-best-shows-of-the-modern-era/

Ellis, Kate Ferguson. *The Contested Castle: Gothic Novels and the Subversion of Domestic Ideology*. Champaign: University of Illinois Press, 1989.

Federici, Silvia. *Caliban and the Witch*. New York: Autonomedia, 2004.

Grant, Barry Keith. *The Dread of Difference: Gender and Horror Films*. Austin: University of Texas Press, 2015.

Mies, Maria. *Patriarchy and Accumulation on a World Scale: Women in the International Division of Labour*. London: Zed Press, 1987.

*Penny Dreadful*. Created by John Logan. Showtime, 2014–2016.

Skal, David J. *The Monster Show: A Cultural History of Horror*. New York: Farrar, Straus and Giroux, 2001.

Springhall, John. *Youth, Popular Culture and Moral Panic: Penny Gaffs to Gangsta Rap, 1830–1996*. New York: Palgrave MacMillan 1999.

Warwick, Alexandra. "Victorian Gothic." In *Routledge Companion to Gothic*, edited by Catherine Spooner and Emma McEvoy, 29–37. New York: Routledge, 2007.

Wolfreys, Julian. "I Could a Tale Unfold or, the Promise of Gothic." In *Victorian Gothic: Literary and Cultural Manifestations in the Nineteenth Century,* edited by Ruth Robbins and Julian Wolfreys, xi–xix. New York: Palgrave Macmillan, 2000.

*Part II*

# MARKET FORCES AND THEIR MONSTERS

*Chapter Five*

# Recession Horror

## *The Haunted Housing Crisis in Contemporary Fiction*

Lindsey Michael Banco

In 2006 and 2007, the first victims of toxic subprime mortgage loans in the United States began losing their homes.[1] Presaging a widespread 2008 economic collapse that has come to be called the "global financial crisis" or "the Great Recession," these initial foreclosures portended millions of American losing their homes, their jobs, or their retirement savings. The apparent unthinkability of this financial meltdown was seen, according to Elena Oliete-Aldea (herself synthesizing the work of April Miller and other scholars of postrecessionary culture) "as a scary, almost apocalyptic scenario where, if too-big-to-fail companies had actually failed, anything could happen."[2] This sense of crisis and anxiety, coming nearly a decade into the War on Terror and just as globalized, placed blame in several places: overextended Americans, on the one hand, who bought into the consumerist myth of the American Dream and could not afford what they had purchased; and deregulated banks, on the other hand, preying on innocent borrowers and symbolizing a larger "maleficent global economy."[3] Into this environment comes the postrecessionary haunted house tale, a type of fictive and filmic narrative in which the American home, the "primary marker of class and our central symbol of domesticity"[4]—the "certificate of the American dream accomplished"[5]—becomes the site of nightmares. In addition to laying blame, however, haunted house novels and films engaging with the economic disorder of the first decade of the twenty-first century are attempting, I argue, to dramatize some of the epistemological issues thrown into relief by the crisis. What, a homeowner whose mortgage is underwater might be forgiven for asking, is going on here?

Dramatizing epistemological uncertainty is a foundation of the horror genre and its Gothic precursors and contemporaries, including haunted-house fiction and film.[6] In a 2008 article on William Peter Blatty, Davide Mana traces an intriguing genealogy between three horror novels with a particular element of the haunted house formula in common, the team of investigators ascertaining the house's supernatural manifestations, to comment on the status of knowledge claims in the postrecession age. Shirley Jackson's *The Haunting of Hill House* (1959), Richard Matheson's *Hell House* (1971), and Blatty's *Elsewhere* (1999) feature groups of characters—physicists, spiritualists, real estate agents—who bring various forms of financial or institutional backing, professional expertise, and epistemological perspectives to bear on a haunted house. Mana writes: "Reading the novels in chronological order, it is evident that through the years it becomes harder and harder—and more expensive—for the person setting up the investigation to gather a full team."[7] "Times have changed," notes Mana, "and what was a purely academic pursuit in the 1950s has become a privately sponsored venture in the 1970s, and an open commercial speculation in the 1990s."[8] Especially in the postcrisis age, Mana is right: "Monetary issues, originally a marginal element of the [haunted house] tale, have become central, pushing scientific curiosity and integrity to the margins."[9] Moreover, the desire to know—the epistemological questions opened up by the horror genre—has not been replaced by financial worries. In fact, in the postrecession age characterized by a volatile and unpredictable free market, monetary issues *are* epistemological issues.

To look to haunted house fiction and film, then, especially in light of the generally "privileged status of dwelling places"[10] and the insistent centrality of the home to the narrative of the Great Recession of 2008, is to draw upon several strands, two of which include: (1) the social, historical, and psychological commentary horror provides, as articulated by a vast body of scholarship generally known as Gothic Studies;[11] and (2) the uncertainty unleashed upon the global market by the esoteric financial instruments of mortgage financing and the epistemological confrontations with this uncertainty that take place in American haunted houses. The effectiveness of a horror story, argues Scott McCracken in his study of pulp fiction, "depends on the reader's inability to rationalise the source of the terror."[12] Horror is notorious for (if not defined by) its withholding of explanation, for its violation of boundaries, binaries, and other principles of cultural organization. Whether such border meltdowns involve primeval psychological taboos (Freud's *unheimlich*, say) or historically inflected anxieties (the burdens of the past, the anxieties of the present projected onto the past), the multiplicity of a Gothic or horror text frustrates that desire to rationalize. Despite the haunted house's long history of evoking the complex relationships between present and past, postrecession haunted house narratives seem to dramatize a slightly different relationship, one which nevertheless proves unrationalizable or inscrutable: the anxieties provoked by the *future*. What will become of us if we lose the house? if we lose our jobs? In a sense, these anxieties are integral to neoliberal capitalism: its ahistorical, unfettered free markets deracinate us from the past, and its obsession with short-term gain obliterates the future. These haunted house tales, for all the anxiety they dramatize, nonetheless help readers grapple with the epistemological uncertainty wrought by the financial crisis: the baffling ingredients of contemporary capitalism—derivatives, credit default swaps, mortgage-backed securities, collateralized debt obligations—get displaced onto comfortably familiar monsters and beasties. At the same time, these monstrosities are rarely vanquished unequivocally. Authors do not simply provide readers with bailouts. Instead, the motif of the haunted house ensures that the question of what, financially, is going on in the twenty-first century remains open.

Whether a place of solace or a millstone around the neck—comfort from the storm or Gothic tomb—houses and the monsters they contain function in postrecession horror fiction and film as "unstable interstitial figures that problematize dichotomous thinking,"[13] as a "symptom of repressed knowledge,"[14] and as "a reminder that the forces of history and the economy create restless spaces whose uses and meanings are constantly being repurposed."[15] The spatialized experiences these texts provide indicate an attempt to lay out, to survey, to appraise in an epistemologically uncertain time the streams of data and specialized knowledges underpinning the recession, but the only knowledge they ultimately affirm is the impossibility of knowing. This bind, antithetical to what is often called "the knowledge economy," underscores the true horror of these texts even as they dramatize attempts to come to terms with economic uncertainty.

This chapter explores the relationship between haunted houses and American financial anxiety. It begins with a short historical survey of some twentieth-century manifestations of this anxiety and then focuses, for the most part, on post-2008 fiction. I do, however, endeavor to put these novels—both early and recent—into conversation with film. Discussions of twenty-first-century haunted house films reveal that movies such as *Paranormal Activity* (2007) can be read "as soothing morality tales in which overleveraged suburbanites are punished,"[16] and a film such as *Drag Me To Hell* (2009) "directly engages with the central issues of the economic crisis—banks' predatory lending practices, home foreclosures, and the brutal divisions between the 99 and 1 percent."[17] Other scholars have called this type of film an "allegory for the credit crisis."[18] Unlike more straightforward morality tales, allegories function on multiple levels of meaning and thus inherently frustrate the desire to map out unequivocal interpretation. Perhaps for that reason, these films have attracted some critical attention of late. I am indebted in this chapter to that work, but because such analyses have not yet been carried out in detail on post–credit-crunch haunted house *fiction*, I take the fundamental instability of allegory as foundational to my focus on fiction in this chapter.

## PREAPPROVALS: THE 1970S

Early twenty-first-century economic anxieties, expressed through the haunted house trope in literature and film, naturally have historical precedent. One of the most influential American haunted house stories, Jackson's *The Haunting of Hill House* (1959), appeared at the end of a decade typically characterized by its affluence and depicts a semiprofessional investigation of supernatural occurrences at deceased patriarch Hugh Crain's sinister Hill House. This trope—in which neither scientific nor intuitive epistemologies, neither psychological nor parapsychological explanations, are sufficient to account for the events—would become legion in haunted house narratives and gets inflected in telling ways in those novels evincing economic anxiety. Robert Wise's adaptation of Jackson's novel, *The Haunting* (1963), acknowledges the new national anxieties dawning in the 1960s with its visual distortions that amplify the novel's epistemological complications and its character Dr. Markway (Wise's version of Jackson's Dr. Montague) confirming the inexplicability of the house's manifestations. Wise's film also retains Jackson's depiction of house guest Eleanor's death by car crash on the Hill House property, emphasizing the troubling obsession with the automobile as the "other" American status symbol. A little over thirty years later, in what Steven Jay Schneider suggests was a cynical time for cashing in on classic horror films following Gus Van Sant's "abysmal"[19] 1998 shot-by-shot remake of Hitchcock's *Psycho* (1960), Jan DeBont remade *The Haunting* (1999) using computer-generated imagery to visually dispel all the ambiguity of Jackson's novel and Wise's film. DeBont also rewrote Eleanor's fate, removing Jackson's biting depiction of a Gothic automobile and reconfiguring Eleanor's death as a self-sacrifice *within* the house—a gesture of containment that ensures the film has a more-or-less "happy ending."

Nevertheless, by the 1970s—a decade of economic stagnation, high unemployment, and skyrocketing energy costs in the United States—the haunted house tale had turned the housing dream into a nightmare. Not surprisingly, that decade saw a dramatic increase in haunted house fiction and film.[20] Matheson's *Hell House* (1971), like Jackson's novel, depicts a team of investigators assessing a haunted house but, in a rather reactionary ploy, seems to lay much of the blame for unexplained events on the hysteria of its female characters and the failure of its male characters to regulate that hysteria. British director John Hough's adaptation, *The Legend of Hell*

*House* (1973), working with a screenplay by Matheson, largely reproduces this conceit. Even more influentially, Blatty's *The Exorcist* (1971), while strictly speaking a possession novel rather than a haunted house tale, nevertheless charted national economic and political anxieties within a fraught domestic setting and, ultimately, sought solace for such national anxieties in the power of traditional religious faith. William Friedkin's adaptation, arriving in the midst of the US recession of 1973 and the impending collapse of the Nixon presidency, became one of the highest-grossing horror films of all time. *The Exorcist* (1973) owes at least some of its success to its rehearsal of the novel's reassuring gestures in uncertain times. Robert Marasco's *Burnt Offerings* (1973), likewise influential in the decade (overshadowed though it was by *The Exorcist*), features the young Rolfe family fleeing the big city—specifically to escape the effects of "the fiscal crisis,"[21] as one of Marasco's characters puts it—and renting a summer home at a price that's too good to be true. Among other manifestations, they contend with a strange mechanical-sounding hum in the house, which Dale Bailey identifies as "nothing less than the eternal and uncaring hum of an economic system which entraps, uses, and destroys its laborers."[22] Their errand into the wilderness ends when the family is consumed by the house, a metaphorical foreclosure on their self-destructive material consumerism in a time of economic stricture. In a possible nod to Jackson's "death car," US director Dan Curtis's film adaptation of *Burnt Offerings* (1976) ends with Marian (Karen Black) throwing husband Ben (Oliver Reed) from a window of the house to his death on the windshield of his car parked below. For Dara Downey, this ending "graphically dramatizes the unreasonable demands which domestic ideology placed upon the middle-class American housewife."[23] Even when characters stay in the city, as Jeffrey Konvitz's do in *The Sentinel* (1974), they remain unnerved by or even disdainful of the financial crisis unfolding around them; Konvitz's aloof New York protagonist, Allison Parker, "walked along the rows of middle-income housing that had sprouted like mushrooms during the past few years, fertilized by federal subsidies,"[24] to what turns out, vengefully, to be a brownstone full of demons. Michael Winner's 1977 film adaptation, which appears to have spent a considerable sum on an all-star cast (Burgess Meredith, Ava Gardner, José Ferrer, Tom Berenger, and others), still punishes its urban, upper-crust heroine (Cristina Raines) with a fate worse than death at the end of the film. The suburbs prove no better, with Anne Rivers Siddons's *The House Next Door* (1978) offering a contemporary spin on the Southern Gothic. Set in a suburb of Atlanta, Siddons's novel dramatized Southern class anxieties—the vexatious presence of the *nouveau riche*, for instance—through the trope of the haunted house. In 2006, Jeff Woolnough directed a television movie adaptation for the Lifetime cable channel. Unlike Siddons's novel, in which the house still stands at the end to haunt the suburbs and trouble its presumed values of exclusivity, Lifetime's adaptation concludes with the destruction of the house and the removal of its threat to suburban normalcy. The final scene of the film, in which another couple wants to rebuild the house, suggests that the "evils" of the suburbs do not extend much further than modern architecture's uncomfortable puncturing of the pretensions of suburban gentility. Toward the end of the decade, as economic woes were being felt more acutely, Jay Anson published *The Amityville Horror* (1977), a blockbuster book of slightly controversial generic status, in which the Lutz family accidentally buys a haunted house for a bargain price, only to experience symbolic manifestations of the financially constrained era: glowing red eyes staring in, unseen forces pressing down on the Lutz's bodies as they sleep, doors and windows damaged, and rooms with mysterious drafts and odors. Stuart Rosenberg's blockbuster 1979 film takes the book's ambiguous description of the last night in the Lutz family's home and revisits the relationship between house and automobile in financial horror texts. George (James Brolin), Kathy (Margot Kidder), and children successfully flee the haunted house in their car, but their buyer's remorse, coming on the heels of what they thought was a way to outsmart the market, suggests that no homeowner in the 1970s—in fiction or film—was going to emerge into solvency from this crisis.[25]

## INHERITANCES: MALFI'S *CRADLE LAKE* (2013) AND *LITTLE GIRLS* (2015)

Thirty years later, many of the same anxieties emerged. A toxic combination of overleveraged homebuyers, underregulated lenders, and predatory Wall Street financiers led to a crisis that, especially in the decade following 9/11, came to seem apocalyptic. Horror novelists and filmmakers of the 2000s and 2010s responded as they did in the 1970s: with haunted house tales. Like their precursors, these texts are fairly heterogeneous in spite of their apparent grounding in formula. Nevertheless, several trends become apparent through a focus specifically on fiction. For one, many of the novels of this recent period foreground the future-oriented anxieties engendered by the economic crisis over the traditional location of Gothic anxiety in the past. Perhaps ironically, the prospective anxiety of postrecession horror fiction seems to draw inspiration from the burden-of-inheritance trope long central to Gothic fiction: contemporary, postrecession families continue to inherit mansions, but rather than a windfall in trying times, the abodes represent an additional, future-oriented economic burden, effectively ruining the lives of the "lucky" inheritors.

The work of Ronald Malfi is emblematic of this trend. A prolific author of horror, mystery, and other genre novels, Malfi positions the haunted country home as an ominous inheritance in *Cradle Lake* and *Little Girls*. *Cradle Lake*'s Alan Hammerstun inherits a house near the Great Smoky Mountains and, like the Rolfe family in Marasco's *Burnt Offerings*, he and his wife escape New York for a "fresh start." The notion of inheritance, often figured ambivalently as both a catalyst for success and freedom and as a dark burden from the past, takes the form of the isolated ranch house, but the real source of nightmares in *Cradle Lake* is the titular body of water in the woods nearby. Like *Burnt Offerings*, Malfi's novel presents the escape from the city as an escape from financial difficulties; Alan and Heather lament their austere, cramped conditions in New York, with Alan seeking specifically to flee the legacy of his father's checkered financial past—"It was amazing," the narration tells us, focalized through Alan, "just how different their lives would be now that they'd left the city behind."[26] In the discovery of a strange, supernatural lake behind the house, however, their flight from New York becomes another entry in the long-standing and misguided fantasy of domesticating the wilderness. As Christine Wilson notes, "Americans view(ed) wilderness space as a much-needed respite from restrictive cultural norms and acted accordingly to preserve what was viewed as an important resource. Stories in which the house itself figures as a natural space tap into this wilderness ethic, while at the same time capitalizing on the profound ambivalence toward this space that historically pervades the cultural imagination."[27] The ending of the novel, encapsulating that ambivalence, has Alan cutting masses of strange, sentient vines out of the attic, as if in a surreal episode of *Fixer Upper*, and burning the place down. This grim ending is reminiscent of the many conflagrations and implosions that claim haunted houses in the American tradition—metaphorical market corrections—from Charles Brockden Brown's ancestral home in *Wieland*, to Poe's House of Usher, to the Freeling family's suburban mock Tudor in *Poltergeist*. Such endings, in which the homeowners sometimes survive and sometimes do not, also speak to the urge to position blame for familial decay, vice, vanity, national decline, the burdens of inheritance, and other expressions of Gothic anxiety on a concrete structure and then eliminate it. In postrecessionary fiction, this desire reveals a profound epistemological nervousness about speculative finance. Modern hypercapitalism is no antidote to old-fashioned financial corruption.

Similarly, Malfi's *Little Girls* features a protagonist, Laurie Gennaro, inheriting her dead father's house and finding out dreadful secrets from his past and from her own childhood. Laurie entertains selling the house and ridding herself of its terrible baggage, but as the characters make clear, the housing market is "lousy"[28] and "crummy,"[29] glib assessments that nevertheless emphasize Laurie's affliction with her unwanted investment. The slippage in Laurie's perspective from "inheritance" to "investment," from the burdens of the past to the anxieties of the future, allows *Little Girls* to mark the slippage in contemporary capitalism from finances based on a coherent narrative of the past to the uncertain and troubling future-oriented bubble of speculative finance. The ghostly children creeping through the novel cannot be confirmed as either real or products of Laurie's anxiety, so in their representational ambiguity (as tatters of the past, as indicators of the future) they too fail to offer a solid foundation for navigating the postrecession future.

## EXTRAVAGANCES: BENTLEY LITTLE'S *THE HAUNTED* (2012) AND *THE HANDYMAN* (2017)

Like this recasting of the notion of the inheritance, many contemporary haunted house novels exhibit another enduring Gothic preoccupation: the pressures of material acquisitiveness—of the proper conspicuousness of one's affluence—endemic to notions of class mobility. Simply put, keeping up with the Joneses becomes significantly more anxiety-provoking in the postrecession age—and one's house, a powerful potential signifier of one's superiority over the Joneses, showcases those anxieties. In Bentley Little's *The Haunted*, for instance, the Perry family is "downsizing" as their suburban neighborhood goes to pot around them. Not underwater, but clearly downwardly mobile and financially constrained, the Perrys buy a house with a feature not included in the real estate listing: a panoply of ghosts. Worst of all, one of the ghosts is a "squatter," the spirit of a homeless man who died in their basement. The lower-class status of the ghost is not only a manifestation of some past financial trauma but also a picture of where the Perrys could end up in the future. Pressed by the changing housing market following the 2008 recession, the Perrys find in their home less certainty and refuge and more a glimpse into a horrific future—an indication of Little's troubling propensity to invoke the abjectness of the lower classes in his depictions of the precariousness of American capitalism.

Little's *The Handyman* demonstrates a similar anxiety about the intrusive power of the lower classes, turning Frank Watkins, the titular handyman and ostensible just-in-time service worker, into a pervasive presence. Real estate agent Daniel Martin, the novel's protagonist, lives with the haunting memory of the strange, incompetent handyman who shoddily constructed the Martin vacation home in Randall, Arizona, when Daniel was a child:

> The economics of vacation home ownership turned out to be not as simple as my parents had originally thought, especially when things started to fall apart.

At first, it was a leaking toilet. The plumber who came to fix it shook his head and said he was surprised it hadn't leaked immediately because the bonehead who had installed it hadn't put in a required gasket. After that, we had a blackout because, the electrician said, Frank hadn't wired the house properly and one of the circuits was being overloaded. Then the roof leaked during a summer monsoon, and the roofer told us, after he had patched the spot, that there should have been a layer of tarpaper under the shingles. . . .

"This damn Frank House," Dad said after each new disaster.[30]

Frank's menace intensifies significantly over the course of the novel, but Daniel's early remarks about class anxiety intersect with Frank's working-class identity: "That year, my father had to get a summer job to make ends meet. There weren't that many part time job openings in Randall for a middle-aged man who was only in town between the last week of June and the last week of August. But he managed to get hired at the lumber yard."[31] Like the Perrys, the Martins count among their greatest anxieties their perilous proximity to the lower classes. Like *The Haunted,* Little's *The Handyman* arranges much of this anxiety around the concept of the house. *The Handyman* identifies the family home—particularly the upper-class signifier of the vacation home—as a potential weak point in the American mythos of upward mobility, a warning (like that of *The Amityville Horror*'s bargain entry into homeownership) against greed and pretensions on the cheap. Such a cautionary tale, Little's work reminds us, reveals how such a mythos is predicated upon a distrust of the working class.[32] In Little's work, the consequences of the recession are clear and dire: don't get left behind at the lumberyard, or you will not be able to embody the appropriate class signifiers.

## SPECULATIONS: *A HEAD FULL OF GHOSTS* (2015) AND *THE FAMILY PLOT* (2016)

Little's emplacement of economic anxiety onto lower-class characters is not necessarily an inevitable component of postrecession haunted house fiction. Within this growing body of work, some novels offer more complex meditations on storytelling itself as an epistemological tool. The texture of this self-reflexivity in contemporary fiction likely owes some of its genesis to early twenty-first-century haunted house films. These films, as Hahner, Varda, and Wilson note in their analysis of the Oren Peli film *Paranormal Activity* (2007), frequently employ electronic surveillance equipment—cameras, in particular—as tropes of self-reflexivity that implicate the viewer in the vicarious consumption of the house as status symbol.[33] Similarly, Emmanuelle Wessels points to the baby monitor in James Wan's

*Insidious* (2010) as a revealing piece of technology in the excavation of that film's depiction of public and private labor in the postrecession age.[34] These films' self-reflexive willingness to highlight representational technologies in the depiction of recession horror translates, it seems, into some of the fiction of the era. Paul Tremblay's *A Head Full of Ghosts*, for instance, features the middle-class Barrett family in dire financial straits (the postrecession manifestation of "the imperiled nuclear family"[35] long considered central to Gothic and horror fiction). John Barrett is unemployed, Sarah Barrett worries constantly about losing the house, eight-year-old Merry Barrett is both naïve and precocious in her understanding of the family's financial problems, and most alarming of all, fourteen-year-old Marjorie Barrett is in the throes of either a schizophrenic episode or demonic possession. Neither clergy nor psychologists seem to be able to help her, but a Discovery Channel reality show called *The Possession* swoops in to offer the family financial relief in exchange for broadcasting their disintegration. Merry, Tremblay's narrator, includes blog entries, ekphrastic and exegetical accounts of the TV show that saved the Barrett house but destroyed the family, and constant references to horror classics from "The Yellow Wallpaper" to *The Exorcist*. These framing devices and textual heterogeneity, as in Walpole's *The Castle of Otranto* or Shelley's *Frankenstein*, result in what McCracken calls an "excess of meaning produced by its various enclosures, each of which discloses some new form of monstrosity."[36] Like *The Exorcist*'s exploration of the anxieties of parenthood, *A Head Full of Ghosts* reveals the disquiet wrought upon children in the postrecession economy—a possession novel in which financial constraints threaten a family's material possessions. It also discloses the contemporary concern with being possessed by popular culture and electronic devices. None of its epistemological realms—religion, finance, psychology, social media, pop culture—ultimately provide transcendent truth. Tremblay suspends the question of whether Marjorie's behavior is schizophrenic or supernatural and affirms only the insufficiency of "reality television" as a guarantor of reality and the dubiousness of the ideal nuclear family in an age of economic downturn. With their competing epistemologies—academic or scientific, psychic or mediatized ways of knowing—postrecession novels like *A Head Full of Ghosts* are animated by the interplay between "the supernatural" and the hypermodernity of digital-capitalism. Moreover, the protagonist of *A Head Full of Ghosts*, and the varied forms of knowledge dissemination she uses (television appearances, blogs, interviews), enables the novel to highlight the ambivalence of the epistemological categories at the center of the recession, ambivalence often covered up in accounts of the decline by the logic of market fundamentalism.[37]

Cherie Priest's *The Family Plot* assumes the appearance of a Southern Gothic tale updated for the twenty-first century while, like Tremblay's novel, also engaging in a self-reflexive exploration of the epistemological stakes of storytelling. Money is a constant source of pressure in the novel, with both families at the center of the plot—the upper-class Withrows and the working-class Duttons—succumbing to the postrecession age. The Faulknerian Withrow family has reached the end of its line, with its last scion Augusta Withrow selling the sprawling estate to a salvage company: Music City Salvage, run by the Duttons, in Nashville. The recession is clearly a juggernaut in *The Family Plot*: not only is the estate being sold for a song, but the salvage company—which profits from the economic fall of others—is itself about to go under. When the Withrow estate appears on the company's radar, "Barry the Finance Guy [...] put his foot down with a hard-ass *no*. Music City Salvage barely had enough cash on hand to keep the lights running and cover payroll. [....] There was absolutely no stray money for sweetheart deals on old estates."[38] Chuck Dutton, the owner of the company, overrules this dire assessment in part to allow his daughter, Dahlia, to prove herself as a capable salvage employee: "It'd be the biggest gamble of his life."[39] This narratorial assessment indicates an awareness that American capitalism is deeply imbricated in luck, gambling, and the willingness to risk everything. Within this context, the house Dahlia Dutton is charged with stripping is covered in metaphorical price tags. The characters constantly assess the salvage value of windows, banisters, fireplaces, tiles, flooring, roofing material, and the bric-a-brac Augusta Withrow left behind. This activity, reminiscent of the way "haunted houses enact the tyranny of domesticity, insofar as they present domestic spaces that require never-ending caretaking, from women, just to maintain the barest amount of livability,"[40] augments caretaking to its absurd conclusion: destruction. The ghostly manifestations in the Withrow estate are all fairly conventional for this genre of fiction.[41] They also have a robust Southern Gothic flavor: "Why shouldn't the Withrow house have a haint or two hiding in the woodwork?"[42] asks one of the Music City Salvage employees. This blasé attitude turns to horror, naturally, but *The Family Plot* is remarkable for its dramatization of the power of economic pressure. Despite the incredible things these characters witness in the house, financial exigencies force them to stay. When one character wants to leave, Dahlia says, "You know we can't do that, and you know *why*."[43] Music City Salvage would go under. When the characters have to remain overnight in the house to contend with, for instance, a force taking "the shape of a girl wearing a smock that had been rent into rags" and "covered in mud, in blood, and in the stink of death,"[44] Dahlia's anxieties are framed resoundingly as economic ones: "She wished she'd pressed her dad for a set of hotel rooms instead of this house with all its anger and unhappiness, though she would've felt bad for spending extra money."[45] Consistent with Dale Bailey's observation that "people in haunted house stories act in consistently unbelievable ways; they remain in the house long after any rational person would leave,"[46] Dahlia's behavior in *The Family Plot* reveals the irrational power of market forces. The absurdity of having to contend with ghosts because of fiscal constraints is part of Priest's depiction of overwhelming financial anxiety in the post-recession period.

At the same time, these working-class characters demonstrate a concerted effort to comprehend the ghostly manifestations, to gather evidence, to learn the truth. They seek out historical records. They uncover buried secrets. They are on mobile phones constantly, scouring the internet for information and deploying the phones as video cameras in positivist efforts to log the reality of their situation. The narrative Dahlia constructs is predicated on a rational, thoroughly technologized epistemology. Like financial speculators and market watchers, these characters believe that more information—empirical data, electronically-mediated records—will provide knowledge of the difficult, confusing circumstance. Ultimately, though, this technology, as in Bernice Murphy's analysis of post-recession film, simply "affirm[s] the impossibility of trying to record, control, or expel malevolent supernatural forces in any strictly 'rational' manner."[47] The unknowability of the ghost is cemented when Dahlia throws away a camera's memory card purportedly containing visual evidence of the apparition and when the novel ends with the lyrics of a murder ballad "explaining" the origins and motivations of the ghost. The ballad, also entitled "The Family Plot," signals itself as lore, as a stylized tale the objective reality of which is always a suspended question and whose main function, like the tales within the tale of Poe's Usher family, is to illuminate *itself* as narrative.[48] In that sense, Priest's novel, in addition to a modern Southern Gothic ghost story, is as much a self-reflexive meditation on the epistemological conflict between "data" and "storytelling." The tale Priest tells of twenty-first-century economic woes is still one of mystification, but the novel's implicit critique of how we tell such tales—how fragile are our evidentiary accumulations, how enmeshed in the past are our stories of progress—marks an awareness of the power of narrative in understanding this fraught historical moment.

## CONCLUSION

The decade of fiscal anxiety and home ownership woes following the economic collapse of 2008 clearly has had an impact on American horror fiction.

Not only has the haunted house trope come back into vogue as it did in the 1970s, attempting now as then to work through the specifically domestic anxieties of economically difficult times, but the especially bewildering nature of twenty-first-century speculative finance has led to fictive and cinematic representations of a crisis at the level of knowledge itself. Wessels, in the context of postrecession horror film, affirms this crisis as a problem of epistemology: "Dealing with the speculative economy in the wake of the crisis, it seems, has opened a door to embracing the irrational and the mystical as methods of controlling the vagaries of the market."[49] Such control seems illusory, at least in these texts, but often the very mechanisms and ontologies of storytelling become possibilities for control. Novels such as Malfi's *Cradle Lake* and *Little Girls* acknowledge the difficulties of predicting the fallout of the recession by taking the Gothic mode's preoccupation with the burden of inheritance and the more American literary tradition of spatializing these concerns into domestic and wilderness settings and then reconfiguring them into a contemporary concern for future economic inequality. In the contemporary moment, in which financial success involves purporting to understand highly dispersed and abstracted global capitalism, these "smaller," domestic tales reveal the absurdity of that proposition.

Furthermore, novels such as Tremblay's *A Head Full of Ghosts* and Priest's *The Family Plot* dramatize competing epistemologies and mediatizations of incomprehensible phenomena, and they lend texture to the difficult process of comprehending the implications of the economic collapse without necessarily assigning blame. Unlike Bentley Little's work, such as *The Haunted* and *The Handyman*, which exhibit considerable discomfort with the working or lower classes (those who have been excluded from and thus haunt the American Dream[50]), Tremblay and Priest seem to take more nuanced views of class mobility and class relations. Moreover, they tend to view economic exclusion and disparity as among the drivers of the recession rather than as instructive lessons in how not to be left behind by the American Dream. The cinematic and the televisual have also again asserted themselves as relevant forms in the postrecession age, with (perhaps not surprisingly) yet another adaptation of Shirley Jackson's novel: Mike Flanagan's Netflix series *The Haunting of Hill House* (2018–). Despite preserving Jackson's mansion in its title, Flanagan's series has reimagined the tale considerably. It is now thoroughly a family drama; Jackson's Hugh Crain, the wealthy, eccentric builder of Hill House, becomes in the series' 1992 story line, a "flipper"—one of the most emblematic (and often reviled) figures of the contemporary housing market—while Jackson's house guests have become siblings, the children of Hugh Crain. Despite the money lavished on the house set, the series locates most of the tale's gothic anxiety in the family rather than in the house. Furthermore, in the series' present-day timeline, several of the Crain children have profited from their paranormal experiences. Shirley Crain (Elizabeth Reaser), a character absent from Jackson's novel, and a clear nod to Jackson herself, has monetized the figure of the house as repository of family strife and become the owner of a funeral home. The eldest Crain child, Steven (Michiel Huisman), has banked on his family's experiences to become a famous author. The series has, in these ways, explicitly juxtaposed the epistemological concerns of Jackson's tale with the economic ones of the twenty-first century. The Netflix Crains are equally baffled and troubled by the goings-on at Hill House, but they have become savvier about profiting from them.

My individual analyses of these texts in this chapter are necessarily brief, but I hope they provide insight into some of the general trends in post-recession haunted house tales. It would seem that at least some of these tales, consistent with their identities in the cultural marketplace *as stories*, allow for the rehearsal of different narrative epistemologies—varied ways of telling the story of the economic collapse and of imagining its future consequences. Stories as items in a cultural marketplace also help inflect, in what I hope are productive ways, larger notions of the market—housing markets, job markets—with values other than the limited neoliberal ones that only serve to concentrate wealth in smaller and smaller numbers of hands. In that sense, perhaps Fannie Mae and Freddie Mac have already felt the icy fingers of the haunted 'hood.

## NOTES

1. Thanks to Ross Bullen, Jason Haslam, Mark McCutcheon, Karen McFarlane, and MacKenzie Read for their comments on the conference paper that formed the basis of this chapter. Thanks also to Len Findlay, who suggested a marvelous alternative title: "Fannie Mae and the Haunted 'Hood."
2. Oliete-Aldea, "The Great Recession," 1167.
3. Ibid., 1169.
4. Bailey, *American Nightmare*, 8.
5. Redding, *Haints*, 30.
6. Such uncertainty is not, it seems, irreconcilable with the notion that horror fiction and other "marginal" genres enable often silenced voices to speak out (as argued in, say, Carpenter and Kolmar's collection of essays on ghost stories by American women).
7. Mana, "It Ain't Over Till the Fat Lady Sings," 152.
8. Ibid., 153.
9. Ibid.
10. Janicker, *The Literary Haunted House*, 82.

11. A comprehensive bibliography of Gothic scholarship would be impossible to attempt here, but for a selection of work specifically on the haunted house motif, especially in a contemporary context, see Bailey, Carpenter and Kolmar, Davidson, Hennelly Jr., Janicker, Lewis and Cho, McCloud, Wilson, and Vidler. On the haunted house motif in film and television, see Beard, Curtis, Hahner et al., Miller, Murphy, Musante, Smuts, Stone, and Wessels. For assessments of the haunted house in the work of specific authors see, for instance, Dziemianowicz, Fuchs, Halttunen, Jameson, Kleinman, Kröger, and Poznar.

12. McCracken, *Pulp*, 128.
13. Weinstock, "Introduction," 4.
14. Ibid., 6.
15. Curtis, *Dark Places*, 14.
16. Hahner, Varda, and Wilson, "*Paranormal Activity*," 362.
17. Miller, "Real-to-Reel," 31.
18. Stevens, "Paranormal Activity."
19. Schneider, "Thrice-Told Tales," 168.
20. I focus in this introductory section on the 1970s, but this precedent for the connection between financial pressure and the haunted house extends to the tale's origins in Gothic literature. Such literature, beginning in the eighteenth century, organizes much of its depiction of visceral horror around the anxieties of inheritance, the burden of class, and the disquiets of ancestral castles (imagine, for instance, trying to get a good variable-rate mortgage on Otranto). In American literature, Poe's "The Fall of the House of Usher" is an early nineteenth-century example of mapping a tale of class decay onto the architecture of a house; Nathaniel Hawthorne's *The House of the Seven Gables* dramatizes at mid-century the anxieties attending inherited wealth and ascendant materialism; while Charlotte Perkins Gilman's "The Yellow Wallpaper" appears at the end of the nineteenth century to provide a tale of class precariousness, of "mere ordinary people" who manage to "secure ancestral halls for the summer." Gilman, "The Yellow Wallpaper," 3.
21. Marasco, *Burnt Offerings*, 8.
22. Bailey, *American Nightmare*, 77.
23. Downey, "Locating the Specter," 158.
24. Konvitz, *The Sentinel*, 71.
25. That the film was remade in 2005, starring Ryan Reynolds and Melissa George, shows the tale speaking to a post-9/11 era in which the retreat from the global into the domestic was starting to be troubled by the housing market woes on the horizon.
26. Malfi, *Cradle Lake*, 14.
27. Wilson, "Haunted Habitability," 201.
28. Malfi, *Little Girls*, 237.
29. Ibid., 266.
30. Little, *The Handyman*, 77.
31. Ibid.
32. Little's early novel *The Mailman* (1991) reveals a long-standing distrust of the working class within his notion of the American family. The postal worker of the

novel's title threatens another young nuclear family with his strange appearance and preternatural knowledge of their lives.

33. Hahner, Varda, and Wilson, "*Paranormal Activity*," 366.
34. Wessels, "A Lesson Concerning Technology," 516.
35. Bailey, *American Nightmare*, 24.
36. McCracken, *Pulp*, 137.
37. As of 2018, Robert Downey Jr. and Susan Downey's production company Team Downey was getting ready to produce an adaptation of *A Head Full of Ghosts*, which will likely lend another layer to the narrative's media self-reflexivity.
38. Priest, *Family Plot*, 15.
39. Ibid., 19.
40. Wilson, "Haunted Habitability," 204.
41. Lights flicker, the sound of a crying baby echoes through the halls, and figures in Civil War uniforms flit through the yard. At one point, the characters find an overgrown cemetery on the Withrow property, and while the space is not on ancient Indian burial ground, they do find (in a likely nod to that old saw) "the skeletal remains of an Indian motorcycle." Priest, *Family Plot*, 70.
42. Priest, *Family Plot*, 162.
43. Ibid., 202.
44. Ibid., 198.
45. Ibid., 217.
46. Bailey, *American Nightmare*, 50.
47. Murphy, "'It's Not the House That's Haunted,'" 239.
48. The murder ballad also warns against feminine wiles: "*For wicked girls will weave a web. / Be sure you don't get caught, / Lest you find yourself one day / Beneath a family plot.*" Priest, 360. Nevertheless, Dahlia's control over the novel's "weaving," like Augusta Winthrow's over the history of the Withrow family, indicates Priest's investment in women's narrative power. The power of Priest's narrative lies in the truths it reveals outside of, or in spite of, the limited epistemology of "masculine" technology.
49. Wessels, "A Lesson Concerning Technology," 512.
50. For a discussion of the haunting and constitutive power of (racial, gender, and class) exclusion, see Goddu, *Gothic America*. For an elaboration of this process of constituting American identity, see Redding, *Haints*.

## BIBLIOGRAPHY

*The Amityville Horror*. Directed by Andrew Douglas. MGM, Dimension Films, 2005.
*The Amityville Horror*. Directed by Stuart Rosenberg. Cinema 77, Professional Films, 1979.
Anson, Jay. *The Amityville Horror*. 1977. New York: Pocket, 2005.
Bailey, Dale. *American Nightmare: The Haunted House Formula in American Popular Culture*. Bowling Green, OH: Bowling Green State University Popular Press, 1999.

Beard, Andrew J. "Horror Begins at Home: Family Trauma in Paranormal Reality TV." PhD diss., University of Oregon, 2012.
Blatty, William Peter. *The Exorcist*. 1971. New York: HarperCollins, 2004.
Boyle, Kirk, and Daniel Mrozowski, eds. *The Great Recession in Fiction, Film, and Television: Twenty-First-Century Bust Culture*. Lanham: Lexington, 2013.
*Burnt Offerings*. Directed by Dan Curtis. P. E. A. Films, United Artists, 1976.
Carpenter, Lynette, and Wendy Kolmar, eds. *Haunting the House of Fiction: Feminist Perspectives on Ghost Stories by American Women*. Knoxville: University of Tennessee Press, 1991.
Curtis, Barry. *Dark Places: The Haunted House in Film*. London: Reaktion, 2008.
Davison, Carol Margaret. "Southern Gothic: Haunted Houses." In *The Palgrave Handbook of the Southern Gothic*, edited by Susan Castillo Street and Charles L. Crow, 56–67. London: Palgrave Macmillan, 2016.
Downey, Dara. "Locating the Specter in Dan Curtis's *Burnt Offerings*." *Cinematic Ghosts: Haunting and Spectrality from Silent Cinema to the Digital Era*, edited by Murray Leeder, 143–158. London: Bloomsbury, 2015.
Dziemianowicz, Stefan. "Horror Begins at Home: Richard Matheson's Fear of the Familiar." *Studies in Weird Fiction* 14 (1994): 29–36.
*The Exorcist*. Directed by William Friedkin. Hoya Productions, 1973.
Fuchs, Michael. "The Black Hole at the Heart of America? Space, Family, and the Black Hallway in *House of Leaves*." In *Placing America: American Culture and Its Spaces*, edited by Michael Fuchs and Maria-Theresia Holub, 103–125. Bielefeld: Transcript, 2013.
Gilman, Charlotte Perkins. "The Yellow Wallpaper." 1892. In *The Yellow Wallpaper and Other Stories*, edited by Robert Shulman, 3–19. Oxford: Oxford University Press, 1998.
Goddu, Teresa A. *Gothic America: Narrative, History, and Nation*. New York: Columbia University Press, 1997.
Hahner, Leslie, Scott J. Varda, and Nathan A. Wilson. "*Paranormal Activity* and the Horror of Abject Consumption." *Critical Studies in Media Communication* 30, no. 5 (2012): 362–376.
Halttunen, Karen. "Gothic Imagination and Social Reform: The Haunted House of Lyman Beecher, Henry Ward Beecher, and Harriet Beecher Stowe." In *New Essays on "Uncle Tom's Cabin,"* edited by Eric J. Sundquist, 107–134. Cambridge: Cambridge University Press, 1986.
*The Haunting*. Directed by Jan DeBont. Dreamworks Pictures, 1999.
*The Haunting*. Directed by Robert Wise. Argyle Enterprises, 1963.
*The Haunting of Hill House*. Created by Mike Flanagan. Netflix, 2018.
Hawthorne, Nathaniel. *The House of the Seven Gables*. 1851. New York: Modern Library, 2001.
Hennelly, Mark M., Jr. "Framing the Gothic: From Pillar to Post-Structuralism." *College Literature* 28, no. 3 (2001): 68–87.
*The House Next Door*. Directed by Jeff Woolnough. Lifetime, 2006.
*Insidious*. Directed by James Wan. Blumhouse, 2011.
Jackson, Shirley. *The Haunting of Hill House*. New York: Viking, 1959.

Jameson, Misty L. "The Haunted House of American Fiction: William Gaddis's *Carpenter's Gothic*." *Studies in the Novel* 41, no. 3 (2009): 314–329.

Janicker, Rebecca. *The Literary Haunted House: Lovecraft, Matheson, King and the Horror in Between.* Jefferson, NC: McFarland, 2015.

Kleinman, Ed. "Henry James and the Haunted House of Fiction: Hawthorne's Influence in *The American*." *Canadian Review of American Studies* 21 (1990): 31–48.

Konvitz, Jeffrey. *The Sentinel.* 1974. New York: Ballantine, 1976.

Kröger, Lisa. "*House of Leaves*: A Postmodern Retelling of Shirley Jackson's *The Haunting of Hill House*." *Journal of the Georgia Philological Association* 1 (2009): 149–156.

*The Legend of Hell House*. Directed by John Hough. Academy Pictures, 1973.

Lewis, Tyson, and Daniel Cho. "Home Is Where the Neurosis Is: A Topography of the Spatial Unconscious." *Cultural Critique* 64, no.1 (2006): 69–91.

Little, Bentley. *The Handyman.* Forest Hill, MD: Cemetery Dance, 2017.

———. *The Haunted.* New York: Signet, 2012.

———. *The Mailman.* New York: Signet, 1991.

Malfi, Ronald. *Cradle Lake.* Aurora, IL: Medallion, 2013.

———. *Little Girls.* New York: Pinnacle, 2015.

Mana, Davide. "It Ain't Over Till the Fat Lady Sings: William Peter Blatty's *Elsewhere* and the Haunted House Formula." In *American Exorcist: Critical Essays on William Peter Blatty*, edited by Benjamin Szumskyj, 150–165. Jefferson, NC: McFarland, 2008.

Marasco, Robert. *Burnt Offerings.* 1973. Richmond, VA: Valancourt, 2015.

Matheson, Richard. *Hell House.* New York: Viking, 1971.

McCloud, Sean. "Mapping the Spatial Limbos of Spiritual Warfare: Haunted Houses, Defiled Land and the Horrors of History." *Material Religion* 9, no. 2 (2013): 166–185.

McCracken, Scott. *Pulp: Reading Popular Fiction.* Manchester: Manchester University Press, 1998.

Miller, April. "Real-to Reel Recessionary Horrors in *Drag Me to Hell* and *Contagion*." In Boyle and Mrozowski. *The Great Recession in Fiction, Film, and Television*, 29–49.

Murphy, Bernice M. "'It's Not the House That's Haunted': Demons, Debt, and the Family in Peril Formula in Recent Horror Cinema." In *Cinematic Ghosts: Haunting and Spectrality form Silent Cinema to the Digital Era*, edited by Murray Leeder, 235–252. London: Bloomsbury, 2015.

Musante, Dewey. "Insidious Forms: Deleuze, the Bodily Diagram and the Haunted House Film." *Horror Studies* 7, no. 1 (2016): 73–93.

Oliete-Aldea, Elena. "The Great Recession and Transnational Horror: Sajit Warrier's Crossover Film *Fired* (2010)." *The Journal of Popular Culture* 49, no. 5 (2016): 1163–1183.

*Paranormal Activity.* Directed by Oren Peli. Performed by Katie Featherston and Micah Sloat, Blumhouse, 2009.

Poe, Edgar Allan. "The Fall of the House of Usher." 1839. In *Collected Works of Edgar Allan Poe*, edited by Thomas Mabbott et al., 392–411. Cambridge, MA: Belknap Press of Harvard University Press, 1978.

Poznar, Susan. "Rocking and Reeling through the Doors of Miscreation: Disequilibrium in Shirley Jackson's *The Haunting of Hill House*." In *Monsters and Monstrosity from the Fin de Siècle to the Millennium*, edited by Sharla Hutchison and Rebecca A. Brown, 144–65. Jefferson, NC: McFarland, 2015.

Priest, Cherie. *The Family Plot*. New York: Tor, 2016.

Redding, Arthur. *Haints: American Ghosts, Millennial Passions, and Contemporary Gothic Fictions*. Tuscaloosa: University of Alabama Press, 2011.

Schneider, Steven Jay. "Thrice-Told Tales: *The Haunting* from Novel to Film . . . to Film." *Journal of Popular Film and Television* 30, no. 3 (2002): 166–176.

*The Sentinel*. Directed by Michael Winner. Jeffrey Konvitz Productions, Universal Pictures, 1977.

Siddons, Anne Rivers. *The House Next Door*. New York: Simon and Schuster, 1978.

Smuts, Aaron. "Haunting the House from Within: Disbelief Mitigation and Spatial Experience." In *Dark Thoughts: Philosophic Reflections on Cinematic Horror*, edited by Steven Jay Schneider and Daniel Shaw, 158–173. Lanham, MD: Scarecrow Press, 2007.

Stevens, Dana. "*Paranormal Activity*: A parable about the credit crisis and unthinking consumerism." *Slate*, October 30, 2009. http://www.slate.com/articles/arts/movies/2009/10/paranormal_activity.html

Stone, James D. "Horror at the Homestead: The (Re)possession of American Property in *Paranormal Activity* and *Paranormal Activity II*." In Boyle and Mrozowski, *The Great Recession in Fiction, Film and Television*, 51–65.

Tremblay, Paul. *A Head Full of Ghosts*. New York: HarperCollins, 2015.

Vidler, Anthony. *The Architectural Uncanny: Essays in the Modern Unhomely*. Cambridge: MIT Press, 1992.

Weinstock, Jeffrey Andrew. "Introduction: The Spectral Turn." In *Spectral America: Phantoms and the National Imagination*, edited by Jeffrey Andrew Weinstock, 3–17. Madison: University of Wisconsin Press, 2004.

Wessels, Emanuelle. "A Lesson Concerning Technology: The Affective Economies of Post-Economic Crisis Haunted House Horror in *The Conjuring* and *Insidious*." *Quarterly Review of Film and Video* 32, no. 6 (2015): 511–526.

Wilson, Christine. "Haunted Habitability: Wilderness and American Haunted House Narratives." In *Popular Ghosts: The Haunted Spaces of Everyday Culture*, edited by María del Pila Blanco and Esther Peeren, 200–212. New York: Continuum, 2010.

*Chapter Six*

# Classism and Horror in the 1970s
## *The Rural Dweller as a Monster*
### Erika Tiburcio Moreno

Rednecks, hillbillies, and similar individuals have been prominently featured as monsters in Hollywood horror films since the 1970s.[1] The turn toward realism that took place within the horror genre during the postwar era—driven by technological advancements and the shifting interests of a new generation of filmmakers—diminished the role of supernatural monsters in favor of explanations of how ordinary human beings became macabre reflections of the qualities that defined the "good citizen." Rural areas became a frequent setting for such stories in Hollywood horror films, and depictions of rural life became vehicles for questioning the human cost of economic opulence and reflecting on the forgotten individuals who lived there in appalling conditions. Isolation and deprivation, the films suggested, produced human monsters.

The aim of this chapter is to analyze the figure of the rural dweller—the "redneck" or "hillbilly"—in American horror films of the 1970s as a figure whose monstrous qualities stem from the structural classism intrinsic to capitalism in the United States. In that sense, the relationship of poverty and rurality was understood as a reflection of the worst vices (sloth, sluggishness) of the American citizen instead of the result of an unequal system in which economic power was the differentiating element. Consequently, "backwardness" is the prevalent idea in the discourse, and the rural serial killer embodies the degeneration that comes of not belonging to the mainstream and the modern, urban world. This chapter uses an overview of the cinematic and historical contexts of those years, followed by case studies of *Deranged: Confessions of a Necrophile* and *Mother's Day*, to illustrate how the economic disruptions of the era created a new type of cinematic monster.

## UNDERSTANDING AMERICAN HORROR IN THE SEVENTIES

During the 1970s, America went through a difficult period in which violence and economic dislocation became real threats. The economic shocks of the era (stagnant wages, inflation, and the oil embargoes, to name a few) revealed the social boundaries that divided America into different classes, with the lower classes suffering most due to their inability to escape from the cycle of poverty. The American capitalist system was structured in ways that made the problem worse, by preventing the lower classes—both rural and urban—from accessing aspects of a better life, such as higher education and good housing, that the upper classes already possessed.

The hopelessness of this endemic situation led members of the lower classes to delinquency and crime (such as drug dealing), resulting in an increasing sense of insecurity among the middle classes, which was subsequently exploited by mass media. Crime in America—paired with television images of American soldiers committing outrageous, indiscriminate acts of violence in Vietnam—reinforced the idea that violence was an ordinary, everyday occurrence. Violence became particularly associated with those individuals who stood on the outskirts of mainstream society—the marginal places where impoverished citizens lived because they could not afford better.

Simultaneously, the film industry's attitudes toward depictions of sex and violence onscreen were changing. The Hays Code, imposed in 1935, tightly restricted both, but as the Studio System broke down in the 1950s, the horror genre became popular with makers of "exploitation films," who added sex or violence to their low-budget productions in order to increase ticket sales. Indeed, Stephen Thrower points out that "unlike the majors, who were always looking over their shoulders at the gossip mags or mainstream press, or worrying about the absurd demands of the Hays Code, exploitation moviemakers could badger away at the limits of what was legally allowed onscreen."[2] In the 1960s, the willingness of the studios to release serious films including profanity (*Who's Afraid of Virginia Woolf,* 1964), nudity (*The Pawnbroker,* 1965), or graphic violence (*Bonnie and Clyde,* 1967) began to erode the Hays Code. In 1968 the industry replaced it with a rating system administered by the Motion Picture Association of America (MPAA). The institution of the MPAA rating system allowed for horror directors to work with taboo topics and content that could only be fit for a mature audience. Horror films involving explicit violence and sexuality—Roman Polanski's *Rosemary's Baby* (1968), William Friedkin's *The Exorcist* (1973), and Steven Spielberg's *Jaws* (1975) thus began to enter the mainstream, produced by major studios and independent ones alike.[3]

The mainstreaming of horror did not, however, eliminate the exploitation film. Indeed, it was followed by a cluster of low-budget movies labeled as "American Gothic," which used graphically sexual and violent stories as metaphors for the issues that affected the country the most.[4] This group of films used more intricate plots than prior exploitation movies, in order to offer a critical reading of contemporary America. Their exhibition in marginal venues—rural and suburban drive-ins and urban "grindhouse" cinemas—allowed them to explore these subjects by introducing their own outlook. Wes Craven's *Last House on the Left* (1972), for instance, tells the story of Mari and Phyllis, two teenagers who are raped and killed. When their murderers end up, unwittingly, in Mari's house, her parents take revenge and slay them. Through this cruel story, based on Ingmar Bergman's *The Virgin Spring* (1960), Wes Craven portrays a critical vision of the American attitude of indifference toward the increasing violence, as well as establishing a metaphor of the Vietnam War and the outrageous crimes that soldiers were performing there.

For the first time, onscreen horror became a mirror in which American society's hidden secrets were made visible, and its taboos (cannibalism, cruelty, shamelessness) were openly explored. The naturalized violence that was part of the history of the United States from its beginning—that helped to maintain white male supremacy within American society—was particularly prominent in such films. They were influenced not only by the country's history of violence, but also by the increasing banalization of violence in American society, mirrored in the surge of interest in (even fascination with) murderers such as Ted Bundy, the Zodiac Killer, John Wayne Gacy, and David "Son of Sam" Berkowitz, whose crimes had no apparent purpose or reason. These killers horrified Americans *because* their crimes were incomprehensible, making them completely impossible to predict and control. Unlike bank robbers or jealous spouses, whose actions could be explained and whose victims were predictable, serial killers turned any member of society into a potential victim. The crimes of Billy the Kid, an outlaw and gunfighter who killed eight men, could be understood in the context of his life. Ted Bundy, on the other hand, seemed to be a normal, handsome, and responsible young man, but—for psychological reasons never understood—sadistically murdered several young women. This new type of monster, by "combining a discourse of madness and monstrous evil" established serial killers as "a powerful symbolic construction of all that had gone wrong since Woodstock."[5]

The social unsteadiness, political upheaval, and economic stresses of the 1970s undermined belief in American exceptionalism—particularly the idea that individualism, nurtured by the freedom and equality that America provided, was the key to achieving wealth.⁶ Widespread disillusionment and dissatisfaction with America's supposedly "exceptional" qualities took many forms—outrage at institutionalized sexism and racism, frustration with political corruption, and despair over economic insecurity—all of which contributed to feelings of alienation. Serial killers, real and fictional, were monstrous embodiments of those feelings. Their crimes implied a sense of alienation so profound that it led them to kill and mutilate for inexplicable "reasons." Simultaneously, the threat they posed—sudden, violent death at the hands of normal-*looking*, but actually monstrous, fellow citizens—intensified Americans' sense that their own lives had grown precarious, and that they were merely commodities that the world could use and cast aside.

"American Gothic" horror films originated from this anger and from the filmmakers' desires to criticize poverty, class divisions, economic insecurity, corruption, and social tensions that—contrary to what defenders of American exceptionalism believed—really did exist in the United States. The importance that the filmmakers placed on showing audiences a hidden reality led them to use a semidocumentary style, made possible in part by use of the still-new Steadicam. Films sought to create a close association between truth and horror, and many—such as *Texas Chain Saw Massacre* and *Last House on the Left*—featured prologues stating that they were based on actual events. This embrace of realism eliminated the distance between horror films and audiences' everyday reality. Fictional fear was no longer tied to fantastic monsters, but derived from the exhibition of concealed, real-world terrors not displayed in other media.

As Hollywood embraced the blockbuster in the late 1970s, it upgraded entertainment to its highest form of fiction, and shifted away using film as a form of social commentary. Horror cinema was influenced by this trend and, eventually, an increasing number of films started to revolve around murders. The slasher subgenre, which emerged in the late 1970s, consisted of a simple formula: a serial killer, who carries recognizable weapons and wears a specific costume—such as Michael Myers in John Carpenter's *Halloween* (1978), or Freddy Krueger in Wes Craven's *Nightmare on Elm Street* (1984)—who chases and kills a group of young people, generally teenagers. Sex and violence were the main enticement for young spectators, who came to such films expecting to watch macabre and imaginative murders. The "American Gothic" movement in horror film thus came to an end, with many experts pointing out that *Halloween* was the transitional film to the following phase. Individual films such as John McNaughton's *Henry: Portrait of a Serial Killer* (1986) continued to use horror as a metaphor for social issues, but it was no longer a predominant trend.

# REDNECKS AND HILLBILLIES: RURAL WORKING-CLASS MONSTERS AS OUTSIDERS

All horror films, regardless of their subgenre, force two distinct concepts into conflict. One is normalcy, which positions the main characters as the embodiment of "good," as defined at the moment when the movie was produced. The second is monstrosity, or otherness—a fearsome element that represents a menace to the established order, and must be defeated in order to render society safe. Both ideas, however, are connected and indivisible because the construction of good is directly built upon the understanding of evil, and on a hierarchical order in which normalcy is morally superior to monstrosity.[7]

Monsters come in many forms—vampires, werewolves, aliens, serial killers, zombies—and thus possess a wide variety of traits, but they divide into two broad categories. Fantastic or surreal monsters threaten society by challenging our idea of reality—either directly, by their own existence, or indirectly, by embodying real-world forces that threaten to negate the principles on which it rests. The alien monsters in Cold War horror films such as *The Thing from Another World* (1951) and *Invasion of the Body Snatchers* (1956) were monstrous both in their own right and as metaphors for Communism. Female vampires (like their male counterparts) subvert humans' accustomed dominance over nature, turning them from predators to prey, but also (by tapping into the "corrupting" power of female sexuality) by inverting men's accustomed dominance over women. Serial killers, on the other hand, leave the structure of our reality essentially intact, but force us to consider either good or evil within our own limits of reality.

The monster considered here—the American rural dweller—is a product of classism. America promotes itself, in its national discourse, as a classless society, but the central roles played by capitalism and private property have transformed it into a strongly hierarchical social order in which wealth is the key to social advancement.[8] Poor people were demonized, blamed for not ascending socially and thus escaping poverty, in order to uphold this principle and keep the myth of equal opportunity intact. Their abject poverty is attributed to their laziness and stupidity, instead of an unfair system. According to Michael Harrington:

> Poverty in the United States is a culture, an institution. There is, in short, a language of the poor, a psychology of the poor, a world view of the poor. To be impoverished is to be an internal alien, to grow up in a culture that is radically different from the one that dominates the society.[9]

Rural dwellers in popular culture embody this "internal otherness" and personify the demonization of the poor—people who had no place in the hegemonic or dominant culture. Their status as outsiders, and society's disapproval of them, are evident in the labels applied to them as a group: "white trash," a derogatory term for those of working-class or lower-class status;[10] "redneck," specifically for poor southern white men; and "hillbilly," applied to residents of the Appalachian or Ozark Mountains. These epithets reaffirm an American mental hierarchy where modernity, an urban or suburban lifestyle, and middle-class values represent the "real" America, and deviations from them suggest laziness, degeneracy, and immorality.[11]

The backwoods-set horror fiction of the 1970s, as Bernice Murphy notes, gave rural outsiders barbarian- and beastlike attributes, portraying them as feral, savage, incestuous, inbred, callous, filthy, cannibalistic, sadistic, insular, uneducated, and psychologically and physically misshapen.[12] Rural horror films of the period took a similar approach, placing "normal" middle-class individuals in settings where they were menaced by monstrous rural dwellers. The oddity of the latter was reinforced by their association with wildness and the woods, their old-fashioned lifestyle, and their simultaneous attachment to tradition and rejection of modernization alike.

*Psycho* (1960) takes place just beyond the outskirts of a major southwestern city, but it was, in a sense, one of the first cinematic examples of this opposition. Firstly, Norman Bates (Anthony Perkins)—who lives with his mother in a Victorian-era house and runs a motel isolated from the recently built modern highway and thus from the modern world—represents the traditional America. Marion Crane (Janet Leigh)—who lives in the city, holds a full-time job, and is hiding at the motel after stealing money from her employer—embodies modernity and middle-class capitalist success. This physical distance is also translated into an insurmountable gulf between their mind-sets. On the one hand, Norman is framed as an outsider for his prioritization of family over money and his lack of adaptation to conventional urban/middle-class social boundaries. On the other hand, Marion's lifestyle reflects that 1960s modernity, where women began to live alone and became more independent, and where money was directly linked to happiness. The scene where they are talking in Norman's office reflects this distinction and presents two different worlds.

Norman's conspicuous domesticity, the meal of milk and sandwiches he offers to Marion, and his subdued voice and personality represent a portrayal of masculinity far removed from 1960s norms, which are embodied by Marion's lover Sam Loomis (John Gavin). The full depth (and monstrosity) of Norman's otherness is revealed in the second half of the film, first by the indiscriminate murders of Marion and the private detective tracking her, and then by the revelation of his transvestism and the preservation of his mother's stuffed corpse in the basement of their home.

This emerging concept of otherness became a sinister mirror of society in the 1970s, where films such as *Deliverance* (1972) and *Texas Chain Saw Massacre* (1974) showed rural dwellers as degenerate monsters eager to murder, torture, rape, or even eat outsiders who wandered into their domain. They were placed at a distance—moral as well as geographic—from the "civil" world of the middle class, and their environment was portrayed as dilapidated, filthy, and backward. Their abject poverty thus became, onscreen, an explanation for their kind of monstrosity—one that fitted neatly into the relentless stereotyping of poor whites, and portrayed their lifestyle as a deliberate choice rather than a result of social and economic forces beyond their control.

As noted here, classism influenced rural poor killers because, unlike urban serial ones, their intrinsic features prevented them from living within normalcy and being capable of concealing their true nature. Cleverness, attractiveness, and apparent normality were associated to urban sophisticated white young men, the only ones allowed to use violence to stand out from the crowd.[13] By comparison, ferocity, brutality, and bestiality were prominent features which turned the rural killer into a dangerous being, and they were described as citizens who could not adapt to social rules. Furthermore, their lack of sympathy for urban dwellers and their willingness to attack them resulted in the creation of a human beast that further distanced them from a normal individual.

Even though we must regard insanity as an important attribute for both types of serial murderers, one of the main reasons why the urban serial killer needs to kill is sexuality, whereas rednecks or hillbillies usually attack victims because of hostility, as in *Two Thousand Maniacs* (1964) and *Madman* (1982). American urban middle-class citizens are seen as aliens who do not belong to the same community and whose arrival is understood as a disrespectful and aggressive attack to their customs. This unfamiliarity is expressed through several narratives. The "American Gothic" works focused on the journey of middle-class urban or suburban characters to a rural world that they *think* is part of "their" America, only to discover that it is an entirely separate world where "normal" rules have no place. Consequently, two kinds of normality are placed against one another, as it is seen in *Texas Chain Saw Massacre*. "Rednecks," meanwhile, see outsiders as noxious Others who have come to disrupt their lives and mock them, and/or as an opportunity to even the score for the harm done to them by society. It never occurs to the locals to treat the outsiders as humans deserving of consideration, because they are from the other side of the gulf separating the two Americas. This difference is not perceived by city folks, but rednecks are never allowed to forget about it. Indeed, rednecks embody everything that America is ashamed of and, according to Jim Goad, they are "a convenient way for America to demonize itself, or, rather, to exorcise the demon and place it somewhere outside of itself."[14]

In other words, rurality was sidelined, and only urban citizens were enjoying earnings in their daily lives—in spite of the national discourse which, in theory, recognized all citizens as deserving of rewards. Thus, they felt oppressed by those newcomers who tried to prevail over them without considering their rights as equal Americans. In this way, the two opponents are reflective of a class struggle in which the forgotten lower-class culture could be annihilated by the middle-class intruders and their invasion of a territory that, although under American sovereignty, does not seem to fit inside its territory.

When horror filmmakers embraced the serial killer as a villain in the 1970s, they did so in ways that reflected the class-based hierarchy that dominated American society in that period. The rural serial killer was different from, and less impressive than, the urban one. The urban serial killer might possess intellect, elegance, and seductive charm (even if he used them for twisted ends), but his "white trash" counterpart was crude, animalistic, and often grotesque. Even in the serial murder, the urban/suburban middle class set standards that the rural poor struggled and failed to meet.

*Deranged: Confessions of a Necrophile* and *Mother's Day* reflect these patterns in 1970s horror films. Both present the rural dweller as a monster, but their starting points and approaches differ. *Deranged* belongs to the "American Gothic" movement and is focused on the serial killer and his life. The story is told in documentary style, without taking a specific stance and forcing the audience to witness Ezra's abhorrent crimes. Through twisted images, the film describes an apparent harmless resident whose strict morality drives him to commit horrible killings in name of decency. This deviant discourse serves as a critique toward the bad consequences of Puritanism and those reactionary responses of some of the population against social and scientific advancements of the time. *Mother's Day,* on the other hand, is a slasher movie, and entertainment is the central purpose of its storytelling. It pits hegemonic normalcy against an unknown monstrosity in the form of a backward rural family, whose members try to imitate a modern lifestyle they are incapable of achieving. The members of the family are stereotyped, and their otherness established, through their house, their manners, and their mental impairment.

## DERANGED: CONFESSIONS OF A NECROPHILE

Directed by Alan Ormsby and Jeff Gillen and released in 1974, *Deranged* is based on the case of Ed Gein, a Wisconsin serial killer and grave-robber known as "the butcher of Plainfield," who became famous for his necrophilia and collecting of body parts to shape into objects and sculptures. The main character, Ezra Cobb (Roberts Blossom), is depicted as an unsophisticated, mentally disabled man whose hillbilly lifestyle is "used to represent a people and culture strangely out of sync with modernity but also to point out the moral and social costs of an increasingly automated and materialistic America."[15] He is deeply religious—a legacy from his mother, whose puritanical principles caused her to see all male-female relationships as sinful. The characters are thus presented as products of a reactionary America whose rigid morality is the main cause of Ezra's insanity.

As Karen Halttunen notes, such films portray the family "as a site of dark mysteries and unspeakable horrors . . . not a haven in a heartless new commercial world, but a bastion of traditional coercion and brutal violence."[16] Ezra's mother is presented as a very possessive woman who does not allow him to develop as a normal individual. He looks childish and his neighbors treat him as such—as if he were a young boy who needs advice. When his mother dies, his inability to face the world alone causes him to hallucinate that she is reprimanding him about his incorrect behavior. Eventually, as Ezra becomes crazy, his behavior and the state of his house convey just how deeply he is deteriorating.

Garbage accumulating inside his home turns it into a house of horrors, with the corpses of his victims sitting upright on chairs, symbolizing his confusion between reality and fantasy. Ezra himself behaves oddly and demonstrates neither intelligence nor strategy in planning his murders, which are depicted as a conjunction of failed ethics and repressed sexual impulses. When Ezra kidnaps Mary and forces her to dine with his corpses and him, it visually appears to be a normal family dinner, in which each seat reveals the occupant's hierarchical position within that household. This recognizable family tradition is transformed, however, into a sign of Ezra's twisted desire to achieve normalcy. His irrational behavior—setting the scene with corpses instead of living people—underscores his otherness.

Ezra's rurality and insanity prevent him from being a powerful monster; he did not have access to higher education, and his danger resides in the fact that he holds his neighbors' trust. As a matter of fact, in the bar where he meets Mary Ransom (Micki Moore), where the customers are all working-class men, the waitress refers to them as people who indiscriminately drink cheap alcohol, thus furthering an urban middle-class stereotype of rural dwellers. Additionally, all the victims that will end up murdered—Mary, Sally (Pat Orr), and Maureen Shelby (Marian Waldman)—embody various elements of modernity (such as Maureen's eastern alternative religious beliefs, and Mary's independence), which run counter to Ezra's intransigent traditionalism.

*Deranged: Confessions of a Necrophile* focuses on a rural dweller whose lack of higher education and strict mother explain his otherness, which, at the same time, places him outside society. The rest of rural dwellers present the same features, but they do not consider murder as an appropriate social act. For that reason, these people see Ezra as another member of their community and it is what helps Ezra go undetected, but his filthy house and its macabre decoration turn him into a monster. His mother's domination leads him to consider all women as outsiders, and those who are independent and sexually active above all. Internalization of her discourse rules him out of putting his congeners in danger.

His monstrosity—a product of his atrocious crimes and twisted thinking—is imbued by classism because his power does not come from either cleverness or adaptation, but familiarity. Obviously, this is less fearsome than a killer who is capable of deceiving a victim of his choosing, who can travel around the country, passing unnoticed like an urban killer such as Ted Bundy could do.

## *MOTHER'S DAY*

Directed by Charles Kauffman and released in 1980, *Mother's Day* is a slasher-style horror comedy where three young women—Jackie (Deborah Luce), Abbie (Nancy Hendrickson), and Trina (Tiana Pierce)— fight for survival against backwoods brothers Ike (Holden McGuire) and Addley (Billy Ray McQuade) and their mother (Rose Ross). Although the portrayal of the rural poor could be considered as a parody of horror-film families (such as the one in the *Texas Chain Saw Massacre*), classism has a strong influence here because the family's portrayal is full of the aforementioned rural stereotypes. The film differs from *Deranged* because it presents normalcy as originating in a different place than the one where the film is set. Indeed, the three main characters are urban girls who behave according to the established social rules, and viewers, who believe themselves to be quite similar to the girls, are forced to relate to them. When the two sides are opposed, the antagonists are described as inferior due to their rural background—they are not as clever as the girls, their behavior is stupid, and their defeat is the consequence of that. Normalcy, in the film, is rooted in modernity, an urban lifestyle, modern technology, fashionable clothes, and new types of leisure. The depiction of the rural family, however, presents them as individuals who seek to imitate trendiness, but are ultimately incapable of assimilating to the hegemonic, mainstream way of life. In other words, urban normality is understood as the role model to which all American citizens should aspire in hopes of leading a better life, ruling out any other alternative.

Regarding the difference between the two concepts, the two men are physically and mentally different. Where the girls are beautiful, sophisticated, well-educated and independent, Ike and Addley are ugly, filthy, disorganized, rude, and do not speak properly, despite having access to a home gym for fitness and a television set where they can watch role models for their behavior and thoughts. Despite their awkward efforts to exhibit normality (they pretend to brush their teeth and use deodorant), the young women—the ones who must recognize them as peers—reject them, because Ike and Addley's crimes distance from being "modern and normal" good citizens.

This mutual hostility is the reason why each group considers the other as aliens who must be killed in order to preserve their own normality. However, the antagonists also display their anger at the denial of their consideration as proper citizens. This sharp distinction between civilization and barbarity (which also delineates what a crime is) masks the social class division between upper-middle and working classes, where lower class reveals itself as abandoned by the protection of the state. One of the main conflicts is that between the state mentality (modern civilization, economic advancement, and middle-class status), embodied by the three women, and the statelessness (security is assured by citizens themselves) personified by the rural family. The first one is associated with concepts such as order and community, security being the objective to which all Americans are assumed to aspire. On the contrary, statelessness is associated with violence, anarchy, and lack of control, which produces animalistic individuals who act according to their survival instincts without respect for civilized rules.[17] Consequently, they will never be able to improve their social status because they are trapped in endemic poverty.

Ike and Addley have the advantage of knowing the territory into which the women have ventured, but—being savage and irrational—they are incapable of planning their crimes carefully. Instead, they follow their mother's instructions. Their dependence on their mother deprives them of autonomy and the freedom to choose their own victims. The dysfunctional rural family at the center of the film twists the picture of the traditional layout of one, in a critique that has been part of American culture since the 1960s. Ike and Addley's otherness is also apparent in their lack of empathy for their victims and the sheer brutality of their crimes. In the rape scene, Jackie is dehumanized until she is turned from a person into a commodity to satisfy them. Their brutality is portrayed as a primitive instinct that, in another social setting, would never have been allowed to surface.

The close link that *Mother's Day* draws between primitivism and poverty reinforces the capitalist idea that poor citizens need stricter discipline to counteract their dangerous behavior. The higher economic classes are presented as the most mature and thus the most fit to rule America, and any act aimed at maintaining the established order—no matter how violent or cruel—is justified by the notion that it is necessary for the common good.[18]

*Mother's Day* ends with Trina and Abbey, the family's surviving victims, killing them. The film treats this as justified because of the dreadful acts that the family has committed, and at the end Trina declares to Abbey that "we were meant to survive," which asserts their power over the situation and so restores normalcy. The importance of preserving the social order validates their actions and justifies actions that might otherwise be seen as abhorrent and criminal, allowing them to be understood as necessary. This case illustrates the fundamental dynamic of such films: preservation of what is important for the middle-class is paramount, and any threat to it posed by the working class will be annihilated.

The middle-class characters' behavior, however, is far from admirable. They show no respect for the owner of the gas station, and they care only for themselves. They enter the building laughing and throw objects around, and blatantly ignore the owner's anger. They decide to sleep by the lake, taking no notice of the potential dangers of doing so, and are consequently kidnapped by Ike and Addley. In this movie, classism is also observed in the depiction of the family, characterized by the degeneration of the working class, which detaches them from being human, so they cannot claim to have a place in the same country as the chosen people. Although this movie shows the same brutality emerging from both classes, mixed with violence on one side (rural family) and revenge on the other (city women), the latter is better understood—and even supported—because of the weight of the stereotype that hangs over rural dwellers, turning them into beasts.

## CONCLUSION

The association between the rural monster and the working class in 1970s American horror films reinforced a discourse of classism that frames the middle class as natural leaders and more prepared to rule the country. The monstrosity of rural serial killers did not, however, extend to their urban counterparts. Urban otherness was associated, in fictional serial killers, with intelligence, charm, and power. Rural otherness rooted itself in feral savagery instead, and violence as means of socializing.

The anger of the rural poor against the urban and suburban middle classes—born out of governmental neglect and the disdain for rural culture—turned into rape, torture, and revenge directed against them. Despite not being responsible for the economic and cultural dislocations of the 1970s, the rural poor became scapegoats for and embodiments of sins possessed by all Americans. For that reason, poverty was associated to an individual failure instead of a social injustice. The rural monsters in both instances are emptied of intelligence and higher qualities; depravity, degeneration, savagery, and deviancy are presented as their defining qualities.

The killers in both films regard their victims as inferior beings—representation of an alien way of life (*Deranged*) or invading foreigners (*Mother's Day*)—who must be destroyed. While Ezra Cobb sees independent women as sinners who are corrupted, the family in *Mother's Day* see the same type of victims as inferior who must suffer and be destroyed in basis of their otherness.

The rural monster thus mirrors, in a sinister way, the rural working-class belief that their unique culture must struggle to not be swallowed by the hegemonic middle-class culture. The films frame working class in distinctly middle-class terms: as a threat, whose members could rise up against the Establishment at any moment. Rural monsters serve as receptacles of the dark side of America: those who are not allowed to have voice or create a valid counter discourse opposed to the hegemonic one. For that reason, rednecks use violence as a revenge against the middle class who rules the country and are oppressing them constantly. Stereotypes around these dwellers, who are blamed for their unlucky faith, conceal the failures of the system. Consequently, characters such as Ezra Cobb or Ike and Addley reflect this classism because they are rejected, misfit serial killers who bear sole responsibility for their own degeneration and will never be able to be accepted as equals by hegemonic society. Poverty is thus the excuse to create depraved monsters that must be isolated and punished and, their very working-class condition, inseparably linked to these crimes, denies the possibility of drawing attention to the unjust class boundaries that divide America.

## NOTES

1. The final copyediting of this chapter was done by Lorena Zúñiga.
2. Thrower, *Nightmare USA*, 13.
3. Cook, *Lost Illusions*.
4. Navarro, *American Gothic*.

5. Poole, *Monsters in America*, 152.
6. Hodgson, *Myth of American Exceptionalism*.
7. Hall, "Spectacle of the 'Other,'" 234–237.
8. Foley, *American Credo*.
9. Harrington, *Other America*, 179–180.
10. Hartigan, "Unpopular Culture," 319.
11. Jarosz and Lawson, "'Sophisticated People versus Rednecks,'" 12–14.
12. Murphy, *Rural*, 149.
13. Cawelti, *Mystery, Violence, and Popular Culture*.
14. Goad, *Redneck Manifesto*, 100.
15. Harkins, *Hillbilly*, 220.
16. Halttunen, *Murder Most Foul*, 169.
17. Clover, *Men, Women and Chain Saws*, 125–133.
18. Newitz, "White Savagery and Humiliation," 152.

## BIBLIOGRAPHY

Cawelti, John G. *Mystery, Violence, and Popular Culture: Essays*. Madison: University of Wisconsin Press/Popular Press, 2004.

Clover, Carol J. *Men, Women and Chain Saws. Gender in the Modern Horror Film*. Princeton, NJ: Princeton University Press, 1992.

Cook, David A. *Lost Illusions: American Cinema in the Age of Watergate and Vietnam, 1970–1979*. New York: Scribners, 1999.

*Deranged: Confessions of a Necrophile*, directed by Alan Ormsby and Jeff Gillen. 1974. Blu-Ray. New York: Kino Lorber, 2015.

Fairclough, Norman. *Language and Power*. London: Longman, 1989.

Foley, Michael. *American Credo. The Place of Ideas in US Politics*. Oxford: Oxford University Press, 2012.

Goad, Jim. *The Redneck Manifesto. How Hillbillies, Hicks, and White Trash Became America's Scapegoats*. New York: Simon & Schuster, 1997.

Hall, Stuart. "The Spectacle of the 'Other.'" *Representation. Cultural Practices and Signifying Practices*, edited by Stuart Hall, 223–290. London: SAGE, 1997.

Halttunen, Karen. *Murder Most Foul. The Killer and the American Gothic Imagination*. Cambridge, MA: Harvard University Press, 1998.

Harkins, Anthony. *Hillbilly. A Cultural History of an American Icon*. New York: Oxford University Press, 2004.

Harrington, Michael. *The Other America. Poverty in the United States*. Maryland: Penguin Books, 1975.

Hartigan, John. "Unpopular Culture: The Case of 'White Trash.'" *Cultural Studies* 11, no. 2 (1997): 316–343. http://dx.doi.org/10.1080/09502389700490171

Hodgson, Godfrey. *The Myth of American Exceptionalism*. New Haven, CT: Yale University Press, 2010.

Jarosz, Lucy, and Victoria Lawson. "'Sophisticated People versus Rednecks': Economic Restructuring and Class Difference in America's West." *Antipode* 17, no. 1 (2002): 8–27. http://dx.doi.org/10.1111/1467-8330.00224

*Mother's Day*, directed by Charles Kaufman. 1980. DVD. New York: Troma Entertainment, 2000.

Murphy, Bernice. *The Rural Gothic in American Popular Culture. Backwoods Horror and Terror in the Wilderness*. Basingstoke, UK: Palgrave Macmillan, 2009.

Navarro, Antonio J. *American Gothic: el cine de terror USA, 1960–1980*. San Sebastián: Donostia Kultura, 2007.

Newitz, Annalee. "White Savagery and Humiliation, or a New Racial Consciousness in the Media." *White Trash. Race and Class in America*, edited by Matt Wray and Annalee Newitz, 131–154. New York: Routledge, 1997.

Poole, W. Scott. *Monsters in America. Our Historical Obsession with the Hideous and the Haunting*. Waco: Baylor University Press, 2011.

Thrower, Stephen. *Nightmare USA. The Untold Story of the Exploitation Independents*. 2007. Goldaming: FAB Press, 2017.

*Chapter Seven*

# All against All

## Dystopia, Dark Forces, and Hobbesian Anarchy in the Purge Films

A. Bowdoin Van Riper

The premise behind the *Purge* trilogy of films (2013–2016) is brutally simple: one night out of each year, the rule of law is suspended for twelve hours, and all crime becomes legal. The nation's collective id is allowed to slip its leash and run wild. "More people will be purging this year than ever before," a radio announcer declares in the opening moments of *The Purge* (2013) as grainy security camera footage of beatings and shootings plays onscreen. "American streets will be running red tonight when people release the beast in record numbers." The camera cuts to a television screen where a man in a white lab coat wraps a pseudo-scientific explanation around the "release the beast" slogan. "History has proven it over and over again," he solemnly declares. "We are an inherently violent species," and we deny that fundamental reality at our peril. The Purge enables us to express our violent nature while limiting the disruption to a single night, and "creates psychological stability by letting us release the aggression we all have inside of us." It is an image of human nature that runs through two thousand years of Western thought: from the Christian doctrine of original sin through Hobbes's vision of primitive society as a "war of all against all" to the savage schoolboys of William Golding's *Lord of the Flies*.[1]

Almost immediately, however, *The Purge* deploys a counternarrative. Other voices—men and women in the street—label the Purge a sham: an attempt by the government to rid society of "undesirable" members: the poor, the sick, and the homeless, by allowing "patriotic citizens" to murder them with impunity. Critics of the Purge contend that it is—though they do not use the phrase—an attempt to enact Social Darwinism on a grand scale. Narrative and counternarrative intertwine throughout the trilogy and, by the third film, merge. It becomes clear, in *The Purge: Anarchy* (2014) and particularly in *The Purge: Election Year* (2016) that—while the wealthy and privileged may believe that the Purge somehow "cleanses" and "purifies" their souls—it is actually a tool for eliminating not undesirable emotions but undesirable people.

The *Purge* films are horror, but horror of a particular sort. There are few conventional jump-scares in the trilogy, and—by genre standards—little graphic violence. Thousands are said to lie dead in the streets each morning-after, but the carnage is reported by newscast voiceovers, rather than shown. Hundreds are mowed down onscreen by gunfire, but the horror of their deaths is muted by distance and darkness. The aesthetic is that of a 1950s western or war film, not the slow-motion surrealism of *Bonnie and Clyde* (1967) or the brutal immediacy of *Saving Private Ryan* (1998): Guns fire, bodies fall, and the story moves on.[2] Characters are threatened, wounded, and killed by melee weapons—maces, axes, machetes, and knives—but editing, camera angles, and (again) darkness mute the effects. None of the films dwell on the details of what can happen when lead and steel meet flesh and bone. The horrors of Purge Night, as explored in the film, are more complex, and ultimately more horrifying—linked not to the fragility of the human body but to the darkness of the human soul.

## A NATION REBORN

The title card that opens the first film in the trilogy establishes the films' shared setting and underlying premise:

> America 2022
> Unemployment is at 1%
> Crime is at an all-time low.
> Violence barely exists.
> With one exception...

The exception is the night of the annual Purge: twelve hours (from 7 PM on March 22 until 7 AM on March 23) when all laws are suspended and all otherwise-criminal acts, including murder, become legal. The Purge is the signature achievement of the New Founding Fathers of America (NFFA), a political party that formed, and rose to power, during a nationwide economic crisis in the mid-2010s. Both the Purge and the party enjoy widespread popular support. They are, as a second title card from the beginning of *The Purge* suggests, accorded near-religious reverence by many:

> Blessed be the New Founding Fathers
> for letting us Purge and cleanse our souls.
> Blessed be America, a nation reborn.

Such support, however, is not universal. Characters in all three films express opposition to the Purge—arguing that its impact falls disproportionately on the poor and vulnerable, and an armed anti-Purge resistance movement emerges in the second film and plays a central role in the third.

The three films that make up the trilogy occur sequentially: the first in 2022, the second in 2023, and the third in 2026.[3] Each begins on the afternoon of Purge Night, and ends the following morning as the sun rises and a warning siren signals the end of that year's Purge. All three follow broadly similar trajectories: introducing a group of characters who intend to spend the night safe and protected behind locked doors, but who find themselves forced to fight for their lives.

*The Purge* (2013) focuses on the Sandins: an upper-middle-class family living in a prosperous suburban neighborhood. James (Ethan Hawke), a successful salesman of high-end home-security systems whose clients include his own family and most of his neighbors, returns home on Purge Night proud of his success during the company's busiest sales period. He arms the house's security systems and settles in with his wife Mary (Lena Headey) and children, but—soon after the Purge begins—finds that his seemingly secure home contains two unwelcome guests. One is Henry (Tony Oller), an eighteen-year-old boy from the neighborhood whose relationship with fifteen-year-old Zoe (Adelaide Kane) he disapproves of; the other is a nameless, homeless, bloodied African American stranger (Edwin Hodge) who is admitted by twelve-year-old Charlie (Max Burkholder) after he pleads for sanctuary. The night quickly spins out of control. Henry shoots and wounds James, and is shot dead by him in return, and a gang of college-age purgers who were chasing the Stranger arrive, threatening to storm the house and kill everyone inside if he is not surrendered.

James agrees to their demands, but is unable to locate the Stranger, who (guided by Charlie) has disappeared into the darkened house along with the traumatized Zoe. The youthful gang carries out their threat with ease—revealing the expensive security systems that James sells to be useless in the face of a determined attack—and James is killed in the resulting melee. The neighbors arrive, mowing down the gang with gunfire, but then bind Mary and the children and prepare to kill them in retaliation for James's history of trumpeting his own success and making them feel inferior. The timely arrival of now-armed Stranger turns the tables. He frees the Sandins and, after Mary declines his offer to execute the neighbors, helps her to hold them at gunpoint until the Purge ends.

*The Purge: Anarchy* (2014) moves the action from the suburbs to the streets of an unnamed city where the lives of three separate groups of characters intertwine. Waitress and single mother Eva Sanchez (Carmen Ejogo) flees her apartment along with her teenaged daughter Cali (Zoe Soul) after they barely escape being being raped by the building superintendent and kidnapped by a paramilitary gang led by Big Daddy (Jack Conley). Shane and Liz, an estranged married couple, are stranded on the streets after their car, sabotaged by a gang of Purgers to make them easy targets, breaks down. Both are ultimately rescued by Leo Barnes (Frank Grillo): an off-duty police officer who temporarily suspends his own Purge Night plans in order to save them. The group flees through the city, encountering gangs, Big Daddy's paramilitary force, wealthy purgers who bid for the right to "hunt" unarmed victims in an enclosed arena using night-vision goggles and state-of-the-art weapons, and members of a guerilla resistance unit led by Carmelo Johns (Michael K. Williams) and his assistant Dante Bishop (Edwin Hodge): the Stranger from the first film. Leo, accompanied by Eva and Cali, makes his way to the suburbs, where he intends to kill Warren Grass (Brandon Keener)—the man who, while driving drunk, ran down and killed Barnes's young son the year before. Leo confronts Grass but chooses to spare his life—a decision soon rewarded when Grass saves Leo and the women by shooting the still-pursuing Big Daddy.

*The Purge: Election Year* takes place in Washington, DC, twenty years after the first Purge. Dante Bishop is now the leader of the resistance, and Leo Barnes is chief of security for Senator Charlene "Charlie" Roan (Elizabeth Mitchell), a leading presidential candidate whose platform includes a promise to abolish the Purge by executive order. Roan is close to Minister Edwidge Owens (Kyle Secor), the NFFA candidate, in the polls and the leaders of the NFFA party—determined to eliminate the threat she poses—lift the Purge-Night immunity previously enjoyed by high-ranking government officials and dispatch a neo-Nazi paramilitary group to kidnap her from her home. She escapes due to Barnes's timely intervention and the two flee into the city, where they struggle to stay alive until morning. Their fates become intertwined with those of African American storekeeper Joe Dixon (Mykelti Williamson), his immigrant assistant Marcos Dali (Joseph Julian Soria), and his protégé Laney Rucker (Betty Gabriel), a notorious former gang member who patrols the streets on Purge Night in an armed, armored "triage van," giving aid to the injured and ferrying them to a makeshift aid station organized by Bishop and the resistance movement.

Laney and Marcos's capacity for ruthless violence, along with Joe's own history as a former member of a street gang, make them formidable allies and guides through the chaotic streets of the capitol. Joe and Marcos rescue Leo and Charlie from a gang of foreign "murder tourists" who have taken them captive and, with Laney's help, try to keep Leo and Charlie safe until morning. Evading the paramilitary forces, they arrive at the aid station, where they meet Bishop and learn that the resistance is planning to use a colonial-era tunnel to penetrate the Our Lady of Sorrows Cathedral and attack the leaders of the NFFA, who have gathered there for Purge Night. Upon learning that the goal of the attack is to kill Owens, Charlie implores them to call the attack off and allow the democratic process to take its course but Bishop declines. Shortly afterward, however, she is captured by the paramilitary forces and taken to the cathedral to be ritually killed by the NFFA, and the raid becomes her only hope of survival. The attack succeeds, with heavy casualties on both sides, freeing Charlie and leaving Owens as one of the few NFFA survivors. Agreeing, at Charlie's insistence, *not* to execute Owens, Bishop warns her: "You'd better fucking win" the election . . . which, the epilogue reveals, she does.

## WITH MALICE AFORETHOUGHT

All crimes committed on Purge Night should, according to the logic of the official explanation, be crimes of passion: acts driven by the sudden, unpredictable explosion of a year's worth of bottled-up animal violence. They should fall, with equal ferocity, upon the just and the unjust alike, proximity and chance alone determining the identities of their victims. In all three films, however, the transgressions shown in horrifying detail and at close range are frequently nothing of the sort. They are carefully premeditated, aimed at a specific target, and driven by particular grievances or desires. Those behind these crimes-that-are-not-crimes know, well before Purge Night begins, precisely what they want and who they want it from.

Every stereotype of teenage masculinity suggests that Henry, sneaking into Zoe's bedroom on Purge Night, should be at the mercy of his raging hormones—heedless of everything but his desire for sex. Instead, he is measured and soft-spoken as he pulls her down onto the bed with him, kissing and fondling her. Still wearing what is presumably her school uniform—a white blouse, loosely knotted tie, and improbably short plaid skirt that simultaneously convey virginal innocence and sexual availability—she responds quietly but enthusiastically to his advances, receptive to what she clearly assumes is a seduction. Henry begins unbuttoning her blouse, exposing her cleavage and the lacy margins of her bra, but then (refuting the "release the beast" rhetoric amid which he was raised) abruptly stops, declaring: "I can't do this." He came to the house, he explains, to see not Zoe but James: "It's time to straighten this out," he tells her. "It's crazy; he *cannot* forbid you from seeing me." Zoe protests that a confrontation will only make the situation worse, but Henry produces a revolver and steps into the hallway, headed for the confrontation that will leave him dead and James wounded.

Eva's coworker and friend Tanya seems, when introduced in the first scenes of *Anarchy,* to be as carefree and playful as Eva is serious. As they leave the diner where they work, she teases Eva about another coworker, Carlos, who (jokingly) declares his intention to "kidnap Eva tonight," and then (seriously) offers her a ride home. "He's a dog," Eva says, and Tanya, grinning, retorts: "I *like* that dog. . . . I'd love the shit outta that dog . . . but he's not interested in me. He only wants to sniff *your* ass." Later that night, when Eva, Cali, and Leo—on the run from Big Daddy's paramilitary crew—arrive at her family's apartment seeking temporary shelter, Tanya enthusiastically takes them in and offers them food and drink, folding them into the extended family already gathered there, which includes her husband, father, and sister Lorraine. It soon becomes clear, however, that Tanya—like Henry in *The Purge*—is tense and distracted, consumed by something she is keeping from the others. She washes down a handful of pills with a glass of red wine, and—in a scathing torrent of words that pours forth like water held for years behind a crumbling dam—calls out her husband and sister for sleeping with each other, and takes long-planned revenge by shooting and killing Lorraine.

Even those purgers seemingly at the mercy of their volcanic emotions are, as they prepare to commit their acts of violence, carrying out premeditated plans aimed at achieving specific goals. We first see Diego, the superintendent of Eva and Cali's building in *Anarchy,* as Eva returns home from work on Purge Night, brushing past him in the hallway and deflecting his

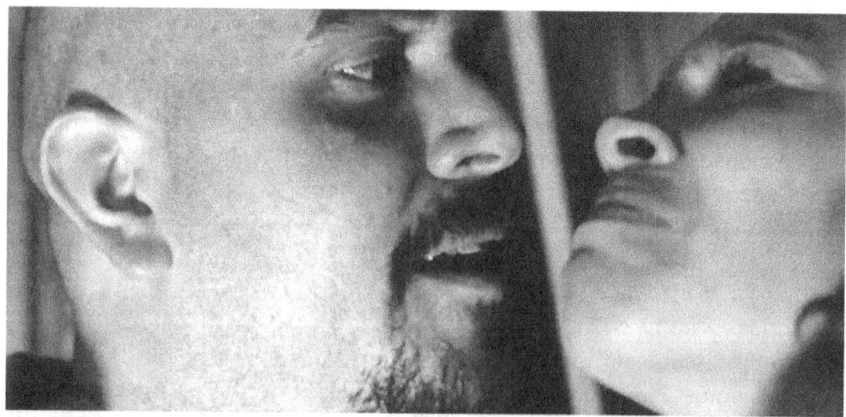

*In* The Purge: Anarchy, *Diego, the building superintendent, explains to his tenant Eva Sanchez that Purge Night is his opportunity to "do anything he wants" to her and her teenaged daughter, Cali.*

"friendly" overtures with a mild, casual remark. The scene appears to be an unremarkable piece of scene-setting until, a few hours later in the evening, Diego breaks into Eva's apartment and declares his intention to rape both her and—as a "little bonus"—Cali. His planned crime, averted by the arrival of Big Daddy's men, is not a random act of violence against whichever women happen to cross his path. It is, rather, an act of revenge: claiming the sexual favors to which he feels his "friendliness" entitles him, punishing Eva for her serial "rejections," and soothing his bruised sense of masculinity and potency. When Leo Barnes comes face-to-face with Warren Grass at the climax of the same film, he can barely contain his rage, but he engineers the encounter with cool, methodical precision. He located and cased Grass's suburban home well in advance, he explains to Eva, sabotaging the security system so that he could—on Purge Night—slip into Grass's bedroom and confront him over his crime.

Groups on both sides of *Election Night* plot to use the upcoming Purge as a pretext to eliminate their opponents and thus ensure their own political ascendancy. Caleb Warrens (Raymond J. Berry) declares to the other members of the NFFA party leadership that "it is time to do some spring cleaning, gentlemen," and to "deal with cocksuckers like . . . Bishop, and that cunt Senator."[4] Bishop plans, with equal determination and similar relish, to release set his anti-Purge guerillas loose on Owens and the rest of the NFFA faithful gathered at Our Lady of Sorrows. Unrolling plans of the cathedral and surrounding area that date to the years before the Revolution, he shows Charlie and Leo the tunnels, created on orders from George Washington, that the group will use to gain access to the building. "The original Founding Fathers," he crows, "are going to fuck over the New Founding Fathers!"

These violent acts—executed or merely planned—recapitulate an evergreen horror-film trope: the protagonist confronted, and menaced, by an invader that threatens to violate their body as it has violated their (seemingly) safe environment. The invaders of the *Purge* films, however, are not the monstrous Others of traditional horror films. They are neither exotically unfamiliar (vampires and zombies) nor psychologically unfathomable (serial killers and alien invaders)—not even agents of chaos who "just want to watch the world burn."[5] They are, rather, part of the fabric of their intended victims' lives—friends, neighbors, customers, casual acquaintances, the man on the street—prepared to inflict horrific violence in retribution for psychic wounds that their victims may be unaware of even having caused. "We have met the enemy," the *Purge* films imply, "and he is us."[6]

## VIOLENCE AND IDENTITY

The violence committed by groups in the *Purge* films is equally premeditated, albeit in more diverse ways. The anti-Purge guerillas in *Anarchy* and *Election Year* are a disciplined paramilitary force committed to—and waging urban warfare in the service of—a shared political ideology. The same is true of the NFFA death squad that hunts Charlie and Leo throughout *Election Year*, whose leader signals their white-supremacist allegiances with emblems on his clothing and tattoos on his shaven head. Each film opens with security camera footage of beatings and shootings that evoke "everyday" muggings and gang violence, but the Purge Night street gangs that the main characters actually encounter engage in elaborate, baroque displays of violence that evoke the costumed gangs of Walter Hill's *The Warriors* (1979).

At one point in *Anarchy,* Leo, Shane, and Liz find themselves menaced by a gang that roars through the streets in armed vehicles that evoke the jerry-built, postapocalyptic hot rods of the *Mad Max* universe, down to a swivel-mounted flamethrower fueled by a large tank of propane mounted on the chassis. Roaring through a highway underpass, the gang members set cars alight and incinerate luckless pedestrians who have nowhere to run. A similar scene in *Election Year* involves a muscle car with helpless prisoners tied to its hood while grinning gang members lean out the windows, brandishing medieval ball-and-chain flails.[7] "It's survival of the fucking fittest!" bellows a member of yet another gang, standing watch at the entrance to a subterranean parking garage where others like him—hulking, muscular, and shirtless—duel each other with medieval axes and swords by the flickering light of torches. "Who's the fittest?" the herald calls into the darkness, addressing no one in particular. "*I'm* the fittest one of all!"

The elaborate, baroque acts of violence that groups engage in on Purge Night streets is performative. The victims are chosen at random—people literally in the wrong place at the wrong time—because their identities are beside the point. The violence is not committed to take revenge for past slights, or advance toward a finite goal, but to build—or maintain—a shared identity. For the street gangs, whether riding in weaponized vehicles or engaging in faux-medieval combat, acts of violence are a performance of strength and toughness. For the resistance and the paramilitary death squads, they are a performance of solidarity and dedication to a cause. For the wealthy and privileged, however, elaborately staged displays of violence are performances of the power that they wield within society.

The youthful gang that pursues the Stranger in the *Purge* are formally dressed—the men in blazers and striped club ties, the women in white dresses—as if they have come directly from a lawn party at the local yacht club. The leader uses a mannered, oddly formal style of speaking that half-mimics, half-mocks upper-class gentility. "We can enter any home we want," he tells James Sandin, addressing the security system's front-door camera and microphone, "and we *will* want . . . because wanting is our will on this fine night. Don't force us to hurt you—we don't want to kill our own. Please let us *purrrrrge*." Their pursuit of the Stranger—chosen apparently at random, and hounded simply because he *is* their chosen victim—has overtones of a fox hunt: the quarry, though blameless, must be hunted down and killed. If it escapes, the hunt loses its meaning, and its value. The gang leader's justification for demanding that the Sandins turn over the Stranger underscores their sense of entitlement: "The man you're sheltering is nothing but a dirty homeless pig—a grotesque menace to our just society who had the audacity to fight back, killing one of us when we attempted to execute him. The pig doesn't know his place, and now needs to be taught a lesson."

In *Anarchy,* a similar sense of entitlement animates the wealthy audience at a black-tie Purge Night auction, who bid for the "services" of prisoners (like Leo, captured by a street gang for the purpose) as targets for them to hunt, and the wealthy family who "buys" Rico (Eva's father and Cali's grandfather) for $100,000 so that they can sacrifice him in the comfort of their palatial home. Writer-director James DeMonaco does not call attention to the obvious historical parallels—enslavement, with its reduction of human beings to a salable commodity or renewable resource—but, especially when the Stranger is African American, Rico is Latino, and every one of the purgers is white, the dots are not difficult to connect. Rico's death occurs off-camera, but the scenes immediately before, in which his formally attired purchasers surround him with gleaming machetes and repeat the "Blessed be . . ." incantation, literalizes the idea of his death as a sacrifice—a ritual killing. Rico, though not *called* "pig" or "filthy swine," is cast in a role traditionally reserved for animals.

The foreign "murder tourist" gang that subdues, captures, and comes within moments of executing Leo and Charlie in *Election Year,* reminds their intended victims that bloodletting and butchery—key elements of traditional animal sacrifices—await them. "We will torture you and violate your flesh," the gang leader tells Charlie, holding a gleaming knife to her throat, "remove your skin and share in your blood." She is rescued at the last moment, but threatened with an all-but-identical fate when, in the climax of the film, she is brought—captive, bound, and gagged—to Our Lady of Sorrows to be sacrificed by Edwidge Owens. Preparing the assembled crowd of NFFA supporters for the sacrifice, Owens whips them into an ecstatic frenzy with a speech reminiscent—not just in its cadences, but in its actual words—of an evangelical preacher exhorting the faithful at a revival meeting. He speaks

Minister Edwidge Owens (far right) waits for other members of the NFFA leadership to join him at the altar and participate in the sacrifice of his opponent, Senator Charlie Roan (second from left) in The Purge: Election Year.

of "our godly duty" and the need to "scour and sanitize our souls," and the crowd, in unison, responds by chanting "purge and purify!"

In the climax of the speech, Owens takes his purification metaphor to its logical conclusion: a bizarre inversion of traditional Christianity. "Jesus died for their sins," he tells the now-ecstatic crowd, "and now our modern-day martyrs will die for our sins!" Politics and religion collapse into a single activity, with Owens positioning himself both as the savior of the nation and of his followers' souls. As his followers grip their knives (blades purified with holy water) and prepare to strike at Charlie, he works himself (fueled by their ecstatic cheers) into a state of all-consuming glee: Jesus, Pilate, and the bloodthirsty crowd that calls for crucifixion collapsed into a single character.

## DYSTOPIAS AND DARK FORCES

The films in the Purge Trilogy borrow freely from multiple genres, most obviously the day-after-tomorrow dystopias that have been staples of science-fiction filmmaking since the days of *Silent Running* (1971) and *Soylent Green* (1973).[8] *The Purge,* in particular, borrows many of the world-building conventions of such dystopias: title cards that provide key facts and figures, radio and television broadcasts that reveal details of "normal" life, and briefly glimpsed rituals (the Sandins display a particular type of blue flower to signal their support for The Purge) that evoke a larger, unseen world. James Sandin's speech to his sensitive young son—"You don't remember how bad it was, Charlie: the poverty, all the crime"—mirrors those of Edward G. Robinson in *Soylent Green* and Peter Ustinov in *Logan's Run* (1976), explaining what life was like "before."[9] The change separating the nightmare-world of the characters from our world is, the films suggest, not war (the *Planet of the Apes* and *Mad Max* films), environmental collapse (*Silent Running, Soylent Green*), or theocracy (*The Handmaid's Tale*), but economic collapse: a free-market Armageddon that makes the Great Depression look like a mild downturn in the market. The "official" argument for why the Purge matters, laid out in the opening scenes of the first film, imply as much. The introduction of the Purge, title cards and media "talking heads" blandly declare, has brought crime and unemployment rates to all-time lows. A television commentator repeats critics' principal argument—that the Purge is merely an excuse to eradicate "the poor, the needy, the sick, those unable to defend themselves"—but immediately pivots to a statement that "the eradication of these so-called 'non-contributing' members of society ultimately unburdens the economy."

All three films reinforce the idea that the real motive for the Purge has nothing to do with human nature and everything to do with class differences and economic inequality. Middle-class suburban father James Sandin reassures his children, "I know bad things can happen tonight, but we can afford protection, so we'll be fine, like always." Rico sells himself to wealthy strangers in *Anarchy* both to bring his daughter and granddaughter a one-time financial windfall and to rid them of the economic burden his failing health places on them. Eva's explanation to Cali frames the transaction—like the offers of cheap firearms and "protection" that she received from street-corner hustlers while walking home from work—is part of a well-established, but unregulated, underground economy: "It's how the wealthy purge, baby. They buy poor and sick people, bring them into their homes in the suburbs, and kill them where it's safe." Joe Dixon, in *Election Year,* also experiences the potentially lethal effects of being poor on Purge Night: An insurance-company representative informs him, hours before the siren sounds, that the premiums for his business are going up, "effective immediately," and his policy will be cancelled if the does not (again, immediately) pay the difference. Critics of the Purge, notably Carmelo Johns in *Anarchy* and Dante Bishop in *Election Year,* are unwavering in their conviction that the Purge is "about money" and the systematic victimization of the poor by the rich. Caleb Warrens appears to agree in *Election Year.* "I'm sick of these idealistic pigs," he declares. "They want the impossible: Everyone to have. Some *cannot* have—not enough to go around."

The world of the *Purge* films is not, however, a Social Darwinist dystopia created by a totalitarian government. It is, save for Purge Night itself, the world in which its viewers live. There are still free elections, an opposition candidate is allowed to run, and repeal of the Purge is (*Election Year* implies) one executive order away. The death squads in *Anarchy* and *Election Year* are not an official arm of the government, but right-wing paramilitary groups that make common cause with it. Religion and politics intertwine in ways that, while disturbing in context, are not far removed from recent American history. Edwidge Owens, with his televangelist manner and shadowy corporate backers, could be a younger, more successful Pat Robertson. The "Blessed be..." incantation that begins each Purge echoes the ritualized ending of countless presidential speeches: "God bless you, and God bless the United States of America." Casual racism and sexism are pervasive—sexual harassment is endemic, and the Gang Leader in *The Purge* calls the (black) Stranger "dirty, homeless pig" and "filthy swine"—but it is exhibited in the words and acts of individuals, rather than social and legal structures.

The horror in science-fiction dystopias is inflicted on the main characters by a corrupt, broken System and those who serve it. The violence in the *Purge* films—*except* for that directed against Charlie Roan in *Election Year*—comes from individuals, with the System merely serving as their enabler by freeing them from the legal consequences of their actions for one (and only one) night a year. The threat to the protagonists of traditional horror films comes from monstrous Others: savage animals, alien beings, deranged killers, or the undead. The *Purge* films, however, are rooted in far more disturbing possibility. There is nothing monstrous about the "monsters." They are, like the members of Reserve Police Battalion 101, profiled by Christopher Browning, "ordinary men."[10] They are us . . . one consequence-fee opportunity away from *being* monsters.

The horror in the *Purge* films has its roots in the infamous Milgram Experiment.[11] It draws from the same well as Shirley Jackson's "The Lottery," the original version of *The Wicker Man* (1976), and *Twilight Zone* episodes like "The Shelter" and "The Monsters Are Due on Maple Street."[12] The cold premeditation of the rapes, murders, and attempted murders that occur when the opening siren of Purge Night sounds, and the baroque violence that breaks out in the streets each year, suggest a Hobbesian universe . . . but not the one implied by the official propaganda surrounding the Purge. It is not that we are instinct-driven, self-aggrandizing savages, held in check and forced to behave by the web of limits that we call "civilization." The savagery exhibited on Purge Night is, the films suggest, a product of civilization itself. It is fueled by the toxic by-products of humans, in large groups, policing one another's behavior: tribalism, entitlement, fear of difference, and confusion of privilege with worth. Our friends and neighbors, the films suggests, are not who we think they are. Given the opportunity, they—and, by extension, we—would do terrible things: loot an unguarded store, rape a neighbor, kill someone who wronged us, or hunt down a stranger in order to improve or secure our place in "civilization." The semi-excuses rejected by the judges at Nuremberg—ignorance, orders, threats—are beside the point. The only answer to "why?" is "because we can."

The single most disturbing scene of violent death in the *Purge* trilogy is glimpsed only briefly, and only from a distance. Rolling through the streets of the city in *Election Year*, Charlie Roan looks out the window of Laney's triage van and sees bodies—lynching victims—hanging from the low branches of a tree, silhouetted by firelight. The framing and lighting are familiar from hundreds of grotesque "souvenir" photographs taken in the Deep South during the early twentieth century. All that is missing is the strains of Billie Holliday's "Strange Fruit" on the soundtrack. Charlie asks softly: "How the hell did it get to this?" The films' chilling answer is that there was no need to "get to this," because the exploitation, abuse, and even outright murder of the poor and vulnerable by the rich and powerful never *stopped* being part of American life. It did not disappear, only slipped into the shadows until the New Founding Fathers—not just tolerating, but celebrating it—gave it license to slouch back into the light for one night a year.

## NOTES

1. Kavka, "Hobbes's War of All Against All," 291–295. Compare, specifically in the context of the *Purge* trilogy, Coates, "The War of 'All Against Them.'"

2. Prince, *Classical Film Violence*, 87–138; Basinger, *World War II Combat Film*, 254–257; Lichtenfeld, *Action Speaks Louder*.

3. The internal chronology of the films is mildly contradictory. Title cards for the first two films establish that they take place in 2022 and 2023, and both the Universal Studios website and the DVD packaging for *Election Year* place its events two years after those of *Anarchy*. The Purge is implied to have been going on for nine years in *Anarchy* but explicitly stated to have been going on for twenty in *Election Year*.

4. The harshness of his language—starkly at odds with his measured tones and the conspicuously upper-class setting of the scene—is a sly bit of characterization. "Cunt" and "cocksucker" remain the most transgressive of George Carlin's famous "seven words"—along with "motherfucker," the ones you *still* can't say on television.

5. Alfred Pennyworth (Michael Caine), describing the Joker (Heath Ledger) in Christopher Nolan's *The Dark Knight* (2008).

6. The expression, a play on Oliver Hazzard Perry's famous report of the outcome of a naval battle in the War of 1812 ("We have met the enemy, and they are ours."), was popularized by cartoonist Walt Kelly, first in a poster for the first Earth Day

(1970) and then in an installment of his *Pogo* comic strip celebrating the second (1971). See Williams, "Pogo the Possum and the First Earth Day."

7. The ball-and-chain flail (sometimes called a "morningstar" or, inaccurately, a mace) is, as medieval historian Paul Sturtevant notes, a fantasy weapon rather than a real medieval artifact. See: "The Curious Case of the Medieval Weapon That Didn't Exist."

8. See, for example, Anderson, *Science Fiction Films of the Seventies;* Berg, "'Goddamn You All to Hell!'"; and Geraghty, *American Science Fiction Film and Television,* 51–68.

9. The characters played by Robinson and Ustinov, however, see the erasure of the past as a profound loss.

10. Browning, *Ordinary Men.*

11. On the Milgram Experiment, with particular relevance to the *Purge* films, see Helm and Morelli, "Stanley Milgram and the Obedience Experiment."

12. Zicree, *The Twilight Zone Companion,* 2nd edition, 90–91, 226–227; Worland, "Sign-Posts Up Ahead," 106–107.

## BIBLIOGRAPHY

Anderson, Craig W. *Science Fiction Films of the Seventies.* Jefferson, NC: McFarland, 1985.

Basinger, Jeanine. *The World War II Combat Film: Anatomy of a Genre.* Middletown, CT: Wesleyan University Press, 2003.

Berg, Chris. "'Goddamn You All to Hell!': The Revealing Politics of Dystopian Movies." *Institute of Public Affairs Review,* vol. 60, no. 1 (March 2008): 38–42.

Browning, Christopher R. *Ordinary Men: Reserve Police Battalion 101 and the Final Solution in Poland.* New York: HarperCollins, 1992.

Coates, Ta-Nehisi. "The War of 'All Against Them.'" *The Atlantic,* October 10, 2012. https://www.theatlantic.com /personal/archive/2012/10/a-war-of-all-against-them/263345/

Geraghty, Lincoln. *American Science Fiction Film and Television.* Oxford: Berg, 2009.

Helm, Charles, and Mario Morelli. "Stanley Milgram and the Obedience Experiment: Authority, Legitimacy, and Human Action." *Political Theory* 7, no. 3 (1979): 321–345.

Kavka, Gregory S. "Hobbes's War of All Against All." *Ethics* 93, no. 2 (1983): 291–310.

Lichtenfeld, Eric. *Action Speaks Louder: Violence, Spectacle, and the American Action Movie,* revised and updated edition. Middletown, CT: Wesleyan University Press, 2007.

Prince, Stephen. *Classical Film Violence: Designing and Regulating Brutality in Hollywood, 1930–1968.* New Brunswick, NJ: Rutgers University Press, 2003.

Sturtevant, Paul. "The Curious Case of the Medieval Weapon That Didn't Exist," *Public Medievalist*, May 12, 2016. https://www.publicmedievalist.com/curious-case-weapon-didnt-exist/

Williams, Karen. "Pogo the Possum and the First Earth Day," *Retroist*, April 22, 2016. https://www.retroist.com/2016/04/22/pogo-the-possum-and-the-first-earth-day/

Worland, Rick. "Sign-Posts Up Ahead: *The Twilight Zone*, *The Outer Limits*, and TV Political Fantasy 1959–1965." *Science Fiction Studies* 23, no. 1 (1996): 103–122.

Zicree, Marc Scott. *The Twilight Zone Companion*, 2nd edition. Los Angeles: Silman James Press, 1992.

*Chapter Eight*

# Motor City Gothic

## White Youth and Economic Anxiety in It Follows *and* Don't Breathe

Russell Meeuf and Benjamin James

After the housing market crash of 2007 and subsequent recession, the city of Detroit solidified its place in the US popular imagination as the exemplar of poverty and despair. Images of its once-thriving but now decrepit middle-class neighborhoods are frequently used in news, documentaries, and popular culture to signify the devastating economic fallout of the Great Recession, providing stunning images of urban decay and the failures of the American Dream.

Such images appear in two recent, Detroit-set horror films that tap into the Gothic potential of Detroit's crumbling neighborhoods: the critically acclaimed indie-slasher homage *It Follows* (2014) and the popular home-invasion film *Don't Breathe* (2016).[1] Each film relies on the spectacle of Detroit's crumbling neighborhoods to tell stories about young, white women who must confront the terrors festering in the dilapidated ruins of

*The iconic once-middle-class but now decrepit neighborhoods of cinematic post-recession Detroit in films such as* Don't Breathe.

the old middle class. Of course, despite the disproportionate impact of the Great Recession on people of color in the United States, and in Detroit in particular,[2] each film uses the images of a Gothic Detroit to tell stories of white Detroiters and the horrors they face in a postrecession world.

In both *It Follows* and *Don't Breathe* the spectacle of a decaying Detroit exposes the nagging fear that white Americans were at risk of losing social standing in Obama's America. In *It Follows*, although the mysterious curse in the film is often interpreted as a reference to sexually transmitted diseases, the shape-shifting monster also dramatizes the stifling economic realities of millennials, especially white teens who face a far more precarious economy than their parents. In *Don't Breathe*, the formerly middle-class family home becomes a Gothic trap (full of secret compartments and monstrous sexual threats) for the poor, white protagonist seeking to escape Detroit and its poverty. In each film, the real horror is that young white folks might not be so out of place against the backdrop of black poverty as they once were.

These racial anxieties make Detroit the perfect Gothic setting for a postrecession America. The Gothic tradition in literature and cinema tends to focus on dilapidated mansions or castles as sites where the horrors of the past can never be truly laid to rest. In the British Gothic of the late 1700s and early 1800s such tales challenged the narrative of progress emerging from the nascent Industrial Revolution, suggesting that a traumatic past will always haunt the present. Similarly, the Southern Gothic tradition focuses on sprawling Southern plantations where the horrors of slavery continue to fester in the post–Civil War South.[3] Detroit's landscape of urban decay, then, provides a glaring reminder of the economic collapse of the mid-2000s, illustrating the persistent presence of this past trauma. This landscape, however, speaks more to a white nostalgia for a thriving middle class than it does to the poor people of color who bore the brunt of the Great Recession. In what we classify as "Motor City Gothic," the crumbling remains of formerly prosperous white neighborhoods are a warning to white youth vying for upward social mobility as they are engulfed by the kinds of urban poverty typically suffered by people of color in the United States.

## *IT FOLLOWS*

The low-budget indie film *It Follows* introduces us to its protagonist, a teenaged girl named Jay, as she wades into her family's aboveground pool, whose water, shaded by the surrounding trees, looks chilly and is peppered with dirt and debris. Enjoying the solitude, Jay notices a small bug crawling on her forearm and slowly immerses her arm into the water as the bug floats away.

Jay's pool is the perfect emblem of her precarious class status in the film. The idea of a built-in backyard swimming pool with the sun glistening off its pristine waters is a prevalent symbol of affluence in the United States (see Clark Griswold's fantasies of installing one for his upper-middle-class family in *National Lampoon's Christmas Vacation*). But the aboveground pool, a cheaper imitation, represents lower social standing: Jay's family aspires to upward mobility, but a dirty aboveground pool is all they can attain.

Despite its shortcomings, Jay uses the pool as a childlike respite from the pressures of the outside world, scoffing at the neighborhood boys who try to peep in on her swimming. But later in the film as she waits for the demon that haunts her, the pool is inexplicably destroyed, a gaping hole in the side having let out all the water. Now, even the pretense of economic stability and the naïve pleasures of childhood have gushed away.

*It Follows* made critical waves in 2014 with its minimalist, low-tech homage to the slasher films of the 1970s and 1980s. In the film, Jay, who lives in the lower middle-class suburbs of Detroit, becomes infected with a mysterious curse after having sex. Now an entity that can take the form of any person (but can only be seen by those who have been infected) slowly stalks her. It can only walk slowly toward her, like a Romero zombie, but it does so relentlessly. If Jay pauses, "It" will eventually catch up with her and kill her, then turn its attention back to the person who initially infected her. With the help of her sister and neighborhood friends (adults exist only on the periphery of this story), Jay must decide if she will pass the curse along to someone else through sex or if she will resort to a life of constant movement to keep "It" at bay.

Given the sexual transmission of the curse, critics were quick to link the film to anxieties about sexually transmitted diseases and youth hook-up culture (although many critics, and the director himself, opt for more open-ended interpretations). Writing for the *Catholic World Report*, one reviewer even promoted the movie as a Christian parable about "tainted sex"—one that highlights the failures of the sexual revolution.[4]

Clearly, sexual anxieties are central to the film's story, and the slasher genre has long intertwined its images of graphic death with anxieties about young people's forays into adult sexuality. But the real dread in *It Follows* centers less on sex than on a more general loss of childhood and the recognition that adulthood won't deliver on its promises of freedom and prosperity. Adulthood in the film delivers, instead, only anxiety and a precarious existence. Jay herself articulates this dread just after she is infected by the young man she has been dating, Hugh. Lounging in the backseat of Hugh's car, a deserted building looming above them as a reminder of Detroit's economic ruin, she laments:

It's funny. I used to day dream about being old enough to go on dates and drive around with friends in their cars. I had this image of myself holding hands with a really cute guy listening to the radio, driving along some pretty road, up north maybe, when the trees started to change colors. It was never about going anywhere, really. It's having some sort of freedom, I guess. Now that we're old enough, where they hell do we go?

She is then violently chloroformed by Hugh and tied to a wheelchair in her underwear as he explains how the curse works, an abrupt end to her reverie about childish fantasies and a forceful reminder that she, in fact, now has nowhere to go without "It."

The film is punctuated by other, similar wistful reflections on lost childhood. Jay's neighbor and friend Paul, who harbors a not-so-secret crush on her, reminisces about being Jay's first kiss in a more innocent time before telling a story about the two of them finding porn and not realizing what the magazines depicted. Jay's flirty neighbor Greg recalls good times spent at the family lake house with his now-absent father as the teens flee to this once-safe place in a time of crisis. On his date with Jay, Hugh expresses a desire to be a carefree child again instead of facing the stress of young adulthood. All the while, their bespectacled friend, Yara, periodically reads them crushingly hopeless passages from Dostoevsky's *The Idiot* as their naïve visions of childhood dissipate in the face of their banal present and future.

Jay is haunted not by the specter of casual sex but rather by the plodding anxieties of becoming an adult in a world of dead-end opportunities. Sex is certainly part of these anxieties. Far from the promises of love and pleasure, sex here is fraught with danger, deception, and obligation. But sex is only one part of a larger realization that the promises of adulthood are empty.

Specifically, *It Follows* explores the dread of white millennials facing a more uncertain economic future than their parents. The teens in the film live in a lower-middle class, white world suffering from economic stagnation. Their neighborhood is a Detroit suburb that appears to have been built in the 1960s—largely brick, ranch-style houses that, while certainly far from derelict, are no longer homes for the upwardly mobile white families that used to occupy them. Jay's home in particular is decorated with 1970s-style wood paneling and floral wallpapers, and looks as if its last redecoration came in the mid-1980s. The teens lounge on sickly yellow couches from the 1970s and watch old horror movies on a black-and-white TV (stacked on top of another, presumably broken, old TV). Hugh drives around in a 1970s sedan, while Greg drives an early 1980s station wagon. The film is peppered with anachronisms like these, juxtaposing landline telephones with Yara's sleek clamshell e-reader.

This retro aesthetic is part of the film's homage to the classic, suburban slashers of the 1970s and 1980s, such as 1978's *Halloween*. But the anachronisms also draw attention to the economic stagnation of the neighborhood. This is a neighborhood whose families, while not poor, have not made significant economic gains for decades and are barely treading water in the neoliberal economy. Its inhabitants are people like Jay's mom, a single mother who is largely absent from her children's lives thanks to an unspecified job that requires her to wake at 5:45 AM and who struggles with alcoholism. She is often passed out in the evenings as the events unfold in her own home. If the film tries to emulate the visual style of 1970s and 1980s slashers, this technique only affirms how little progress middle-class whites have made in recent years.

What really pursues Jay throughout the film, then, are a range of economic circumstances that haunt young people today: the prospect of student loan debts, low rates of home ownership, the need to move to high-cost cities to find low-paying jobs, a gig economy that won't provide stable employment, a skimpy social safety net. Like "It" in its pursuit of Jay, these economic conditions creep along—they won't cause bankruptcy overnight—but they are steadily and relentlessly eroding young people's chances of social mobility. No matter how hard young people work, they can't shake the nagging threat of financial disaster that follows them.

In this way, the conceit of *It Follows*—with its slow-moving but persistent threat—mimics the sensations of living paycheck-to-paycheck in near-poverty felt by the working poor. Jay is unsettled and exhausted by the constant cycle of frantic escape followed by restless waiting (as are her compatriots, who are constantly seen sneaking in naps when they can). Jay is constantly on the move looking for opportunities and solutions, but she never makes headway.[5]

Gothic images of Detroit's crumbling neighborhoods are interspersed with the teens' struggle against their persistent foe. As they explore the city at different moments in the story, the film lingers on long tracking shots of run-down neighborhoods with crumbling, formerly middle-class homes and boarded up storefronts. Sometimes, black men stand on the corners of these neighborhoods. Such images highlight the racial anxieties that are intertwined with white economic anxieties. As the teens contemplate Jay's uncertain future, the images of a poor, implicitly black Detroit taunt them, insinuating that the seemingly horrific poverty that is supposed to be endemic to black communities may not be off limits to them. They even contemplate these racial and economic borders as they wander through a poorer part of town:

> YARA: When I was a little girl my parents told me I wasn't allowed to go south of 8 Mile [Road]. I didn't even understand what that meant. It wasn't until I

got a little older that I realized that was where the city started and the suburbs ended. I started thinking how weird and shitty that was. I had to ask permission to go to the state fair with my best friend and her parents just because it was a few blocks past the border.

JAY: My parents said the same thing to me.

Yet, as they remember the old parental directives to avoid the poor (and black) parts of Detroit, the teens transgress these borders, crossing through the city to get to the public pool to set a trap for "It." The old boundaries that their parents so desperately enforced between a white middle-class life and black poverty are now meaningless to the teens. Swimming pools again mark Jay's downward social trajectory. Gone are the pretenses of even the aboveground pool as she now seeks out the public pool, and one in the city to boot.

It is not simply social and economic standing that are at stake for Jay and her crew, but their racial standing as well: their attempts to evade "It" are bound up in their efforts to elude the stigma of becoming so-called "white trash." Because of persistent racial inequalities in the United States, poverty is often imagined as being specific to people of color, especially in the specter of crime-ridden, mostly-black inner cities such as Detroit. The image of poor white people disrupts this racial vision of poverty: US culture stigmatizes poor whites as white trash, people whose core whiteness is called into question by imagining them as messy, uncouth, and lazy.[6] The othering of poor white folks as trashy attempts to imagine them as somehow distinct from more affluent white people, whether culturally (poor taste, shoddy living conditions) or even physiologically (dirtier, more apt to be missing teeth).

Mirroring the culture's anxieties about trashy whiteness, "It" almost always takes the form of abject white bodies. Although it sometimes appears as someone close to its victim (for example, as Yara or Jay's absent father), more often "It" manifests in white bodies that undermine the cultural norms associated with whiteness and beauty: naked, middle-aged men and women; an unusually tall, gaunt man; a sallow-faced old woman in a ratty dressing gown; a pale-faced, almost feral little man. "Its" manifestations are mostly grotesque, white bodies that suggest low social class. One of the most memorable versions of "It" is a young woman, around Jay's age, with dark eyes and missing teeth, wearing a tattered bra with one side pulled down, a short skirt, and one tube sock. She pees down her leg as she walks toward Jay in her kitchen. The missing teeth, repellant hygiene, and suggestions of sordid sexuality are all exaggerated white trash stereotypes, terrifying Jay with an image of what she might become.

*"It" takes the form of a young woman who embodies the specter of trashy whiteness in* It Follows.

As a result of their encounters with "It" and its specter of trashy whiteness, the young people in the film are forced to linger in a world of unseemly poverty. Hugh—whose real name is Jeff—embraces a transient existence, squatting in dilapidated houses in abandoned urban neighborhoods, rigging up his hovel with makeshift security alarms built from empty bottles and cans. Once he has passed "It" on to Jay, he, like so many other millennials, moves back to the suburbs with his mom. The last we see of him he is sitting cross-legged in the grass of his parent's backyard, wearing sweatpants that resemble a child's pajamas.

Similarly, after the teens attack "It" at the city pool but are unsure about the entity's survival, Paul convinces Jay to pass the curse along to him. Once they have sex, he heads into an abandoned industrial zone in the city and sleeps with a poor, white prostitute (who, with dark shadows under her eyes, a cheap push-up bra, and tube socks, bears a slight resemblance to the form that "It" took in Jay's kitchen). Here, Paul reinforces not only the literal but also the social distance between himself and "It" by (one assumes secretly) infecting the prostitute and her future clientele with the curse. Because of "It" and its pursuit, Paul is forced to dally in the world of white poverty and trashy values, and he assumes that this action will at least buy him some time with little thought for the lives of those he deems socially beneath him and therefore unworthy of his consideration.

In the final scene, Paul and Jay walk morosely, hand-in-hand down their street. Unfocused in the background, a figure appears, following them. Is this "It"? We don't know, nor does it matter, because for the rest of their lives, Jay, Paul, and the other teens will always look over their shoulders, just as they will never escape the unrelenting horrors of the neoliberal economy. They grew up being promised the fantasies of constant upward mobility for white folks in the US economy, but instead they will always be on the move, seeking one dead-end job after another, entering into meaningless relationships as they attempt to keep the horrors of white poverty at bay.

## *DON'T BREATHE*

While *It Follows* tells a story about white teens on the bottom rung of the middle-class, tormented by the possibility of poverty in their futures, *Don't Breathe* flips this story on its head. *Don't Breathe* focuses on poor white teens in Detroit struggling to move up in the world but blocked by economic and moral decay. The film first introduces us to Rocky, a young woman desperate to escape Detroit and her own poverty, as she breaks into a modern, upscale home. Aided by her boyfriend, Money, and another friend, Alex—who provides access to the houses they rob through keys and security codes purloined from his father, an employee of a local home security firm—the trio ransack the house in their own ways. Alex, wedded to strict rules and ethics (no cash, don't steal items totaling over $10,000), quickly and carefully grabs electronics that can be sold easily. Money, an impulsive borderline-psychopath, purposefully breaks vases and masturbates on the kitchen floor.[7] But Rocky heads to one of the bedrooms in the house, clearly used by an affluent teen girl, and tries on her clothes. While the others rob the house, she flops on the bed in her new outfit, a cute stuffed bunny just over her shoulder. More than the others, she longs for escape, to become the carefree, upper-middle-class young woman, doted on by loving parents.

Rocky's wish to escape Detroit with her little sister and head to the beaches of California lead her, Money, and Alex to one last job, this one outside of the careful rules that Alex has established to protect them from more severe penalties if they are caught (and to protect his father's job). Money learns about an old man living alone in an abandoned neighborhood who won a huge settlement from a rich family whose daughter was driving drunk and killed the old man's daughter. The rich-daughter driver avoided jail time, but the grieving father now supposedly keeps his settlement locked away in his house in cash. As they prepare for their home invasion, they also learn that the old man is a blind veteran who lost his vision in one of the US wars in Iraq. Alex at first wants nothing to do with the high-stakes job, but his simmering crush on Rocky and the idea of running away with her leads him to reluctantly accept.

Naturally, this is a huge mistake on Alex's part. Once inside, the heist goes wrong, and Money is shot by the Blind Man (we never learn his name), who is a well-trained army veteran able to masterfully navigate his own house.

Alex and Rocky are locked inside the house with its owner, and a tense cat-and-mouse game ensues as the two try to find a safe route to escape. Although the audience might at first root for the Blind Man against his teenaged tormentors, soon Rocky, Alex, and the audience discover why the Blind Man has so much invested in security: he has kidnapped the wealthy young woman who killed his daughter and is keeping her in his basement, having artificially inseminated her with his own semen in the hopes that she will deliver to him a new child. Confronted with the Blind Man's horrific secret, Rocky and Alex have to decide what is more important to them: escaping with the money or getting caught by calling the police but bringing the Blind Man to justice.

Just as in *It Follows*, *Don't Breathe* uses Gothic images of decaying, formerly middle-class neighborhoods as a backdrop to its violence. In a brief montage-tour, the film makes a spectacle of Detroit's economic ruin and presents the Blind Man's neighborhood as a symbol of it. The houses, mostly two- and three-story brick homes that once housed the upper middle classes of a more prosperous Detroit, are literally crumbling around the Blind Man's house, a last vestige of the white families that used to occupy the space. Boarded-up windows, collapsing roofs, and unclaimed furniture piled in yards are being slowly overgrown as the vegetation reclaims the land. Whatever past prosperity these neighborhoods held is long gone as the film shows that the remains of the white, middle-class American Dream are haunted by a tortured monster with a psychotically deranged sense of entitlement.

Rocky, meanwhile, lives the kind of squalid life that the teens in *It Follows* feared was in their future, one marked by white-trash stereotypes. She and her young sister share a tiny trailer with their abusive mother, whose lazy boyfriend is living with them while out of work. Lined with tacky wood paneling and ratty carpeting, the trailer is littered with Rocky's mother's empty beer and malt liquor bottles. Knowing that Rocky has been saving money on the side, the mother implies that Rocky has been giving blow jobs for money. Trevor, the unemployed boyfriend, sports a swastika tattoo on the back of his hand, a reminder of their status as poor whites who retain a sense of their racial superiority over blacks, Latinos, and others.

This spectacle of horrific, white poverty makes it easy to sympathize with Rocky's fantasy of escape, especially thanks to her adorable little sister, Diddy. But Rocky and the other teens soon find that the road to upward mobility is treacherous and passes through the remnants of the middle class that have been forsaken by the neoliberal economy. The Blind Man's neighborhood provides a visual reminder of the fickle economic forces that can devastate whole communities, but it also illustrates the monstrous effects of neoliberalism and the free market on morality, as well as the vicious competition at the heart of contemporary capitalism.

What draws the teens to the neighborhood, after all, is its freedom from rules and regulations. While casing the Blind Man's house, they describe the neighborhood as a "ghost town," and Money notes that they won't have to worry about the police here: "No people means no 5-0 on patrol." On their other jobs, Alex enforces strict rules about whom they steal from and what they steal, hoping to create petty, almost victimless robberies. But this job takes them to a space without those constraints, one with higher rewards but, as they soon find out, much higher risks. By making the decision to enter that space and steal from a blind war hero whose daughter had been murdered, the trio enters a realm of unfettered greed and distorted morals. As the devastated neighborhood reminds us, though, the greed of the poor, desperate burglars exists alongside the greed of the capitalist system. The neighborhood is a visual reminder of the greed of executives, bankers, and brokers who would destroy whole neighborhoods in their quest for never-ending wealth during the housing bubble.

The Blind Man has also come to accept the failures of liberal systems to protect people from the excesses of capitalism. He has embraced the brutal freedoms of his abandoned neighborhood to pursue his own forms of monstrous justice. After capturing Rocky, the Blind Man delivers an extended monologue that indicts the freedoms of the wealthy in capitalism: "Rich girls don't go to jail," he notes. He has seen that systems designed to instill justice have no meaning in neoliberal capitalism. Rich people don't follow the rules, he reasons, so why should he? Freed from the logic and rules of civil society, he rejects all authority and morality, declaring the godlessness of his dilapidated world and, therefore, his right to unfettered violence to accumulate whatever he wants, in this case a new child.

The film's use of blindness highlights this disregard for the rules of civil society. The Blind Man's impairment is, of course, a common Gothic trope. Relying on stereotypes of disability in storytelling, his grotesque body signifies his villainy.[8] But the blindness also signifies his disregard for the rules and ethics of the world. The injustices wrought upon him have blinded him to traditional morality, leaving only his own vengeful justice. His blindness also indicates the myopia of neoliberalism: his crumbling neighborhood is a place where no one is looking and no one cares.

The Blind Man's house is the perfect Gothic house for postrecession America. Like other houses in the Gothic tradition, it is full of labyrinthine passageways (his cluttered basement with rows and rows of metal shelves), hidden compartments (the unusually large ductwork through which Rocky attempts to escape, his basement dungeon), and dark, sexual secrets that have their roots in a traumatic past. A convoluted and treacherous space in which the horrors of the past impinge on Rocky's future, the creaky and dingy house is a microcosm of the economic collapse of Detroit and the moral collapse of neoliberal capitalism. The white, middle-class home, once a symbol of stability and prosperity, in *Don't Breathe* is now a bastion of repressed fears about the degraded state of white, patriarchal authority and the horrific challenges hindering upward social mobility.

In the face of the brutal logic of the Blind Man's world, then, Rocky and Alex must reevaluate their commitment to upward mobility and their own morality. At several points in the film, the teens have to choose between ruthless and dangerous individualism and the justice system of a civil society that they know doesn't have their best interests at heart: try to make it out with the money, or alert the police and save their lives but face legal consequences? This dilemma assumes that upward mobility necessarily means abandoning one's morality, and that the only path upward for poor, young people is to embrace the same kinds of unethical behavior used by the capitalist elite to decimate Detroit's middle class in the first place.

This dilemma provides the tension of the film's final scene. After knocking The Blind Man down his basement ladder with a crowbar and seemingly killing him, Rocky (the film's "Final Girl") escapes the house with the money. We then see Rocky, her face still bruised from her traumatic escape, and her sister, Diddy, waiting at the train station for their departure for California, when a news report catches her attention. The local news is reporting on her break-in, covering it as a remarkable survivor story in which a blind veteran killed two erstwhile robbers, showing that the Blind Man survived the home invasion but stating that "no goods were reported stolen by the victim." As Alex had suggested earlier, the Blind Man is buying Rocky's silence, knowing that reporting the money stolen would lead to Rocky and the revelation of his crimes.

Rocky's upward mobility, then, is contingent upon her silence, leaving the Blind Man to live, recover, and possibly strike again. Facing this dilemma, Rocky and Diddy march out of the station following the arrow toward "Departures," suggesting that she has chosen ruthless individualism over morality. If she wants to move up in a competitive, neoliberal world, she can't play by the rules, even if that means the denial of justice for the Blind Man.

## CONCLUSION

In their explorations of white teens and economic standing, both *It Follows* and *Don't Breathe* feature prominent, shocking scenes of taboo sexuality. In *It Follows*, Jay agrees to pass her infection to Greg to test its reality. While Greg at first says he hasn't seen any stalkers, one night, Jay sees a figure who looks like Greg wearing white long johns break into Greg's house. Fearing that the figure was the entity, she follows it into Greg's house, where it has now taken the form of Greg's mom, wearing a sheer nightgown with her breasts hanging out. When the real Greg opens his bedroom door, the entity pounces, and Jay watches in horror as it extracts the life from Greg by erotically rubbing its genitals on Greg while still in the form of Greg's mother.

In a similarly troubling scene in *Don't Breathe*, Rocky finds herself captured by The Blind Man after his former prisoner had been shot as Rocky and Alex tried to free her. Hung from the ceiling in a body harness, Rocky listens helplessly as The Blind Man tells her that he had artificially inseminated the young, wealthy woman in order to extract a child from her. Now that she is dead, he plans to do the same to Rocky. He approaches her with a turkey baster dripping with his semen, freshly defrosted over a nearby camp stove. He grips the squirming Rocky, using scissors to cut out the crotch of her pants, but Alex arrives in time to knock him to the ground and free Rocky as they make another attempt at escape.

These scenes dramatize each film's concern with sex and power, using sexual violence to highlight generational tensions. Both graphically depict a member of an older generation committing unspeakable, implicitly incestuous acts of violence (Rocky is probably about the age that the Blind Man's daughter would have been, had she lived). Underpinning each scene is a disturbing sense of betrayal, with parental figures becoming monstrous foes who must be overcome, a theme affirmed in *It Follows* when the entity takes the form of Jay's absent father in the film's climax at the city pool.

Images of Detroit's poverty and decay draw out this generational conflict in each film, providing not simply stark visions of economic collapse but a deeply nostalgic musing on the perceived fall of the white middle class. The brooding shots of decaying neighborhoods in each film are a reminder of what the Baby Boomer generation threw away in its pursuit of neoliberal capitalism: thriving communities that could have supported the teens in these stories. Instead, like other millennials, the protagonists must face an economic reality starkly different than that enjoyed by the generation that came before them, and the scenes of incestuous violence underscore a sense of betrayal as millennials face the precarious economy created by their parents' generation.

This betrayal is felt mostly by white youth grappling with economic realities vastly different than what their parents' generation had promised. Detroit resonates not simply because of its poverty but because of its nostalgia for a time with a vibrant manufacturing base and thriving, middle-class white communities. In the shadow of those stable communities, many of which are now decimated by the neoliberal economy, young, white folks face dwindling opportunities. Young people of color, of course, face an even more precarious economy, as well as long-standing discrimination, but they have never really been promised the American Dream. In the Motor City Gothic, however, the decaying ruins of the city's middle-class haunt young white people as they mourn the loss of a past stability that their culture has taught them to feel entitled to claim.

## NOTES

1. Similar images of a deteriorating Detroit are used in Jim Jarmusch's 2013 vampire film *Only Lovers Left Alive*, but as the film doesn't fit neatly into the horror genre, the primary focus here will be on *It Follows* and *Don't Breathe*.
2. Department of Labor, "The African-American Labor Force."
3. Marshall, "Defining Southern Gothic."
4. Olszyk, "Pope Paul VI Makes a Horror Movie."
5. For more on the representation of precarity in *It Follows*, see Kelly.
6. Newitz and Wray, *White Trash*.
7. Coincidentally, Money is played by Costa Rican actor Daniel Zovatto, who also played Greg in *It Follows*.
8. Longmore, "Screening Stereotypes."

## BIBLIOGRAPHY

Kelly, Casey Ryan. "*It Follows*: Precarity, Thanatopolitics, and the Ambient Horror Film." *Critical Studies in Media Communication* 34, no. 3 (2017): 234–249.

Longmore, Paul K. "Screening Stereotypes: Images of Disabled People in Television and Motion Pictures." In *Why I Burned My Book and Other Essays on Disability*, 131–148. Philadelphia: Temple University Press, 2003.

Marshall, Bridget M. "Defining Southern Gothic." In *Critical Insights: Southern Gothic Literature*, edited by Jay Ellis, 3–18. Ipswich, MA: Salem Press, 2013.

Newitz, Annalee, and Matt Wray, eds. *White Trash: Race and Class in America*. New York: Routledge, 1997.

Olszyk, Nick. "Pope Paul VI Makes a Horror Movie." *The Catholic World Report*, April 14, 2015. http://www.catholicworldreport.com/2015/04/14/pope-paul-vi-makes-a-horror-movie/

US Department of Labor. "The African-American Labor Force in the Recovery." February 29, 2012. https://www.dol.gov/_sec/media/reports/BlackLaborForce/BlackLaborForce.pdf

*Part III*

# IDEOLOGY: YOU JUST HAVE TO BELIEVE

*Chapter Nine*

# Gothic Neoliberalism in 1980s British Horror Cinema

Fernando Gabriel Pagnoni Berns, Juan Juvé, and Emiliano Aguilar

Neoliberalism is a political/economic philosophy that celebrates individualism and is dedicated to the extension of market forms of governance—such as free trade, privatization, and the reduction of reliance upon government for provision of services—across all spheres of social life.[1] The rise of Margaret Thatcher in the United Kingdom marked a decisive moment in the history of neoliberalization. Thatcher became leader of the Conservative Party during the bleak "Winter of Discontent" that defined British politics and culture in the late 1970s, and served as Prime Minister from May 1979 until 1990. "Thatcher fashioned a neoliberal resurgence with an evangelical fervor expressed in the refrain, 'There Is No Alternative'"[2] and her reforms had a deep impact upon many aspects of British society.

The political and economic doctrine of neoliberalism came together in Britain with an extreme conservative ideology which, at that moment, proved to be complementary. Thatcher and her followers espoused both neoliberalism and a social-conservative endorsement of traditional gender roles, which promoted so-called family values and the holiness of the nuclear family. Thatcher used this moral rhetoric in her speeches even when talking of economy; in fact, translating politics into moral terms was one of her great strengths.[3]

Another characteristic of the late 1970s and the 1980s was that the prominence of British horror films diminished; Hammer ceased exports to United States, and smaller studios like Amicus and Trigon struggled financially. Even so, the Thatcher years saw the release of Clive Barker's seminal *Hellraiser* (1987) and several other significant but less-familiar horror films. With American slasher films dominating the global market and the attention of critics in the 1980s, little space has been given to these lesser-known efforts. These overlooked British films, however, reflected

Thatcherite neoliberal doctrines in the ways in which the role of women, class mobilization, enterprise culture, and the traditional family were actualized. They invite critical re-evaluation, especially from the perspective of Gothic studies, as they explore what lies behind the surface of the neoliberal age. The Gothic sensibility is foregrounded in an era in which the nuclear family was conceptualized as an equal to the individual, since, for Thatcher, there was "no such thing as society, only the individual and his family."[4] Further, according to Thatcherite doctrine, the individual and the family must be free from the meddling of state intervention, rather than protected by it. "Thatcher's statements suggest the primacy of the individual and the promotion of the ideology of the family as if the family and society are at odds;"[5] *enemies* rather than companions. Regarding society and entrepreneurship, Thatcher argued: "It doesn't matter who you are, where you come from. If you can build up a fortune to yourself, jolly good luck to you, because in doing so you will help create jobs for others. And I want the successful people here, not an envious society but a go-getter society."[6] For Thatcher, "society" was an ambiguous concept tied to the policies of the government-supervised welfare state, which turned society "softer" and was thus the enemy of personal initiative. For her, society was comprised of men, women, and families, all working as the foundation of free society by helping one another succeed in their respective lives. It was thus the family, rather than society, that was depicted as under threat in British horror cinema during the neoliberal decade.

The theme of a home and family under siege underlies not only *Hellraiser*—a story in which female sexuality produces a string of horrors within the home—but also films such as *Scream for Help* (1984), which revolves around a home invasion carried out by lower-class citizens, and *Dream Demon* (1988), a Gothic tale of doomed marriage that allegorizes Princess Diana's role in contemporary British culture. This chapter analyzes the ways in which neoliberal policies and Gothic tropes intersect in these horror films, exposing neoliberal British anxieties of the 1980s.

## NEOLIBERALISM IN THE UK IN THE 1980S

By the 1980s, neoliberalism had come to mean an approach to economics favoring reduction of overall government spending and support for free trade as a central economic policy.[7] This led to the numerous privatizations of hitherto state-owned enterprises (such as British Gas and British Petroleum) as well as significant reductions in government spending on social programs. Firmly believing that state intervention stifled entrepreneurship, Thatcher's government cut the income tax. Simultaneously, it enacted a number of measures that weakened the role of unions, leading to the government's victory in the Miners' Strike of 1984. Many of these reforms were unpopular at first; after a rocky start in 1979–1982, however, Conservatives won majorities in 1983 and 1987 and remained in power until 1990. The Falkland War, the last war fought and won by the British alone, was key to Thatcher's victory in 1983, increasing her popularity and burnishing her reputation as a brave leader, while creating a climate of national euphoria.

The economic restructuring and deindustrialization of the British labor market in the 1980s, however, brought contradictions. With factories and traditional industries closing, and both inflation and unemployment on the rise, many men were unable to provide for their families along traditional lines. Indeed, housewives increasingly had to go to work to support their husbands, who stayed at home, unemployed. Further, the neoliberal ethos pushed people to become successful, encouraging women who might otherwise have stayed home to become career women. This contradicted the Thatcherites' support for a traditional gender binary that assigned men the role of going out into the public sphere to compete with other men for resources in order to support themselves and their families, and women the role of keeping the home clean and in proper order. The neoliberal ethos of personal freedom and economic independence thus created a disturbing sense of instability about what it meant to be a "good woman."

This contradiction was solved by creating the image of the idealized neoliberal/conservative woman, who worked outside home to support her family rather than for some selfish ideal of personal fulfillment. Being a wife and mother devoted to the care of husband and family thus remained a woman's most important social role. This new attitude toward women complemented what have been termed the "anti-feminist"[8] agenda which came to put women at their "rightful" place after the cultural shifts of the 1960s and 1970s and radical feminism. The different feminist collectives had encouraged women to abandon their "proper" role as homemakers and caretakers, so it was time to put Britain on the right track again regarding gender.

Neoliberalism in Britain was accompanied by conservative policies that proclaimed that the dire state of the country was due not only to welfare state policies, which promoted laziness, but also to the moral decline that had begun in the 1960s.[9] In other words, neoliberalism and conservative ethos united together to "solve" what were argued to be two "problems:" first, to end a state that maintained "parasites" (neoliberalism) and, second, to end the "moral decline" embodied in progressive social forces (conservatism). The evident contradiction in the formulation that there are only families and individuals was resolved by "the intersection of neoliberalism with conservatism."

If conservatives ontologize the individual and sexual difference "there is no actual contradiction between individuals and families, because the focus is on the individual who can move easily between the public market space and the private domestic sphere."[10] Thatcher, basically, presupposed a masculine citizen who can be an individual (work) while existing within the domestic space (the patriarchal figure). Women, on the other hand, faced a more complex situation, as women were considered as upholders of moral values and defenders of family and social order.[11]

Thus, behind the neat surface of family values lurks a Gothic reality shaped by anxiety about the impossibility of fitting into this new paradigm, a disconnect between image and reality which threatens to destroy any attempt made by women to conform to neoliberal politics. Linnie Blake calls "neoliberal Gothic" the "rendering of the monstrous dislocations that free market economics have inflicted on selfhood and society"[12] after the 1980s. The neoliberal politics of the 1980s presupposed the erasing of all the progressive thinking of the 1960s and 1970s in the name of a bright conservative future. According to Japhy Wilson, the neoliberal ethos and the Gothic mode are fitting companions: neoliberal ideology "has always been driven by an anxious desire to hide the ugly realities of capitalism beneath a fantasy of harmonious order."[13] The horror films of the 1980s actualized Gothic narratives of beautiful, young, and naïve heroines living in gorgeous mansions that are rife with skeletons-in-the-closet. In fact, all the films involve young women moving into, or already living in, spacious, lovely places where a threatening male presence lurks in the corners, hiding behind the mask of a perfect husband. In the intersections of the nuclear family and radical individualism on one hand and the logic of free market and personal subjectivities in the other, the Gothic finds its place of haunting.

Each of the three films considered here simultaneously embodies and, to varying degrees, critiques the neoliberal values of the Thatcher era. Both *Hellraiser* and *Dream Demon* exhibit a highly Gothic awareness of repressed sexuality and explore—in very different ways—its intersection with Thatcherism's celebration of the nuclear family and traditional gender roles. *Scream for Help* shifts the focus from gender to class, staging a nightmarish scenario in which bourgeois conformity is assaulted through the irruption of the working-class, but ending with the Thatcherite status quo comfortably restored. The fragmented gender- and class-based identities displayed in these films suggest the extent to which, far from finding comfort in the neoliberal sociocultural landscape of the 1980s, Britons were haunted by their own inability to meet the demands placed on them, creating situations drenched with horror and anxiety.

## HAUNTING CONFORMITY

Neoliberal subjects are informed by the politics of entrepreneurism, which favors consumption and links it to self-transformation.[14] On the other hand, Thatcherite femininity is shaped by the traditional values of conservative gender regimes through which women are identified with domestic space. In this sense, unrestricted female sexuality is a threat in both Gothic fiction and neoliberal politics. Women were expected both to reproduce and—as part of making the home a safe, comforting space for their husbands to come home to—be sexually available to their spouses at whatever times, and in whatever ways, the men wanted it. It is the need of women to satisfy their own desires that made them morally suspicious. Nonreproductive sexuality is a threatening presence toward masculine integrity because it denies the "essential" (that is, controlled) roles of women in society.

Made to capitalize on the American success of Wes Craven's *A Nightmare on Elm Street* (1984) and its blending of dreams and reality, *Dream Demon* (1985) revolves around an anxious bride-to-be whose nightmares begin to materialize in her real life. Even as an imitative product, the film can be read as an example of the "Female Gothic:" an exploration of women's fears about entrapment within domestic spaces.[15] Jemma Redgrave plays Diana, a woman just a few days away from marrying Oliver (Mark Greenstreet), a hero of the Falklands War whose distinguished war record has made him a national figure. It is implied that marrying him will make her famous, as well. Diana's marriage to a war hero parallels that of a more famous woman with the same name: Diana, Princess of Wales. At the start of the 1980s, the campaign to find a suitable wife for the Prince of Wales came to an end. "A wave of popular enthusiasm greeted the 'fairytale' royal wedding" where "impeccable chastity was a prerequisite."[16] Both Dianas would become the locus of national pride, any sense of real personal fulfillment replaced by their newfound celebrity status. Both women were, actually, marrying an idealized representation of British nationhood. Thus, the pressure on them to conform to officially expected norms (like chastity and complacency) was vastly increased.

The film opens with a bucolic sequence that emphasizes the virginal character of the soon-to-be bride. During the opening credits, which use sacred music as background, Diana is ritually dressed in dazzling white, symbolic of the fact that she is a virgin. Like the real Diana, the fictional Diana finds no fairy tale in her marriage. She harbors some unspecified doubts about her marriage (Social pressure? Lack of real commitment?) but only dares to reject Oliver in her dreams. When she does so, Oliver brutally slaps her and the dream quickly turns into a bloody nightmare: she punches and, in doing so, decapitates him, producing a geyser of blood that turns her white dress into a gory mess. In another dream, she appears scantily dressed in front of Oliver's conservative parents, provoking his fury and violence. In still another of her nightmares, she is raped by Oliver. Yet, Diana continues with the wedding plans. The reason is clear: Oliver is the perfect husband. Young and handsome, he is recognized throughout Britain as a hero of the Falklands War. She has no reason to give him up. The pressure to marry him, considering that Diana's family does not appear in the film, is clearly social rather than familial. Even if she has doubts, Diana wants to hone herself into the perfect commodity, someone who can complement national pride through the management of her public persona and her sexuality. For Thatcherite neoliberals, it is the woman's "job" to find a perfect man and marry him, thus "winning" in the competitive market of women seeking husbands from among suitable bachelors. When Diana's anxieties about the impending marriage begin to take the form of horrible nightmares, it is clear that she is doubtful about her compromise but reluctant to express her fears. The dreams become an outlet for doing so.

The Falklands War enters the picture when Diana reluctantly agrees to an interview conducted by two seedy journalists, played by Timothy Spall and Jimmy Nail. At one point, the interview becomes unpleasant when the journalists observe that "it must be very exciting to marry a man who had killed a lot of Argentines. That turns you on, right?" The film does not treat the intersection of war, heroism, and violent death in depth, but the journalists' crass question highlights the bloody nature of Oliver's "heroism" and destabilizes the image of national heroism and pride that the public sees in the wedding. Diana is marrying a hero but, also, a killer; in her nightmares both images merge. Inside the perfect husband hides, in fact, a killer. After her meeting with the journalists, her nightmares start to revolve around them rather than Oliver. In her nightmares, both reporters start to haunt her as she moves through her spacious house, their faces overtaken by rot. Their putrid appearances are reminders of the rot behind British pride, as the heroism of her future husband has been built on spilled human blood. Further, Diana states that she has been not able to get a good night sleep after moving to the luxurious and *pristine white* mansion Oliver bought for them to live in together after marriage. The enormous house works as a reservoir of Diana's anxieties, reminding her of her virginity and her socially approved "proper role" within the domestic space.

## DESTABILIZING SEXUALITY

The horror in *Dream Demon* stems not from fear of sexuality—Diana, certainly, feels sexually attracted to Oliver—but from the politics of power and subjugation in a highly public relationship about which Diana has very little to say. In *Hellraiser*, on the other hand, sexuality is central to the film. Gothic plots are traditionally seen as "narratives of emergent female sexuality,"[17] and Julia (Clare Higgins)—the principal female character in *Hellraiser*—is the archetype of a Gothic heroine. Her repression is embodied in the house that she inhabits, and her sexual activity is monstrous and destructive, even though, like Diana, she tries desperately to channel her sexuality into traditional forms consistent with conservative "family values."

The film opens with Julia moving with her husband, Larry (Andrew Robinson), to his family home. A close shot of Julia's face reveals that she is not as enthusiastic as he is about this choice. She is clearly just doing what a good conservative wife must do: please her man. It is equally clear that the couple's marriage is troubled, and that they see the move as their last hope for a new beginning. At home, Julia will face ghosts from her past that occupy some of the desolate, dirty rooms. Larry's brother, Frank (Sean Chapman), was briefly Julia's lover, and she is still emotionally attached to him. Unknown to everyone, Frank died in the house after opening a mysterious box called the Configuration of Laments, which opened a gateway to another dimension and brought forth a race of creatures called Cenobites, who killed him. While Julia and Larry are repairing the house, an accident causes Larry's blood to drip on the floorboards and awakens Frank, who is now a living corpse—skinless after his fatal encounter with the Cenobites—in need of more blood so that his body can be fully restored. Upon discovering that Frank has returned to life, Julia—to whom he has promised a life together, once he is fully alive—becomes his accomplice, picking up men in bars and bringing them to the house, where she murders them and collects their blood to feed to Frank.

The Cenobites re-enter the film when Kirsty (Ashley Laurence), Larry's daughter by his first (now deceased) wife, finds the puzzle-box. Kirsty embodies both sides of Thatcherite ethos. On one hand, she embraces neoliberalism in her rejection of economic dependence and her determination to make her own way in the world. Larry criticizes Kirsty's desire to not live with them in the family house, as well as her decision of get a job when, according to him, it is unnecessary. His insistence in keeping his daughter within the familial home reveals his fears of being coded as somehow "lacking" sufficient manliness to support his wife and daughter. On the other hand, Kirsty rejects the socially conservative side of Thatcherism as well, neither remaining in her father's household nor retaining her virginity.

Julia, the other main female character, is an entire catalog of social-conservative nightmares. She has sex with her future husband's brother days before the wedding (lying on top of her wedding dress), seduces men in order to kill them and steal their blood (to continue the illicit affair), and continually satisfies her own desires (and her lover's) rather than those of her husband, who remains unsatisfied at home. Because both Julia and Kirsty continually subvert traditional feminine roles, they ruin any attempt made by Larry to form a family that embodies the conservative values of Thatcher's Britain. Both women, Kirsty and Julia, unleash evil into the world, the former by opening the puzzle-box, and the latter by using her sexuality to kill men.

The regimes of desire of neoliberal culture—to produce more, to consume more, to enjoy more—that Kirsty tries to embrace (by, for example, having premarital sex with her boyfriend), reveal the impossibility of fulfilling this self-regulated image. At one point in the film, having barely survived an attack by the still-skinless Frank, Kirsty wanders—dazed and aimless—through the streets. Significantly, the only people that she encounters in her wanderings are a couple of nuns, who (perhaps mistaking her shock for a drug-induced high) look at her with reproach. Kirsty and the nuns juxtapose the moral regime promoted by Thatcherites with the 1960s legacy they hoped to erase: the traditional values of subordination and service to others in opposition to the radical, pleasure-seeking individualism of youth.

Within the realm of family values, the concept of adolescence remains central. Kirsty represents another of Thatcher's enemies: an unruly teenager.[18] One of the forces that publicly opposed British conservatism, especially among adolescents, was the punk movement. The economic transformation linked with conservative thinking was mocked by punk, which interlinked the political with the personal. Punk was, among many other things, a call for authenticity in a world obsessed with surfaces and fake images of personal success.[19] When, in *Dream Demon,* Diana's nightmares start to bleed into reality in the form of otherworldly landscapes and sinister presences, it is no coincidence that the only person willing to help her is Jenny (Kathleen Wilhoite), a punk girl. She is the only one able to demystify the figure of Oliver, and willing to mock the public's image of him as the perfect husband. Oliver, for his part, immediately dislikes Jenny and her punk attitude. Unlike Diana, she wears mostly black and belongs to the working class. If Diana is a mirror of the future Princess of Wales, Jenny reflects the "minority of cynics and 'women's libbers' [who] took up the slogan 'Don't do it, Di.'"[20] Unlike that minority, however, Jenny is able to help Diana dominate the supernatural presences who live in the mansion's cellar (as in so many Gothic stories) and separate her from Oliver. What is privileged at the film's end is feminine sisterhood, a far cry from the traditionalist, antifeminist agenda of Margaret Thatcher and the conservative movement she led. As the neoliberal decade was coming to its end, *Dream Demon* reenacted Diana Frances Spencer's marriage as a horror story.

Unlike the punk, the neoliberal and conservative female is "disciplined in her work, but also disciplined in her body."[21] Julia appears, in the opening scenes of *Hellraiser*, dressed in clothes that convey a polished, professional look, but that image quickly dissolves. The flashbacks that recount her affair with Frank show her with her hair unbound and flowing, and later—when committing murders on Frank's behalf—she is perpetually disheveled and constantly blood-stained: a Gothic figure defined by overwhelmed sexuality and decay. She is the embodiment of the neoliberal contradiction: the perfect wife and the perfect ambitious, thrill-seeking individual, the impossibility of this combination marking her Gothic persona.

After Frank's resurrection, Julia becomes an evil caricature of the career woman, wearing sophisticated clothes—including hats and sunglasses—and cruising bars in search of men whose blood she can use to feed him. In a Gothic inversion, her career is that of a sex worker, a woman who sleeps with other men in exchange for material, rather than emotional or familial, gain. The fact that she does not want their money but rather, their blood—their life—only deepens the sense of horror. This distorted mirror of the successful self-identity promoted by neoliberalism has her turning the body into commodity. On a symbolic level there is one final, deeper horror: Julia creates a "bait trap" where she takes men to her house in order to (apparently) satisfy her own sexual desires, only to send them instead into the embrace, not just of another man, but of a grotesque caricature of a man. The Thatcher years saw a strong antigay backlash in Britain, but one that distinguished between good and bad homosexuals. There was a "limited toleration" for the "good," meaning "closeted," homosexual, but revulsion for those who "flaunted" their sexuality in public.[22] Frank is the perfect embodiment of the perverted man who lives (literally) in the closet. Still, through Gothic inversion, he is truly monstrous and damaging, even if he does not come out of the house at any time during the film.

The main female characters of *Hellraiser* embrace, like Diana in *Dream Demon*, the glossy surface of the sophisticated self-made woman, ignoring the tensions it creates with the traditional values of the family and the nation. Their self-images are inseparable from a Gothic reversal: external "symbols" such as pure whiteness and expensive clothes hide a reality of fleshless men and national heroism drenched in blood.

## RADICAL INDIVIDUALISM AND CLASS MOBILITY

The neoliberal imagery of class mobility signaled by expensive clothes and luxury brands, together with radical individualism, informs *Scream for Help*.

Christie Cromwell (Rachael Kelly) is a hyperactive upper-class teenager who is convinced that her handsome-but-vicious stepfather Paul Fox (David Brooks) intends to kill her mother Karen (Marie Masters) and run off with the family fortune. Christie tries to warn her friends, as well as the police, about a variety of failed murder attempts, but no one believes her. Christie's suspicions prove to be accurate, and *Scream for Help* turns into a home-invasion film as Paul returns to the house accompanied by a pair of cold-blooded killers.

Karen's "crime" lies not in favoring her second husband over the daughter of her first marriage, but in choosing to marry a man from the working class. She knows far too little about Paul, thus setting in motion the perfect Gothic plot of a woman endangered by a husband—a plot fraught with machinations for murder. The presence within the family of an external "other" threatens to undermine any sense of security and boundaries, introducing the crucial Gothic quality of transgression. After the death of Karen's first husband, Paul—a tradesman already employed by the family—seduced and married the still-young widow with murder in his mind. Like Julia in *Hellraiser*, he thus acts as a horrifying embodiment of neoliberal success. Determined to achieve success in a market saturated with competitive attitudes and individualism, Paul is willing to embrace even premeditated murder, and the film suggests that, rather than being an extreme exception, he represents the neoliberal norm. The Gothic fragmentation of the "stable social order,"[23] is made literal in *Scream for Help*, which revolves around the intrusion of a man from the lower classes into a bourgeois household.

After Paul's murderous plan is revealed, he runs from the house but returns during the night and, with the aid of two companions—Brenda (Lolita Lorre) and Lacey (Rocco Sisto)—takes Karen and Christie prisoner. Jobless and morally degenerate, the pair live together in a small, shambling house, and spend their days watching television. Brenda is married to Lacey but simultaneously maintains her relationship with Paul, cheating on both men. When Lacey discovers his wife's unfaithfulness, however, he does not give it much thought. Both, along with Paul, are examples of the kind of unproductive, lazy, unambitious citizens that Thatcherism blamed for the problems of the welfare state.

Paul and his friends, leeching on the middle class, are the film's version of "the figure of the parasite [that] becomes paramount within Gothic precisely because it is an internal not an external danger that Gothic identifies and attempts to dispel."[24] Paul is a skeleton in the closet, an anomaly within the house. He is capable of thinking about his situation in big-picture terms, formulating a "class warfare" narrative to explain his situation, holding a grudge about it, and acting on that grudge. Unlike his accomplices, Paul wants to "fix" class inequality by cheating rather than working hard, as neoliberalism demands. He is thus a contradictory figure, on one hand embodying ambition and will and, on the other, remaining somehow the ultimate working-class enemy of Thatcher's neoliberal vision for Britain: lazy, unproductive, and parasitic.

*Scream for Help*, like *Dream Demon* and *Hellraiser*, thus becomes an example of the female Gothic, in which the domestic space of the home becomes a "paranoid space, each object turning into a possible threat, a betrayal."[25] Bourgeois fears of the loss of private property are underscored when Paul and his accomplices invade Cromwell's home, intending to take Karen and Christie's lives as a step toward taking their money and possessions. Ownership is a central theme in Thatcherite Britain, as private property is the emblem of individual freedom and the reward (in the eyes of neoliberalism) for individual initiative. The Housing Act of 1980, an early initiative of the Thatcher government, was designed specifically to promote home ownership, the ultimate form of private property. Thatcher's rise to power represented a specific moment in the class struggle, involving a defeat of the working class by the bourgeoisie. The conflict is embodied in the relationship between Karen and Paul: he claims that his attempt to kill her is not only motivated by greed but because he had always hated the economic welfare of the Cromwell's family and, by extension, the unearned economic advantages of all those belonging to the middle and upper classes. The film invites us to assume, however, that the Cromwell family's wealth represents hard work and success, and that Paul is lazy and parasitic—a drain on those willing to earn their success through hard work.

Throughout the film, the house itself is made a mortal trap as Paul uses his working-class knowledge to turn gas leaks, high stairs, electricity, and other seemingly mundane parts of the Cromwells' house into the ingredients of a "perfect accident" that kills both women without raising suspicions. Paul insinuates himself not just into the family (a traditional Gothic trope), but into the house itself. He does not just corrupt the social fabric of the Cromwells' world but also the physical fabric of their home—the totem of their upper-middle-class identity. As a member of the working class, he is able to "fix" the house so that it turns against its wealthy female occupants; his social background becomes a weapon. At the film's climax, however, Paul, Brenda, and Lacey have all been killed and the status quo has been restored.

Issues of parasitic nature are also on display in *Hellraiser*. Frank, like Paul, is a leech. He needs other men to restore his body, but he also lives—contributing nothing—in his brother's house. While Larry is depicted as the typical bourgeois father, Frank is a nomad without property or income. He is first seen in Morocco, buying the magic box which—the seller promises him—will satisfy his desire for ever-more-thrilling experiences with its "transgression of the boundaries between pleasure and pain."[26] Still, like Paul in *Scream for Help*, Frank exhibits traits of radical neoliberalism: the pursuit of individual gain without the constraints of "artificial" limits imposed by society, and without concern for the harm potentially done to others in the process. The box is, in a sense, the perfect embodiment of Neoliberalism: an object which is bought and sold as a kind of mechanism that offers individualistic self-satisfaction. Its existence reminds us that, on a truly free and open market, even sexual gratification is reducible to a commodity.[27]

Even a heroine such as Kirsty engages in radical individualism, saving herself at the expense of another. Once the box is opened, Kirsty is visited by the Cenobites, who want to take her with them. To save her life, she offers to deliver Frank, her uncle, and their escaped captive, to them by leading them to his hideout. In the UK of the 1980s, the film suggests, life itself is subject to market forces.

## CONCLUSION

Behind the sanitized, glossy surface of huge mansions that symbolize economic success, the horrors surfacing in *Hellraiser*, *Scream for Help*, and *Dream Demon* disrupt many of the social and cultural values central to Thatcherism.

Thatcher and her supporters sought to achieve the "recuperation" of the nuclear family, and to rescue it from the devastating effects of what they saw as the poisonously progressive 1960s and 1970s. Family, the Thatcherites argued, was the moral basis of society, with women and children its fundamental figures. Thatcher's insistence on the restoration of traditional moral values clashed, however, with progressive elements of British society that could not be fully rolled back: sexual freedom, expansion of the rights of minorities, and broadening of the options available to women. The New Right's sought-after restoration of the nuclear family was thus rendered unstable, and British horror cinema of the 1980s explored the fears generated by that instability.

Oliver, Frank, and Paul are all perfect embodiments of Gothic anxieties regarding female entrapment. In Thatcher's vision, individual and family were one and the same, and as such, if family were in danger because of an internal disorder, society could be in danger too. The Gothic thus offers a nightmarish vision of fragmented individualism "dissolved into predatory and demonic relations that cannot be reconciled into a healthy social order."[28] This lack of a familiar social order is a given because sexual femininity clashes with the "essential" chastity of women, as seen in Diana's secret desire to reject marriage to Oliver that frames *Dream Demon*. At the end of the film, Diana chooses sisterhood (with a punk) rather than proper marriage, threatening the fabric of family (and by extension, society itself).

The three films here analyzed share themes of "properly fitting" into the neoliberal and conservative home. The gorgeous houses are visible symbols of a competitive race. The Thatcher's affirmation that "everybody can win a fortune" can be read as a Gothic one: "everybody" means that borders are downplayed and intrusion, like that carried out by Paul and his friends, is enacted. As in classical Gothic narratives, the lumpen, foreign, dirty body, like that of Frank, can reach spheres previously negated. While Gothic narratives present such intrusions as the exception, suggesting that the lower-class creature only can worm into higher-class spaces occasionally, Thatcher invited everyone to attempt this violation. Thus, Diana is marrying not just Oliver but a new status as the wife of the UK, while Paul and Frank usurp roles alien to them. This infringement is literal in Frank's case, as he steals his brother's face (and thus his place in society) at the film's climax—a way of becoming the neoliberal subject so cherished by Thatcher. Still, the neoliberal ethos of self-control and self-image as paths to success is constantly undermined, offering twisted reverses of these values though Gothic narratives that present the cracks appearing through the neat surface.

These three films express themes that run through much 1980s British horror. Their adaptation of Gothic elements to an age of neoliberalism turns women from victims of dark secrets hidden in crumbling manor houses to agents of destruction whose inability to fit into "proper" family structures and gender roles threatens to provoke the collapse of the social order. Further, the class mobilization proposed by Thatcherism shaped a landscape of porosity and potential intrusion by foreign elements, from whom the families Thatcher herself exalted were the main group under attack. The Gothic and neoliberalism intermingle in these films through figures of uncooperative women and ambitious, self-centered men, who threaten to provoke the collapse of the proper order.

## NOTES

1. Our gratitude to Amy Davis, who helped us in the making of this chapter.
2. Whitehead, "Religion and Criminal Justice," 201.
3. Grimley "Thatcherism," 88.
4. Abott, *Family Affairs*, 146.
5. Ventura, *Neoliberal Culture*, 31.
6. Eliason, "Margaret Thatcher," 81.

7. Fry, *The Politics*, 74.
8. Gamer, *Women and Gender*, 225.
9. Nunn, *Thatcher*, 44.
10. Canning, "When Will They Hear," 211.
11. Nunn, *Thatcher*, 40.
12. Blake, "Neoliberal Adventures," 167.
13. Wilson, "Neoliberal Gothic," 596.
14. Scharff, "Gender and Neoliberalism," 218.
15. Smith, *Gothic Literature*, 31.
16. Abbot, *Family Affairs*, 144.
17. Norton, *Gothic Readings*, 2000.
18. Nunn, *Thatcher*, 21.
19. Dee, "The Brutal Truth," 60.
20. Abbot, *Family Affairs*, 144.
21. Ussher, *The Madness of Women*, 91.
22. Burak and Wilson, "Constructing Christian Right Enemies," 140.
23. Hendershot, *The Animal Within*, 1.
24. Halberstam *Skin Shows*, 15.
25. Fay, *Theaters of Occupation*, 144.
26. Aldana Reyes, "Gothic Horror Film," 397.
27. On the other hand turning sex into the ultimate individualistic act frees its (male) owner from the need to seek a wife as a sexual partner, and thus undermines (one aspect of) Thatcherism's conservative moral agenda.
28. Kilgour, *The Rise of the Gothic Novel*, 12.

## BIBLIOGRAPHY

Abbot, Mary. *Family Affairs: A History of the Family in 20th Century England*. London: Routledge, 2003.

Aldana Reyes, Xavier. "Gothic Horror Film, 1960–Present." In *The Gothic World*, edited by Glennis Byron and Dale Townshend, 388–398. New York: Routledge, 2014.

Blake, Linnie. "Neoliberal Adventures in Neo-Victorian Politics: Mark Hodder's Burton and Swinburne Novels." In *Technologies of the Gothic in Literature and Culture: Technogothics*, edited by Justin Edwards, 166–178. London: Routledge, 2015.

Burak, Cynthia, and Angelia Wilson. "Constructing Christian Right Enemies and Allies: US, UK and Eastern Europe." In *Remoralizing Britain?: Political, Ethical and Theological Perspectives on New Labour*, edited by Peter Manley Scott, Christopher Baker, and Elaine Graham, 136–155. New York: Continuum, 2009.

Canning, Charlotte. "When Will They Hear Our Voices? Historicizing Gender, Performance, and Neoliberalism in the 1930s." In *Performance, Feminism and Affect in Neoliberal Times*, edited by Elin Diamond, Denise Varney, and Candice Amich, 203–214. New York: Palgrave Macmillan, 2017.

Dee, Liam. "The Brutal Truth: Grindcore as the Extreme Realism of Heavy Metal." In *Heavy Metal Music in Britain*, edited by Gerd Bayer, 53–72. New York: Routledge, 2008.

Eliason, Marcus. "Margaret Thatcher Marks 60th Birthday." *Bangor Daily News*. 11 October 1985

Fay, Jennifer. *Theaters of Occupation: Hollywood and the Reeducation of Postwar Germany*. Minneapolis: University of Minnesota Press, 2008.

Fry, Geoffrey. *The Politics of the Thatcher Revolution: An Interpretation of British Politics, 1979–1990*. New York: Palgrave Macmillan, 2008.

Gamer, Karen. *Women and Gender in International History: Theory and Practice*. London: Bloomsbury, 2018.

Grimley, Matthew. "Thatcherism, Morality and Religion." In *Making Thatcher's Britain*, edited by Ben Jackson and Robert Saunders, 78–94. New York: Cambridge University Press, 2012.

Halberstam, Judith. *Skin Shows: Gothic Horror and the Technology of Monsters*. London: Duke University Press, 1995.

Hendershot, Cynthia. *The Animal Within: Masculinity and the Gothic*. Ann Arbor: University of Michigan Press, 1998.

Kilgour, Maggie. *The Rise of the Gothic Novel*. New York: Routledge, 2013.

Norton, Rictor. *Gothic Readings: The First Wave, 1764–1840*. New York: Continuum, 2000.

Nunn, Heather. *Thatcher, Politics and Fantasy: The Political Culture of Gender and Nation*. London: Lawrence & Wishart, 2002.

Scharff, Christina. "Gender and Neoliberalism: Young Women as Ideal Neoliberal Subjects." In *The Handbook of Neoliberalism*, edited by Simon Springer, Kean Birch, and Julie MacLeavy, 217–226. New York: Routledge, 2016.

Smith, Andrew. *Gothic Literature*. Edinburgh: Edinburgh University Press, 2000.

Ussher, Jane. *The Madness of Women: Myth and Experience*. New York: Routledge, 2011.

Ventura, Patricia. *Neoliberal Culture: Living with American Neoliberalism*. London: Routledge, 2012.

Whitehead, Philip. "Religion and Criminal Justice in Canada, England and Wales: Community Chaplaincy and Resistance to the Surging Tide of Neoliberal Orthodoxy." In *Organising Neoliberalism: Markets, Privatisation and Justice*, edited by Philip Whitehead and Paul Crawshaw, 201–228. London: Anthem Press, 2014.

Wilson, Japhy. "Neoliberal Gothic." In *The Handbook of Neoliberalism*, edited by Simon Springer, Kean Birch, and Julie MacLeavy, 592–602. New York: Routledge, 2016.

*Chapter Ten*

# Infringing on Cycles of Oppression

## *Artisanal Bricolage and Synthesis in Mumblegore*

Brandon Niezgoda

In one tale from the Time's Up Movement, Harvey Weinstein, the man who had progressively monopolized the independent niche film market through his company Miramax, brought struggling young actress Lupita Nyong'o to his family's mansion in order to discuss a project which, he promised, would be perfect for her.[1] With the other household members safely tucked away in a screening room where no one could hear, Weinstein pressured Nyong'o to have sex with him in an upstairs bedroom. As she was fleeing the house, Weinstein's assistant trailed after her with a bizarre fulfillment of his original offer: a DVD set of HBO's *The No. 1 Ladies' Detective Agency*, which had not been on the air for years. Weinstein's mansion became, for Nyong'o, the "terrible place" in a real-life horror story, whose elements echoed Hollywood plot devices.[2]

Hollywood has allowed aspiring female actors—and, to a lesser extent, men and children as well—to be preyed upon by those who hold power over them. Mumblecore, however, serves as an alternate production model. A genre spawned from early 2000s South by Southwest festivals, Mumblecore quickly evolved into a movement characterized by networked collective conscience and designed to prevent the sort of studio-system horrors that women like Nyong'o have described. The genre's films offer stirring and vivid images, taking on the undercurrents of a system that leaves its victims objectified, alienated, and abject.[3] Mumblecore, as both movement and genre, provides responses to stories such as that of (then) twelve-year-old Eliza Dushku, who was sexually abused by stunt coordinator Joel Kramer and, after confronting him about the abuse, was suspiciously injured on the set. Significantly, in her exposé, she blamed not an individual but the industry, declaring: "Hollywood failed to protect me."[4] Before considering the corrective offered by Mumblecore, then, one must ask: How is Hollywood failing?

## CONSTRUCTING THE HOLLYWOOD MARKET

Alternative models buried, the mainstream American film industry has been historically structured in ways that allow sexual predators to get away with their abuse. Despite Edison's patent-enforcement crusade, which caused production companies to flee New York for California, the production mode of early Hollywood was, in many ways, collaborative.[5] Even as the industry progressed from serving the working class in nickelodeons to serving the middle class in movie palaces, women played noticeably important roles and exercised significant influence. Eventually, however, the success of select talkie films, coupled with the Great Depression, brought about change. Many female-headed independent production companies went bankrupt, and investors in the burgeoning conglomerates that gradually came to dominate Hollywood believed that women could not handle the complex business aspects that the industry now involved. With a handful of exceptions like Mary Pickford, a joint founder of actor-led production company United Artists, women found little room for progress within the producer-led studio system. Five major and three minor studios, all headed by men, dominated the industry through their ownership of theater chains, which facilitated practices such as block booking, blind bidding, zoning, and price discrimination. The studios were thus able to control not only the financing and production of films, but also their distribution and exhibition.[6]

Rather than collaboration, this new system fostered compartmentalization and isolation. The unions that subsequently formed within the industry battled less against studio owners than against competing unions for jurisdiction over work functions.[7] Those outside of the industry suffered as studios worked to make "amateurs" inconsequential.[8] Women trying to break into one of the Hollywood studios were at particular risk due to their vulnerability. Employed as "extra-girls" without contracts to protect them, they were hounded at stag parties and sales conventions by men who promised to help them get their big break.[9]

In order to avoid job insecurity or unemployment, actresses in the studio system would often submit to studios' demands, allowing themselves to be molded into salable commodities to the point that their private and public lives became blurred. As Simpson notes, the studio system's treatment of women was not far removed from that of the pornography industry.[10] Even famed actress Judy Garland reported being repeatedly abused by producer Louis B. Mayer, the cofounder of Metro-Goldwyn-Mayer Studios. Being forced to participate in "meetings" while seated in his lap was part of a pattern of psychological belittlement that drove her, like many other women in Hollywood, to the brink of suicide.[11]

With the rise of television and the Supreme Court's ruling in United States v. Paramount, which forced the studios to divest themselves of their theater chains, the studios' role in the filmmaking process changed. Rather than maintaining large staffs of actors and production workers on long-term contracts, they became "nerve centers" of vertically dis-integrated production networks, assembling "packages" on a film-by-film basis by leasing a variety of services from specialized firms. Utilizing and exploiting these freelance agents, the studios sought to compete with television by producing less numerous, but more grandiose, films.[12] Within the system, the success of past methods and vestigial unionized labor pools encouraged old divisions of labor to continue. Auteur-driven films enjoyed marked success in the 1970s and 1980s, but this did not lead to more funding for directors, actors, or production staff. Instead, in an industry where business and filmmaking continued to mix, it made them increasingly dependent on studio financing to produce and distribute the blockbuster films favored by the market.[13]

While participation in the "indie scene" that emerged in the 1990s might have seemed to serve the needs of unknown filmmakers by providing much needed visibility and an alternative model to Hollywood, outlets such as the Sundance Film Festival and the Weinstein brothers' Miramax Films still functioned capitalistically.[14] Once signed by an "independent" producer or distributor, a rising filmmaker could easily feel indebted or become afraid to criticize that person for fear of retribution. Quentin Tarantino, for example, who rose from Blockbuster Video employee to independent auteur-provocateur, owed much of his success to Miramax distribution, and refused to completely cut ties with the company when he heard of Harvey Weinstein's sexual assaults.[15] "Independent" distributors are frequently not independent at all, but rather subsidiaries of major studios, created to market niche material (e.g., Paramount vintage).[16] Many of these subsidiary companies closed in the post-2008 recession, and those that survived came to give preference to films with bankable stars, as "tentpole" films deliver almost all of the market share in order to remain competitive and lucrative. Selection committees at Sundance and other festivals do the same. In such a competitive business, hotel "casting room" meetings are set up even if the agents who do so all but know they are sending their clients into a trap.[17]

## MUMBLECORE RISES

In the early 2000s, as the United States faced two ongoing wars and an approaching recession, the "cast" of Mumblecore coalesced from a group of young people drifting through their early twenties. Ti West was at New York

University, the only student in Kelly Reichardt's class who was interested in horror; E. L. Katz and Adam Wingard were at a dingy for-profit trade school in Florida; and A. J. Bowen was attending the University of Georgia after switching his major from music to acting, and so losing his scholarship, at his previous college. There was every possibility that they would be chewed up by, or disappear into, the mainstream film industry, if they were able to break into it at all. Through collaboration and a determination to eschew industry norms, however, they escaped that fate. Indeed, they openly confronted the industry, and its record of abuse, through the content of their films.

Ti West was introduced by one of his NYU professors to genre veteran Larry Fessenden. Fessenden—himself defying Hollywood norms, under which a producer would rarely, if ever, offer funding to an untested student director—took West's word that for $50,000 he could make a quality film. The result, *The Roost* (2005), tells the story of four friends traveling to a wedding who fall prey to bloodthirsty bats when their car breaks down. A hokey and parodic plot presented in a vintage movie-of-the-week format, the film demonstrates the positive affordances horror movies offer independent filmmakers: they can be made relatively cheaply, they don't need bankable stars (since spectators are more interested in visceral effects),[18] and they have a built-in and enthusiastic audience.[19]

*The Roost* (2005) premiered at South by Southwest, a then-new and influential film, music, and culture festival. While attending the festival, West met Joe Swanberg, who was there to showcase his first feature film, *Kissing on the Mouth* (2006). Swanberg had graduated from the University of Southern Illinois at Carbondale with a film degree, specializing in video production.[20] His digital aesthetic, defined by handheld cinematography and the talky performances of nonprofessional millennial actors, was shared by fellow festival-circuit filmmakers including Mark and Jay Duplass and Andrew Bujalski.[21] The name "Mumblecore" was sarcastically bestowed on their shared style by the sound editor of Bujalski's *Mutual Appreciation* (2005), who noted in an interview that he could never hear the dialogue of musician-turned-actor Justin Rice. The term has since come to characterize not only the production network that began in these early years, but a style combining naturalistic acting, an emphasis on dialogue over plot, and a focus on characters' relationships. The merging of this style with horror elements has been termed "Mumblegore."

The Duplass brothers' *Baghead* (2009) integrated genre-horror elements into a plot involving a group of struggling filmmakers and actresses who parodied the mannerisms of sycophantic film festival itinerants they had encountered.[22] Starring Greta Gerwig (who had appeared the previous year, along with Duplass and Bujalski, in Swanberg's *Hannah Takes the Stairs*), the title of the film comes from an indistinct figure in the woods who voyeuristically spies on one of the actresses—a manifestation of her "worst fear." The figure is eventually revealed as a ruse devised by two of the men in order to create a movie and win fame.

In Florida, E. L. Katz switched his major from music recording to film, bonding over horror films with fellow misfit Adam Wingard. After college, Katz found himself once again despondent over lack of prospects. With the promise to make a movie together, Wingard offered Katz a place to stay at his already packed family home. Their film *Home Sick* (2007) was a slightly bloated production (resulting from a mismanaged allocation of money by producers after Wingard serendipitously landed cult actor Bill Mosley), but an aesthetically unique horror film. Soon after the production they met freelance writer Simon Barrett while covering a production for the horror website *Fangoria*.

Katz, West, Wingard, and West sought—with relative success—to avoid participating in industry trends that they regarded as demeaning. Katz worked for two years writing spec scripts for Sam Raimi's Ghost House Pictures, but found the experience alienating and praiseless.[23] The frustration of writing for-hire scripts led him, along with Wingard, to start a writing group. Given the opportunity to direct *Cabin Fever 2* (2009)—the sequel to Eli Roth's successful, offbeat 2002 feature premiere—West found the process so disaffecting that he wanted his name removed from the project.

Following his second feature *Pop Skull* (2007)—a bare-bones, no-budget portrayal of isolation and drug dependency starring, and based on the lonely life of, his friend Lane Hughes—Wingard was selected to be a contestant on Fox's 2007–2008 filmmaking-based reality show *The Lot*. He took note, early on, of the show's exploitive dynamic, which left struggling independent artists all but begging judges like Brett Ratner (later accused of sexual harassment during the Time's Up movement) for the literal gates of Hollywood to be opened for them by Steven Spielberg in the season finale. Wingard refused to play along, and when it was time to pitch what he saw as an asinine movie concept for the judges, he deliberately sabotaged himself by presenting a plot that mocked such high-concept fare.[24] *Pop Skull* (2007), however, brought Wingard not only attention and "opportunity" from Fox but praise from Travis Stevens, a cinephile who held film screenings and meetings for aspiring filmmakers in his Los Angeles apartment.[25] With all the members of Stevens's circle living within ten minutes of each other, a clique was established. As the group spent time appreciating anti-Hollywood aesthetics, Katz became aware of *The Signal* (2007). An anthology film starring charismatic actor A. J. Bowen, it had had little potential of ever being made, let alone seen, without supporters willing to take collaborative and collective risks.

At the University of Georgia, Bowen had united with upstart MTV alumnus Jacob Gentry, as well as David Bruckner. As theater students, they had made films by borrowing cameras from the university's journalism school. After graduation, they joined with others to create the POPfilms Collective. *The Signal*, a horror story about a television signal that made people volatile and violent, emerged from this collective and premiered at the Sundance Film Festival in 2006. The insidious form in which the titular signal penetrated the brains of its victims was central to its atmosphere of horror. Like the harassment victims who participated in the Time's Up movement, the characters were trapped in a world that made it difficult to tell when they were in danger, or if they were ever safe to begin with.

The premiere of *The Signal* helped the collective establish a connection with Roxanne Benjamin, a fan of alternative horror who sought to participate in a style filmmaking that was more democratic and less exploitative than traditional Hollywood productions, and to filter out the "terrible misogyny" of typical horror-film conventions.[26] After working for some time as an intern at Paramount Vintage, Benjamin was eventually hired by the rising film website *Bloody Disgusting*. The bare-bones enterprise was run by Brad Miska, a participant in screenings held by Travis Stevens, who introduced her to Wingard and the others.

## THE FILMS OF MUMBLEGORE

Harboring a shared passion to create films, the networked members decided to embark on a project. The result was *A Horrible Way to Die* (2010), a dark, joyless tale focused on a recovering alcoholic, whose serial killer ex-boyfriend stalks her like a specter. The film was produced by Stevens, written by Barrett, and directed by Wingard, with principal roles played by Lane Hughes from *Pop Skull*, Joe Swanberg, and Amy Seimetz, an actress recognized for her work in independent film. On Katz's suggestion, they hired A. J. Bowen to play the key role of the ex-boyfriend.[27]

The project was followed by *V/H/S* (2011), an anthology Miska created by reaching out to filmmakers whose work he had discovered and found interesting while touring festivals. The group involved in the film came to include, among others, Wingard, Barrett, West, and Swanberg. With his Directors Guild of America minimum fees too high for the low-budget production to pay, Gentry recommended fellow POPfilms Collective member and *Signal* anthology segment director David Bruckner to contribute. Miska described the mode of production for *V/H/S* as a "trust-fall," in which the group of filmmakers were given the freedom to create their projects as they wished.[28] The actors and directors were so at ease during filming *V/H/S*, that Sophia Takal, star of the segment directed by West, participated in the minimalist production—staying in a motel with Joe Swanberg and Kate Lyn Sheil, and doing karaoke every night—without even being aware that the finished project would be sent to festivals.[29]

A segment titled "Tape 56" frames the film, following a group of malcontents who are hired to steal a rare VHS tape. While searching a decrepit house for the McGuffin, the group, along with viewers, are subject to film after film of violence, many of which deconstruct narrative and patriarchal scopophilia. Bruckner's segment "Amateur Night," for instance, follows three "bros" who have rented a motel room for a night out. The two more outwardly masculine members, Patrick and Shane, have purchased a set of camera glasses and coerced their slightly more well-intentioned friend Clint into wearing them so that they can record an unsuspecting woman during sex. Lisa, one of the two women they bring home, soon passes out while having sex with Patrick. The other, Lily, remains aloof, despite her apparent affinity for Clint and ominous glances toward the three friends during the intermittent periods of camera glasses buffering. She is eventually revealed to be a demon, who strikes just as Shane, aggressive and undaunted, comes on to her.

Over the course of the film the characters from the framing segment disappear one by one, seemingly swallowed whole by the decrepit house or killed by the aged, decomposing man who stalks them. Their fate, the film suggests, is well-deserved. Earlier in the day, in broad daylight, they seized a young woman in a parking lot, exposing her breasts and filming her so that they could sell the footage to a pawnshop or amateur porn producer. Their subsequent discussion of the price they will charge for the footage (fifty dollars) underscores the film's critique of the objectification and exploitation of women in films and by filmmakers.

Ti West followed up *The Roost* with two films in which he reified the alternative aesthetic and production mode that he had begun to establish in it. *House of the Devil* (2009) deconstructs the familiar horror-genre trope of scantily clad women killed off one by one in a slow, plodding film about cash-strapped college student who takes a babysitting job in a dangerous house on the night of a full moon. Davis describes the film's aesthetic as "VCR style" horror, filled with incidental, leisurely, and quotidian scenes in which the action is paused to both capture the mundane pace of everyday life and build tension.[30] In *The Innkeepers* (2011) the protagonist Claire is played by Sarah Paxton, a young woman often objectified in her appearances in other films.[31] Claire and her partner Luke, played by Pat Healy, are working at a soon-to-close inn during its final weekend in business, at the request of their boss, who is vacationing in Barbados. Her character is developed throughout the film, and established as a person with anxieties, fears, and goals. She searches the hotel for a ghost, but also for any sign that her existence has importance and meaning, eventually suffering a painful, tragic death in the climax of the film. Trapped in a cellar after Luke deserts her in fear, she bangs ineffectually on the door, seeking escape as the ghost of a forgotten woman who haunts the house inches closer and closer. Claire, an asthmatic, is found the next day with her inhaler beside her, leaving open the question of what actually caused her death . . . or whether it matters.

Snoot Entertainment (another small production company that had made the rounds at film festivals and would later hire Benjamin as head of development and acquisitions) provided a million-dollar budget for *You're Next* (2011), with Wingard as director and Barrett penning the script. The cast and crew were rounded out by other members of the network, including West, Swanberg, Seimetz, Fessenden, Bowen, and Hughes. Barrett, a film school graduate, crafted the lead female character as a reflection of the work of Carol Clover, which he had studied.[32] After premiering at the 2011 Toronto Film Festival, *You're Next* was bought for distribution by the Weinstein company, which shelved it for two years. Instead of becoming indebted to the Weinsteins, however, the Mumblecore network created opportunities, markets, and distribution techniques that made their lack of interest inconsequential. Swanberg struck a deal with Brooklyn distributor Factory 25 for his four 2011 films to be released quarterly, packaged with memorabilia in a model designed to make film viewing more personal while deconstructing a system of distribution focused on immediacy and disposability.

Included in the set was Swanberg's *Silver Bullets,* a Mumblegore film that maintains the ambience of horror in every scene while tracing the alienation and abjection of an aspiring young actress. It emerged from two-and-a-half years of off-and-on filming of encounters between an objectified aging actress (Jane Adams playing a version of herself) and a series of ex-lovers. The project evolved as Swanberg shifted its focus to the politics of his own production method. In the film, he plays a character similar to himself: a low-budget director named Ethan, who makes intimate films centered on relationships. His girlfriend and artistic muse, Claire (Kate Lyn Sheil), an actress who typically works on his films, has been recently cast as a werewolf in a horror film by another director (Ti West, also playing a version of himself).

The werewolf metaphor invites alternative perspectives. One reads it as Swanberg's own self-reflexive choice: his effort to confront the incipient jealousy and competitive power struggles he, as a director, felt toward actors who are given the chance to transform in their roles.[33] Ethan is portrayed in a negative light, and the werewolf can be seen as a positive, and powerful, figure—paralleling the themes of werewolf fantasy novels, and acting as an antithesis to the behavior of directors recently exposed as having taken advantage of their power.[34] A second, opposing perspective reads the werewolf as an abject female, a monstrous feminine figure that is "hounded and harassed."[35] When Claire returns from a makeup test, Ethan greets her with suspicious questions. Later that night, he reviews footage—reflecting the traditional, probing male gaze—from a scene that he shot of Claire in a shower, as a haunting violin score by Orange Mighty Trio accentuates the malice and control in his gaze. The next day Claire has drinks with her friend and fellow actress Charlie (Amy Seimetz), who expresses praise for Claire's new role, but is solemn about pressures she will face from the established, patriarchal industry.

When Ethan decides to cast Charlie in his new film, the act strikes Claire as hurtful—reducing her to an interchangeable object. Ethan gets closer to Charlie and, sitting on his bed, they discuss his working method and his thoughts on the business. Movies don't make him happy, he explains, nor do prizes. In fact, he relates that nothing makes him happy other than the ability to get closer to people. His self-reflexive dialogue acts here as a reflection of Swanberg's filmmaking aspirations, particularly when situated against Harvey Weinstein's drive for Academy Awards.[36] In a parallel scene, Claire and West bond over his early horror film after a photo shoot in West's own family basement. West grabs an old werewolf mask used in his first short film *Prey* (2001) from a dusty top shelf, and has Claire put it on. The mask is soon taken off, her hair brushed away from her face as West kisses her. She stops him, and as he gets up, he places the macabre mask back on her face. He walks upstairs, while Claire, with the mask still on, remains silent

*Claire's emotions are hidden under an abject façade in* Silver Bullets *(2011).*

and motionless—suggesting that she now considers herself as a monstrous female: shocking, terrifying, horrific, and abject.[37]

*Silver Bullets*, like other Mumblegore films, embraces the horror genre fully in its last act. Forlorn after her encounter with West, Claire adorns herself with makeup and the werewolf mask, then dances violently and horrifyingly in front of Ethan in an effort to get his attention, suggesting that she has internalized a perspective of herself that is both demeaning and demoralizing.[38] After narrative turns that include Claire's murder of Charlie and a sexual encounter with West, the film ends with Claire, on a high-budget film shoot, putting on makeup as she looks directly at the camera. By the end of the shot tears stream down her face, and she is left with the agony and betrayal of a position—a starring role in what is likely to be a successful film—that leaves her no consolation.[39] The long shot deconstructs notions of the fetishized object; Claire derives no satisfaction from the "pleasure and privilege of the invisible guest" that the camera's gaze represents, but suffers from losing her own sense of self.[40]

## THE MUMBLEGORE MODEL

Kickstarter has also served as an alternative production model that has spawned more oppositional pictures by Mumblecore networked participants. Dennis Widymer and Kevin Kölsch ran a campaign from February 25 to March 27, 2013, seeking $50,000 to complete their proposed project Starry Eyes, which they pitched as a "feature film of paranoia and possession."

Partly produced by alternative-cinema enthusiast Travis Stevens, and directed by Dennis Widymer and Kevin Kölsch, the film's version of Hollywood is merciless and hierarchical. You are either part of the cultlike film industry, or you are left to struggle on the periphery.[41] Shot with a Red Digital Cinema camera, which has given independent filmmakers the aesthetic of film without the price, the film traps its main character, Sarah, in a dark, color-saturated Los Angeles with little sunlight.

An aspiring actress with few successes and no prospects, Sarah pays the rent on her decrepit apartment complex by displaying her starved body in a skimpy top and low-cut pants as a waitress at "Taters." Off work she finds little solace. Her "friend" Erin, for example, holds back a smirk at a party when she tells Sarah of being chosen for a small-yet-paying role for which Sarah also auditioned. The culture of patronization drives her to try out for *The Silver Scream*, produced by Hollywood institution Astraeus Pictures. After the ominously solemn casting directors dismiss her, one of them happens to be present when she breaks down in the studio bathroom and pulls her own hair in frustration. Intrigued, she invites Sarah back onstage to repeat the breakdown for the other directors, which earns her a callback. Quitting her waitressing job to fully commit herself to acting, she is blinded by a spotlight during the second audition—forced to strip and "fully let herself go" in order to prove her willingness to "do anything" that the film requires. The experience confuses and tortures, but also emboldens her. Dazed by the experience, she lets a laugh slip when one of the girls sycophantically parading beside her apartment complex pool, hoping to be the star of a web series, falls and breaks her nose.

Intrigued by what he has seen in recordings of her auditions, the head of Astraeus calls Sarah in for a private meeting. After spending an immense amount of time getting ready, Sarah walks past the gaze of complex residents with perfectly set hair and glistening skin. When she reaches the office, the studio head's assistant lets her in and—aware of what the meeting entails—locks the door behind her. The old and powerful producer, regarding her with a sinister glare and a grim sneer, tells her that the part is hers if she is willing to give him her body. Like many women of the Time's Up movement, she is dismayed at the proposition, and bangs on the door to be let out.[42]

Sarah returns to her job at Taters, but after discontent seeps in, she reluctantly agrees to another meeting with the head of Astraeus.[43] Once the office door is again locked behind her, he asserts his dominance over her, forcing her head downward, and reinforcing the idea that her body is simply a collection of parts for the use of (or consumption by) others.[44] The film glosses over the details of the encounter, but it becomes clear that the producer's intentions involve not just the sexual, but the supernatural. Sarah spends the next days locked in her dingy apartment. Her beauty becomes tarnished and then

*A sinister studio head propositions Sarah (Alexandra Essoe) in* Starry Eyes *(2014).*

begins to deteriorate: teeth break, fingernails snap, and clumps of hair fall out as her body becomes abject.[45] Her roommate is disgusted by the smell of her decaying flesh, and the two argue about what Sarah's time with the producer involved. The director of *Silver Scream* calls and mocks her cries, telling her to embrace her transformation or die. In the end of the film she is reborn in a ceremony staged by a demonic cult that uses the film production company as a front. Her sins and history are hidden away by makeup and a wig, and she becomes Other at the price of her own life.[46]

## CONCLUSION

The Mumblecore network provides a case study of a production network oppositional to the hierarchical Hollywood structure, removed from the Hollywood "cult" and commenting on it in films like *Starry Eyes* and West's *The Sacrament* (2014), in which Bowen, Swanberg, and Mumblecore actor/director Kentucker Audley face off against a Jim Jones-like cult leader. Refusing to compromise, E. L. Katz finally made his independent feature film debut directing *Cheap Thrills* in 2013. It depicts the antithesis of the process that formed the Mumblecore network, tracing the breakdown of a longtime friendship as offers of money for increasingly demeaning and grotesque exploits place the two friends in competition rather than causing them to join together in solidarity as Katz and Wingard did in their writing group.

Now that Barrett and Wingard have signed deals with mainstream studios, figures like Joe Swanberg are making their work for alternative platforms like Netflix, and Lupita Nyong'o has starred in the groundbreaking *Black Panther*, it is possible that Mumblecore's democratic ethos will be extended into a changing Hollywood. Forager Films, cofounded by Swanberg, continues to provide microbudget filmmakers an outlet for production with a democratic and feminist emphasis, while Kentucker Audley founded NoBudge as a premiere alternative to an increasingly competitive, and oversaturated film festival market.[47]

On the other hand, Adam Wingard's production of such high-concept studio pictures as *Godzilla vs. Kong* (2019) calls into question how much creative choice some of the filmmakers truly have. *V/H/S* has now seen two sequels, the second of which, *V/H/S 3: Viral* (2015), makes it clear that the original film's political edge is gone. That Mumblecore alumna Greta Gerwig has recently received an Academy Award nomination, a capstone in a long line of Mumblecore actresses—Sophia Takal, Kris Swanberg, and Josephine Decker among them—who moved into directing themselves, provides some consolation, as does Roxanne Benjamin's continued prominence in the industry as a producer of independent films and director of segments for ambitious projects like *XX* (2017): an anthology of "four short horror films directed and written by women." Also promising is the continued work of the trio Radio Silence in the production network. The group of filmmakers, who also contributed to *V/H/S,* has moved away from Hollywood-style auteurism in favor of a cooperative and collective production model.[48]

Along with Roxanne Benjamin and David Bruckner, Radio Silence contributed films to the anthology *Southbound* (2015), the segments of which are interconnected stories played out on a timeless highway. Throughout the film, dark secrets and morally bankrupt decisions bind the characters to one another and trap them in a suffocating, never-ending cycle of oppression and deceit. The closing segment loops back to become the introduction for the first, suggesting that—as in Hollywood itself—the all-too-familiar cycle will be played out into eternity unless something is changed.

## NOTES

1. Nyong'o, "Lupita Nyong'o: Speaking Out about Harvey Weinstein."
2. Clover, "Her Body, Himself."
3. Tyler, "Against Abjection." Kristeva's theory on abjection builds from Lacan's consideration of the mirror stage, theorizing that once someone recognizes themselves in the mirror, they are split from the maternal and into the world of the symbolic.
4. See Fox and Singletary, "Eliza Dushku."
5. Bordwell, Staiger, and Thompson, *Classical Hollywood Cinema.*
6. Malone, *Backwards and in Heels.*
7. Ibid.
8. Fox, "Rethinking the Amateur."
9. Kenaga, "Making the 'Studio Girl'."
10. Simpson, "Coming Attractions."
11. Rosenwald, "I'll Ruin You."
12. Whitney, "Vertical Disintegration."
13. Lewis, *New American Cinema.*
14. Ortner, *Not Hollywood.*
15. Kantor, "Tarantino on Weinstein."
16. Newman, "Indie Culture."
17. Gonzalez and France, "Rachel McAdams, Selma Blair."
18. Tudor, "Why Horror?"
19. See, for instance, Cherry, "Screaming for Release," 56.
20. Belton, "Digital Cinema."
21. Aymar, "Joe Swanberg, Intimacy, and the Digital Aesthetic."
22. Ponsoldt, "Good in the Sack."
23. Nicholson, "Mumblegore."

24. Collis, "You're Next."
25. Nicholson, "Mumblegore," p. 6.
26. Ibid.
27. Ibid.
28. Nigel Smith, "Bloody Disgusting Founder."
29. Takal, "Interview."
30. Davis, "Speed of the VCR."
31. Eisenberg, "Writer/Director Ti West."
32. Barrett and Wingard, "We Are Adam Wingard and Simon Barrett."
33. Kramer, "Interview."
34. Du Coudray, " Cycle of the Werewolf," 60.
35. Este, *Women Who Run with the Wolves,* 4.
36. Twohey et al., "Weinstein Complicity Machine."
37. Creed, "Horror and the Monstrous-Feminine."
38. Fredrickson and Roberts, "Objectification Theory."
39. See, for instance, Holloway, "'One Tree Hill.'"
40. Mulvey, "Visual Pleasure and Narrative Cinema."
41. Cattani and Ferriani, "Core/Periphery Perspective."
42. See, for instance, Teal, "Harvey Weinstein Caught on Tape."
43. McRobbie, "Clubs to Companies."
44. Fredrickson and Roberts, "Objectification Theory."
45. See, for instance, Thrope, "Brave."
46. See, for instance, Dobuzinskis. "He Did All Kinds of Unpleasant Things.'
47. Kohn, "Joe Swanberg's Filmmaking Factory."
48. Working as part of a collective has been historically seen as an active and conscientious choice to disavow Hollywood structures. See, for instance, Eshun and Sagar, *Ghosts of Songs.*

# BIBLIOGRAPHY

Barrett, Simon and Adam Wingard. "We are Adam Wingard and Simon Barrett—Director and Writer of the Film The Guest. Ask Us Anything." Reddit.com. 2015. https://www.reddit.com/r/IAmA/comments/2gh1yk/we_are_adam_wingard_and_simon_barrett_director/?st=jhgh3607&sh=f326f23c

Belton, John. "Digital Cinema: A False Revolution." *October* (2002): 98–114.

Bordwell, David, Janet Staiger, and Kristin Thompson. *The Classical Hollywood Cinema: Film Style & Mode of Production to 1960.* New York: Columbia University Press, 1985.

Cattani, Gino, and Simone Ferriani. "A Core/Periphery Perspective on Individual Creative Performance: Social Networks and Cinematic Achievements in the Hollywood Film Industry." *Organization Science* 19, no. 6 (2008): 824–844.

Cherry, Brigid. "Screaming for Release: Femininity and Horror Film Fandom in Britain." In *British Horror Cinema,* 56–71. London: Routledge, 2001.

Christian, Aymar Jean. "Joe Swanberg, Intimacy, and the Digital Aesthetic." *Cinema Journal* 50, no. 4 (2011): 117–135.

Clover, Carol J. "Her Body, Himself: Gender in the Slasher Film." *Representations* 20 (1987): 187–228.

Collis, Clark. "You're Next: Mumblegore Goes Mainstream." *Entertainment Weekly*, August 17, 2013. http://ew.com/article/2013/08/17/youre-next-adam-wingard-ti-west/

Corvino, Deborah. *Amending the Abject Body: Aesthetic Makeovers in Medicine and Culture*. Albany: University of New York Press, 2004.

Creed, Barbara. "Horror and the Monstrous-Feminine: An Imaginary Abjection." In *Horror, the Film Reader*, edited by Mark Janovich, 75–84. London: Routledge, 2002.

Davis, Glyn. "The Speed of the VCR: Ti West's Slow Horror." *Screen* 59, no. 1 (2018): 41–58.

Debruge, Peter. "Interview with Joe Swanberg," *Variety*. March 5, 2008. http://variety.com/2008/music/markets-festivals/interview-with-joe-swanberg-1117981936/

Dixon, Wheeler Winston. *Death of the Moguls: The End of Classical Hollywood*. New Brunswick, NJ: Rutgers University Press, 2012.

Doane, Mary Ann. "Film and the Masquerade: Theorizing the Female Spectator." *Screen* 23, no. 3–4 (1982): 74–88.

Dobuzinskis, Alex. "He Did all Kinds of Unpleasant Things—Actor Uma Thurman Accuses Harvey Weinstein of Sexual Assault." *News North America*, April 5, 2018.

Du Coudray, Chantal. "The Cycle of the Werewolf: Romantic Ecologies of Selfhood in Popular Fantasy." *Australian Feminist Studies* 18, no. 40 (2003): 57–72.

Eisenberg, Eric. "Writer/Director Ti West Talks about Creating Atypical Horror Film The Innkeepers." *Blend*. 2012. https://www.cinemablend.com/new/Writer-Director-Ti-West-Talks-About-Creating-Atypical-Horror-Film-Innkeepers-29210.html

Eshun, Kodwo, and Anjalika Sagar. *The Ghosts of Songs: The Film Art of the Black Audio Film Collective*. Liverpool: Liverpool University Press, 2007.

Este, Clarissa Pinkola. *Women Who Run with the Wolves: Contacting the Power of the Wild Woman*. London: Rider, 1992.

Fox, Broderick. "Rethinking the Amateur." *Spectator* 24, no. 1 (2004): 65–79.

Fox, Jeremy C. and Kenneth Singletary. "Eliza Dushku Says She was Sexually Assaulted as Child During Filming." *Boston Globe*, January 13, 2018.

Fredrickson, Barbara, and Tomi-Ann Roberts. "Objectification Theory: Toward Understanding Women's Lived Experiences and Mental Health Risks." *Psychology of Women Quarterly* 21, no. 2 (1997): 173–206.

Gonzalez, Sandra, and Lisa Respers France. "Rachel McAdams, Selma Blair Accuse James Toback of Sexual Harassment." *CNN Wire Service*. October 6, 2017. https://www.cnn.com/2017/10/26/entertainment/rachel-mcadams-selma-blair-james-toback-allegations/index.html

Holloway, Daniel. "'One Tree Hill' Cast, Crew Accuse Showrunner Mark Schwahn of Sexual Harrasment." *Variety* (Online) November 13, 2017.

Jones, Candace. "Careers in Project Networks: The Case of the Film Industry." In *The Boundaryless Career: A New Employment Principle for a New Organizational Era*, edited by Michael Bernard Arthur and Denise M. Rousseau. 58–75. Oxford: Oxford University Press, 1996.

Kantor, Jodi. "Tarantino on Weinstein: 'I Knew Enough to Do More Than I Did.'" *New York Times* (Online), October 19, 2017. https://www.nytimes.com/2017/10/19/movies/tarantino-weinstein.html

Kenaga, Heidi. "Making the 'Studio Girl': The Hollywood Studio Club and Industry Regulation of Female Labour." *Film History: An International Journal* 18, no. 2 (2006): 129–139.

King, Geoff. *Indie 2.0: Change and Continuity in Contemporary American Indie Film*. London: IB Tauris, 2013.

Kohn, Eric. "Joe Swanberg's Filmmaking Factory: How the DIY Filmmaker Is Supporting a Community of Directors on the Rise." IndieWire.com, October 27, 2016. http://www.indiewire.com/2016/10/joe-swanberg-forager-films-support-indie-film-1201740588/

Kramer, Gary. "Interview: Joe Swanberg Talks Silver Bullets, Mumblecore, and More." *Slate*, October 25, 2011.

Lewis, Jon, ed. *The New American Cinema*. Durham, NC: Duke University Press, 1998.

Malone, Alicia. *Backwards and in Heels*. Miami, FL: Mango Media, 2017.

Marie, Michel. *The French New Wave: An Artistic School*. West Sussex: John Wiley & Sons, 2008.

McRobbie, A. "Clubs to Companies: Notes on the Decline of Political Culture in Speeded Up Creative Worlds." *Cultural Studies* 16, no. 4 (2002): 516–531.

Mulvey, Laura. "Visual Pleasure and Narrative Cinema." *Screen* 16, no. 3 (Autumn 1975): 6.

Murray, Gabrielle. "Hostel II: Representations of the Body in Pain and the Cinema Experience in Torture-Porn." *Jump Cut* 50 (2008): 32–37.

Newman, Michael Z. "Indie Culture: In Pursuit of the Authentic Autonomous Alternative." *Cinema Journal* 48, no. 3 (2009): 16–34.

Nicholson, Amy. "Mumblegore." *LA Weekly*, October 24, 2013. http://features.laweekly.com/mumblegore/

Nyong'O, Lupita. "Lupita Nyong'o: Speaking Out about Harvey Weinstein." *New York Times,* October 19, 2017.

Oakes, Kaya. *Slanted and Enchanted: The Evolution of Indie Culture*. Holt Paperbacks, 2009.

Ohikuare, Judith. "Screen Actors Guild Bans Work Meetings in Hotel Rooms & Homes." Refinery29.com. April 13, 2018. https://www.refinery29.com/2018/04/196337/screen-actors-guild-awards-changes-rules-for-meetings

Ortner, Sherry B. *Not Hollywood: Independent Film at the Twilight of the American Dream*. Durham, NC: Duke University Press, 2013.

Ponsoldt, James. "Good in the Sack." *Filmmaker Magazine*, Summer 2008. https://filmmakermagazine.com/archives/issues/summer2008/baghead.php

Rogers, Katie. "5 Harassment Takeaways from Ashley Judd and Times Reporters." *New York Times,* December 6, 2017.

Rosenwald, Michael. "I'll Ruin You: Judy Garland on Being Groped and Harassed by Powerful Hollywood Men." *The Washington Post,* November 14, 2017.

San Filippo, Maria. "A Cinema of Recession: Micro-Budgeting, Micro-Drama, and the 'Mumblecore' Movement." *Cineaction* (2011): 2–8.

Scott, Allen. "A New Map of Hollywood: The Production and Distribution of American Motion Pictures." *Regional Studies* 36, no. 9 (2002): 957–975.

Simpson, Nicola. "Coming Attractions: A Comparative History of the Hollywood Studio System and the Porn Business." *Historical Journal of Film, Radio and Television* 24, no. 4 (2004): 635–652.

Smith, Nigel. "Bloody Disgusting Founder and 'V/H/S' Producer Brad Miska on Why the Found Footage Movie is Here to Stay." Indiewire, January 22, 2012. http://www.indiewire.com/2012/01/bloody-disgusting-founder-and-vhs-producer-brad-miska-on-why-the-found-footage-movie-is-here-to-stay-49609/

Takal, Sophia. "Interview: Versatile Indi Actress Sophia Takal Makes Directorial Debut in 'Green.'" HollywoodChicago.com, September 5, 2012. http://www.hollywoodchicago.com/news/19793/interview-versatile-indie-actress-sophia-takal-makes-directorial-debut-in-green

Teal, Josh. "Harvey Weinstein Caught on Tape Forcing Actress to Watch Him Shower." *Unlad,* October 8, 2017.

Thorpe, Vanessa. "Brave: Rose McGowan, the Angry Voice who Pursued Hollywood's Beasts, tells Her Story." *The Guardian,* January 7, 2018.

Tudor, Andrew. "Why Horror? The Peculiar Pleasures of a Popular Genre." *Cultural Studies* 11, no. 3 (1997): 443–463.

Twohey, Megan, Jodi Kantor, Susan Dominus, Jim Rutenberg, and Steven Eder. "Weinstein Complicity Machine." *New York Times,* December 5, 2017.

Tyler, Imogen. "Against Abjection." *Feminist Theory* 10, no. 1 (2009): 77–98.

Whitney, Simon N. "Vertical Disintegration in the Motion Picture Industry." *The American Economic Review* 45, no. 2 (1955): 491–498.

Widmyer, Dennis. "Starry Eyes—A Feature Film of Paranoia and Possession." *Kickstarter,* March 2013. https://www.kickstarter.com/projects/parallacticpictures/starry-eyes-a-feature-film-of-paranoia-and-possess

*Chapter Eleven*

# Faith as Confinement
## *Alejandro Amenábar's* The Others *(2004)*
María Gil Poisa

In 2001, a movie by one of Spain's most promising young directors, Alejandro Amenábar, achieved both national recognition and international attention. A Spanish-American-French-Italian coproduction, shot in Northern Spain with a Spanish crew and an Anglo cast led by Nicole Kidman, *The Others* combined the British Gothic tradition with a skeptical Spanish vision of the Catholic faith, creating a ghost story with a clear undertone of religious criticism.

The film is set during World War II on a small British-ruled island in the English Channel. A young woman called Grace—an interesting name, given her role in the story—lives with her two young children in an enormous, isolated, labyrinthine house where they wait for the return of the father, who has gone off to war. The children, Anne and her young brother Nicholas, are photosensitive, and Grace devotes most of her life to keeping their environment safe and controlled by closing doors and windows in their path as they move through the house. She is also a devout Catholic, and has raised the children in the faith.

One day a group of servants—Ms. Mills, Mr. Tuttle, and the young mute girl Lydia—arrive at the door, saying they had worked at the house in the past, and are in need of a job. Since Grace's own servants have abandoned the family, she allows the trio to stay. From the very beginning, however, she starts to feel a strange presence in the house that, she believes, is trying to kill her children. Fearing that she is the only one who perceives the uncanny attack, Grace starts to believe that she is losing her mind, and gradually pulls the children into her delusion as well. Anne, the prepubescent daughter, also seems to be receptive to supernatural happenings and talks about the presence of a boy, Victor. She is the only one able to connect with "the others." At one point in the story, Grace enters in the room where her daughter is playing—wearing a first communion dress, the symbol of the child's voluntary acceptance of Catholicism—but when Anne turns around to look at her, the child's face is that of an old woman, who laughs at her.

During one of her panic episodes, Grace decides to walk to the nearest village and get help, but becomes lost in a foggy forest that lies beyond the house. There, she finds her husband Charles, wearing his military uniform and also confused and lost. She brings him home and they spend the night together, but the next morning he tells her that he needs to return to the front and, disregarding her pleas, leaves the house and disappears into the fog outside. Despairing over this new loss, Grace begins a new downward spiral into madness. Her refusal to face trauma impedes her from leaving the house, even as it tries to expel her family.

Meanwhile the children discover that sunlight does not actually hurt them, and leave the house for the garden, where they find an old tomb. The names carved into the stone reveal, both to them and to the audience, that the new servants are actually ghosts: the spirits of former employees who died of tuberculosis decades ago. Shortly afterward, the film reaches its climax as Grace, with the children beside her, challenges the monstrous spirits she believes are invading her home, only to discover the truth: Grace, Anne, and Nicholas are the actual ghosts. "The others," whom they perceive as haunting the house, are members of a living family who have been trying to contact them with the aid of a spiritualist medium. The moments when Anne turns into an old woman are moments when the medium succeeds, for a second, in breaking through into the sprit realm. Grace, the story reveals, went insane from isolation and solitude after her husband's death in the war and, in her insanity, killed her children and then herself, like a modern-day Medea.

## LIMINAL MONSTERS

In *The Others*, Amenábar designs a classic Gothic story but then twists the conventions of the genre, transforming a traditional Protestant/Anglo story into a rationalist distortion of a Catholic tale. Following an established tradition within the genre, he gathers well-known Gothic elements—a determined, independent heroine and an apparently haunted house—and relocates them from the typical ruined medieval castle in a superstitious and menacing Catholic country to a more contemporary setting: the mansion of a Catholic family on a small British island.[1] As in many other Gothic narratives, the house is the center of the action, but—contrary to traditional ghost stories—the invasion of the uncanny comes from inside, rather than outside, since the protagonists are revealed at the end to *be* the ghosts who are haunting the house. Gothic tales consistently treat the invaders of the house as monsters, and Grace, the heroine, ultimately finds herself forced to acknowledge that she and her children are, in fact, the monsters who are invading the house, even though the monstering process is not shown.[2]

Throughout *The Others,* the audience is encouraged to follow events only through Grace's eyes, and so to establish an identification with her.[3] The camera, which guides the spectator through the film, is always behind or ahead of the characters as they (and it) move around the house. It is never at the same level as they are, acting instead like a spy who invades the intimacy of the house. It forces the audience to feel like an invader who identifies with Grace, but still is not like her. When the film reveals that Grace is actually a ghost, this identification causes the monster to be humanized as the two figures blend. Grace and the children are monstered not because of their physicality or morality but because of their liminality—the fact that they have dragged the audience across the line separating life from death. In *The Others*, that line has already vanished, and the characters cross it without being aware they are doing so: "Ghosts are, after all, liminal entities whose existence (meaning) paradoxically asserts their nonexistence (death, nonmeaning) as well."[4] It is not that Grace rejects the loss; she has not noticed it, so for her it has not happened. It may, in fact, be her repressed trauma that envelops the house and calls the spirits of the dead servants to it.

The ghost is the classic liminal monster—one trapped between life and death. As incarnations of the memory, ghosts represent the denial of both death and eternal life. As Gillian Beer notes: "Ghosts are not the resurrection, but the insurrection of the dead"[5]—the rebellion of memory against oblivion. Ghosts, by refusing to abandon the spaces they once inhabited, claim the insides of those spaces as a personal refuge, seeking control of the space as a means of controlling their own (non-)life, but their control through possession implies a feeling of property. Walter Benjamin claims that human activity leaves a trace in objects through property—what he calls "traces of inhabitation"[6]—and the ghost reverses the dynamic by leaving a trace of the person who refuses to leave what he or she considers private property. Liminality, in this case, comes from the actions of the living, and therefore has a moral tenor: "Nonorganic locales of the murders, as buildings, corridors and rooms are impregnated with the force of the hero/heroine's fear and the victim's anguish and pain."[7] Here, the impregnation of the space takes place through violence: Grace, like a modern Medea or Llorona, kills her children, and that violence links them to the house. The film gives no explanation for the presence of the servants' ghosts, but the obvious parallel with Henry James's *The Turn of the Screw* suggests that they, too, are bound to the house by their personal stories. In both cases there is a material link between person, memory, and space. Charles Rice argues, picking up on Benjamin's idea of traces, that the process "sets up a charged and ambivalent relation between an inhabitant's objects, and the inhabitant's subjectivity."[8] In Western cultures, the tenant's subjectivity inhabits the space in the form of memories, and when an inhabitant is closely linked to a house, their ghost may refuse to leave it. The ghost *occupies*—that is, haunts—the house but it *is* not the house, as it is in some non-Western traditions like that of the Japanese. In this sense, it is interesting to note that the characters in *The Others* always perceive the place as property. They declare that "this house is ours" and that "no one will make us leave this house," both expressing clear material links with the space that are very characteristic of Western thought.

This is the case in *The Others*, where the characters possess the house in much the same way that demons—more in the Catholic imaginary than in the Protestant—are said to take possession of individuals' bodies. In the film, the ghosts possess the house and are one with the building, but the house remains its own entity. The two physically coexist, and the house beats and manipulates them: the doors attack Grace, and the curtains disappear, or so it appears to her and thus to the audience that shares her point of view. The curtains play a twofold role in the story. They are, Grace believes, the only way she has of protecting her children, but the darkness they create also hides the realities of her life from her. Once the blinds are removed, she rediscovers her house and herself, feeling vulnerable because both have been violated. From their own perspective, of course, the living inhabitants of the house feel that something similar is occurring. The events that make Grace feel invaded in her own home are the actions of the living people, who see themselves suffering, simultaneously, from the invasion of what they consider *their* own place.

The physical manifestations in the house are thus episodes in a constant confrontation between Grace and "the others" that culminates when Grace, and the audience that has been led to identify with her, actually *become* "the others." When Victor and his parents—the house's new, living owners—remove the curtains, they are opening the house not only to their own lives but also to Grace and the children's deaths. The film is about a battle for the space, in which every change made by one side necessarily affects the other, and underscores the existence of both, reinforcing the separation of the Other.

## A PRISON INSIDE: HOUSE AND MIND

Catholicism is a constant presence in *The Others*, not only in the details of its plot, but also in its overarching narrative. This presence forms the background to a discourse that questions the use of religious doctrines to achieve control.

The Catholic faith imbues the story from the very beginning. The film opens with Grace telling her children: "Now children, are you sitting comfortably? Then I'll begin," suggesting that what is going to be introduced is a fairy tale. However, the audience immediately realizes it is not a children's tale, but the Biblical tale of Genesis as the beginning and origin of everything, including this film. On one hand, the scene points out the religiosity of her character. On the other hand, the fact that Grace is introduced as the narrator through an apparently fictional children's story suggests two other points: she is not a reliable narrator (indeed, at the end we find out she has been wrong the whole time), and the story has an antireligious tone in that it implicitly compares Genesis with a fairy tale. When Grace reads the Bible to the children as if it was a fairy tale, she is in some way denying the reality of the doctrine in which she believes, just as her own presence as a ghost, even if she does not know it yet, undermines her beliefs.

The film also constantly mentions the Christian afterlife—specifically the Catholic version: heaven, hell, and limbo—yet the very existence of the characters denies that possibility; they have crossed the line between life and death, but do not know it yet—a possibility inconceivable in the Catholic worldview. The details of their postdeath world also undermine Grace's worldview. If limbo is the place for unbaptized children, and hell is for murderers (as Grace herself explains to her children), where are they? Their very presence in the house denies Catholic doctrine, which has no word or concept for the liminal space they occupy between both levels. When they must face that fact, Grace's rigid and unyielding faith shatters; her sense of certainty deserts her, and she states, "I don't know if there is even a limbo."

In reality, we can say there are two limbos in the film, neither of which is that referenced in Catholic doctrine. The first one is the spiritual, but not material, space Grace and the children occupy in the house. The film sets the audience on the side of the "I," inside the house, from the beginning, but when Grace leaves it, the spaces and the identities are reversed, and "I" becomes the Other. The second limbo is the physical space, specifically the forest, surrounding the house, which separates Grace and her family from the external-material world. The forest is a disorientating place, with no reference points and no boundaries other than the limit of the fog. It is the light at the end of the tunnel—the light that the characters must find in order to finally die. It is in the forest that the two sides approach one another, and the forest is also the place of Grace's catharsis, when she is forced to face her own nature and her crisis of faith—the crisis that invades her life and renders her monstrous.

Death is the crisis: the true invader that Grace is not aware of, and the force that turns her and the children into monsters. It is presented in the film, however, more like a cognitive act than a fact.[9] In the eyes of the audience, Grace and the children do not "die" until they—and thus the audience—realize that they are dead. Their physical state does not change with that realization, but their mental state does, and when it does they need to choose between crossing the line and remaining where they are. Their relationship with the space they inhabit does not change, but the way they relate to "the others" does. They considered the invaders to be monsters, and once they realize that they themselves are the ghosts, this classification does not change, they are already monstered.

The realization of their own monstrosity terrifies Grace, since it goes against her religious beliefs, and makes her own continued existence a denial of the doctrine at the core of her faith. This is why she is terrified of the dead, to the point of throwing away Victorian-era albums of postmortem photographs that the children find in the house. Death is a taboo in the film—a presence that the characters understand but refuse to deal with and thus cannot recognize—one that transfers its liminality from the subjects to the space, monstering the house and transforming it into an uncanny place devoid of the familiarity of life.

This transformation from a domestic space to one that no longer belongs to the inhabitant is precisely what makes a home a haunted house. Anthony Vidler notes that World War I produced such feelings of estrangement on a mass scale, leaving many Europeans feeling unsafe in their own homes.[10] For Ng, the transformation from house to haunted house is a subjective experience originating either in wishes or trauma.[11] Amenábar, by setting his story in the context of World War II, clearly ties it to the latter, evoking both the general unease captured by Vidler as well as the feeling of loved ones away at war, perhaps never to return. Over the course of the film, Grace experiences the traumatic moment, over and over, stopping her from leaving the house. Freud describes some patients' reaction to psychoanalytic therapy as hostile, and an impediment to them facing their problem: "The same struggle during the analytic treatment opposes anew the efforts to carry this unconscious thought over into consciousness. This process we felt as a resistance."[12] Grace's abandonment by her husband and murder of her children, even when she is not fully conscious of them, have left deep wounds in her psyche, permeating her mind and the interior of her personal space, the house. The domestic space she inhabits is impregnated with trauma and has thus been "de-domesticated."[13] The mansion is now a space of mourning for both the absent father and the dead protagonists.

The house is, therefore, a double of the characters: a product of the split existence born of their grief.[14] A double is an extension of the subject in the form of an alter ego. The house is the double of Grace because it has two main functions: to protect her children from light and to shield Grace herself from the external influences that can threaten her beliefs, and thus her way of life.[15] The house, as the traditional maternal symbol, protects its inhabitants and is immediately linked to Grace, who needs to fight against her own house to avoid the entrance of the light that harms the children. The haunted house is usually interpreted as a uterus, an "uncanny womb,"[16] and in this case Grace's home is the uterus where she gestates her insanity, a product of the growing religious feeling that she believes is the only protection for her family. The invasion of her house/womb by "the others" parallels her children's growing skepticism about the faith in which they are being raised, which they develop against Grace's wishes. She transfers her trauma to the house, monstering the invaders—assuming that they want to harm her children—in order to avoid facing the actual truth.

The house is a claustrophobic interior space, containing other interior spaces (basement, closets, attic) that have no connection to the exterior. Those internal spaces are created by the house itself, an exclusive parallel world for the inhabitants who control them—shelter and grave at the same time. The house seems to exist outside of time, and the servants—dead a century ago—do not seem out of place. Nothing looks anachronistic, everything remains, nothing changes, and the family cannot escape.[17] The house contains more than fifty doors, each of which—even that for the cover over the piano keys—needs to be unlocked. The family thus lives under the pressure of constantly confronting open and closed doors. The doors represent danger, but they are also the link between the worlds inside and outside the house.

The house's enormous windows also function as barriers. They are made for the light to come in, but the curtains are always closed to prevent that from happening, leaving the interior as quiet and dark as a grave: "The only thing that moves here," Grace says at one point, "is the light." Even so, the house—dark as it is—always remains lighter than the exterior, a fenced and foggy, perpetually gloomy land. Even during the day, the world immediately beyond the walls of the house stays dark and gray, and the light that comes from the exterior seems brighter in the living room than it does when any of the characters actually steps outside. The games that Grace continually plays with the light further obstruct the domestic space and contribute to the confinement of the family.

## AN IMPENETRABLE TEMPLE

The house is, for Grace, like a temple or a church: a space where she feels safe and comfortable, and a place she trusts to protect her family. It also, however, reflects the negative qualities that the film associates with the Catholic Church: immobility, repression, and patriarchy. The house cannot change because Grace does not allow it to change, just as the faith she follows does not allow the family to move or regenerate, leading to the personal and familial repression that rules her life.[18] The house is also, like the Catholic Church, governed by a system of patriarchal control.[19] Grace's power over the house is a result of Charles's absence; when he comes back, the house is not his anymore, but hers. He loses his place when he leaves, and he can only return for his farewell; he cannot stay because it is no longer his space. His homecoming, therefore, is another representation of the uncanny; the reunited family defamiliarizes the domestic space because he is no longer a part of it, even though being in control of it is his "natural" role. Like his family, he does not know he is dead until he comes back and realizes that he is there to say good-bye. Death has taken him there, but there is nothing to keep him with them.

Consistent with the extremely religious environment she has established, Grace makes an effort to protect her family from any exterior influence. The world beyond the house, she believes, can only corrupt the world she has created within. It is a world in which religion controls every aspect of their lives, and no other influence is allowed to gain a foothold. The intellectual impenetrability of the family is reflected in Grace's control of the house: light, laicism, and rationality are banned from the place. She tries to fight the children's questioning of her rules, and the presence of the servants/ghosts, whose appearance casts doubt on the nature and logic of her religion. Grace cannot, however, control everything; she cannot, for example, control the glimpses of light (symbolic of reason) that enter the house every time "the others" open the door. When Grace's final confrontation with the new tenants and the medium takes place, it happens through a door: when she opens it, she finds herself facing reason—the other side. The door serves as her first link between the two physical levels of existence, and her first contact with the medium and the possessed Anne. This is the only moment in which the spectator's point-of-view momentarily separates from Grace's and moves exclusively to the other side. It is a liminal moment—when both levels converge and there is light and reason—as well as an epiphanic moment for Grace and the children, who realize their true nature and discover together that they can expose themselves to the light.

The house, despite its hermetic quality, is a porous universe. The others, "the invaders," pass through the doors that connect the two sides, crossing the line that separates the living from the dead as Grace and her children did. This permeability is balanced, however, by their isolation, which prevents them from relating with anyone else: "The house is continually locked and fortressed against the outside. [...] Grace is caught between the world of the living and the dead, highlighting the porosity of her home."[20] The house is effectively Grace's grave—a confinement she cannot leave. She refuses to allow her children to leave it because she is simultaneously frightened of the outside and afraid to remain alone. The exterior walls of the house define the physical limits of their world, confining them in death as religion has confined them in life. The mansion is a cemetery, its dark and eerie grounds bounded by a fence that represents the absolute boundaries of their world.

The house, as the physical representation of Grace's Catholicism, simultaneously protects and imprisons her. She uses her faith—as she uses the house's doors, locks, and curtains—to protect the children, not realizing that, in doing so, she is imprisoning them and repressing their attempts to reach beyond the constraints she has imposed. The house, as a space, needs to be adapted to the needs of the children, but they cannot control it because they cannot open and close the doors by themselves. Anne and Nicholas, having never been home alone, are frightened by the prospect. They cannot be independent because they always need somebody to look after them, to open the doors and close the curtains. It is an enormous gathering of interior spaces to which only Grace has access. The control that Grace continually exercises over the family reduces the children's autonomy, and prevents them from thinking for themselves. When the children, especially Anne, question Grace's religious beliefs and controlling rules, they are punished by being made to read the Bible, making religion their penalty as well.[21]

The storage room—the setting for the pivotal scene where Grace faces the invasion and her fears—is the antithesis of the house: a small, bright, crowded space, full of covered things. It is a space of truth, with hidden uncanny presences. The first thing Grace uncovers in it is an image of Christ, symbol of the religion that isolates her and hides reality; the last thing is a mirror wherein she sees her reflection and confronts the need to face herself and the reality that she and the children are ghosts (beings often depicted as being covered by a sheet)—that *they* are "the others." The storage room embodies the mother's transferred monstrosity and offers a way out of the house that has become, for them, an impenetrable temple: sacred but oppressive.

## LINKING "THE OTHERS"

The house is, throughout the film, a space of conflict between Grace and "the others": the place that she is linked to and "the others" invade. Grace is not a link but a shield, rejecting any attempts at contact by the others, who challenge her religious perception of life. The children, more receptive to the others' presence because of their open-minded questioning (rather than rigid acceptance) of religion, are the channel between worlds that Grace, blinded by her faith, cannot be. Anne is thus the one who can connect with the others, who tries to find the truth, and who tries to jump out of the window—the source of light (and reason)—to escape from Grace's strict limits.[22] Anne's escape is the only time the children leave the house in search of the truth. Facing the cemetery, they experience their own cathartic moment without crossing the fence. The house has, for Anne, been like the cavern in Plato's "allegory of the cave": a world of misleading shadows cast by their mother's faith, which they accept because they have never been given an alternative. Once they escape from its confinement, they are free to face the truth and challenge the imposed beliefs that once limited and channeled their minds.

Grace's own moment of catharsis arrives when she tries to leave the house and finds that she cannot. Her world becomes a maze that reflects her own liminal state because, lost in the fog, she is neither inside nor outside the house: The fog won't let her go any farther, she realizes, and at that moment, she is forced to face herself. It is a transitional moment, when the "dialectic inside vs. outside, I vs. the others" is established.[23] When she crosses the fence for the first time, leaving the limits, the camera is set at an extreme high angle, almost a bird's-eye view, that observes and follows her from above, like a god judging, but not stopping or punishing, her. She has been abandoned by her own God: a foreshadowing of the film's ending, when she will be forced to abandon her beliefs. As she crosses the fence, she is crossing her faith boundaries as well. When, at the end of the film, the family is finally free—when there is no fog and they can leave the house—they remain trapped because they have nowhere else to go. Then they discover, at this moment, that there is no judgment for their souls, and that neither heaven nor hell awaits them.

That discovery triggers an identity crisis for Grace, who now understands that—although there is an afterlife—it is not the Christian afterlife in which she fervently believes. There are ghosts, she herself *is* a ghost, and therefore there is no God and no heaven as she understands them. The solid foundations of her life vanish, like fog, along with the certainty of Catholic doctrine. The ghostly life in which Grace finds herself is a distortion of the wished-for eternal life her faith had led her to expect. She has been dragged into this new, strange, unwanted life by her own home, her space. The house, haunted by the family, is the materialization of their monstrosity, and their personal transformation modifies that space: monstering it through invasion and, at the same time, forcing them to face a reality they have always wanted to ignore: They themselves are monsters in the eyes of the living. They are the others.

## NOTES

1. Oakes, "Ghosts in the Machine," 7.
2. Jordan, "Alejandro Amenábar and Contemporary Spanish Horror," 148.
3. It is, however, an independent though slanted narrative; sometimes the spectator learns things that she does not know, as when the graveyard is discovered by the camera but not the character.
4. Ng, *Women and Domestic Space*, 168.
5. Quoted in Ng, *Women*, 166.
6. Benjamin, "Paris, the Capital of the Nineteenth Century," 9.
7. Powell, "A Touch of Horror," 175.
8. Rice, "Rethinking Histories of the Interior," 279.
9. Briefel, "What Some Ghosts Don't Know," 97.
10. Vidler, *Architectural Uncanny*, 7.
11. Ng, *Women and Domestic Space*, 11.
12. Freud, "Resistance and Supression," 254–255.
13. Ibid., 158.
14. Ibid., 149.
15. It is interesting to think of the meaning of Grace's name. According to the *Oxford English Dictionary*, "grace" is "(in Christian belief) the free and unmerited favour of God, as manifested in the salvation of sinners and the bestowal of blessings."
16. Creed, *Phallic Panic*, xiii.
17. This is also the reason why the space itself is a temporal limbo and the servants, despite being ghosts, cannot go through closed doors; they are in the phantom space to which they belong, the postlife one.
18. In "Resistance and Suppression," Freud describes the repression case of a patient that is comparable to Grace's: "Instead of recalling, he actually goes again through the attitudes and emotions of his previous life which, by means of the so-called 'transference,' can be utilized as resistances to the physician and the treatment" (251).
19. Giral and Ibáñez Rosales, "Otherness," 279.
20. England, *Breached Bodies*, 359–360.
21. Aviva Briefel ("What Ghosts Don't Know," 103) reads Grace as a Catholic figure through her frigidity, the religious woman who rejects her own body and sexuality.
22. When Anne realizes that the servants are dead, she tells Nicholas: "Don't talk to them, they're dead," something that her mother would have never accepted so easily.
23. Imbert, *Cine e imaginarios sociales*, 535.

## BIBLIOGRAPHY

Allmer, Patricia, Emily Brick, and David Huxley, eds. *European Nightmares: Horror Cinema in Europe since 1945*. New York: Wallflower, 2012.

Benjamin, Walter. "Paris, the Capital of the Nineteenth Century." In *The Arcades Project*, 3–14. 1935. Cambridge, MA: Belknap Press of Harvard University Press, 1999.

Briefel, Aviva. "What Some Ghosts Don't Know: Spectral Incognizance and the Horror Film." *Narrative* 1 (2009): 95–110.

Creed, Barbara. *Phallic Panic: Film, Horror and the Primal Uncanny*. Carlton, VIC: Melbourne University Press, 2005.

England, Marcia. "Breached Bodies and Home Invasions: Horrific Representations of the Feminized Body and Home." *Gender, Place & Culture* 13, no. 4 (2006): 353–363.

Freud, Sigmund. "Resistance and Suppression." In *A General Introduction to Psychoanalysis*, 248–261. 1920. New York: Horace Liveright, 2015.

Giral, Anabel Altemir, and Ismael Ibáñez Rosales. "Otherness in *The Others*: Haunting the Catholic Other, Humanizing the Self." In *Roman Catholicism in Fantastic Film: Essays on Belief, Spectacle, Ritual and Imagery*, edited by Regina Hansen, 275–289. Jefferson, NC: McFarland, 2011.

Imbert, Gérard. *Cine e imaginarios sociales: El cine posmoderno como experiencia de los límites (1990–2010)*. Madrid: Cátedra, 2010.

Jordan, Barry. "Alejandro Amenábar and Contemporary Spanish Horror." In Allmer, Brick, and Huxley, eds., *European Nightmares*, 141–151.

Ng, Andrew Hock-Soon. *Women and Domestic Space in Contemporary Gothic Narratives: The House as Subject*. New York: Palgrave Macmillan, 2015.

Oakes, David A. "Ghosts in the Machines: The Haunted Castle in the Works of Stephen King and Clive Barker." *Studies in Weird Fiction* 24 (1999): 25–33.

*The Others (Los otros)*. Directed by Alejandro Amenábar. 2001.

Powell, Anna. "A Touch of Horror: Dario Argento and Deleuze's Cinematic Sensorium." In Allmer, Brick, and Huxley, eds., *European Nightmares*, 167–177.

Rice, Charles. "Rethinking Histories of the Interior." *Journal of Architecture* 9, no. 3 (2004): 275–287.

Vidler, Anthony. *The Architectural Uncanny: Essays in the Modern Unhomely*. Cambridge, MA: MIT Press, 1992.

*Part IV*

# HISTORY NEVER DIES

*Chapter Twelve*

# The Pursuit of Certainty

## *Legends and Local Knowledge in* Candyman

### Cynthia J. Miller

"You are not content with the stories, so I was obliged to come." In 1890, legend has it, the love of a black man for a white woman brought about horrific destruction; a century later, as the cautionary tales of death and dismemberment accompanying his fate are dismissed as "modern oral folklore," the horror reemerges. Fear—the driving force behind the lore—must be sustained, or its lesson will be lost.

In 1992, Bernard Rose's film *Candyman* reminded audiences that the tale's lesson continued to be relevant, and that desire across racial boundaries was still something to be feared. Weaving together horrors of the past and horrors of the present, the film tells the story of Helen Lyle (Virginia Madsen), a beautiful but reckless PhD student studying urban legends in the housing projects of Chicago. When Helen investigates a series of murders in the Cabrini-Green project, she learns the story of Candyman, a supernatural figure credited with the killings, and spreads the disbelief that brings about his reappearance. When the powerful, mesmerizing figure appears to her, Helen finds herself unable to resist. As those around her begin to die, her marriage, her sanity, and her life all hang in the balance and are ultimately forfeit, until she is revealed to be the reincarnation of the woman whose love caused him to be mutilated, tortured, and burned to death.

On the surface, this late-twentieth-century film presents a clear cautionary tale about the intermingling of race, gender, class, and violence. Moral messages about interracial coupling are upcycled from the Civil War era to the audience's present day, using a contemporary form of the Bloody Mary myth as their vehicle. As the literature demonstrates, the cinematic telling—and subsequent critical and box office success—of *Candyman*, regardless of the setting and plot points, signals the continued relevance of racist interdictions about the disastrous consequences of interracial romance, suggesting that, at the cultural level, less progressive social change may have occurred in the hundred years between the life of the Candyman and the lives of the film's audiences than we might think. In a way similar to other oral forms of storytelling, urban legends such as this are highly plastic tales that rely on the deep cultural truth of their narrative message, rather than specific details of a given iteration, endowing them with a timeless significance that is easily recognized.

Approaching the tale from a different perspective, however, we see that *Candyman* is also a story about the cultural and social force of what Wendy James has termed "the pursuit of certainty"—claims to knowledge about identities, histories, and events—as well as the social and cultural consequences that result when certainty is challenged, or its claims are perceived to be ideologically threatening.[1] This chapter argues that the film highlights the vital role played by certainty in the everyday lives of its characters, and that the figure of the Candyman is, in both the narrative's past and present, a manifestation of competing claims to certainty in an uncertain world.

## CRISIS, CONFLICT, AND CATASTROPHE

Loosely based on Clive Barker's short story "The Forbidden," *Candyman* presents a horrifying collision of class, race, and gender that has been drawing scholarly attention since its release. At the outset, the main narrative, set in a university, makes clear that a sharp divide of knowledge, resources, authority, and power inheres within the confines of the school as well as in the city beyond its campus. This dynamic is one that is familiar to most who have experienced, or even simply read about, urban universities. Articles such as *The Atlantic*'s "Should Urban Universities Help Their Neighbors" and *The Chronicle of Higher Education*'s "How to Market a College in a Troubled Locale" have been exploring this issue for decades, as prestigious institutions of higher education, such as New York University, Yale, University of Detroit, Princeton, UCLA, the University of Chicago, and countless others have historically stood as islands of both affluence and influence in the midst of great need.[2] The narrative focus on anthropology and folklore—two fields that have traditionally featured Caucasian researchers advancing their careers by studying the lifeways, stories, and beliefs of their cultural Others—only accentuates this divide. The faculty and students who initially set the stage for this horror tale are white, and appear confident, relaxed, and ambitious, while the service staff is comprised of hard-laboring, congenial, but cautious workers who are black. The stage for tension in certainty is already set. Helen, along with her friend and research partner Bernadette (Kasi Lemmons), is embarking on a project interviewing freshmen about urban legends—shared frames of reference about fantastic tales of blind, albino alligators living in the sewers or babysitters who roast their infant charges in the oven, and a murderous figure known as the Candyman who, much like Bloody Mary, is conjured by repeating his name five times while looking in the mirror. This is modern oral folklore, Helen's husband Trevor (Xander Berkeley) tells his freshman class: "the unselfconscious reflection of the fears of urban society." Some researchers such as Jan Brunvand, Gary Alan Fine, Michelle Hall, and others have argued that legends like these succeed because they provide insightful social commentary about the cultural or economic context.[3] Others, such as Alan Dundes, have suggested that it is shared psychology that drives their persistence, while still others point to their ability to tap into shared emotional states.[4] The pursuit of certainty maps across all these explanations, drawing together social norms, culture, psychology, emotion, economics, and so much more, as individuals navigate the waters of their daily lives and identities. Whether urban legends provide practical or moral information, increase social capital, or address anxieties, they provide some degree of comfort or reassurance in an uncertain world.

As the film illustrates, though, not all uncertainty is created equal, and some worlds are more uncertain than others. Trevor's lecture on the nature of these tales taints Helen and Bernadette's research pool. As a dismayed Helen transcribes her notes, now rendered pointless, however, Kitty (Sarina C. Grant), a member of the custodial staff, overhears the mention of Candyman and affirms her knowledge of his existence. He is, she relates, a bogeyman credited with committing a series of grisly murders in the nearby housing project known as Cabrini-Green. She questions the woman:

Helen: What have you heard?

Kitty: Everybody's scared of him once it get dark. He live over at Cabrini—my friend told me about him.

Helen: Cabrini-Green?

Kitty: Yeah, in the projects. I live on the South Side, so I don't know much about it, but my friend she know all about it. Her cousin live at Cabrini.

When the woman summons her friend Henrietta (Barbara Alston) to tell her story to Helen, she relates that the most recent Cabrini death was that of a young woman named Ruthie Jean. It was reported that Ruthie Jean heard "banging and smashing" and called the police, terrified, claiming that someone was "coming through the walls." Her story was met with disbelief, and she called again, begging for help. When the police finally arrived, Ruthie Jean was dead, her torso sliced open with a large hook.

Henrietta's tale, a classic friend-of-a-friend story, explicitly draws together class, race, violence, and irrationality, as it sets up a visible dichotomy between the well-to-do PhD student and her working-class counterpart. The story frames Cabrini-Green—one of Chicago's many low-income housing sites—as part of a racialized underworld, safely set apart from more affluent white communities; a "geography of evil" where this recent murder is only the most visible offense. As Sorcha Ni Fhlainn points out, the black community of the film is firmly placed in a "ghettoized space" where it can be "collectively ignored by those unaffected by poverty," such as Helen and her colleagues.[5] When, early in the film, Helen realizes from an old newspaper photo that her own condominium building was initially constructed as low-income housing, and once even resembled Cabrini-Green, she quickly sees that it was converted to its current upscale status because there was no "natural barrier" between it and Chicago's "Gold Coast," an affluent neighborhood bordering on Lake Michigan defined by stately old homes and upscale shopping. The "El" tracks and the highway, however, stood between the historic area and Cabrini-Green, creating a barrier that isolated the housing project and poverty from the rest of the city, and placed its residents socially "beyond" the mainstream community.

Cabrini-Green's troubles, however, go much deeper. We learn that the projects stand on the site of a historic tragedy. Professor Philip Purcell (Michael Culkin), a folklorist in Helen's department, provides Helen with the story of Daniel Robitaille—a black artist, murdered for his romance with a white woman—which first appeared in 1890:

> Candyman was the son of a slave. His father had amassed a considerable fortune from designing a device for the mass-producing of shoes after the Civil War. Candyman had been sent to the best schools and had grown up in polite society. He had a prodigious talent as an artist and was much sought after when it came to the documenting of one's wealth and position in society in a portrait. It was in this latter capacity that he was commissioned by a wealthy landowner to capture his daughter's virginal beauty. Well, of course, they fell deeply in love, and she became pregnant. Hmm . . . poor Candyman. The father executed a terrible revenge. He paid a pack of brutal hooligans to do the deed. They chased Candyman through the town to Cabrini-Green, where they proceeded to saw off his right hand with a rusty blade. No one came to his aid. But this was just the beginning of his ordeal. Nearby there was an apiary. Dozens of hives, filled with hungry bees. They smashed the hives and stole the honeycomb . . . and smeared it over his prone, naked body. Candyman was stung to death by the bees. They burned his body on a giant pyre and then scattered his ashes over Cabrini-Green.

Cabrini, it would seem, is cursed with the angry, tortured soul of the murdered artist, who now lashes out at the living. The invocation of these stories about the Candyman in the face of murder among the disenfranchised speaks to what Fredrick Koenig calls "Three C's—crisis, conflict, and catastrophe"—events that lead to extreme emotional arousal, which in turn generate contemporary urban legends as explanatory devices and coping mechanisms.[6]

While the residents of Cabrini-Green believe that Candyman is responsible for the murder of Ruthie Jean and many others, the media attributes them to the work of a serial killer still at-large ("Death Toll 21" as one headline reported). As Helen researches the events of this most recent slaying, newspaper headlines make clear the connection between poverty and violent death: "What Killed Ruthie-Jean? Life in the Projects." Bernadette concurs: "I won't even drive by that place." Helen relates the legend of Candyman and his summoning, and the two begin the required five recitations of his name in the mirror, but Bernadette stops at four, unwilling to tempt fate. When she leaves the room, however, Helen finishes the cycle, switches off the light, and the intertwining of real and supernatural horrors begins.

## CERTAINTY AND IDENTITY

Helen is convinced that the story of Ruthie Jean's death and the Candyman are the sort of urban legend artifacts that will propel her and Bernadette to

*Helen (Virginia Madsen) and Bernadette (Kasi Lemmons) enter the world of Cabrini-Green in* Candyman.

scholarly acclaim. She attempts to convince her fearful (and defensively armed) friend that the project is too enticing to walk away from, arguing for the significance of circumstances where "an entire community starts attributing the daily horrors of their lives to a mythical figure," and Bernadette concedes.

As the two women venture into the dim interior of the housing project to investigate, it seems that every inch of wall is covered beneath layers of graffiti. The dark recesses of the staircase they use to avoid being accosted by a group of young thugs are filled with the stench of decay. When they finally arrive at Ruthie Jean's former apartment, it bears no resemblance to a dwelling place, full of dried blood and filth. Helen removes the bathroom medicine chest to reveal a gaping hole, leading directly into the apartment next door; she crawls through, and discovers a shrine to Candyman, apparently created by fearful residents of the building. Viewers see, long before she does, that a mural of the deadly figure has been painted around the hole, and she is emerging from its mouth. Here, in Candyman's lair, finding an offering of candy containing razorblades, she is momentarily overcome, and viewers are left to wonder about the psychic connection that the two now share.

This surreal moment, however, quickly passes, and the focus shifts back to the project's harsh realities as Helen returns to Bernadette and the two meet Anne-Marie, a young African American mother who lives down the hall with her baby Anthony, who harshly reminds her that she doesn't belong there: "You know whites don't never come here, 'cept to cause us a problem." When Helen, painfully unaware of her arrogance, replies that she is "doing a study," Anne-Marie retorts: "What you gon' study? That we bad? Hmm? We steal? We gang-bang? We all on drugs, right? We ain't all like them assholes downstairs, you know."

This exchange is, perhaps, the most explicit marker of the film's commentary on racism, and once the lines are uttered, the narrative focus shifts, temporarily, to the two women's shared humanity, rather than their differences. Helen begins to develop relationships with Anne-Marie and young Jake (Dejuan Guy) who helps her explore further, but this entrée into the world of the projects emboldens her and both real and supernatural horrors escalate. After Helen is brutally beaten by a gang leader who uses Candyman's identity to enhance his reputation, Jake fears that he will be Candyman's next target. Helen tries to reassure him that the thug who beat her was of flesh-and-blood and now behind bars, and that the mythical Candyman he fears isn't real—that the crimes were committed by a bad man using his name. The scene closes with a close-up of the confused little boy, quietly questioning "He's not real?"

This brief, understated scene is the pivotal moment of the film: a confrontation of knowledge systems. For young Jake, a belief in Candyman is a natural

*Helen (Virginia Madsen) begins to develop a relationship with young Jake (DeJuan Guy) in* Candyman.

and taken-for-granted part of his everyday existence. Helen asserts her reality—her belief in what appear to be objective facts—over that of the boy, sowing seeds of doubt in a member of the Cabrini-Green community. Even more significantly, Jake is not just *any* resident of the projects, he is the next generation; the generation that will carry the legend forward or abandon it in favor of other explanatory devices. His belief in—and certainty about—the essential truth of the legend of the Candyman is vital to the continuity of the culture of his community. It is, in Wendy James's terms, part of his "local self-knowledge"—part of his identity as a resident of Cabrini-Green.[7] If we understand "culture" to be a constellation of learned, shared ideas about behavior and the workings of the world, then the production and transmission of this local knowledge and place-based identity is critical to the culture of Cabrini-Green as an autonomous community.[8] James argues:

> The wider range of cultural practice, imagery and representation . . . are the new defining images of ethnic, cultural and national authenticity as a universal fount of singular self-knowledge and a justification for the oppositional classification of others.[9]

The confusion in Jake's eyes when he hears Helen's reassurances that the Candyman is not, in fact, real signals a shift in the young boy's understandings of the monstrous figure's status as "natural" and taken for granted. Questions emerge; and questions breed doubt; doubt signals loss of certainty; and lacking certainty, solidarity, identities, and worldviews can unhinge. Certainty is not, as James continues, "the equivalent of truth," but

> In fusing, as it may, emotion and intellect, language and action, the abstractions of ideology and the concreteness of [material] claims can certainly be morally and politically threatening.[10]

In this case, the risk is significant: that of a young, black boy raised in the projects, losing certainty about an element of his community's shared culture and adopting the perceived "truth" of a privileged, white outsider. As an isolated instance, such a shift might simply create conflict; writ large, however, this is the face of assimilation.

So, Candyman becomes manifest. The horrors, which should logically abate, thus intensify, instead, with an increasingly unstable Helen at the center. Candyman (Tony Todd) finally appears to her in a parking garage, calling her by name and asserting "I came for you." Elegant and seductive, yet the embodiment of abject black masculinity, Candyman is a stereotypical focal point for monstrosity.[11] As film critic Judith Halberstam observes, "[m]onstrosity, in this tired narrative, never becomes mobile; rather it remains anchored by the weight of racist narratives."[12] Mesmerized and unable to resist, Helen allows him to approach. A powerful figure in contrast to her slight frame, he moves closer, and continues: "You were not content with the stories, so I was obliged to come." He pins her against her car, and murmurs a soft command: "Be my victim." As Diane Hoeveler observes, the young woman responds "with a gaze in which we see a merging of willingness and fear, desire and loathing."[13] This encounter marks the beginning of a powerful sense of erotic terror that accompanies the monstrous figure's presence throughout the film.

Helen loses consciousness and awakens in Anne-Marie's apartment, only to find that she has become *part* of the stories, laying in a pool of blood, as agonizing screams fill the air. Anne-Marie's dog has been decapitated, and baby Anthony is missing, his crib stained crimson. Helen, who picked up the cleaver used to kill the dog to defend herself before investigating Anne-Marie's cries, is arrested and jailed. Once she is released on bail, the monstrous figure and his horrors return, this time claiming Bernadette and again implicating Helen, who is now committed to a psychiatric institution.

Here, it is Helen's certainty that comes into question. She begins to doubt her sanity, her senses, and all that she knows as "truth." Her belief that she could not possibly murder is shaken by the absence of memory. Could she truly be evil? Candyman appears in her isolated room, looming over her hospital bed as she struggles to free herself from her restraints, and screams for help: "He's here! He's under the bed!" He further erodes her confidence in herself and the moral order, asking "What do the good know, except what the bad teach them by their excesses?" Not long after his appearance, she is confronted with another set of competing knowledge claims: evidence of the institutional "truth" about her experiences. When her doctor shows her a surveillance tape of these moments, she stares in disbelief at images that show her completely alone in the room, apparently in the midst of a psychotic episode. Helen's reliability as a narrator is formally called into question here. Are her knowledge-claims valid? Adopted from a divergent cultural worldview—that of her cultural Others—they have already been summarily rejected by the characters in Helen's own social world. In this moment, both she and the film's viewers grow increasingly uncertain about the existence of a monster that may not exist outside of Helen's fantasies.[14]

## RUMOR AND REBIRTH

Numerous scholars have pointed to the film's clear moral message about miscegenation, inherent in the tension between Candyman and Helen. As Pinedo asks,

> What does it mean when the genre violates conventions by locating violence in the city where it is most expected, and furthermore plays openly on prevailing cultural anxieties by marking the monster as a racial Other?[15]

While Candyman (in life, a well-educated, genteel artist) is a monster clearly created by society and then vilified for the result, Robin Means Coleman observes that the film avoids framing Candyman as the tragic—and sympathetic—figure he might otherwise be by "playing on fears of the big Black boogeyman coming in and taking away a White woman."[16] This, as Jessica Baker Kee points out, creates a highly complex character, positioned as both victim and monster.[17] A sensual, compelling, yet grotesque figure, Candyman unmistakably seduces an unwilling but powerless Helen, using what producer Alan Poul has described as "very loaded imagery," much drawn from Barker's source manuscript.[18] When the two finally kiss on screen, it is made horrifying by imagery of bees pouring forth from the monster's mouth into Helen's, simultaneously suggesting penetration and pollution. As Pinedo notes, this moment of body horror is used "to undermine the acceptability of interracial romance."[19] In Barker's story, however, the scene is even more powerful, recalling the erotic tension filling the film's parking garage scene:

> And she was almost enchanted. By his voice, by his colours, by the buzz from his body. She fought to resist the rapture, though. There was a monster here, beneath this fetching display; its nest of razors was at her feet, still drenched in blood.[20]

In truth, however, what Candyman really desires is not Helen's body so much as her belief—to be made "real" and vested with power by reframing her knowledge base. He continually asks her "Do you believe?," urging her to cast aside both her cultural upbringing and her academic training to accept and endorse his existence. He tempts her with a subtle version of immortality, assuring her that if she were to be slaughtered as yet another of his infamous victims, she would live forever as part of his legend. Helen, however, resists what she recognizes as a seduction, and retorts that she would "prefer to be forgotten than [to] be remembered like that." He punishes her for eroding the Cabrini-Green community's certainty about him by menacing and murdering those for whom she cares—making an example of them—and confesses: "Your disbelief destroyed the faith of my congregation. Without them, I am nothing."

Candyman's dark attempts to win Helen display a deep understanding of the cultural and psychological work of urban legends, highlighting the ability of the unknown to effortlessly elicit fear and wield power:

> Why do you want to live? If you had learned just a little from me, you would not beg to live. I am rumor. It is a blessed condition, believe me. To be whispered about at street corners. To live in other people's dreams, but not to have to be. Do you understand?

He promises her an eternity to which few aspire, and yet, his words convey the complexity of overpowering horror—the rush of emotion that characterizes both terror and ecstasy: "Your death will be a tale to frighten children, to make lovers cling closer in their rapture. Come with me and be immortal." Gregory Kershner writes about this menacing, yet compelling, quality of Gothic horror to "unite the poles of life and death, being and nothingness, fullness and emptiness. . . . They are dissolved like subject and object in the insensible totality of darkness. . . . The totality of nonexistence."[21] Candyman offers Helen the ecstasy of an agonizing, intimate death that will lead to the unimaginable power that comes of being legend and rumor—the ability to be everywhere, and nowhere; all things, and nothing.

In the film's climax, after a month of drug-addled institutionalization, Helen summons Candyman in order to prove to his existence. He brutally eviscerates her doctor, breaks her restraints, and hurls himself through a window, once again leaving her to take the blame. Helen, however, escapes. She returns home to find that her philandering husband has already moved one of his beautiful young students into their home. This last vestige of her life gone, Helen goes to find Candyman, submit to him, and end her torment. The two make a deal, trading her life for that of baby Anthony, but Candyman reneges and vanishes with the infant, ultimately placing him inside a pyre being prepared for a community bonfire. Using a hook much like Candyman's, Helen clambers into the rubble, and struggles against the ghoulish figure to save the baby. Impaling him with a flaming stake, she succeeds, and crawls from the blaze with the infant in her outstretched arms, but quickly succumbs from her own massive burns. In the chaos, only young Jake spies the flaming form of Candyman amidst the burning pyre.

Helen's sacrifice, however, embeds her in both the real and mythic histories of Cabrini-Green. Her graveside funeral is essentially unattended, until the residents of the housing project appear, dressed in black, walking single-file across the cemetery with Jake, Anne-Marie, and baby Anthony in the lead. Jake tosses Candyman's hook into the grave in tribute, and the procession departs. The scene cuts to sometime later, as a distraught Trevor, wracked with guilt over his affair and his wife's fate, looks in the bathroom mirror and laments "Helen . . . Helen . . . oh, Helen." At the fifth utterance of her name, she appears like a vengeful wraith, wielding Candyman's hook. Hearing his agonized cries, his girlfriend runs down the hallway and opens the bathroom door to find Trevor's mutilated body lying in a pool of blood.

The film's closing images gradually fill the screen with a mural on the wall of an abandoned apartment in Cabrini-Green. It is an image of Helen, clothed in her white burial shroud with arms outstretched, flowing blonde locks ablaze, rising up from a bonfire's flames. The visual narrative gives testimony to her triumph over evil, and her place in the lore of the projects. Her mythic status affirms that the community has duly processed and informally commemorated the events that saved baby Anthony, but it also does a good

Jake (DeJuan Guy), Anne-Marie (Vanessa A. Williams), and baby Anthony pay tribute at Helen's funeral in Candyman, dropping the defeated Candyman's hook in her grave.

bit more. Helen, herself, has become the stuff of contemporary urban legend, joining the Candyman in the lore of the community.

Are Candyman and Helen now supernatural reincarnations of a tragic interracial love story, as his intonations of "It was always you, Helen" suggest? Is the monstrous figure a product of her own fractured psyche? Are the murders at Cabrini-Green the work of a flesh-and-blood killer, rather than a vengeful specter? Ultimately, the "truth" behind these questions matters very little in the world of the film, at least in terms of objective knowledge of reality. As philosopher Ludwig Wittgenstein wrote, "The difference between the concept of 'knowing' and 'being certain' isn't of any great importance, except where 'I know' is meant to mean 'I *can't* be wrong.'"[22] Of far greater significance here is the struggle for social and cultural power behind the competing truth-claims—the pursuit of certainty.

The struggle for the ability to define the way individuals experience the world moves the narrative, from start to finish. The steadfast belief in the Candyman by black, impoverished residents of the projects is deemed "superstitious" and "ignorant" by the wider, more affluent society, and his story labeled "contemporary urban myth" worthy of study by white (or "whitened") members of the university community; the experience of his presence deemed "psychotic" by the medical community. At the film's outset, each of these communities is living their own truth, framed by a range of explanatory devices and evidence. Each embraces those notions of truth as part of their learned, shared ideas about the workings of the world, and none require, or create space for, complementary perspectives. The horror, then, happens when the boundaries between those worlds become permeable—when competing claims to certainty attempt to occupy the same cultural space—and characters must grapple with counterviews and contradictions.

The story is told through Helen's eyes, and so, privileges a particular academic worldview, right from the outset. She intrudes upon the world of Cabrini-Green with unflagging certainty in the nature and function of urban legends, and in an extended act of scholarly hubris, asserts the authority of her own knowledge claims, even as she expresses a desire to learn from the project's residents. She is then chided (in a way equivalent to sanction) by her husband and Professor Purcell for seeming to soften and give the slightest glimmer of credence to their tales. However, as contact between the respective cultures continues, the waters muddy: unexplained occurrences continue, fear mounts, relationships evolve, claims to certainty are shaken, and positions shift. Jake's belief falters, and Helen's grows, causing her to be vilified and rejected by those whose worldview she once shared. Knowledge, power, and social discipline are all drawn into question in ways that appear to be straightforward issues of race, class, or gender, but are, in fact, far more nuanced and broadreaching. On the surface, the film presents a straightforward, multilayered cautionary tale about racism, miscegenation, poverty, and privilege, but each of these elements points to larger systems of knowledge and social identity in tension. As Fred Botting argues, rather than endorsing or explicitly challenging the racist and sexist stereotypes that fuel its horror, the film "presents them as representations, as projections to be interrogated, and highlights the role of representation in generating fear and maintaining social tensions."[23]

*Candyman* thus suggests, following Kee, that "the ultimate frontier of abjection is not the existence of Othered identities within the exclusionary social matrix, but a corruption of the boundaries of identity itself by unknowable and unbearable affects of difference."[24] So, by the film's end, we see Helen, completely existentially transformed. Losing all of the certainty granted by her privileged, white academic worldview, her orientation—and her identity—fully shifts to align with that of the residents of Cabrini-Green. She acknowledges her belief in the Candyman, and then sacrifices her life to save baby Anthony from the blaze. Burned almost beyond recognition, she is dead to her former life and her former worldview—perhaps even narratively punished for her disavowal of its knowledge-claims—yet lives on for eternity as a darkly heroic and terrifying figure in the lore of a new community that acknowledges her truth, in ways that her former world never will.

## NOTES

1. James, *Pursuit of Certainty*.
2. Gardener, "How to Market a College"; Semuels, "Should Urban Universities Help Their Neighbors?"
3. See, for example, Brunvand, *Vanishing Hitchhiker*; Fine, "Kentucky Fried Rat"; and Hall, "Great Cabbage Hoax."
4. Dundes, "On the Psychology of Legend," 21–36.
5. Ni Fhlainn, "Sweet, Bloody Vengeance," 187.
6. Koenig, *Rumor in the Marketplace*.
7. James, *Pursuit of Certainty*, 3.
8. Heider, *Ethnographic Film*.
9. James, *Pursuit of Certainty*, 4.
10. Ibid.
11. Kaplan, *Looking for the Other*.
12. Halberstam, *Skin Shows*, 5.
13. Hoeveler, " Postfeminist Filmic Female Gothic Detective," 2.
14. Kuhn, "'What's the matter, Trevor? Scared of something?'"
15. Pinedo, *Recreational Terror*, 112–113.
16. Coleman, *Horror Noire,* 189.

17. Kee, "Black Masculinities and Postmodern Horror," 52.
18. Ibid., 190.
19. Pinedo, *Recreational Terror*, 131.
20. Barker, "The Forbidden," 243.
21. Kershner, "Horror and Eroticism."
22. Wittgenstein, *On Certainty*, 3e.
23. Botting, *Limits of Horror*, 72.
24. Kee, "Black Masculinities and Postmodern Horror," 53.

# BIBLIOGRAPHY

Barker, Clive. "The Forbidden." *Books of Blood*, 227–246. www.clivebarker.com/html/visions/bib/book/books/barker.pdf

Botting, Fred. *Limits of Horror: Technology, Bodies, Gothic*. Manchester, UK: Manchester University Press, 2008.

Brunvand, Jan. *The Vanishing Hitchhiker: American Urban Legends and Their Meanings*. New York: Norton, 1981.

Coleman, Robin Means. *Horror Noire: Blacks in American Horror Films from the 1890s to the Present*. New York: Routledge, 2011.

Dundes, Alan. "On the Psychology of Legend." In *American Folk Legend: A Symposium*, edited by Wayland D. Hand, 21–36. Berkeley & Los Angeles: University of California Press, 1971.

Fine, Gary Alan. "The Kentucky Fried Rat: Legends and Modern Society." *Journal of the Folklore Institute* 17, no. 2–3 (1980): 222–243.

Gardner, Lee. "How to Market a College in a Troubled Locale." *The Chronicle of Higher Education*. January 1, 2018. https://www.chronicle.com/article/How-to-Market-a-College-in-a/242130

Halberstam, Judith. *Skin Shows: Gothic Horror and the Technology of Monsters*. Durham, NC: Duke University Press, 1995.

Hall, Michelle. "The Great Cabbage Hoax: A Case Study." *Journal of Personality and Social Psychology* 2, no. 4 (1965): 563–569.

Heider, Karl G. *Ethnographic Film*. Austin: University of Texas Press, 2006.

Hoelever, Diane Long. "The Postfeminist Filmic Female Gothic Detective: Reading the Bodily Text in *Candyman*." In *Postfeminist Gothic: Critical Interventions in Contemporary Culture*, edited by Benjamin A. Brabon and Stephanie Genz, 99–113. Basingstoke, UK: Palgrave-Macmillan, 2007.

James, Wendy, ed. *The Pursuit of Certainty*. London: Routledge, 1995.

Kaplan, E. Ann. *Looking for the Other: Feminism, Film and the Imperial Gaze*. New York: Routledge, 2012.

Kee, Jessica Baker. "Black Masculinities and Postmodern Horror: Race, Gender, and Abjection." *Visual Culture & Gender* 10 (2015): 47–56.

Kershner, "Horror and Eroticism: Bram Stoker's Dracula." *Hofstra Horizons*, 2006. https://news.hofstra.edu/2006/10/09/horror-and-eroticism-bram-stokers-dracula/

Koenig, Frederick. *Rumor in the Marketplace: The Social Psychology of Commercial Hearsay*. Santa Barbara, CA: Praeger, 1985.

Kuhn, A. "'What's the matter, Trevor? Scared of something?' Representing the Monstrous-Feminine in *Candyman*." *Erfurt Electronic Studies in English*, 1 (2000). http://webdoc.sub.gwdg.de/edoc/ia/eese/artic20/kuhn/kuhn.html

Ni Fhlainn, Sorcha. "Sweet, Bloody Vengeance: Class, Social Stigma, and Servitude in the Slasher Genre." In *Hosting the Monster*, edited by Holly Lynn Baumgartner and Roger Davis, 179–196. Amsterdam: Editions Rodopi, 2008.

Pinedo, Isabel Cristina. *Recreational Terror: Women and the Pleasures of Horror Film Viewing*. Albany, NY: SUNY Press, 1997.

Semuels, Alana. "Should Urban Universities Help Their Neighbors?" *The Atlantic*, January 19, 2015. https://www.theatlantic.com/business/archive/2015/01/should-urban-universities-help-their-neighbors/384614/

Wittgenstein, Ludwig. *On Certainty*. Edited by G. E. M. Anscombe and G. H. von Wright. Translated by Denis Paul and G. E. M. Anscombe. Oxford: Basil Blackwell, 1969.

*Chapter Thirteen*

# "Nothing Is What It Seems"

## Montage and Misread Histories in Nicolas Roeg's Don't Look Now (1973)

### Thomas Prasch

A girl in a red raincoat (Christine Baxter, played by Sharon Williams) plays with her ball by a pond in the English countryside; a white horse gallops past behind her; a boy (her brother Johnny, played by Nicholas Salter) rides at the edge of the nearby woods on his bike. Inside, beside a warming fireplace, a couple, the parents we presume (John and Laura, played by Donald Sutherland and Julie Christie), seem wrapped in domestic tranquility; he is looking at slides of stained-glass church windows (and what is that red-hooded figure that keeps cropping up in the corner, that draws his, our, the camera's eye?), while she thumbs through a book, looking for an answer to her daughter's question ("If the world is round, why is a frozen pond flat?"). It turns out, she reports, that if the pond is big enough—a great lake, say—it is not flat after all. "Nothing is what it seems," John chuckles. Why, in this idyllic opening sequence of bourgeois comfort, do we already feel a creeping dread? Is it the elegiac edge to the background piano music? Is it the oddness of the militaristic messages that Christine's camo-clad-but-clearly-girl doll spouts every time she pulls the doll's string ("Action man patrol. Open fire")? Perhaps we are still unsettled by the unclarity of the two-shot credit sequence that precedes this opening, shots that anchor (although we cannot know it yet) the two locations of the film: the first, of a pond as rain is falling (it is the pond the girl plays by, but the rain comes later, as John and Laura leave after Christine's death); the second, a more mystifying shot accompanied by a bell tolling and a man humming, proves to be the window of the couple's hotel room in Venice (we finally see it, and hear the humming, and recognize the shimmer as an effect of the water in the canal outside, twenty-seven minutes later, just before the infamous love scene).[1] Or maybe we just worry about the unaccompanied girl playing so near the water; one of her first actions, after all, is to throw her ball into the pond.

Of this opening sequence, Neil Sinyard writes that it "illustrates practically every facet of montage as an expressive device in the cinema." He notes, as the film "cross-cuts between" interior and exterior, that Roeg is careful to show "the *spatial* relationship (the fragile geometry of space?)," to underline the distance John will have to travel to try to save his daughter; that "the action is represented sequentially but is also fragmented when the film momentarily concentrates of a particular detail"; that "[t]he linking of shots is mainly chronological, but sometimes shots are linked by association" or "by similarity or contrast of shape and physical appearance."[2] Mark Sanderson, who provides a full recapitulation of the hundred-shot, seven-minute sequence, calls it a "textbook example of compression and encapsulation."[3] But the montage also does much of the work of creating our creepy sense of impending disaster. Sinyard notes: "By establishing connections between two apparently unconnected places of action, the montage generates atmosphere and suspense. Two seemingly realistic events become weird and uncomfortable because the montage insists on their unaccountable similarities."[4] Yet this montage is, at the start, almost languorous; no frenzied staccato jump-cutting here.

The pace quickens as we come to the moment of crisis: a shot of Christine stepping in water cuts to one of Johnny's bike breaking a pane of glass. When John spills a drink onto his viewing table, the water gets on a slide, and the red-hooded figure bleeds out over the church window; unsettled by something, John rushes to the door as Christine sinks, face up (like Millais's Ophelia), into the water. (And what exactly is the shape of that bleeding dye? John Izod, in his Jungian reading, offers a range of meanings: "The outline [of Christ's halo in the mosaic he is working on in Venice] has the familiar foetal shape identified in Christine's corpse, John's smudged slide, and a brooch worn by Wendy."[5] Neil Feineman adds that the form is echoed in "an icon on the bishop's office wall" and that, at the end of the film, "John's blood will coagulate into the same shape."[6] Neil Sinyard sees "the shape of Venice, as seen later on the map on the Inspector's wall."[7]) The end of the opening sequence both speeds and slows: the cuts come at a more rapid pace, but John's dive for his daughter, his mournful cry as he emerges with her corpse, his efforts to revive her, are all in slow motion.[8]

Finally, Laura emerges from the house and, at last seeing, emits a (very Hitchcockian) short scream, nearly interrupted by a jumpcut to Venice, to the piercing sound of a drill digging into stone. Mark Sanderson observes: "The jump-cut ... mirrors the cut in *The Thirty-Nine Steps* (1935) when a woman's terrified scream merges with that of a steam train's whistle."[9] Neil Sinyard adds that Roeg "was insistent on retaining the specific sound-cut that bridges the sudden jump in the narrative both in time (some months have passed) and space (from England to Venice)—that is, the cut from Julie Christie's short scream on seeing her daughter, taking in the tragedy *instantly,* to the drill her husband is using in his work on the church in Venice. It is a cut that fires the viewer like a bullet into the future: future *shock* will be one of the film's main themes."[10] A montage that to this point has presented, albeit in fractured, multiple perspectives, a single episode in the family's life suddenly widens to undermine our confidence as viewers in the stability of place and time.

In the midst of the sequence, as Roeg himself has pointed out, John has unveiled the whole premise of the movie: "Nothing is what it seems." John's character is given to such pronouncements, declarations that refer in nondescript ways to immediate circumstances but resonate more broadly. When he meets Laura in a restaurant in Venice, for example, he tells her, in reference to his restoration project, "The deeper we go, the more byzantine it gets."[11] (Laura's response is equally open to double reading: "It's incredible that you can't change course.") Roeg explains: "You remember the scene at the beginning and the film . . . [when] Donald Sutherland says, 'Nothing's what it seems'? That isn't in the dialogue of Daphne du Maurier's story . . . but it is the key to the whole premise, and is exactly the feeling I have about life anyway."[12] As he told Mark Sanderson: "I like to start with a premise rather than a plot. . . . I liked the original story very much and it struck me that nothing is what it seems. I remember daring myself to put it into the mouth of one of characters."[13] So he did.

That central premise of *Don't Look Now* can be interpreted in a range of ways. It can be understood as a study in the differential forms grief can take and the impact of such mourning on a couple. Roeg observed, decades later: "It's a strange idea to make grief into the sole thrust of the film. Grief can separate people I've seen it happen. Even the closest, healthiest relationship can come undone through grief."[14] It can be seen as a story about John's second sight and the consequences of his rationalist refusal to accept what he sees, complicated by the presence of the two older English sisters in Venice, Heather and Wendy (played by Hilary Mason and Clelia Matania). Heather, blind, also claims second sight, reassuring Laura about the happiness of her dead child, and telling her that John has "the gift," and warning her that he is in danger in Venice. Laura is convinced; John remains deeply skeptical. It can be viewed as a cathartic takedown of a happy couple, a perspective that corresponds to Roeg's description of them as a "golden couple"—"I thought a lot about the Kennedys when I was doing the film"—a "couple with whom nothing is wrong. They're happy. Their life has gone well" until "life dealt dreadful blows."[15] It can be taken as an exploration of different forms of faith (from John's firm rationalism to the sisters' spiritualist Anglicanism to the bishop's mildly skeptical Catholicism to Laura's uncertainty; she answers the bishop's query about whether she is Christian, "I don't know; I'm kind to children and animals"). It can be summed up as a film about inexorable fate, John as unable to get out of the way of his own death as Oedipus is unable to avoid his prophecy.[16] Whichever interpretation one chooses, the film is also about the dislocation and displacement of time and expected meaning—and that is the work of Roeg's use of montage.

## MONTAGE AND TIME

"Montage . . . [is] the nerve of cinema,"[17] declared Sergei Eisenstein, who did so much in the dawning years of cinema to define the ways in which such intercutting could drive plot, create tension, and illuminate character. For Eisenstein, who compared the form to the creation of complex ideograms in Chinese writing and imagist poems, montage was like "an internal combustion engine, driving forward its automobile or tractor. . . . The dynamics of montage serve as impulses driving forward the total film."[18] But Eisenstein insisted as well that "montage is conflict," and for that matter he insists as well that "*art is always conflict.*"[19] He differentiated between two understandings of montage, the one he designated the "epic principle," in which montage simply serves to drive plot ("montage is the means of *unrolling* an idea with the help of single shots"), and his own preferred "dramatic principle," where montage operates as a form of dialectic: "In my opinion, however, montage is an idea that arises from the collision of independent shots—shots even opposed to one another."[20] Minus the Marxist dialectical baggage, it is that kind of collision and conflict to which Roeg commits himself.

Michael Dempsey includes Eisenstein in his own discussion of how Roeg's "montage is not quite like anybody else's." Dempsey argues that "Eisenstein's montage creates or demonstrates connections," while "Roeg's montage does not say that two shots are connected; it says that they might be. Eisenstein's editing aims for certainty; Roeg's for uncertainty. When his rapid juxtapositions outrun our ability to sort them out, we tumble into an uncertainty. . . . He uses them to undercut our total allegiance to reason, our dogged confidence that we are standing on solid ground."[21] For Roeg this mystification goes to the heart of the cinematic experience, to its sheer magicality: "A lot of filmmaking can be linked to *prestidigitateur*, you know—a shuffling of cards. And that's a marvelous thing. But if you say [adopts campy voice] 'Oooh, shall I show you how I do that?' Then it kills the wonder."[22] Montage seems a lot like that shuffling of cards, and John Baxter appears to embody that "total allegiance to reason."

Baxter's book might be titled *Beyond the Fragile Geometry of Space*, but his training is in art history, not filmmaking. For Roeg, time, rather than space, gets destabilized in the dialectic work of his montages. As Stephen Farber notes: "One of Roeg's unique talents . . . is his original approach to cinematic time. In some key scenes Roeg suspends time. . . . At other moments, Roeg uses crosscutting to give us the sensation of being in two places—or two times—at once."[23] Roeg's perspective on time and cinema coincide: "There's no such thing as seeing into the future because the future is already here. A premonition is just a way of confirming something you know. And I think film is the perfect medium to show this paradox. It's a time machine."[24] As Kathleen Carroll puts it: "One loses a sense of time. Present terrors, future terrors, real or imagined terrors blend together in a single nightmare."[25] As Anton Bitel notes of the "many jarring, at time violent cuts . . . forging strange associations across time and space": "Like some manic slasher on the loose, Nic Roeg . . . cuts compulsively, severing the natural arteries between cause and effect to expose a more irrational kind of narrative continuum. Flashbacks, flashforwards, and a suggestive series of recurrent images (a child's ball, a red mackintosh, breaking glass, a body pulled from water) allow both the Baxters' past tragedy and their future destiny to infect what we see in the film's diegetic present."[26] The montage work places the viewer in the same position as John: unable to differentiate past from present, present from future.

The confusion has real consequences: It is because he does not recognize, when he sees Laura, whom he has just put on a plane back to England, ride

*A body is dragged from the canals, causing John to flash back to the death of his daughter in* Don't Look Now.

*In* Don't Look Now, *John (Donald Sutherland) grieves at the drowning of his daughter, Christina.*

by on a boat with the two English women, that this is future not present (his own funeral procession, in fact) that he reports the women to the local police, which will lead to the jailing of the blind woman. Taking her back to her hotel, as he tries to undo his mistake, leads to John's separation from Laura, and his pursuit of the red-cloaked figure, in the final movement of the film. But, as Tom Milne observes, "The whole film . . . is predicated upon the subtle two-way traffic in time with its mosaic of associations, recollections and intimations."[27] Present and future routinely commingle in the film, as in the sex scene which intercuts the actual sex with the afterglowy dressing for dinner, or in that red-hooded figure on the slide, which both cues John to Christine's drowning and prophesies his own murder.

Roeg amplifies the effects of his intercutting with another tactic: reflection. Mirrors, glass, and water figure promiscuously through the film. Roeg, in a chapter of his memoir devoted to mirrors, highlights one especially striking usage in *Don't Look Now*:

> There's a sort of truth in mirrors—a sort of surreal truth. . . . The mirror is, for me, very much part of film, cinema and retention of the image. On *Don't Look Now* in Venice, when Julie Christie goes to the ladies' room, two old women

interrupt her there, and the scene is all shot in the room's three mirrors. She's reflected twice, and the women are reflected differently and at different times in different shots—as one leaves, the other comes back into the mirror. I think something so mundane and ordinary as seeing the scene through a mirror somehow sets up a mystery or a revelation of something.[28]

Glass and water similarly work as reflective surfaces as well, with one critical difference, as John Izod notes in relation to the juxtaposition of Christine's splash and Johnny's bike breaking the glass in the opening sequence: "As they break their difference is revealed. For of course the fracturing of glass is final; by contrast water quickly returns to its own level. *Don't Look Now* exploits this structural difference symbolically. On both occasions that it happens, the breaking of glass coincides with death."[29] Izod is thinking, beyond the scene with the bike, of John kicking out a transom window in his death throes (although he forgets the broken glass that accompanies John's near fall when the scaffolding collapses). Roeg notes: "Apart from any symbolic quality, glass sets off a sensation of fear, of something dangerous and brittle. This is built into everyone. . . . Mirrors and glass, glass especially, so fragile . . . so firm at one moment and so dangerous the next, it's frightening."[30] The reflective qualities of water figure especially heavily in the film. In both the opening sequence, and in John's final pursuit of the red-cloaked figure in Venice, we see the red coats reflected in the water (pond and canal, respectively) nearly as often as we see them directly.

Pauline Kael, in her review of the film, rather disliked the disturbance to her field of perception, complaining: "His entire splintering style affects one subliminally. The unnerving cold ominousness that he imparts to the environment says that things are not what they seem, and one may come out of the theatre still seeing shock cuts and feeling slightly dissociated. The environment may briefly be fractured; for me ten minutes or so passed before it assembled itself and lost that trace of hostile objectivity." This reflects, she recognizes, Roeg's worldview: "Roeg has an elegant, edgy style that speaks to us of the broken universe and our broken connections, of modern man's inability to order his experience and to find meaning and coherence in it. The style speaks of the lesions in our view of the world."[31] Kael may not like the way it makes it feel, but her description sounds like success for the filmmaker.

## ADAPTATION AND ACCIDENT IN GOTHIC VENICE

"Don't look now" is the opening line of Daphne du Maurier's 1971 novella (also called *Don't Look Now*), spoken by John at the Venetian restaurant where he meets Laura. He continues: "but there are a couple of old girls two tables away who are trying to hypnotize me.'"[32] The words do not occur in the film, although we can see where they would have: John notices the sisters' stare in the restaurant. The absent clue of the missing title offers one of the more playful examples of adaptive shifting between story and film.

More significantly, du Maurier's story occurs entirely after Christine's death, which she attributes to meningitis. Starting the film with her death, and making it a drowning, changes the tenor significantly, "providing a much more dramatic start," as Mark Sanderson notes.[33] Roeg changes Christine's coat from blue to red; switches Johnny's injury (which leads Laura to return home) from appendicitis to concussion (an injury during a fire drill); and gives John a job to do in Venice, a church restoration. In du Maurier, the couple were merely vacationing there.

Roeg also, for a director whose films appear so carefully put together, was strikingly open to improvisation and last-minute fiddling. Most notably, the sex scene was not in the script, but added at the last minute because Roeg felt its need for the characters he was developing: "Originally it wasn't in the script. We hadn't thought about it before. So we started shooting and, as the film developed, the characters . . . seemed to be arguing all the time. Of course, there were reasons for their bickering—the death of a child, stress— but I thought, 'This story needs something, their plight needs a pause, a breath. There needs to be some kind of intimacy between them.'"[34] As he put it elsewhere: "Without that love scene, you never see them happy together; they're always rowing. . . . And when I put the scene back in, suddenly you can't get confused about them. They're like a married couple."[35] The sex scene also contains an unscripted secret (no, not that the sex was real; everyone involved denies that old rumor[36]):

> It was only after we shot the scene, later that day, that I got the sense that maybe it was the first time they'd made love with that degree of giving and romance since the death of their child. That it was the perfect moment for a child to be conceived—which would be some kind of comfort in their grief. A new life, making up for the death of their child. When we were shooting the final scene when Julie is on the funeral barge, I told her to lift the veil from her face. When she asked why, I said that she knew she was pregnant and she should have a slight smile on her face.[37]

Not a word in the script reveals this. Similarly, the dialogue between the couple in the church was unscripted, based on Sutherland and Christie's first response when they entered the location.[38]

But it is that shift in the use of Venice, from vacation spot to work site, which most deeply affects the film. Roeg reveals how accident figured into things in his discussion of the search for locations:

The church was situated on the Isle of Dusoduro, right on the western tip, and was, at the time, in a rather run-down area that was being restored. The church was named after St Nicolo dei Mendicoli (St. Nicholas of the Poor and the Beggars!). What could be more inviting than that? The bones of the saint were in a casket at the foot of the altar and the complete restoration of the church was being funded by the English 'Venice in Peril' fund—which could almost be a subtitle for *Don't Look Now*. Fate and Chance had begun to take over the movie. One other seeming 'coincidence' was that on the wall of the church, close to the entrance, there was a film poster advertising an old Charlie Chaplin film that was showing at the local cinema.... [W]e track past it as John (Donald Sutherland) and the Bishop (Massimo Serato) walk away from the church. The Italian title on the poster was *Uno Contro Tutti* [*One Against All*]. How true that turned out to be.[39]

Roeg makes similar use of other accidental opportunities: another poster promises "Sciopero generale" ("General Strike"), appropriate to the near-empty winter city John roams as he passes it; he also crosses the Ponte dei Miracoli, or Bridge of Miracles, on his search.[40]

Aside from such details, however, it is a very different city from du Maurier's vacation destination—or from more touristically inclined films—that Roeg presents us. "Wintry Venice ... has exactly the crypt-like patina called for by such a tale of cloistered terrors," Roy Frumkes writes.[41] Sinyard suggests: "In Roeg, it is a city in peril, stagnant and submerging and in the process ... dragging up fearsome things from its hidden depths—rats, corpses."[42] Pauline Kael calls it "rotting Venice, with its crumbling, leering gargoyles."[43] "Venice, that haunted city, has never been more melancholy than in *Don't Look Now*," Roger Ebert observes. "It is like a vast necropolis, its stones damp and crumbling, its canals alive with rats."[44] It is in Italy, Sanderson reminds us, that Horace Walpole first situated the Gothic, in his *Castle of Otranto* (1765), and "Venice—its Renaissance masterpieces and Gothic façades sinking slowly into the sea—is the perfect setting for a story of physical and psychical ruin and restoration."[45] Roeg's Venice presents a complex, layered (and decaying and sinking) visage; John tells Laura, of his restoration project, "I'm restoring a fake," but "the options are restore the fake or let it sink into the sea." His restoration work, in one sense, will add a new layer to the fakery, another layer of falsified history. It may all be some distance from du Maurier's vision, but it suits Roeg's purposes.[46]

## MONTAGE AND MEANING

Five distinct instances of dramatic montage feature in the film, and they provide a full understanding of the ways in which Roeg deploys the tactic: the opening sequence; the moment Laura faints in the restaurant; the sex scene; the point at which the scaffolding collapses beneath John; and his death, finally confronting the red-cloaked figure. Two of them, it is worth noting, were affected by external circumstances: the opening sequence by problems with a child actor who did not want to sink into the pond,[47] and the sex scene by problems with the censors.[48]

I have treated the opening montage in some detail above. Suffice it to say here that it functions to set up much of the film's basic mechanics: the source of the grief, the suggestion of John's second sight, the obscure link between the two red-coated figures. It also establishes Roeg's cinematic tactics.

The fainting scene is the briefest (just a minute of screen time), and the most self-contained. It comes just after Laura has led Heather and Wendy to the restroom, and thus after Heather tells her: "I've seen her, and she wants you to know she's happy. I've seen your little girl, sitting between you and your husband, and she was laughing." The pair leave the restroom before Laura; she spends some time in the restroom by herself (or by herself with the attendant, who sits mute throughout the proceedings). Returning to the table, to eerie violin music, she sits, rises again, saying "I've got to stand up," and then falls, over the small table, spilling it and its assorted contents to the floor. A series of quick cuts shows her fall, the table's tip, her husband reaching out to her, her landing, things from the table falling over her, spilled oil and vinegar mixing on the tile floor. The effect is startling, but it mostly serves to mark a key moment: of her conviction that Heather was telling her the truth, her move from sadness to a new sense of recovered joy.

The sex scene, four minutes long, intercuts scenes of lovemaking with the couple's separate activity getting dressed to go out afterward. Sutherland, speaking not long after Roeg's death, recalls: "He was a genius, Nic. A visionary. He made a love scene between a grieving wife and her husband with no cries of passion, no sounds of orgasm, no words. All you hear is Pino Donaggio's music as Nic intercuts their making love with them getting dressed to go out to dinner. Magical. You don't see that scene as a voyeur. You watch it and it reminds you of yourself, of you loving and you being loved."[49] Following a sequence in which the couple are casually naked—bathing, she noticing his love handles, he brushing his teeth—it above all underlines the natural intimacy of the couple, restoring, as was Roeg's intent, their sense of love. But it also embodies a dual time, during and after crosscut with each other ("eros and its afterglow merge into a timeless fluidity," Bitel writes of the scene[50]), one moment purely present and another anticipatory and future-directed (they are getting dressed for what comes next).

The scaffolding collapse, like the fainting scene, is short—just a couple minutes—and almost self-contained, though significantly preceded by a

*The scaffolding collapses, nearly killing John in* Don't Look Now.

moment in which John, climbing up to the scaffold, sees Heather's face. A spar falls from above, in slow motion and, after its first release, in darkness, so that we almost think we might not have seen anything ("I wanted the audience to feel . . . maybe doubtful, maybe that they'd missed something, maybe that it didn't happen. And then to think 'Oh, Christ!' and to have the time to get together with their time sense," Roeg said[51]). Then the spar crashes through the sheet of glass above John's head, destabilizing the scaffold so that it collapses, all its contents (the mosaic tiles John is testing, most notably) spilling, and John left dangling until he can be pushed into a swinging that leads him to a safe perch. Combining multiple perspectives and shifting time frames (parts in slow motion, parts at regular speed), the montage mostly simply encapsulates the near disaster in stunning fashion. With Heather's appearance immediately before, however, it also reminds us of her prophecy: that John is in danger in Venice.

The final sequence can be seen one of two ways: as commencing when Heather, in the midst of a fit, starts pleading with Wendy to "Bring him back" after Wendy pushes John out of their room (it is a six-minute sequence that includes those pleas, John chasing the red-caped figure, the bishop startling awake in his bed, Wendy arriving too late and chasing after John, and John finally cornering the caped figure in a winter-fogged deserted church); or as beginning when, flashing back to the figure in the slide, John mutters "Wait" and the caped figure turns, shakes her head as if to say no, and pulls out her knife, from which point his death will take four minutes. The lead-in is a stunning chase scene, but the death scene really takes the montage tactics to a new extreme. John, bleeding out, recalls everything that has gone before, against a cacophony of bells, over which we hear a familiar elegiac piano tune: the red-caped figure on the slide, the drowning, the sex, the slide's image bleeding out, the fall, his future vision of Laura, so much else; Sanderson details a seventy-shot sequence between the dwarf's turning and John's foot kicking out the transom window in his final moment, ending with the jump cut to his funeral barge.[52] Bitel observes: "The shock of this film's *giallo*-esque climax—expressed in an orgasmic explosion of cuts that links virtually every scene of the film together—is one that John, and the viewer too, should have seen coming. All the signs have been there all along, as evident as they are irrational, but they are readable only with the second sight furnished by retrospect (or indeed by multiple viewings)."[53] John Kenneth Muir similarly writes: "When John dies, images flash in front of the camera: images of life and death, of love and fear, of pain and joy, but for John his death represents a moment, a summit, of understanding. The tangle of images in the montage suggest this is how it was *meant* to be."[54] The dense fatalism of the story reaches its crescendoed climax in the promiscuous profusion of images.

Or else John's life just flashed before his eyes, as cliché calls for in dying. For Roeg himself, the final scene has another purpose: "I like absurdity. The thing that won me instantly to Daphne du Maurier's story is the last line, 'What a bloody silly way to die.' It's superb, but it didn't fit. I wanted that to come out of the visuals."[55] Dark irony in seventy shots.

## NOTES

1. Scott Salwolke underlines how the sequence disturbs our sense of time: "Already the present and the future coalesce" (*Nicolas Roeg Film by Film*, 38). Neil Sinyard also notes: "In retrospect, these two shots will serve as an indicator of the way the film plays with present and future time" (*Films of Nicolas Roeg*, 43).
2. Sinyard, *Films of Nicolas Roeg*, 46–47. The parenthetical question refers to the title of a book by John Baxter that we see on the couch beside Laura.
3. Sanderson, *Don't Look Now*, 37. His shot-by-shot summary (102 shots, since he includes the 2 in the credit sequence) follows, 37–46.
4. Sinyard, *The Films of Nicolas Roeg*, 47. The most obvious similarity is the red coat on the daughter and the mysterious figure in the slide, but Sinyard notes others: "The mother makes a gesture with her fingers over her mouth, and the daughter outside makes a similar gesture; the son bends over his bike, and the father bends over his transparency" (47). Christine tosses her ball, John tosses Laura her cigarettes.
5. Izod, *Films of Nicolas Roeg*, 81.
6. Neil Feineman quoted in Salwolke, *Nicolas Roeg,* 46.
7. Sinyard, *Films of Nicolas Roeg,* 48.
8. Sinyard also addresses the "manipulation of tempo," *Films*, 47.

9. Sanderson, *Don't Look Now*, 18; Salwolke, *Nicolas Roeg*, 37. Roeg was an admirer of Hitchcock's, as Sanderson notes; Daphne du Maurier, author of the source text for *Don't Look Now*, was source for three Hitchcock films. As birds swirl around John on his solitary meanderings in Venice, we might catch an allusion to one of them.

10. Sinyard, *Films of Nicolas Roeg*, 43.

11. In Venice, it is worth noting, "byzantine" has a second meaning. The cross the bishop examines later in the film is clearly Byzantine (Roeg notes as much; see Milne, Houston, and Roeg, "*Don't Look Now*," 5), and the mosaics John is working on suggest those roots.

12. Milne, Houston, and Roeg, "*Don't Look Now*," 3; final ellipsis in original.

13. Sanderson, *Don't Look Now*, 82. He later recalled: "For me, the basic premise is that in life, nothing is what it seems. That's it, really. I felt for the idea so much I put the line into the actual script" (Sean O'Hagan, "Sexual Power and Terror").

14. O'Hagan, "Sexual Power and Terror."

15. Roeg quoted in Kathleen Carroll, "Everything to Fear from Him," 7.

16. Anton Bitel also finds an echo of Oedipus in John: "Nothing, however, can make John change course as, Oedipus-like, he ignores the words of a blind seer and rushes inexorably towards a fate that he cannot properly understand" (Bitel, "*Don't Look Now*").

17. Eisenstein, "Dialectic Approach to Film Form," 46.

18. Eisenstein, "Cinematographic Principle," 34.

19. Ibid., on montage; "Dialectic Approach," 46, on art.

20. Eisenstein, "Cinematic Principle," 49.

21. Dempsey, "Reviews: *Don't Look Now*," 40–41.

22. "Nicolas Roeg on Don't Look Now" [Film4], brackets in original text.

23. Farber, "Movies: 'Don't Look Now' Will Scare You Subtly."

24. Lanza, *Fragile Geometry*, 92. For Vincent Canby, practically the same understanding of the nature of film and time undermines the movie: "The point, I guess, is that if you can see into the future, it's often difficult to keep your mind on the present.... One of the problems with 'Don't Look Now' is that second sight does not easily translate as a terrifying talent for a film character to possess. It simply looks like a flash-forward, which, along with the flashback, the jumpcut and the face, are standard story-telling devices in movies" (Vincent Canby, "Film: 'Don't Look Now,' a Horror Tale").

25. Carroll, "Everything to Fear from Him," 7.

26. Bitel, "*Don't Look Now*."

27. Milne, "*Don't Look Now*," 237.

28. Roeg, *The World Is Ever Changing*, Kindle edition location 1577–1586. Roeg slightly errs on the circumstances, however. The two women do not "interrupt" Laura; she has in fact led them there.

29. Izod, *Films of Nicolas Roeg*, 73–74.

30. Milne, Houston, and Roeg, "*Don't Look Now*," 4.

31. Kael, "Labyrinths," 68. Kael concluded, after grumbling about the film's creaky Gothic tone: "It's a masterwork. It's also trash" (71).

32. Quoted in Salwolke, *Nicolas Roeg,* 37. See also Sanderson, *Don't Look Now,* 34.

33. Sanderson, *Don't Look Now,* 13, and for the other differences discussed here, 14–15. See also Sinyard, *Films of Nicolas Roeg,* 42.

34. Roeg, *The World Is Ever Changing,* locations 1494–1503.

35. Salwolke, *Nicolas Roeg,* 43.

36. See, for example, Richmond in "Nicolas Roeg's 'Don't Look Now' is a special kind of supernatural thriller that aptly deals with subjects far from supernatural" [Cinephilia & Beyond] and in Richmond and Risker, "The Consciousness of the Camera: An Interview with Anthony Richmond."

37. Roeg, *The World Is Ever Changing,* location 1511. Elsewhere, Roeg is coyer about the point: "Laura is in a state of grace, that's why she smiles. It is beyond their knowledge. . . . Laura is smiling at some secret memory" (Sanderson, *Don't Look Now,* 85).

38. Roeg, "Sex had to be on the menu;" and "Nicolas Roeg's Don't Look Now" [Cinephilia & Beyond].

39. Ibid., locations 2100–2105; my translation of the Chaplin film title. If that title rings no bells, do not bother searching for it on IMDb, where it does not appear. It was an Italian compilation film of Chaplin shorts, released in Italy in 1961; see the Italian film database www.cinematografo.it/cinedatabase/film/uno-contro-tutti/32579/ for details. Roeg tells a similar story in Sanderson, *Don't Look Now,* 78.

40. The English location, the country house, was also an accidental discovery, but it too embodies a sensibility that fits with the film, as Roeg recalled: "The house is half wood and half brick; it was right in line with the idea that this couple hadn't finally made up their minds about how they wanted to live, hadn't decided on Georgian, Tudor or modern" (Milne, Houston, and Roeg, *Don't Look Now,*" 3).

41. Quoted in Muir, *Horror Films of the 1970s,* 257. It is also noteworthy that such wintry pallor figured into the color scheme. Tony Richmond recalls: "We took all the red out of it. The only red on the set was the little girl's jacket, the dwarf's scarf, the dwarf's jacket and the red in Donald's scarf." (He forgets one pair of red longjohns hanging on a laundry line, but that cues one of the appearances by the red-caped figure.) The blood, he recalled, "was redder than normal blood. That was what we wanted" ("Nicolas Roeg's *'Don't Look Now'*" [Cinephilia & Beyond]).

42. Sinyard, *Films of Nicolas Roeg,* 50.

43. Kael, "Labyrinths," 68.

44. Ebert, *"Don't Look Now* (1973)."

45. Sanderson, *Don't Look Now,*

46. Roeg was quite insistent, however, that du Maurier approved the final film, quoting from a letter she sent him. *The World Is Ever Changing,* location 528; Sanderson, *Don't Look Now,* 86.

47. Roeg discusses the problem, with both the main actor and a handy substitute, and the solution of working in a water tank in Sanderson, *Don't Look Now,* 80.

48. Roeg, "Sex had to be on the menu."

49. Quoted in "Nicolas Roeg's 'Don't Look Now'" [Cinephilia & Beyond].

50. Bitel, *"Don't Look Now."*

51. Milne, Houston, and Roeg, "*Don't Look Now,*" 5.
52. Sanderson, *Don't Look Now,* 71–74.
53. Bitel, "*Don't Look Now.*"
54. Muir, *Horror Films,* 261.
55. Milne, Houston, and Roeg, "*Don't Look Now,*" 7. See also "Nicolas Roeg on Don't Look Now." [Film4]

## BIBLIOGRAPHY

Bitel, Anton. "*Don't Look Now* (1973)." 29 April 2015. *Projected Figures: Film Bits and Bobs.* https://projectedfigures.com/2015/04/29/dont-look-now-1973/

Canby, Vincent. "Film: 'Don't Look Now,' a Horror Tale." *New York Times,* 10 December 1973. https://www.nytimes.com/1973/12/10/archives/filmdont-look-now-a-horror-taledonald-sutherland-and-julie-christie.html?searchResultPosition=5

Carroll, Kathleen. "Everything to Fear from Him." *Evening News,* London, 23 December 1973, 7. University of California Berkeley Art Museum & Pacific Film Archive CineFiles. https://cinefiles.bampfa.berkeley.edu/cinefiles/FilmDetail?filmId=pfafilm5866

Dempsey, Michael. "Reviews: *Don't Look Now.*" *Film Quarterly* 27, no. 3 (Spring 1974): 39–43.

Ebert, Roger. "*Don't Look Now* (1973)." 13 October 2002. https://www.rogerebert.com/reviews/great-movie-dont-look-now-1974

Eisenstein, Sergei. "A Dialectic Approach to Film Form" (1931). In *Film Form: Essays in Film Theory.* New York: Harcourt Brace Jovanovich, 1949.

———. "The Cinematographic Principle and the Ideogram" (1929). In *Film Form.*

Farber, Stephen. "Movies: 'Don't Look Now' Will Scare You Subtly." *New York Times,* 23 December 1973. https://www.nytimes.com/1973/12/23/archives/-dont-look-now-will-scare-yousubtly-movies-this-disturbing-thriller.html?searchResultPosition=2

Izod, John. *The Films of Nicolas Roeg: Myth and Mind.* New York: St. Martin's, 1992.

Kael, Pauline. "Labyrinths." *New Yorker,* 24 December 1973, 68–73. https://www.newyorker.com/magazine/1973/12/24/labyrinths

Lanza, Joseph. *Fragile Geometry: The Films, Philosophy, and Misadventures of Nicolas Roeg.* New York: PAJ Publications, 1989.

Milne, Tom. "*Don't Look Now.*" *Sight and Sound,* Autumn 1973, 237–238. University of California Berkeley Art Museum & Pacific Film Archive CineFiles. https://cinefiles.bampfa.berkeley.edu/cinefiles/FilmDetail?filmId=pfafilm5866

Milne, Tom, Penelope Houston, and Nicolas Roeg. "*Don't Look Now*: Nicolas Roeg interviewed by Tom Milne and Penelope Houston." *Sight and Sound,* Autumn 1973, 2–8. University of California Berkeley Art Museum & Pacific Film Archive CineFiles. https://cinefiles.bampfa.berkeley.edu/cinefiles/FilmDetail?filmId=pfafilm5866

Muir, John Kenneth. *Horror Films of the 1970s.* Jefferson, NC: McFarland, 2002.

"Nicolas Roeg's *Don't Look Now* is a special kind of a supernatural thriller that aptly deals with subjects far from supernatural." Cinephilia & Beyond. https://cinephilia beyond.org /nicholas-roegs-dont-look-now/

"Nicolas Roeg on Don't Look Now." Film4. www.film4.com/features/article/nicolas -roeg-on-dont-look-now

O'Hagan, Sean. "The Sexual Power and Terror That Produced a Classic." *Guardian,* 8 April 2006. https://www.theguardian.com/film/2006/apr/09/features.review

Richmond, Anthony, and Paul Risker. "The Consciousness of the Camera: An Interview with Anthony Richmond." *Cinéaste* 42, No. 3 (Summer 2017): 4–9.

Roeg, Nicolas. "Sex had to be on the menu." *Guardian,* 2 February 2008. https://www.theguardian.com/film/2008/feb/03/observerfilmmagazine.observer filmmagazine18.

———. *The World Is Ever Changing.* New York: Faber and Faber, 2013; Amazon Kindle edition, 2013.

Salwolke, Scott. *Nicolas Roeg Film by Film.* Jefferson, NC: McFarland, 1993.

Sanderson, Mark. *Don't Look Now,* 2nd ed. London: BFI/Palgrave Macmillan, 1997.

"SCRIPT TO SCREEN: Nicolas Roeg's Don't Look Now." *Film Strategy.* 9 December 2013. http://www.filmstrategy.com/2013/12/script-to-screen-nicolas -roegs-dont.html

Sinyard, Neil. *The Films of Nicolas Roeg.* London: Charles Letts, 1991.

*Chapter Fourteen*

# "Tens of Thousands of Men Died Here"

## *Desire, Revenge, and Memories of War in Edgar G. Ulmer's* The Black Cat

### James J. Ward

Ten minutes into Edgar G. Ulmer's 1934 film *The Black Cat,* American newlyweds Joan and Peter Alison (Jacqueline Wells and David Manners), their honeymoon interrupted when the van carrying them to the Hungarian town of Gömbös crashes in a rainstorm, are confronted by the sight of a huge hilltop residence built above ruined fortifications and abandoned graveyards. The van driver has already told them that these are the remains of Fort Marmaros, where Austro-Hungarian and Russian troops fought for months in one of the bloodiest battles of the First World War. "Tens of thousands of men died here," the driver declared. "The ravine down there was piled twelve deep with dead and wounded men. The little river below was swollen red, a raging torrent of blood." Their traveling companion, Dr. Vitus Werdegast (Bela Lugosi), then explains that they are looking at the home of engineer Hjalmar Poelzig, who has constructed a futuristic mansion upon the broken battlements. Admitted to the house by a mute majordomo, the travelers are greeted by Poelzig (Boris Karloff) with a display of old-world hospitality that momentarily masks the history he and Werdegast share. They also share an interest in Joan—Werdegast for motives that are not entirely innocent, Poelzig for ones that are more sinister and perverse.

Poelzig and Werdegast had served together at Fort Marmaros, Poelzig as its Austrian commander, Werdegast in one of the Hungarian regiments garrisoned there. When the fort could no longer be defended, Poelzig negotiated its surrender on terms that ensured his own escape and condemned his soldiers to years of captivity in Russia. Werdegast was sent to the Kurgal prison in Siberia, where, he later recounts, "the soul is killed slowly." Now, fifteen years later, he has returned to settle the score with Poelzig, but before that to learn the fate of his wife and daughter, both of whom he last saw before the war. Werdegast's tortured expression as he describes his experience conveys the suffering endured by the thousands of men Poelzig betrayed:

> One heard the shells whistle through the air and explode one after another; the entire fortress shook. The incessant booms caused the windows to rattle and the iron doors to shake. The blasts destroyed glass while the salvos of the last firing cannons and heavy mortars created incredible noise.... Troops serving outside the fortress walls suffered from cold and dampness and wished death to end their misery. Rising flames and clouds of smoke could be seen at the fortress rings. The troops that returned from the March 19 travesty [a failed breakout attempt] were nothing but skin and bones, tattered uniforms hung off them—the last horses have been slaughtered, tears welled in the soldiers' eyes. They had given their last efforts, the inhuman pain they suffered kills us.[1]

This description, however, is not from *The Black Cat*. It is from the diary of one of the 18,000 civilians who had taken refuge in Fortress Przemyśl, a sprawling ring of fortifications in the Austrian province of Galicia less than twenty miles from the Russian frontier, in the first months of World War I. When ill-planned Austro-Hungarian offensives into Russian territory in August and September 1914 were disastrously routed, Przemyśl became the crucial strongpoint blocking a Russian advance through the Carpathian Mountains into the heart of the Dual Monarchy. In the six-month siege that followed, 200,000 Habsburg soldiers died or were wounded, while the Russians suffered casualties of 115,000 men. When Przemyśl was surrendered in March 1915, 117,000 Polish, Hungarian, and Ukrainian troops, many of them sick and starving, were taken into captivity. The loss of Fortress Przemyśl—in what would become known as the Verdun of the Eastern Front—was a blow from which the Austro-Hungarian Empire never recovered.[2]

In all the academic and critical scholarship that has grown up around *The Black Cat* and its director Edgar G. Ulmer, Przemyśl has escaped mention even though, as a boy living in Vienna during the war, Ulmer cannot have been ignorant of the fighting in Galicia. Even in the censored press at the time, stories of the suffering, sickness, and starvation that accompanied the defense of Przemyśl must have filtered back into the public consciousness, already shaken by the defeats Habsburg armies had faced at the hands of the Russians. In an interview they shared in 1970, two years before his death, Ulmer told Peter Bogdanovich that the setting he conceived for *The Black Cat* was inspired in part by Fort Douaumont, over which the French and Germans battled at Verdun during World War I. The idea had originated with Gustav Meyrinck, author of *The Golem* (1914–1915), Ulmer explained, who was thinking about writing a play that would incorporate the horrors experienced by the soldiers who fought at Douaumont. The play was never completed, and

Ulmer most likely heard about it in Berlin where he claimed to have worked with Paul Wegener, whose film version of *The Golem* was released in 1920. Even by the standards of the First World War, the combat at Fort Douaumont was particularly gruesome. German assault troops captured the fort unopposed in February 1916, the defenders having abandoned it in the belief that it could not withstand shelling by the Germans' heavy artillery. After repeated attempts, the French retook the fort in October at a cost of over 100,000 lives. According to Bogdanovich, Ulmer described the French commander as "a strange Euripedes figure" who had later gone mad from his memories of the place, as "he had walked on that mountain of bodies."[3]

The stories that Ulmer may have heard about Fort Douaumont would have provided sufficient horrors—slaughter, claustrophobia, madness—to inspire both the plot and the setting for *The Black Cat*. Still, it is hard to believe that he was not also thinking of the equivalent horrors that were experienced at Fortress Przemyśl. In his recent of biography of Ulmer, Noah Isenberg cautions against an overdetermined reading of *The Black Cat*, but allows that "the film's sustained preoccupation with the aftershocks of the First World War appears to have been dredged up from the director's experience of war as a youth in Vienna."[4] Combined with accounts Ulmer likely heard from German soldiers who had survived the fighting on the Western Front, Douaumont and Przemyśl could easily have fused in his mind, forming an inventory of monstrous images he would draw upon a decade later in Hollywood.[5] At an even deeper level, the long centuries of war, invasion, and conquest that shaped the historical consciousness of the peoples living in—to use historian Timothy Snyder's term—"the bloodlands" of central and eastern Europe cast a pall of gloom and dread over this landscape of steppes, mountains, and valleys more pervasive than anything known in the West.[6] By tapping into this "deep memory," Ulmer achieved a dimension of dread and revulsion that sets *The Black Cat* apart in the catalog of Universal Pictures' 1930s horror franchise.

## THE ARCHITECTURE OF DESTRUCTION: CURRENTS AND CROSSCURRENTS OF MODERNISM

Working in Berlin as an apprentice scene designer in the first years after the war, Ulmer—if his own accounts are to be believed—met and learned from some of the giants of early German cinema. There are references in *The Black Cat* to Robert Wiene's *The Cabinet of Dr. Caligari* (1920) and F. W. Murnau's *Nosferatu: A Symphony of Horror* (1922). The most notable influence, apparently, was that of the German architect Hans Poelzig, with whom Ulmer, still in his teens, worked in designing the sets for *The Golem*. Uneasily situated between Expressionism and Modernism in the history of early twentieth-century German architecture, Poelzig had his most important works behind him when he was contracted to do the sets for Wegener's film.[7] Engineer Poelzig's name in *The Black Cat* is obviously not accidental, and his hilltop mansion—glimpsed only briefly in a backlit painted glass panel— evokes the clean industrial style of architecture associated with the Bauhaus movement of the 1920s. Ulmer himself attributed the sets he designed for *The Black Cat* to his "Bauhaus period," and scholars since have engaged in some inventive wordplay based on these connections.[8] In his study of the production history of *The Black Cat*, Gregory Mank proposes that Ulmer's sketches for the exterior of the Poelzig mansion were also based on Frank Lloyd Wright's 1924 Ennis-Brown House in Los Angeles, a National Register of Historic Places landmark that has been referenced in dozens of films, including Ridley Scott's *Blade Runner* (1982) and *Black Rain* (1989).[9]

By the 1930s, the pioneering work that Hans Poelzig—together with Bruno Taut, Erich Mendelsohn, Hans Scharoun, and other architects associated with the Bauhaus—had accomplished in the preceding decade no longer found favor in Germany. Hitler's appointment as chancellor in January 1933 cleared the way for a purge of left-wing artists and architects from teaching positions they held in Berlin, Frankfurt, Dresden, Stuttgart, and other cities.[10] While some chose to leave Germany, Poelzig remained in Berlin. Ironically, Poelzig's last major project, the headquarters complex for the chemical giant I. G. Farben outside Frankfurt (1929–1931), displayed a clean industrial modernism that would influence such later Nazi edifices as the Reichsbank building (1934–1938) and the Reich Air Ministry (1935–1936), both in Berlin. These connections have complicated the academic discussion of Ulmer's use of the architect's name in *The Black Cat*. Whatever their relationship in the 1920s, it is difficult to credit the assertion that Ulmer was paying a note of respect by naming Karloff's character Hjalmar Poelzig. In her history of German cinema in the Third Reich, Sabine Hake has suggested that Ulmer wanted to express his unease with the architectural modernism of which Poelzig had been a prominent representative, believing that its theoretical and social influence had contributed to the rise of fascism in central Europe.[11]

Ulmer's apparent ambivalence about the modernist style in which he received his early artistic training extends to the plot of *The Black Cat* as much as it colors the architecture and the atmosphere of Poelzig's mansion. In a provocative 2009 essay Herbert Schwaab compares the film with Pier Paolo Pasolini's essay in cinematic depravity, *Salo, or the 120 Days of Sodom* (1975). The paintings by well-known Cubist and Futurist artists that decorate Pasolini's Fascist torture chambers are only a step or two removed from stark antiseptic surfaces where Hjalmar Poelzig embalms the bodies of his dead wives and displays them in an underground necropolis. "Ulmer's human monsters haunt a new and stylish world of white walls," Schwaab writes,

> with clear geometric lines and abstract ornaments. . . . [But] the film can be read on more than one level. It cannot be reduced to stylish architecture and the 'art for art's sake' mentality of Poelzig and his inhuman, detached approach to life. It also involves the more progressive forces of Dr. Werdegast, Hungary's greatest psychiatrist (that is, before he is driven out of his mind). . . . Does the film answer the question of whether Poelzig's degeneration can be traced back to his attitude toward modernism? The film may be subversive in enabling us to raise such questions, but it is too hybrid, too uneven, too campy to really answer such questions.[12]

The vexed relationship between the modernist movement in architecture and National Socialism is outside the scope of this chapter. However, any reductionist reading that equates the "style" of Nazi buildings with the atavistic classicism seen in such showpiece projects as the arenas and marching grounds that Albert Speer erected in Nuremberg misses the point; the Nazis were far more eclectic in their choice of architectural influences. For the famous "architecture of light" he employed at the 1934 Party Congress, Speer drew upon the work of Poelzig and other modernists in illuminating theaters and department stores in the preceding decade.[13] In *The Black Cat*, Hjalmar Poelzig's mansion—"a masterpiece of construction built upon the ruins of a masterpiece of destruction," Werdegast calls it—combines the experimental modernism associated with his namesake with the inhuman brutalism at the core of Nazi ideology and the buildings it inspired. The reduction of Poelzig's home to a pile of ruins at the film's conclusion thus serves as an uncanny premonition of the fate of Albert Speer's buildings little more than a decade later.

## SEX, SADISM, AND SATANISM IN A HIGH-TECH SETTING

His youth and early adulthood shaped in the hothouse environments of prewar Vienna and postwar Berlin, Ulmer arrived in Hollywood in the mid-1920s with an exaggerated sensitivity to the obsessions and compulsions that ran like fault lines just beneath the conventions of acceptable behavior.[14] Offered the opportunity by Universal Pictures to take over the troubled process of adapting Edgar Allan Poe's *The Black Cat* to the screen, Ulmer and cowriter Peter Ruric scrapped the previous iterations of a screenplay and fashioned a script that retained Poe's title and his story's atmosphere of claustrophobia and morbidity, but little more. Instead, Ulmer drew upon his memories, active or suppressed, of World War I in central Europe, his experiences in the febrile setting of the German film industry in the first postwar years, and such contemporaneous sensations as the accusations leveled against English occultist Aleister Crowley to compound a singular tale of sexual obsession, sadistic intent, and illicit rituals. Crowley's esoteric writings and exhibitionistic behavior had previously captured the attention of Somerset Maugham, who patterned the demonic character in his short novel *The Magician* (1908) on him, and Crowley's well-publicized excesses were such that in 1923 the new Fascist government in Italy evicted him from the residence he had established in Sicily. In 1926 Rex Ingram had directed a silent film adaptation of *The Magician*, with Paul Wegener in the titular role, and is likely that Ulmer knew Ingram's film through his previous association with Wegener when they had worked together in Berlin. Various scandals and lawsuits kept Crowley in the news, and Ulmer may have felt some sympathy for the English eccentric because of his perennial money problems, his notorious libertinage, and his advocacy of sex magic as a cure for the world's ills. Ulmer's own erotic impulses, along with his inclination to sadism, became apparent in the filming of *The Black Cat*, and the character of Hjalmar Poelzig—while certainly a fiend—was also an artist, as evidenced in the design of his house, the display of the bodies of his dead wives, and the choreography of the Black Mass ceremony that ultimately costs him his life.[15]

The first impression viewers get of Poelzig, rising slowly, almost robotically, from his bed recalls both the somnambulist Cesare in *The Cabinet of Dr. Caligari*, emerging from the eponymous box in which he is kept, and the vampire Nosferatu awakening from his slumber in the film that carries his name. Next to Poelzig is his sleeping wife, Karen (Lucille Lund), her body seemingly naked beneath the sheet. The next image of Poelzig, as he greets his unexpected visitors, explicitly references Karloff's first appearance as the Creature in *Frankenstein*, cold and cadaverous and clad in what viewers today might find a strangely Hugh Hefner-ish outfit. Poelzig's attraction to Joan, whom Dr. Werdegast has sedated following their road accident, is immediately off-putting; but no more so than Werdegast's obsessive stroking of Joan's hair as she slept in the train compartment they shared. Recent production histories of *The Black Cat* record the rewritings of Lugosi's character that Universal Pictures required, in each case meant to make him appear less menacing. As a result, Karloff's Poelzig became steadily more pathological and repulsive; the progression through necrophilia, pedophilia, and incest, which the film reveals to constitute Poelzig's history, eradicates any initial sympathy his overly mannered self-presentation may have engendered. Yet even with these changes, and with the cuts Universal made after the first screenings for the Motion Pictures Producers and Distributors of America, the industry's morality watchdog, the two antagonists match one another in their barely concealed sadistic impulses.

Three days of retake shooting softened the more threatening aspects of Lugosi's character, although enough remains to make viewers uneasy. Werdegast's fixation on Joan in the railway compartment, for example, draws a look of reprimand from her husband, and his attention to the injury she suffers in the crash of their van insinuates an unpleasant intimacy that is repeated the following morning when he inspects the wound. Karloff, under no such constraints and clearly enjoying his role as the personification of any number of sexual pathologies, is relentless in his determination to torture his old comrade-in-arms. Not only does he know of Werdegast's intense horror of cats; he also knows that the secrets of his cellar and his bedroom will destroy his vengeance-seeking adversary. Belying the solicitude he shows his American guests, Poelzig can barely contain his attraction to Joan, sublimated in the famous scene where he reflexively clenches a nude female statuette as he watches Joan—awakened but under the influence of Werdegast's sedative—amorously embrace her husband.[16] Werdegast's recognition of Poelzig's

*Poelzig (Boris Karloff) gazing at the beauty of his former wife in a macabre gallery of the dead in* The Black Cat.

intentions toward Joan leads to the equally famous chess game between the two, with Joan's life at stake and Peter wandering about as if in a daze.

With Joan and Peter dispatched to their separate bedrooms, Poelzig makes a nocturnal visit to the underground casements upon which he has constructed his house. Holding a black cat in his arms and stroking its fur, the architect pauses, one after another, at a series of glass cases, each of which contains the preserved body of one of his wives. The women are suspended by their hair and are clad in semitransparent gowns.[17] In this bizarre mausoleum, Poelzig's fetishism is revealed as full-fledged necrophilia, and the delight he takes in his collection of corpses explains his fascination with Joan, intended to be his next sacrifice.

Later the same night, Poelzig again descends into the crypt, this time with Werdegast who has demanded to know the fate of his wife Karen. When Werdegast sees Karen's (again, Lucille Lund) body, and learns that Poelzig had married her after telling her that her husband was dead, he recoils in pain and horror. Only the reappearance of the black cat prevents him from shooting Poelzig on the spot. As the camera appears to float through the catacombs beneath Fort Marmaros, Poelzig explains their common fate:

> Are we men or are we children? Of what use are all these melodramatic gestures? You say your soul was killed and that you have been dead all these years. And what of me? Did we not both die here at Marmaros fifteen years ago? Are we any the less victims of the war than those whose bodies were torn asunder? Are we not both the living dead? And now you come to me, playing at being an avenging angel, childishly thirsty for my blood. We understand each other too well. We know too much of life.

Returning to the upstairs residence, Poelzig retires to his bedroom where the younger Karen, Werdegast's daughter, lies in bed unaware of her father's presence in the house. Evidently under a hypnotic spell, this Karen conflates with her entombed mother, implying that Poelzig's necrophilia coexists with an even more alarming pedophilia. Werdegast has suggested as much, when he confuses his wife and his daughter in accusing Poelzig of illicit desires when they knew each other before the outbreak of the war.

In the literature on *The Black Cat*, the ultramodern interior spaces and furnishings of Poelzig's home are cited as a visual counterpoint to the psychosexual dynamics at work among the principals. The sweeping main staircase, the wall of translucent glass blocks, the recessed lighting, the chrome and steel furniture—none of these would have been out of place in a high-end office building in New York or Los Angeles at the time.[18]

Designed by Ulmer and his art director Charles D. Hall, the sets fit into the cinematic tradition that extends from Fritz Lang's *Metropolis* (1927) to

*Featuring angular walls, art deco stylings, and the most modern of substructures, Poelzig's domain in* The Black Cat *manifests deep historical trauma.*

Alexander Korda's *Things to Come* (1936). As these titles suggest, *The Black Cat* might be considered as much a work of science fiction as of horror, even if it lacks the elaborate scientific apparatus of the first *Frankenstein* films.[19] Similarly, the modernist architecture and furniture of Poelzig's mansion can be seen as a parallel to the historical horrors introduced at the beginning of the film and the intellectual and psychological efforts undertaken to exorcise them in the 1920s and 1930s—efforts which, like Poelzig's determination to preserve the beauty of his dead wives in their glass cases, were only to end in failure and an even greater catastrophe.[20]

## FROM CALIGARI TO KUBRICK: *THE BLACK CAT* AND THE FARTHEST DIMENSIONS OF DESIRE

In the last twenty minutes of *The Black Cat* the tensions that connect the principals are ratcheted up to the breaking point. Karen, having emerged from her semicomatose state to encounter Joan, learns that her father is alive and present in the house. For this transgression, Poelzig murders her, another revelation of his innate monstrosity; presumably the second Karen will join the first Karen in the underground mausoleum where Joan, too, is soon going to be installed. Unaware of his daughter's presence, Werdegast has agreed to serve as a surrogate host for the Satanic ritual planned for that night, with Poelzig enacting his high priest role. As the guests assemble, forming an ensemble of deracinated central European aristocrats, the still virginal Joan is taken against her will to the sacrificial chamber which forms the center of Poelzig's infernal residence. At once the Bauhaus references are dropped, and the viewer confronts an Expressionistic world straight out of *The Cabinet of Dr. Caligari*.[21] Standing behind a tilted double cross, symbolic of the medieval Kingdom of Hungary, Poelzig intones a series of Latin nonsequiturs as the black-cloaked celebrants kneel before him. A close-up of Poelzig's face, as he approaches Joan, bound to the cross and unconscious, leaves little question about his intentions. A sudden scream by one of the cultists, startled by something she sees outside the camera's range, interrupts the ceremony and distracts Poelzig. Taking advantage of the confusion, Werdegast and his manservant free Joan and carry her into one of the underground casements.

Ulmer's staging of the Satanic ritual has been referenced in numerous films, but rarely with such veracity as in Stanley Kubrick's final film, *Eyes Wide Shut* (1999). Even before the elaborate masked ball sequence, the centerpiece of the film, Kubrick had quoted *The Black Cat*—perhaps inadvertently—when he showed the married couple played by Tom Cruise and Nicole Kidman arriving at a lavish Christmas party held in a Manhattan mansion. As they are welcomed by the host, Cruise and Kidman are framed against a grand curving staircase that recalls the one leading to the upper story of Poelzig's residence. The similarity between the two scenes is further accentuated by the gleaming wall of white lights that backgrounds the staircase, echoing Poelzig's wall of glass blocks, and the two silhouetted figures who ascend the stairs, just as Poelzig and Werdegast do in *The Black Cat*.[22]

The masked ball sequence in *Eyes Wide Shut*, replete with Satanism, orgiastic sexuality, and a sacrificial murder, is a much more explicit extrapolation from the ritual scene in *The Black Cat*. Descriptions of the production history of *The Black Cat* ascribe considerably more sexual content to Poelzig's celebration of the Black Mass in the initial cut—frames that had to be edited out to satisfy both studio officials and censors. Not unrelatedly, digital alteration of the most explicit scenes of nudity and fornication in *Eyes Wide Shut* were necessary to avoid an NC-17 rating; Kubrick, who died before the film's release, would almost certainly have resisted these changes.[23] Even excluding the editing, opinion remains divided whether Kubrick intended *Eyes Wide Shut* to be a high-art sex film or a horror thriller whose graphic nudity was meant to have a deadening effect.[24] In *The Black Cat* Joan is to become the latest victim of Poelzig's amatory predations but is saved literally at the last moment. Yet when she escapes Poelzig's doomed residence with Peter, she reestablishes the sexual allure to which he, Poelzig, and Werdegast had all responded on the previous evening, with a risqué display of her undergarments.

The concluding scenes of *The Black Cat* accelerate at an almost hysterical pace. Told by Joan that his daughter Karen is alive and is now Poelzig's wife, Werdegast bursts into Poelzig's embalming chamber only to discover her dead body. His sanity destroyed, Werdegast grapples with Poelzig as Joan looks on. Assisted by his manservant, Werdegast shackles his antagonist to the embalming rack and initiates the film's most horrific moment. The original shooting script makes clear what Ulmer intended viewers to see:

> An effect as if Werdegast was splitting the scalp slowly, pulling the skin over Poelzig's head and shoulders. . . . Werdegast finishes, straightens and surveys his work with eminent satisfaction; his insane eyes turn to Joan. He starts toward her. . . . Peter raises the Luger and fires. . . . Werdegast staggers, falls. Joan is still trying to pry the key out of Thamal's hand in background. Poelzig, sans skin, is struggling on the rack. By a superhuman effort he frees himself and falls to the floor. . . . Werdegast raises himself on one elbow and stares at Poelzig, He laughs hysterically, insanely. . . . Poelzig raises his hideous body—his eyes focused dully, expressionlessly, on Joan. He laboriously, painfully crawls to her. As he comes closer, Joan, with redoubled strength, gets the key, rises, and runs to the door. . . . Poelzig, with the last vestige of his strength, turns and starts crawling to Werdegast. . . .[25]

The scene was apparently never shot, and Ulmer may have included it only as a bargaining chip to use with studio and industry officials. Instead, the skinning of Poelzig is shown by shadows, with close-ups of his manacled hands twisting in pain and his animal-like bleats serving to convey the horror of his punishment. Fatally wounded by Peter, who mistakenly thinks he is assaulting Joan, Werdegast utters his last line—"It has been a good game"—as he pulls the switch to ignite the explosives that still underlie the former fortress.

Scenes of torture, vivisection, and dismemberment had been, along with those involving sex, the film studios' favored means of attracting audiences in the early 1930s. The more lurid and scandalous the images, the higher the ticket sales that could be expected, at least among moviegoers who preferred shocks and thrills to jokes and laughs in their entertainment.[26] Ulmer did not go as far as Robert Florey, who added a suggestion of bestiality to the torture and gore he depicted in *Murders in the Rue Morgue* (1932), or Erle Kenton, who included even more overt implications of interspecies sex in *Island of Lost Souls* (1932), adapted from H. G. Wells's novel *The Island of Doctor Moreau*. But the themes of fetishism, incest, and necrophilia that are central to *The Black Cat* were sufficient to accomplish the same purpose.

## CONCLUSION: WOMEN IN CRYPTS

Almost any discussion of *The Black Cat* will include the exchange between Peter Alison and Vitus Werdegast after the psychiatrist has tried to explain Joan's strange behavior when she briefly awakened from her narcotic-induced sleep. Peter: "It sounds like a lot of supernatural baloney to me." Werdegast: "Supernatural, perhaps. Baloney, perhaps not." Werdegast's next line—"There are many things under the sun..."—recalls John Barrymore's recitation of the line from *Hamlet* in the 1931 Warner Brothers' production, *Svengali*: "There are more things in heaven and earth than are dreamt of in your philosophy." Adapted from the 1894 novel *Trilby*, by George Du Maurier, and directed by Archie Mayo, *Svengali* provided Barrymore a much-needed opportunity to resuscitate his career, which had declined since his stage and screen successes in the early 1920s. Gifted again with the grotesque makeup that had served him well in *Dr. Jekyll and Mr. Hyde* (1920), Barrymore's performance as the sinister music teacher Svengali exploited multiple anxieties that were current at the time, most notably the unease many people felt about the practice of hypnosis—both medically and as popular entertainment—and the even greater discomfiture occasioned by large numbers of immigrants and refugees arriving from the ghettos of Poland, Hungary, and other eastern European countries.[27]

If Karloff's Poelzig presents an exotic appearance, with his black lipstick and demonic haircut, Barrymore's Svengali looks as though he had emerged from a menacing back alley or, even worse, out of a sewer in Warsaw or Budapest. The hypnotist-charlatan-predator was already a familiar cinematic stereotype, thanks to *The Cabinet of Dr. Caligari* and Fritz Lang's *Dr. Mabuse, the Gambler* (1922). Although much in demand in Paris music circles for his uncanny ability to coax passable performances from untalented vocalists, Svengali—a Polish Jew, given to leers and cackles—looks the part of a rag dealer or a kleptomaniac. His attempts to seduce the artist's model and would-be stage singer Trilby, played by Marian Marsh, by use of his hypnotic powers are ultimately successful, as she falls under his control in much the same way that the younger Karen is dominated by Poelzig in *The Black Cat*. While Trilby may not end up on an embalming slab or in a glass container, Svengali's determination to possess her, psychologically as well as erotically, brings him close to the control Poelzig exercises not only over the younger Karen, but over the virginal Joan as well.[28] In *Svengali*, the exhausted mesmerist, after directing a last triumphant performance by Trilby in a Cairo nightclub, dies with his love for her still unrealized; in *The Black Cat*, prevented from completing his blasphemous ritual, the devil-worshipping sadist is tortured and crucified while Joan escapes his clutches.

If the connections between Barrymore's Svengali and Karloff's Poelzig are tenuous at best, the latter's underground vaults recall another lurid melodrama more directly—one that Ulmer himself would bring to the screen well after his career with Universal Pictures had ended. In May 1918 Béla Bartók premiered his one-act opera *Bluebeard's Castle*, with a libretto by fellow Hungarian Béla Balázs, in Budapest. Drawing upon the legend of Bluebeard, which had enjoyed a revival among fin-de-siècle aesthetes in London and Paris, Bartók created a latter-day Symbolist dreamscape—both he and Balázs knew the plays Maurice Maeterlinck had written in the 1890s—in which the heroine, Judith, cannot save herself from the fate the hero-villain's previous wives have suffered.[29] Inside his castle, seven locked doors conceal the secrets of Bluebeard's kingdom; persuading him to open the doors one by one, Judith discovers her new husband's hidden armories, torture chambers, and treasuries, all drenched in blood. The final door, which Bluebeard resists to the last to open, reveals his three former wives, alive but silent, costumed in glittering jewels. These are the wives Judith will join, disappearing into the seventh room as the opera concludes. In this brief description, the women in *Bluebeard's Castle* might seem more suggestive of the three vampire wives Jonathan Harker encounters in the 1931 version of *Dracula*; but the emphasis on the menacing atmosphere of Bluebeard's abode, and on its locked, secret rooms, anticipates in far greater measure the crypt in which Poelzig keeps his perpetually preserved victims.[30]

Ulmer got the chance to try his hand with the Bluebeard story, which he had been interested in for years, in 1944, well into the Poverty Row stage of his career. Working for PRC (Producers Releasing Corporation) and with a screenplay by Pierre Gendron, Ulmer had the good fortune to have John Carradine cast in the title role.[31] Carradine needed a career boost after having played a mad Nazi scientist in *Revenge of the Zombies* for Monogram Pictures the year before, and he provided Ulmer what many critics still believe is one of his best performances. While he was certainly familiar with Bartók's interpretation of the Bluebeard story, Ulmer chose to rely primarily on the Faust legend, evidently under the influence of Charles Gounod's 1859 opera of that name, a miniaturized version of which he incorporated in his film.[32] The Bluebeard character, the painter and puppeteer Gaston Morrell, may at first appear more sympathetic than the sadistic wife murderer and Satanic priest in *The Black Cat*, especially as played with the elegant flair that Carradine would display again in his impersonations of Dracula in Universal's *House of Frankenstein* (1944) and *House of Dracula* (1945); but his obsession with ideal beauty and his string of victims are taken right out of the Poelzig book—Poelzig, after all, is also a serial murderer. Both Poelzig and Morrell are egomaniacs, each with a strong Nietzschean bent, creating their own moral universe that pays no heed to that of "ordinary" individuals; and each inhabits his own underworld, Poelzig prowling the cellars of his fortress home so that he can admire his mummified wives, Morrell surrounded by his puppets and disposing of his victims in the sewers of Paris.

The embalmed wives kept in glass cylinders, the crooked cross used for Satanic rituals, the torture rack on which Poelzig is skinned alive, Werdegast, his victim and his torturer—all perish in the explosion that destroys Fort Marmaros, only Peter and Joan escaping with their lives. The climax of *The Black Cat* can be described in vivid terms:

> The walls began to cave in upon one another, all of the works raised their terrible voices simultaneously, all of the exterior and interior walls. A constant rolling wave formed in the air. Windows rattled, steel girders shook.... All the sounds of hell rang out. You would think it was a volcano exploding.... Every thunderclap a cry of the dead, the bleeding, the starving. Every thunderclap a cry of the hundred thousand martyred souls that gave up their blood for this fort. And so it went the entire night.[33]

Again, this passage does not describe the end of *The Black Cat*, although it could. Instead, it is one of the last diary entries written by a civilian trapped in Fort Przemyśl, as the Russians aimed their final bombardment at the doomed citadel. Edgar Ulmer was not there. He may not even have known the grim details of the fortress's last hours. Yet they informed his imagination as he conceived, designed, and directed his most famous film.

## NOTES

1. A civilian diary entry during the last days of fighting at Fortress Przemyśl in March 1915, quoted in Tunstall, *Written in Blood*, 285.

2. Tunstall, *Written*, 339. See also Tunstall, *Blood on the Snow*, and Schindler, *Fall of the Double Eagle*.

3. "Edgar G. Ulmer," in Bogdanovich, *Who the Devil Made It?*, 575–576.

4. Isenberg, *Edgar G. Ulmer*, 72.

5. On these German accounts, see Kaes, *Shell Shock Cinema* and, with particular attention to *The Black Cat*, Gemünden, *Continental Strangers*, 38–47.

6. Snyder, *Bloodlands: Europe between Hitler and Stalin*. See also Segal, *Genocide in the Carpathians*. Ulmer may have taken the name Marmaros from the northeastern Hungarian district of Máramaros, over which the Hungarians and Russians battled during World War I.

7. An essential source remains Clarke, "Expressionism in Film and Architecture." According to Clarke, Poelzig was happy to take the work on *The Golem* since the economic circumstances in Germany precluded most large-scale building projects.

8. Bogdanovich, *Who the Devil Made It*, 576. For the scholarship on *The Black Cat* see, for example, Peirse, "Bauhaus of Horrors;" Cantor, "The Fall of the House of Ulmer."

9. Mank, *Karloff and Lugosi*, 168.

10. Petropoulus, *Artists under Hitler*, 25.

11. Hake, *Popular Cinema of the Third Reich*, 238–239. Cf. the essays by Ross Wolfe, "Return to Horror: Hans Poelzig's Nightmare Expressionism, 1908–1935" and "Scary Architecture: The Early Works of Hans Poelzig."

12. Schwaab, "On the Graveyards of Europe."

13. James-Chakraborty, *German Architecture for a Mass Audience*, 90–95.

14. The details of Ulmer's early career in America remain obscure despite the best efforts of his biographers to pin them down; apparently there were a number of trips back and forth to Europe before Ulmer became established in California. See Isenberg, "Perennial Detour: The Cinema of Edgar G. Ulmer and the Experience of Exile." Ulmer had lots of company among Hollywood's émigré and exile filmmakers, especially those from central Europe. See Koepnick, *The Dark Mirror: German Cinema between Hitler and Hollywood*.

15. For Ulmer's interest in Crowley, see Mank, *Karloff and Lugosi*, 157–160; Weaver et al., *Universal Horrors: The Studio's Classic Films, 1931–1946*, 87–95. For Ulmer's behavior toward actress Lucille Lund during the filming of *The Black Cat*, see Hoffman, "A Good Game: 1934's 'The Black Cat.'"

16. Here, more than in any other scene in the film, Ulmer's indebtedness to the Vienna of his youth—that is, the Vienna of Sigmund Freud—shows itself. How well-versed in Freudian theory Ulmer may have been remains unclear. Paul A. Cantor, in "The Fall of the House of Ulmer" (159), argues for a conversational familiarity, without citing any direct evidence. Reynold Humphries's psychoanalytically informed *The Hollywood Horror Film* is silent on the subject. For a Freudian reading of *The Black Cat*, see Turbrett, "The Devil's Contract." See also Isenberg, *Edgar G. Ulmer*, who is skeptical about any direct influence by Freud on Ulmer's filmmaking.

17. For Ulmer's addition of the underground tomb scene, see Mank, *Karloff and Lugosi*, 172–173.

18. Or in an expensive sanatorium in Switzerland or Scandinavia as imagined by Thomas Mann in *The Magic Mountain* (1924) and built by such modernist architects as Josef Hoffmann and Alvar Aalto. See Gregory, "Comfortably Numb."

19. Meehan, *Tech-Noir: The Fusion of Science Fiction and Film Noir*, 57–59.

20. Cantor, "The Fall of the House of Ulmer," 148–149. See also Schwaab, "On the Graveyards of Europe," 41–42.

21. Compare, for example, the ritual scene in *The Black Cat* with the images reproduced in Darsa, "Art House: An Introduction to German Expressionist Films"; Hendrickson, "Mad Berlin: Revisiting *Dr. Caligari* in the Wake of Fascism."

22. The similarity of these opening scenes is so striking that it is difficult to dismiss it as coincidental. Yet it does not appear to have been picked up in the critical commentary on *Eyes Wide Shut*. See, for example, the relevant chapters in Rhodes, ed., *Stanley Kubrick: Essays on His Films and Legacy*, and Ljujic et al., *Stanley Kubrick: New Perspectives*. Isenberg, *Edgar G. Ulmer* (73–74), notes the connection

between the ritual scenes in *The Black Cat* and *Eyes Wide Shut*, but does not comment on the earlier arrival scenes. See also Herzogenrath, "Ulmer and Cult/ure" (28), who notes the connection with *Eyes Wide Shut* but does not expand on it.

23. Lewis, *Hollywood v. Hard Core*, 1–3.

24. On the film's contested critical reputation, see Ransom, "Opening *Eyes Wide Shut*: Genre, Reception, and Kubrick's Last Film." On the contextualization of the orgy scene in *Eyes Wide Shut*, see Williams, *The Erotic Thriller in Contemporary Cinema*, 397–400.

25. Towlson, *The Turn to Gruesomeness in Horror Films*, 17–38; Doherty, *Pre-Code Hollywood*, 295–318.

26. Edwards, "'House of Horrors': Corporate Strategy at Universal Pictures in the 1930s."

27. On popular perceptions of hypnosis in the years before and after World War I, see Andriopoulos, *Possessed: Hypnotic Crimes, Corporate Fiction, and the Invention of Cinema*. On the depiction of hypnosis in *Svengali*, see Berenstein, *Attack of the Leading Ladies*, 115–118. For a detailed discussion of *Svengali*, see Mank, *The Very Witching Time of Night*, 28–65.

28. On the popularity of the Bluebeard legend among Symbolist poets and playwrights in Paris at the turn of the century, see Tatar, *Secrets behind the Doors*, 144–155.

29. In Bartók's opera, Judith's insistence on learning her husband's past—with its strong sexual undertones—might be seen as an anticipation of Werdegast's determination to know the fate of his wife and daughter, which ensnares him in the dark web of Poelzig's perversions.

30. On the production history of *Bluebeard*, see Isenberg, *Edgar G. Ulmer*, 146–149, and Rogers, "Remaking the B Film in 1940s Hollywood," 149–150. According to Bernd Herzogenrath, *Bluebeard* was originally intended to be a Universal Pictures' production, filmed after *The Black Cat* was completed and with Boris Karloff in the lead role. Ulmer's break with Universal, for personal reasons, put an end to that project until it was revived for PRC ten years later. See Herzogenrath, "Ulmer and Cult/ure," 33–36.

31. Carradine had an uncredited part in *The Black Cat*, as the organist with his back turned at the celebration of the Satanic ritual.

32. Hanke, "Puppets and Paintings: Authorship and Artistry in Edgar G. Ulmer's *Bluebeard*." On the thematic connection between *The Black Cat* and *Bluebeard*, see Ulman, "Edgar G. Ulmer."

33. A civilian's diary entry on the surrender of Fort Przemyśl, quoted in Tunstall, *Written in Blood*, 286.

# BIBLIOGRAPHY

Andriopoulos, Stefan. *Possessed: Hypnotic Crimes, Corporate Fiction, and the Invention of Cinema*. Translated by Peter Jansen and Stefan Andriopoulos. Chicago: University of Chicago Press, 2008.

Berenstein, Rhona J. *Attack of the Leading Ladies: Gender, Sexuality, and Spectatorship in Classic Horror Cinema*. New York: Columbia University Press, 1996.

Bogdanovich, Peter. *Who the Devil Made It? In Conversation with Legendary Film Directors*. New York: Ballantine Books, 1998.

Cantor, Paul A. "The Fall of the House of Ulmer: Europe vs. America in the Gothic Vision of *The Black Cat*." In *The Philosophy of Horror*, edited by Thomas Fahy, 137–160. Lexington: University Press of Kentucky, 2010.

Clarke, John R. "Expressionism in Film and Architecture: Hans Poelzig's Sets for Paul Wegener's *The Golem*." *Art Journal* 34, no. 2 (1974): 115–124.

Darsa, Alissa. "Art House: An Introduction to German Expressionist Films," *ArtNet*, December 26, 2013. https://news.artnet.com/market/art-house-an-introduction-to-german-expressionist-films-32845

Doherty, Thomas. *Pre-Code Hollywood: Sex, Immorality, and Insurrection in American Cinema, 1930–1934*. New York: Columbia University Press, 1999.

Edwards, Kyle. "'House of Horrors': Corporate Strategy at Universal Pictures in the 1930s." In *Merchants of Menace: The Business of Horror Cinema*, edited by Richard Nowell, 13–29. New York: Bloomsbury, 2014.

Gemünden, Gerd. *Continental Strangers: German Exile Cinema, 1933–1951*. New York: Columbia University Press, 2014.

Gregory, Anne. "Comfortably Numb." *The New York Times Style Magazine*, March 4, 2018, 104–111.

Hake, Sabine. *Popular Cinema of the Third Reich*. Austin: University of Texas Press, 2001.

Hanke, Steffen. "Puppets and Paintings: Authorship and Artistry in Edgar G. Ulmer's *Bluebeard*." In *Edgar G. Ulmer: Detour on Poverty Row*, edited by Gary D. Rhodes, 181–194. Lanham, MD: Lexington Books, 2010.

Hendrickson, Edward. "Mad Berlin: Revisiting *Dr. Caligari* in the Wake of Fascism." *Walker Art Center Magazine*, August 30, 2017. https://walkerart.org/magazine/mad-berlin-revisiting-dr-caligari-in-the-wake-of-fascism

Herzogenrath, Bernd. "Ulmer and Cult/ure." In *Edgar G. Ulmer: Essays on the King of the B's*, edited by Bernd Herzogenrath, 23–38. Jefferson, NC: McFarland, 2009.

Hoffman, Matthew C. "A Good Game: 1934's 'The Black Cat.'" *Screen Deco*, May 2012: 48–59. https://screendeco.wordpress.com/2012/05.

Humphries, Reynold. *The Hollywood Horror Film, 1931–1941*. Lanham, MD: Scarecrow Press, 2006.

Isenberg, Noah. *Edgar G. Ulmer: A Filmmaker at the Margins*. Berkeley & Los Angeles: University of California Press, 2014.

———. "Perennial Detour: The Cinema of Edgar G. Ulmer and the Experience of Exile." *Cinema Journal* 43, no. 2 (2004): 3–25.

James-Chakraborty, Kathleen. *German Architecture for a Mass Audience*. New York: Routledge, 2000.

Kaes, Anton. *Shell Shock Cinema: Weimar Culture and the Wounds of War*. Princeton, NJ: Princeton University Press, 2009.

Koepnick, Lutz. *The Dark Mirror: German Cinema between Hitler and Hollywood*. Berkeley & Los Angeles: University of California Press, 2002.

Lewis, Jon. *Hollywood v. Hard Core: How the Struggle over Censorship Saved the Modern Film Industry*. New York: New York University Press, 2000.

Ljujic, Tatjana, Peter Krämer, and Richard Daniels, eds. *Stanley Kubrick: New Perspectives*. London: Black Dog Publishing, 2015.

Mank, Gregory William. *Karloff and Lugosi: The Expanded Story of a Haunting Collaboration with a Complete Filmography of Their Films Together*. Jefferson, NC: McFarland, 2009.

———. *The Very Witching Time of Night: Dark Alleys of Classic Horror Cinema*. Jefferson, NC: McFarland, 2014.

Meehan, Paul. *Tech-Noir: The Fusion of Science Fiction and Film Noir*. Jefferson, NC: McFarland, 2008.

Peirse, Alison. "Bauhaus of Horrors: Edgar G. Ulmer and *The Black Cat*." In *Edgar G. Ulmer: Detour on Poverty Row*, edited by Gary D. Rhodes, 275–288. Lanham, MD: Lexington Books, 2010.

Petropoulos, Jonathan. *Artists under Hitler: Collaboration and Survival in Nazi Germany*. New Haven, CT: Yale University Press, 2014.

Ransom, Amy J. "Opening *Eyes Wide Shut*: Genre, Reception, and Kubrick's Last Film." *Journal of Film and Video* 62, no. 4 (2010): 31–46.

Rhodes, Gary, ed. *Stanley Kubrick: Essays on His Films and Legacy*. Jefferson, NC: McFarland, 2007.

Rogers, Maureen. "Remaking the B Film in 1940s Hollywood: Producers Releasing Corporation and the Poverty Row Programmer." *Film History* 29, no. 2 (2017): 138–164.

Schindler, John R. *Fall of the Double Eagle: The Battle for Galicia and the Demise of Austria-Hungary*. Lincoln, NE: Potomac Books, 2015.

Schwaab, Herbert. "On the Graveyards of Europe: The Horrors of Modernism in *The Black Cat*." In *The Films of Edgar G. Ulmer*, edited by Bernd Herzogenrath, 39–52. Lanham, MD: Scarecrow Press, 2009.

Segal, Raz. *Genocide in the Carpathians: War, Social Breakdown, and Mass Violence, 1914–1945*. Stanford: Stanford University Press, 2016.

Snyder, Timothy. *Bloodlands: Europe between Hitler and Stalin*. New York: Basic Books, 2010.

Tatar, Maria. *Secrets behind the Doors: The Story of Bluebeard and His Wives*. Princeton, NJ: Princeton University Press, 2004.

Towlson, Jon. *The Turn to Gruesomeness in American Horror Films, 1931–1936*. Jefferson, NC: McFarland, 2016.

Tunstall, Graydon A. *Blood on the Snow: The Carpathian Winter War of 1915*. Lawrence: University Press of Kansas, 2010.

———. *Written in Blood: The Battles for Fortress Przemyśl in WW I*. Bloomington: Indiana University Press, 2016.

Turbrett, Dion. "The Devil's Contract: The Satisfaction of Self-Destruction in Edgar G. Ulmer's *The Black Cat*." In *Edgar G. Ulmer: Detour on Poverty Row*, edited by Gary D. Rhodes, 289–300. Lanham, MD: Lexington Books, 2010.

Ulman, Erik. "Edgar G. Ulmer." In the "Great Directors" series, *Senses of Cinema*, no. 24 (2003). http://sensesofcinema.com/2003/great-directors/ulmer

Weaver, Tom, Michael Brunas, and John Brunas. *Universal Horrors: The Studio's Classic Films, 1931–1946.* 2nd ed. Jefferson, NC: McFarland, 2007.

Williams, Linda Ruth. *The Erotic Thriller in Contemporary Cinema.* Bloomington: Indiana University Press, 2005.

Wolfe, Ross. "Return to Horror: Hans Poelzig's Nightmare Expressionism, 1908–1935." *The Charnel House*, August 17, 2015. https://thecharnelhouse.org/2015/08/17/return-to-the-horrorhaus-hans-poelzigs-nightmare-expressionism-1908-1935

———. "Scary Architecture: The Early Works of Hans Poelzig." *The Charnel House*, November 11, 2013. https://thecharnelhouse.org/2013/11/25/scary-architecture-the-early-works-of-hans-poelzig

*Chapter Fifteen*

# Peril, Imprisonment, and the Power of Place in Jordan Peele's *Get Out*

Michael C. Reiff

It's 1946. World War II has ended. For millions of returning veterans, the American Dream can truly begin.

Unless you're black.

As Richard Rothstein writes in *The Color of Law*, when African Americans returned home from the war, they faced a very different homecoming than their white brethren. The federal government excluded blacks from major elements of the GI Bill.[1] Blacks were explicitly deemed a liability by the Federal Housing Administration and were blocked from housing grants.[2] Blacks couldn't buy property in heavily subsidized new suburban communities ranging from the iconic Levittowns in New York and Pennsylvania to countless other new suburbs from Kansas to California.[3]

This system—written into federal programs created under the iconic liberal administration of Franklin Delano Roosevelt—affected blacks in the North as well as the South. It was not, however, the only method of control black Americans faced in the postwar era. Sometimes bureaucratic oppression didn't work. Sometimes, there was violence.

In 1951 Harvey Clark, a black Air Force veteran, attempted to move his family into the all-white Chicago suburb of Cicero. The police attempted to arrest him. They ordered Clark to "get out" of Cicero.[4] When that didn't work, a mob of thousands descended on the apartment building. Stones were hurled. Firebombs burned the Clarks' belongings. Not a single rioter was indicted. Instead, a grand jury indicted Harvey Clark.[5]

In 1987, it happened again. An African American family attempted to move into the suburb of Cicero. They were greeted by more firebombs and, this time, rifle shots. No one was convicted for these crimes. Following these attacks, the suburb's council president claimed that "the area is well-secured."[6]

Well-secured for whom?[7]

Jordan Peele's 2017 film *Get Out* opens with a young black man walking through a suburb at night. His name is Andre Hayward. The suburb street is filled with substantial homes and leafy trees. Street lights illuminate the sidewalks in calming hues.

Andre, however, isn't calm. He's trying to find a specific house, but his smartphone app is leading him in circles. He feels as though he's trapped in a maze. He feels like he needs to get out of this "creepy-ass suburb."

A pure white sports car passes him, turns around in the road, and pulls up next to him. Andre doesn't have to look. He knows there is a threat. "Not today" he says, turning around and heading in the other direction.

Then, suddenly, he is attacked. The driver of the car appears out of nowhere, puts Andre in a chokehold, and drags him to the car. The young black man disappears into the white car's trunk. After this brief shock of violence, the sounds of suburban tranquility return. The suburb is once again at peace.

Jordan Peele films the opening scene of *Get Out* as a tracking shot, in one continuous take. From Andre Hayward walking alone to his body being stolen away into the trunk of the car, we experience each fleeting second as Andre experiences it. We see how quickly his life changes, and how quickly the suburb changes from a place of anxiety into a hunting ground of horror.

No one steps in. No one stops the abduction. The suburb is well-secured.

The opening sequence to *Get Out* is jarring, immediate, and violent. It is a cinematic synecdoche that previews the structure of the film to come and showcases Peele's exquisite control of cinematic tone and craft. The actions in the opening also reverberate beyond the confines of the film. Its raw immediacy speaks to today's climate of vigilantism in suburban spaces. Its layered

*Andre Hayward is abducted from the midst of a "peaceful" white suburb in* Get Out.

symbolism echoes our national past, from the predation of black bodies for exploitation to the exclusion of black bodies from iconic American spaces.

Which is worse: to be targeted by a single assailant, a mob, or an entire system?

Or all of them at once?

Recently, a number of writers—from Ta-Nehisi Coates to Richard Rothstein—have begun to uncover and recontextualize a history of the post-1945 United States that is often ignored—one that shows the dark and violent intersection of housing, racism, and violent oppression against African Americans in the United States. But a firmer understanding of our shared history can only get us so far. It sometimes takes story, fiction and genre to jolt us into a different understanding of our current situation and its historical antecedents.

*Get Out* does this.

Peele's debut film, a combination of horror genre elements and psychological thriller structures, has been rightly praised for its assured technical prowess and its deft, complex, and stirring script—one that made Peele the first African American in ninety years to win the Academy Award for Best Original Screenplay. One element of *Get Out* is particularly crucial, however, to the film's resonance with American history and contemporary issues.

That element is the importance, and peril, of place.

Peele focuses this critique of places, setting, and homes around two key characters. The first is the film's protagonist, Chris Washington: a young African American photographer who is visiting his girlfriend's parents' home for the first time. The second is Andre Hayward, who—after being violently kidnapped in the first scene of the film—returns later, seemingly transformed. Using these two characters, Peele examines key motifs of peril, property, and imprisonment—elements of the African American experience that reach from the beginnings of the Atlantic Slave Trade to the deaths of Trayvon Martin and Eric Garner.

The history of imperiled and imprisoned black men and women in the United States is long and complex. A full explication of how *Get Out* wrestles with this history could fill an entire book. This chapter, therefore, will focus on how the role of place and ideology in *Get Out*—visible in the recurring motifs of peril, property, and imprisonment—reflects the deeper structures of America's past. The experiences of Chris and Andre in *Get Out* are rooted in the centuries-old experiences of the African slave fort, the slave ship, and the American plantation—as well as in the mind-set of the enslaved and imprisoned. Though technically set over a brief weekend in a single country home, *Get Out* shows the power of place, physical and mental imprisonment, and systemic ideologies over those targeted for powerlessness.

## A NEW SLAVERY

Agents of peril and methods of imprisonment are woven throughout *Get Out*. After the prologue (described above), Peele's focus shifts to Chris preparing to meet his girlfriend Rose's parents. Rose is white, and Chris realizes her parents do not know he is black. He is uncomfortable with this situation, but she puts him at ease to lure him to her parent's house.

The "house" proves to be a palatial estate inhabited by Rose's father, mother, and brother along with two black servants—a male groundskeeper and a female maid. When Chris attempts to interact with the latter, he finds them oddly placid and uncannily "pleasant."

During his first night at the house, Chris sneaks out to smoke a cigarette. Rose's mother discovers him and lures him into her office. A trained psychiatrist, she pushes him first to remember the day he lost his mother, and then seemingly entraps him in a hypnotized trance. He envisions himself in a "sunken place"—falling through darkness, with a small window on the outside world above him. Chris wakes up the next morning questioning the events of the previous night.

On the second day, a party of family friends arrives. This large group of affluent, mostly white people are supposedly there for an annual reunion. But Chris is on the defensive yet again. The guests quickly begin to physically poke and mentally prod him about his identity and abilities as a black man.

Chris also sees Andre Hayworth, an erstwhile acquaintance, at the party, and suspects Hayworth is the same black man who disappeared some weeks back. Andre is now transformed. His attire reflects an affluence and "whiteness" that is new to him. He is now dating an older white woman. He talks with a strange, dreamlike affectation.

After a long, anxious day filled with demeaning and covetously racialized comments and questions, Chris attempts to leave the house early with Rose. It's at this point that Chris begins to suspect that Rose has had a number of relationships with other black men, though she has told Chris that he is her first black boyfriend. As Chris attempts to flee the house, Rose's mother puts him back into a trance, and he is carried into the basement.

In the basement, Chris wakes up, strapped to a chair. A TV in front of him turns on and off autonomously. At one point it plays a seemingly decades-old family advertisement, showing Rose's grandfather talking about a process he's invented called "The Coagula." Later, the TV turns on to show a man he met at the party—a blind, white art dealer. The man is in a medical smock. He clearly and cheerily explains Chris's situation.

Soon, Chris will have most of his brain removed, and the art dealer's brain will be put into his skull. The art dealer will then control Chris's body's actions. He will use Chris's body as a new, more able shell. But Chris will still "exist" inside of himself. Chris's consciousness—his identity—will remain in a sunken, repressed state. He will only be able to glimpse the outside world from a mental basement. Chris will be permanently in the "sunken place." Chris's body will be rendered an object, an exoskeleton, for his new white owner. Chris's physical eyes will help the white art dealer take beautiful pictures. But Chris's mind will also be enslaved, repressed and bottled within his own body. Chris's mind—conscious, aware, writhing in mental darkness—will not be erased. Like the slaves of the antebellum American South, his physical body will be commodified, while his mental identity will be repressed, relegated though not removed.

The art dealer also makes plain what Chris already suspects. He isn't the first to be used in this way. The Armitage family—seductive Rose, her chokeholding brother, her hypnotizing mother, and her lobotomizing father—have created a system. They've been capturing black men and women, replacing most of their original brains (though keeping their identities in a repressed state) with new, "white" brains. The groundskeeper's body houses the grandfather's brain. The maid's body houses the grandmother's. Andre Hayward contains elements of the original Andre, but also hosts a new, white brain. There seem to be countless others, as Chris discovered. Whether born out of greed, racism, or a quasi-spiritual belief in "The Coagula," their system has been at work for years, ensnaring and dehumanizing a population of black men and women. Like the black cars that the Armitages' friends arrive in,[8] and the black "molds"[9] that are in the Armitages' basement, the Armitages have created a system of literally refashioning black bodies into commodified and utilized vessels for white brains.

They've created a new form of slavery.

Chris escapes by picking the cotton stuffing[10] out of the arm of the leather chair he is strapped to and stuffing the cotton into his ears so that he can block out the auditory signal that puts him into a trance. He kills the family and burns down their mansion, including its basement dungeon and scientific instruments of enslavement. On the road out, he confronts Rose a final time. As he is about to strangle her and end her family's system of enslavement forever, Chris sees police car lights. He pauses. She smiles. Positioned as he is, a black man crouching over a white woman with his hands on her neck, with Rose crying out "Help!" she anticipates—as the viewer does—that Chris is about to be shot or, at best, arrested and imprisoned.[11] But the police car is actually driven by his friend Ron, a black TSA agent, who whisks him to safety. The film ends with Chris in Ron's car, staring out the window at the woods surrounding the Armitages' plantation.[12]

Peele dabbles with jump scares and psychological horror throughout *Get Out*, but only unleashes blood and violence at the level of a slasher film in the climax. Each phase of the film, however—from the initial, subtle perils Chris is subjected to, through his treatment as a dehumanized object of curiosity and consumption by the family and partygoers, to his final understanding of the depth of his imprisonment—evokes eras and places and phases in American history. The events of *Get Out* can be situated within a wider historical context. The Armitages' estate, for example, acts as a visual metaphor, or a historical echo of West African slave trade forts, slave ships, and American slave plantations. This interweaving of past and present spaces facilitates the layered readings of the film that Peele seems to invite.

## "FRAUD AND VIOLENCE"

In 1776, as the Thirteen Colonies declared their independence, James Field Stanfield completed a two-year stint on British slave ships that operated off the coast of West Africa, acquiring black men and women by "fraud and violence."[13] Stanfield notes in his book *Observations on a Guinea Voyage* that many Africans were not "prisoners of war" (as was widely believed to be the case) but had been stolen away from their villages by "nomadic, independent . . . raiders." These raiders would attack villages, kill any opposition, and drag away men, women, and children to slave-trading fortresses, like the one where Stanfield was stationed on the British-controlled "slave coast."[14] Not all enslaved Africans, however, were taken by force. The naïve and unsuspecting were, as Stanfield and contemporaries noted, also stolen away by "trickery."[15] Africans like the Nigerian Ukawasaw Gronniosaw were lured to the Gold Coast slave forts through "mesmerizing" stories of European power.[16] Regardless of how they were ensnared, however, once brought to the slave forts, Africans became dehumanized property.

Rose's brother Jeremy Armitage clearly fits Stanfield's description of the "nomadic" slave trader who relies on "violence" as his principal method of capture. The opening scene features Jeremy hunting for prey, not in a fixed location, but roving in his white car. Later in the film, Jeremy threatens, and then uses, violence to subdue Chris—at dinner the first night, wielding a lacrosse stick the second night, and then in the climactic sequence, attempting to incapacitate Chris with the same chokehold he uses on Andre in the first scene of the film. Jeremy taps into the vision of slave traders we may have in our minds—violent, repressive, and dehumanizing from the outset.

Rose, on the other hand, never lifts a finger against Chris, preferring "trickery" to violence. Along with their romantic and sexual relationship, Rose uses persuasion and projection—her parents are supposedly "woke" white people, her Dad "would have voted for Obama a third time" if he had had the chance—to entice Chris to her parent's estate. Tellingly, of course, Rose's character quickly switches when the ruse is exposed. When Chris finally confronts Rose as he attempts to flee her house, Rose instantly exposes herself to be yet another enslaver, as cold and calculating as anyone else. There are no lingering feelings of affection in Rose—there never was affection to begin with. The result, in any event, is the same: Chris ends up in the Armitages' basement and Jeremy and Rose have, through "violence and fraud," delivered yet another human being to the Armitages' slave fort.

Peele goes to some lengths to show that Chris's abduction is not a one-off event, but a single repetition of a larger system. An overheard conversation between the Armitages indicates that Jeremy often damages his prey too much when abducting them. Even the blind art dealer, a client of the Armitages, is aware of Jeremy's notorious track record. When Chris attempts to escape the Armitage estate in Jeremy's car, he finds a spiked, medieval-looking helmet, evoking the brutal garb Jeremy likely wears on some of his hunts.

Peele also suggests that Rose's emotional "fraud" and "trickery" has been used on multiple victims in multiple ways. When Chris finds the box of photographs in Rose's room, he notices that each photo depicts Rose with a different black man (and even one black woman, likely the one that has become the maid Georgina or the "mold" for the grandmother's brain). Each photo shows Rose dressed and acting differently, indicating that her deceptions shift depending on the target. Even though Chris hasn't even undergone the Coagula operation, we see Rose immediately resume her part of the system. Peele shows Rose perusing social network profiles and online pictures of other black men—new targets. The system is not only continuous but rapacious; Chris hasn't even left the basement of the slave fort, hasn't even been converted by the Coagula system, and she is already on the hunt again.

The Armitage estate itself evokes the slave forts that dotted the West Coast of Africa. Minutes after Chris arrives at the Armitages' house, Rose's father Dean leads him on a tour, pointing out sculptures and artifacts he's "brought back" from his trips overseas. He declares that he's "a traveler," by nature and that he "can't help it—I keep bringing souvenirs back," undermining his subsequent statement that "it's such a privilege to be able to experience another person's culture." His encounters with other cultures are, the collection suggests, ultimately about acquisition and possession: bringing home trophies of other cultures rather than understanding, let alone empathizing, with them. The house's first-floor collection eerily echoes the travelling British slave traders Field's narrative describes—individuals who were able to visit places, steal bodies, and profit from other peoples.

The typical layout of the slave forts, with British nationals quartered on the upper floors and captured Africans hidden away in stygian dungeons, warehoused next to other goods for trade and unseen by the outside world,[17] is also reflected in the Armitages' home. Once captured, Chris is held captive in the basement, a space previously off limits to him and unseen by the audience. The basement is also where the bloody and brutal brain transplants occur, and where, presumably, the victims of those transplants are kept before and after the operation—a parallel of the forts, which Yussuf Simmonds aptly describes as "warehouses of black humanity."[18]

Peele also visually and metaphorically foreshadows the Armitages' home as a place of peril in his first establishing shot of the home. When Chris and Rose pull up to the house, Peele gives us one of the first truly wide shots of the film. The house is shot from the front, with Greek Revival-style columns flanking windows and a central door. The shot is so large that Chris and Rose's red car is small and to the left of the frame, with Chris and Rose appearing as even smaller figures as they enter the house. Rose cheerily greets her parents who respond in kind, while Chris quietly walks through the door.

The *mise-en-scène* of the image can be read simply—a house, a car, an arrival—but as the camera slowly pulls back, the viewer is confronted with something else. Metaphorically, Chris's tiny body being led into darkness evokes the African captive being led into the West African slave fortress. Chris seems powerless in the face of his captors and the enormity of the building—both at a superficial, social level (he *must* meet the parents at *some* point) and at a deeper, symbolic level (the house, and his body, have a far deeper and more disturbing relationship that this shot also hints at). The visual symbolism of the house extends the metaphor even further, with the columns of the porch suggesting teeth and the gabled windows and eyes, turning the house itself into a monstrous thing, consuming life. The blood-red car evokes a piece of meat (and, indeed, the car is already splattered with actual blood from a deer they hit during the drive to the house.) Chris, in this metaphorical reading, lacks the distance from (and perspective on) the house that would allow him to register the house's true nature. He is being consumed by something far larger, far more sinister, than he can possibly conceive of at this point.

## FREEMAN'S "NEW LOT"

Once Chris and Rose are inside the house, and particularly during the Armitages' reunion party, the estate takes on the aspect of a different, though equally horrific, location in African American history: the Southern plantation.

The historical idea of plantations may call to mind brutal working conditions and even worse punishments, as described in Frederick Douglass's memoirs and depicted in Steve McQueen's film *12 Years A Slave* or the television series *Roots*. Indeed, the first person Chris and Rose see when they arrive at the Armitage estate is Walter, the permanent "hired" groundskeeper whose life appears to consist of nothing *but* work. The fact that Walter is only seen toiling outside the house, never inside it, evokes the field workers of antebellum American plantations. Once the audience knows that Walter's body and a shard of the original African American's mind are under the control of Rose's grandfather, post-Coagula operation, this slave iconography is doubled.[19] Peele's primary focus in *Get Out*, however, is not on forced labor but on an arguably even more insidious, phenomenon: the marketing, examining, and selling of black bodies as property.[20]

Peele has noted that the scenes of Chris at the party are meant to evoke modern-day microaggressions: the submerged racism that pervades everyday interactions even in liberal social settings.[21] The same scenes, however, also echo the overt commodification and sale of the black body in earlier periods of American history. At first, it seems as though Rose is introducing Chris to her parent's friends, a courtesy to her fish-out-of-water boyfriend. Some members commit microaggressions: they ask if he knows Tiger Woods, ask him to show them his golf swing (assuming he can play golf, like Tiger), and comment on the darkness of his skin. Some members are more aggressive—a woman grips his arm and implies, in comments to her husband and to Rose, that he's sexually virile.

These interactions drive away Chris from the party, and seemingly cause a rupture between him and the Armitage family. In fact, however, his leaving the party is part of the plan. Once he is away from the group, being comforted and cajoled by Rose to return later that evening, the true purpose of the

*Auctioning black bodies in the twenty-first century of* Get Out.

"party" begins. Now that the product—that is, Chris—has been examined, a silent auction is conducted. Dean Armitage presides, standing next to a life-sized photo of Chris. The partygoers who examined him place bids, and the blind art dealer wins the right to dominate Chris's body.

The sequence echoes Solomon Northrop's description of his experiences at his captor's plantation in Northrop's autobiography *12 Years A Slave*. Like Chris, Northrop is a talented, free black man at the time of his abduction. Unlike Chris, he knows that he is being sold by his master, Mr. Freeman. The details of Northrup's account are eerily similar to what Chris experiences, however. Northrop notes that before examination he is "required to wash thoroughly . . . to shave,"[22] an echo of the first shot of Chris in *Get Out*, preparing for his trip to the Armitages' by washing and shaving his face. Northrup is then examined by potential buyers as a member of Freeman's "new lot." He describes how "customers would feel our hand and arms and bodies, turn us about, ask us what we could do,"[23] further echoing the behavior of the Armitages' partygoers and their true intentions in talking with Chris.

Furthermore, Northrop notes that the men being sold were "furnished with a new suit each," consisting of "hat, coat, shirt, pants and shoes," and "paraded and made to dance."[24] Chris isn't formally showcased in this way, but Andre Hayward is. Chris makes note of how Andre is now dressed in a hat and suit (garments he wouldn't have worn before) and how at one point, to Chris's shock, he twirls and dances for his white admirers.[25]

Accounts of American plantations like Frederick Douglass's *Narrative* provide vignettes of human beings deprived of their dignity, given only scraps of clothing to better demean and dehumanize.[26] But Northrup's account, and Peele's vision of human objectification, are different. In the party sequence in *Get Out*, as in Northrup's descriptions of human sale in *12 Years A Slave*, the Armitages' estate and the American plantation are spaces of commodification. These are spaces where the dressing of human beings is done not to dignify but to objectify.

The hat and suit aren't worn to grant dignity to a human life, but to dress up a body as an object, like a dressing a doll. The partygoers' questions aren't asked to illuminate Chris's unique personality, but to evaluate him as commodity. The Armitage's home is a modern-day selling stage, echoing back to the plantations of eighteenth-century America.

The most chilling element in *Get Out*, however, is that this is an ongoing, annual process. Each reunion is simply one more opportunity to gather, objectify, and bid on a live human body, a black life, for future vivisection and consumption and control. However, instead of the Armitages' estate being a mere piece in a wider scheme, it combines a number of historical elements in the historical slave trade system. The estate evokes the West

African slave fortress (where future slaves are housed, Chris's situation), the East Coast US slave markets (where men like Chris are examined and bid upon), and the plantation itself (where "Walter" and "Georgina" now live and work). More importantly, however, the ideology that underpins this horror is bound up in the Armitages' estate. In the Coagula advertisement, Rose's grandfather—the proginator of this process and idology—emerges from the front door of the iconic and omnipresent estate. Therefore the estate acts as a fourth, crucial historical locale, one which the historical slave fortress or market likely did not embody—the creation of dehumanizing, racist ideologies, bureaucracies, and systems.

## "THE FEW CUBIC CENTIMETERS INSIDE YOUR SKULL"

In George Orwell's *1984,* the protagonist Winston is a slave to his society. He lives under the constant watchful lens of a severe police state and is acutely aware that he is influenced by years of Pavlovian conditioning, brainwashing, and hypnotism. His body and most of his mind are not his own. But, while Winston understands that "nothing [is] your own," he takes solace in "the few cubic centimeters inside your skull."[27] There, in those few centimeters, Winston can still think, can still rebel, can still *be*.

In *Get Out*, however, that "few cubic centimeters," that tiny space where you know you are yourself, is not a place of solace, but a prison. The "sunken place" Chris is trapped in isn't a space of comforting solitude, but a form of mental solitary confinement with a tiny window onto a world he can no longer control. In one of the final sequences, Chris becomes aware of the full scope of his impending doom. Not only will his body be brutalized and commodified, but a piece of his consciousness will remain in the sunken place

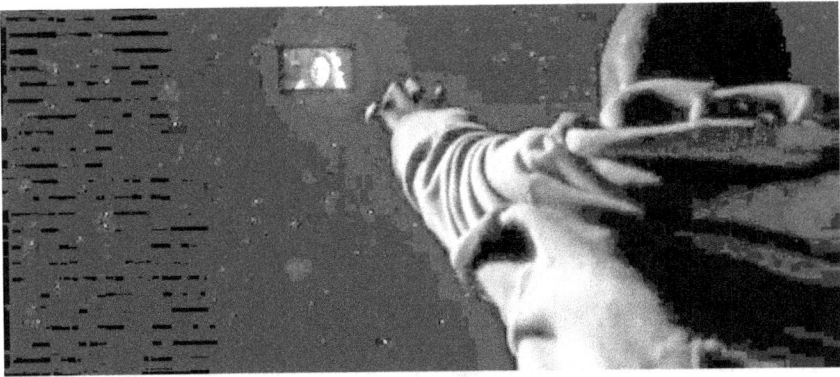

*Chris strains to escape the sunken place in* Get Out.

forever—or, at least for the lifetime of his body—with no hope or opportunity to escape. The true horror of the Armitages' scheme isn't just the gruesome past it evokes or the cold, dehumanizing present that it suggests, but the way it turns the bodies of its victims into prisons for their minds.

Peele's vision of the "sunken place," precise and evocative, is revealed in two ways. One is through wide shots, which depict Chris floating in a dark void, his clothing loosely whirling around him. Chris reaches up to a small window of light, as though he is caught in a viscous liquid—unable to swim up, incapable of falling further. The other is through shots that look down on Chris directly. The camera is a few feet from his face in such shots and we can see the panic and anguish on his face. The light illuminating his features evokes the floodlights in the Armitages' backyard when he is caught earlier in the film, right before Missy Armitage hypnotizes him. Peele's precise *mise-en-scène* of "the sunken place" also evokes other iconic images in American history, notably that of a person hunted at night—such as an escaped slave caught in the dark, struggling alone.

This striking *mise-en-scène*, the only touch of abstract or surreal imagery in the film, reflects two other key "locations" from the history of American slavery. James Stanfield notes in his journals that, once loaded aboard a slave ship, enslaved Africans were often confined below decks for "sixteen hours of darkness" with only a small "aperture," like the opening to a "cave" through which a tiny amount of sunlight shined down each day upon the mass of humanity.[28] Stanfield describes the slave ship as a "floating dungeon,"[29] and even defenders of the slave trade likened it to a "mobile prison."[30] The Armitages' system transforms each victim's body into a slave ship of one—a slave ship of the mind. Peele creates a startling vision wherein the enslaved maintain a shred of their mind, but are forever aware, eternally trapped, in a mental, mobile and solitary prison of their own bodies.

The "sunken place" imagery evokes another element of the experience of enslavement, however. It functions, in the film, as a visual representation of what Frederick Douglass calls the mind of an aware slave. Throughout his *Narrative,* Douglass provides examples of slaves who have been stripped of their autonomy and rebellious natures through adult conditioning, childhood manipulation, and interpersonal rivalries.[31] He himself experiences his most existential grief, however, when he reads Catholic abolitionist tracts and becomes *fully aware* of his plight. Douglass begins to understand the depth of his enslavement, the severity of his loss. He begins to see that he has been in a "sunken place," or as he writes a "horrible pit," for years and has lost a life of mental and physical freedom up until this point:

> As I writhed under [this knowledge], I would at times feel that learning to read had been a curse rather than a blessing. *It had given me a view of my*

*wretched condition, without the remedy. It opened my eyes to the horrible pit, but to no ladder upon which to get out.* In moments of agony, I envied my fellow-slaves for their stupidity. I have often wished myself a beast. I preferred the condition of the meanest reptile to my own. Any thing, no matter what, to get rid of thinking! It was this everlasting thinking of my condition that tormented me.[32]

Chris, of course, is experiencing this awareness from the opposite direction—he began life free, like Solomon Northrup, and now faces a life of eternal imprisonment. But the visuals of Douglass's prose and Peele's camera echo each other, person to person. Just as Peele has discussed how the worst fears that can antagonize us often come from within,[33] Chris is realizing that the ultimate place of peril and imprisonment isn't an entire estate or a single dungeon—it's in the mind of the enslaved.

## CONCLUSION

To end, let's return to the beginning.

*Get Out* could have begun with Chris. The first scene could have simply been Chris shaving, talking to Rose about her parents, and then driving out to the Armitage house. While seeing Andre's abduction adds detail to the plot, it isn't strictly necessary—Ron tells Chris and the viewer everything they need to know about what happened to Andre in a later scene.

So why have this prologue? Why show us the abduction of Andre Hayward?

Because in the prologue we don't know that he's "Andre Hayward." He's just a black man, living his life—and then he's attacked.

For the majority of the opening scene Andre's face is obscured. When walking through the suburb, the shadows of trees obscure his face. When he is put in a chokehold, his head is outside the frame of the shot. When Andre is most in peril, we can't see his face at all.

We can't see Andre's face. Andre could be Andre. But he could also stand in for countless other black Americans.

Andre could be the black men and women who were driven from exclusively white suburbs in the 1950s. The choking of Andre could echo the death of a young black boy who swam at a public beach that was "generally understood to be for whites' use only" and drowned after being pelted by rocks thrown by a white youth.[34]

Some see Trayvon Martin in Andre.[35]

I see Eric Garner, who was put in a chokehold on a Staten Island sidewalk for resisting arrest—a chokehold that killed him.

Peele has noted that many scenes in *Get Out* are designed to appeal to both a specifically black audience, but also a wider, more universal audience.[36] Only some people know what it's like to be black and meet the white parents of your girlfriend for the first time. But many of us probably *do* know how uncomfortable it is to meet our partner's parents for the first time. Peele designed his script this way in order to build empathy—to engage a wider audience's experiences first, before focusing in exclusively on Chris's perspective as a black individual toward the end of the film.

*Get Out*'s prologue isn't just a visual allegory for contemporary incidents of racial violence. It evokes the centuries of dehumanization African Americans have experienced throughout United States history. The abduction of Andre echoes the stolen African lives of the eighteenth century. The prologue evokes the abduction of Solomon Northrop, a free black man living in America in the nineteenth century. It echoes the black men and women lynched in America in the twentieth century. It echoes twenty-first century killings of black men and women by police, many brought to our attention by Peele's own favored tool: the camera.

In the final shot of *Get Out*, Chris is driven away from the Armitages' house. He stares into the dark forest surrounding their estate. We can't see what lurks in the darkness, and neither can he. But Chris's suspicions and fears from the beginning of the film have been validated. In a final stroke of empathetic filmmaking, after all we've experienced through Chris's eyes, after all of the horrors we've shared with him, we may all now feel his lurking terror as our own.

## NOTES

1. Richard Rothstein expanded on these details in his 2017 interview with Terry Gross on NPR's *Fresh Air*, noting, "Housing was a big area where African-Americans were excluded. The Veterans Administration, established under the GI Bill, adopted all of the FHA racial exclusion programs when it began to insure mortgages for returning veterans." Terry Gross, Interview with Richard Rothstein, "A 'Forgotten History' of How the U.S. Government Segregated America," *Fresh Air*, Podcast audio, May 3, 2017, https://www.npr.org/2017/05/03/526655831/a-forgotten-history-of-how-the-u-s-government-segregated-america.
2. Rothstein, *Color of Law*, 71, 85.
3. Ibid., 71–73.
4. Ibid., 145.
5. Coates, "Case for Reparations," 191. Also, see Rothstein, *Color of Law*, 145.
6. Rothstein, *Color of Law*, 145.
7. For the purposes of this chapter, I have only described a select few incidents of racial violence and systemic exclusion out of the myriad that occurred over centuries

in the United States. I have chosen to include these particular events for their alignment with the themes and motifs of *Get Out*. Further reading is likely required to understand the full scope and breadth of this history. I recommend, obviously, Richard Rothstein's *The Color of Law*, Ta-Nehisi Coates's collection of essays *We Were Eight Years in Power*, and Michelle Alexander's *The New Jim Crow*.

8. In an online *Vanity Fair* video, "Jordan Peele Breaks Down 'Get Out' Fan Theories," Peele answers questions from viewers of the film. One viewer questions whether the Armitage guests arriving in exclusively black cars is meant to echo their intention/desire to be transported by black bodies, or shells. Peele agrees with this reading.

9. In the same Vanity Fair video, another viewer wonders if the reference to "black mold" in the Armitage basement (meant as a subterfugal "health warning" toward Chris to keep him out of the Coagula laboratory) may also be in reference to the black bodies that the Armitages use to "mold" around white brains. Peele jocularly agrees with this reading, likely unintentional, but still interesting.

10. Finally, one other question in the *Vanity Fair* piece asks about the symbolism and irony of Chris picking cotton from the armchair he is strapped to in the Armitages' basement. To the question "Anyone think it was intentional that [Chris] was freed by picking cotton?" Peele answers, "Um, yeah. We had a special arm of the chair made with cotton stuffed in it so that we could have the grand irony of him being freed by cotton. You get it."

11. In particular, this moment seems to evoke the death of Tamir Rice, a twelve-year-old boy shot and killed by Cleveland police two seconds after they arrived at a public park where Tamir was holding a toy gun. This linkage, among many others, has been commented upon in analysis of *Get Out* (including Brent Staples's piece "The Movie 'Get Out' Is a Strong Antidote to the Myth of 'Postracial' America" for *The New York Times* and Amma Marfo's piece "*Get Out* and the constraints on black violence, even in black-made art" for the *Pacific Standard*) as well as by Peele himself in previous sketch comedy work (in the *Key and Peele* musical sketch "Negrotown").

12. Indeed, Peele did film an alternative ending in which Chris was arrested and sent to jail. You can see this ending on Vimeo ("*Get Out*—Alternative Ending"). However, in a joint interview for *Vulture* with the cast of *Get Out* and Jordan Peele, Peele and company felt that while the original ending might pack a realistic punch, or critique mass incarceration in the United States, the final ending in the film itself was stronger, and more "honest" to Chris's experience.

13. Rediker, *Slave Ship*, 146.
14. Ibid.
15. Ibid., 104.
16. Ibid.
17. St. Clair, *Door of No Return*, 186.
18. Simmonds, "African Slave Castles."
19. The same, of course, goes for Georgina. At first, the permanent, "hired" live-in servant evokes mid-century American maids, epitomized in Kathryn Sockett's 2009 novel *The Help*, and the 2011 film adaptation. Again, when we realize that "Georgina" is actually Rose's grandmother inside of a stolen black body and mind, "slave," not "the help," is the proper term for this character.

20. Quentin Tarantino's film *Django Unchained* also features highly detailed scenes of the seemingly refined, yet obviously dehumanizing exhibition, examination, and sale of human bodies at the Candyland ranch.

21. The entire interview is outstanding. In conversation with host Terry Gross, Peele also discusses how the entire film, though particular to African American experiences, can apply to other minority groups who often feel singled out and stigmatized, including women and gay individuals. Terry Gross, Interview with Jordan Peele, "*Get Out* Sprang from an Effort to Master Fear, Says Director Jordan Peele," *Fresh Air*, Podcast audio, January 5, 2018, https://www.npr.org/2018/01/05/575843147/get-out-sprang-from-an-effort-to-master-fear-says-director-jordan-peele.

22. Northrup, *12 Years A Slave*, 48.

23. Ibid.

24. Ibid., 47–48.

25. Of course, by this point, Andre's body has already been commandeered by a white owner. Therefore, the parallel isn't quite exact, but the behavioral, sartorial, and social cues are decisive. Additionally, one could imagine that if a person sees a human being as a piece of property before purchase, they would see them even more so afterward. Therefore, to imagine Andre's new "host" as wanting to "show off" his purchase fits within the film's textual and historical context.

26. Douglass, *Narrative*, 6.

27. Orwell, *1984*, 27.

28. Rediker, *Slave Ship*, 150.

29. Ibid., 45.

30. Ibid.

31. Douglass, *Narrative*, 11, 12, 16.

32. Ibid., 24, emphasis added.

33. Gross, Interview with Jordan Peele.

34. After this drowning, "policemen at the scene refused to arrest the attacker" (Rothstein, *Color of Law*, 144).

35. Gross, Interview with Jordan Peele.

36. Ibid.

## BIBLIOGRAPHY

Coates, Ta-Nehisi. "The Case for Reparations." In *We Were Eight Years in Power*, 163–208. New York: One World, 2017.

Douglass, Frederick. *Narrative of the Life of Frederick Douglass*. Mineola, NY: Dover Editions, 1995.

*Get Out*. Dir. Jordan Peele. Universal Pictures Home Entertainment, 2017. DVD.

Gross, Terry. Interview with Jordan Peele. "*Get Out* Sprang from an Effort to Master Fear, Says Director Jordan Peele." *Fresh Air*. Podcast audio. January 5, 2018. https://www.npr.org/2018/01/05/575843147/get-out-sprang-from-an-effort-to-master-fear-says-director-jordan-peele

———. Interview with Richard Rothstein. "A 'Forgotten History' of How the U.S. Government Segregated America." *Fresh Air*. Podcast audio. May 3, 2017. https://www.npr.org/2017/05/03/526655831/a-forgotten-history-of-how-the-u-s-government-segregated-america

"Jordan Peele Breaks Down 'Get Out' Fan Theories from Reddit." *Vanity Fair* video, 9:59. December 1, 2017. https://video.vanityfair.com/watch/jordan-peele-breaks-down-get-out-fan-theories-from-reddit

Northrup, Solomon. *12 Years A Slave*. New York: Penguin Books, 1808.

Orwell, George. *1984*. London: Signet Classics, 1966.

Rediker, Marcus. *The Slave Ship: A Human History*. New York: Penguin Books, 2007.

Rothstein, Richard. *The Color of Law*. New York: Lighthouse Publishing Corporation, 2017.

St. Clair, William. *The Door of No Return*. New York: BlueBridge, 2006.

Simmonds, Yussuf J. "African Slave Castles." *Los Angeles Sentinel*. August 27, 2009. https://lasentinel.net/african-slave-castles.html

*Part V*

# THE HORRORS OF PLACE

*Chapter Sixteen*

# The Hovel Condemned

## *The Environmental Psychology of Place in Horror*

Jacqueline Morrill

Depictions of twisted familial relationships, and of the home as a physical site of violence, have been staples of the horror genre for decades. Alfred Hitchcock's *Psycho* (1960), Tobe Hooper's *The Texas Chainsaw Massacre* (1974), and John Carpenter's *Halloween* (1978)—along with countless imitators of the tropes and plotlines they introduced to the genre—invited audiences to imagine an America in which the boundary between safe spaces and lethally dangerous ones was poorly marked, if indeed it was visible at all. Imprisonment, torture, and death at the hands of deranged killers could, the films suggested, be waiting behind any door, including the door to one's own home. Even as they undermined the traditional association of "home" with safety and security, these films did the same for "family." The first victims of Norman Bates in *Psycho* and Michael Myers in *Halloween* were those closest to them, and the murderous cannibals of *Texas Chainsaw Massacre*, are a nightmarish parody of an idealized 1950s nuclear family.

Horror films' assault on the idea that home *or* family could guarantee safety and security—one thread in the development of "savage cinema"—was nearly a half-century old when director Rob Zombie made his feature film debut, just after the turn of the millennium.[1] His film *House of 1000 Corpses* (2003) and its sequel, *The Devil's Rejects* (2005), drew on the "family of terror" archetype deployed in *Texas Chainsaw Massacre*. His third feature, a remake of *Halloween* (2007), retained the characters and suburban Illinois setting of the original, but transformed Michael Myers from a quasi-supernatural being to a young man (not unlike Norman Bates) who was both completely human and irredeemably psychotic—the product of a horrific childhood that relentlessly pushed his unstable mind deeper into darkness, triggering his first murderous rampage.

Michael is physically removed from his home and placed in the care of Dr. Sam Loomis at a psychiatric institution, but his traumatized childhood prevents him from moving on. His mind, and his soul, continue to haunt the halls of his childhood home, and when he escapes, his murderous acts inevitably circle back to the location of his original sins: his adolescent home town and house. While the abuse that takes place within the Myers's residence is glaringly prominent in *Halloween*, similar familial trauma is also suggested in *House of 1000 Corpses*. Otis's relationship with his father, Captain Spaulding, is strained at best; flashbacks hint at more than just sexual innuendo between Baby and her older brother Rufus; and Tiny, the gigantic son suffering from deformations and burn scars, is left to fend for himself in the basement of the home, his role in the family little more than that of a pet dog. The cumulative damage done to the members of the Firefly family eventually turn their ranch into another house of terror—one that, like Michael's once-and-future home, waits to ensnare the unwary and plunge them into a nightmare of pain and death.

Zombie's films reached the screen at a time—the first decade of the new millennium—when audiences had more reasons than ever before to feel unsafe and insecure in their homes. The 9/11 attacks, the subsequent "War on Terror," and the emerging security state to which they gave rise constantly reinforced the message that the homeland was under siege by shadowy Others who hid in plain sight and were capable of unleashing violence and brutality on innocent Americans without warning. School and workplace shootings, the DC sniper attacks, and other mass-casualty attacks, though unconnected to any terrorist group, deepened the sense of unease and the growing perception that the familiar, public spaces of an individual's everyday life—"home" in the broad sense—were no longer safe. Media narratives of the power of domestic abuse, bullying, and similar psychological trauma to push individuals past their breaking point, reinforced the idea that home might, for some, be the least-safe space of all. This chapter, then, considers how Zombie's millennial films—with their images of savage violence and twisted family dynamics—simultaneously reinforce and interrogate our twenty-first-century nightmare that home is no longer a refuge from the terrors of the wider world ... and, if we are unlucky, may harbor even worse terrors of its own.

## AN INVITATION TO FIREFLY RANCH

What is a home, if not the ground upon which security, comfort, and family are built? Home suggests a place to retire from the daily spells of societal exhaustion; it is a location that, typically, breeds togetherness and love. In the cinematic world of homicidal maniacs, however, the home is transformed into a den of savage violence. The Firefly family of *House of 1000 Corpses* decorate their home with the remains of their murdered victims. Bedrooms house caged women dressed in cheerleader uniforms. The wrap-around patio boasts headless dolls, hats, and other accessories taken from those unable to escape, and the toolshed out back conceals a bona-fide torture chamber, filled with blades; body parts; and, of course, a blood-spattered chainsaw.[2] Zombie's set design becomes a character itself; without even knowing those whose home it is, the audience already dreads what dwells inside.

*House of 1000 Corpses* begins, like many horror films, by following two college couples traveling the country. They are in search of strange, off-highway sideshow attractions and ultimately stumble upon a gas station doubling as haunted house. Beyond its loading dock are cells holding animatronic replicas of infamous killers, including one infamous in local folklore: Dr. Satan. Though the owner of the station, Captain Spaulding, is creepy and seemingly untrustworthy, the young protagonists emerge from the haunted house alive and resume their journey—that is, until their car breaks down after picking up (who else?) a hitchhiker. The group is eventually lured to Firefly Ranch with the promise of a warm, dry house and repairs to their automobile.

Upon meeting the members of the Firefly family, we immediately notice that they occupy familiar archetypal roles: caring mother, cantankerous grandfather, tough and rebellious older brother, beautiful and spoiled younger sister, and isolated middle child. These roles, however, are grotesquely distorted. Baby, the spoiled sister, lures the innocent travelers to the ranch with her good looks and charm, where the mother invites them to stay for a candlelight dinner to celebrate (fittingly enough) All Hallows Eve. It isn't until after their meal, when their car has supposedly been repaired and they are preparing to leave, that the couples are brutally assaulted and dragged back by brother Otis.

The dinner scene, and the familial tension within it, directly parallel those found in Hooper's earlier film, where a nameless all-male family, known only as Grandfather, Old Man, Hitchhiker, and Leatherface, join together around a dining table to bond, eat, and terrify the only remaining victim of a group of travelers, a young woman named Sally. In similar fashion, the members of the Firefly family exchange knowing glances across the table while their guests politely eat their last meal. Unlike Sally, who has witnessed the death of her entire group and helplessly fights against the rope that binds her to the dinner table, Zombie's college students have no idea of what awaits them. Indeed, Zombie replaces the character of Sally not with his protagonists, but with the audience. We know the danger to come, and have already witnessed death at the hands of the Fireflys. Thus, it is we who sit knowingly under the watchful guise of this particular evil.

The dynamics of the Firefly family are more concretely depicted in *The Devils Rejects,* and the characters' relationships are more fully developed. Captain Spaulding and Mother Firefly are implied to be the parents of Rufus, Otis, Baby, and Tiny, and—even if there is no biological tie between them—Captain Spaulding acts as a father figure to Otis and Baby after the destruction of the ranch and the capture of Mother Firefly. One scene of the three riding in the family van, with Otis and Baby playing a game of "copycat," seems deliberately designed to evoke mid-century images of middle-class families "seeing America" through their car windows on long driving vacations. The two siblings pick and poke at each other until a stop for ice cream puts an end to the argument. Their sibling rivalry reflects the persistent lightheartedness that Otis and Baby display throughout the film. Even while taunting their victims, they banter and joke with them and each other.[3] The playful teasing and classic-rock soundtrack behind such scenes soften the fear and dread that the audience would normally be feeling, by suggesting that the Firefly clan feels loyalty, familial affection for one another. As with the dinner-table scene in *House of 1000 Corpses,* however, the audience remains fully aware of what the family is capable of, and—when they do, inevitably, arrive—the scenes of torture and murder are all the more jarring because of the playful banter that precedes them.

The humanization of the Firefly family is critical to the plot of *The Devil's Rejects,* in which the murderous family is forced out of the security of their home by Sheriff Wydell, a fanatical lawman bent on their destruction. Seeking vengeance, rather than justice, and he leaves no doubt that his intention is to eradicate them:

> You listen to me, and you listen good! I am gonna kill every member of your family! I'm gonna hunt them down like the animals they are, and I'm gonna skin 'em alive! They are going to feel the pain and suffering of every last victim! They're gonna crawl on their hands and knees, and they're gonna beg me for mercy! But all I'm gonna have for them is pain! Pain and death!

Wydell soon begins making good on his threats, killing Rufus, taking Mama Firefly into custody, and later stabbing her to death. Later, having captured Otis, Baby, and Captain Spaulding, he brings them to the Firefly Ranch and—with the help of a pair of ruthless bounty hunters— tortures them. Releasing Baby so that he can hunt her down for sport, he sets fire to the house with Otis and Captain Spaulding inside, intending to burn them alive.

It is here, in the confrontation between the Fireflys and Wydell, that Zombie evokes millennial society's growing fear that there are no more truly safe places. The Firefly family are grotesquely exaggerated, white-trash versions of the Others said—in the post-9/11 world—to be the gravest threat to the "ordinary" Americans. They are, despite their friendly banter and obvious affection for one another (as they are being tortured Baby, Otis, and Captain Spaulding each endure additional pain in an effort to spare the others), psychopathic killers responsible for over seventy-five deaths. Yet, the forces of law and order—embodied by Sheriff Wydell—engage in torture and brutality just as freely, destroying property and shooting prisoners. Wydell's motives (bringing the Fireflys to justice) may be admirable, but his methods are as terrifying as theirs.

Having crossed the line from peacekeeper to vigilante, he stands front and center in a pre-Trayvon Martin country, where children are gunned down and brutalized because of their race, religion, or sexual orientation. The campaign he wages against the Fireflys—a family of poor, countercultural "white trash" ruralites—is not a law-enforcement operation but (by his own admission) a war of extermination, designed to eradicate a group of undesirable Others before they taint the idyllic image of "his" small Texas town. Zombie does not dwell on the possibility that such "justice" might subsequently be unleashed on additional groups of "undesirable" Others who were branded a threat, but—few millennial viewers would have missed the implication.

Zombie's success in establishing his cannibal family as vaguely sympathetic characters bridges the gap between the costumed killers of 1990s teen-horror films and the inventive "torture porn" films of the new millennium, just as Tobe Hooper's seminal film "bridged the gap between *Psycho* and what became traditional slashers" by introducing the trope of a psychopath who butchers young people one by one.[4] Films such as *Saw* (2004) and *Hostel* (2005), released before Zombie's debut, also play upon the reemergence of a single killer out to torture and punish young adult invaders; however, these slashers are individual characters without ties to family members with the same fatal appetite. Therefore, the Fireflys of *House of 1000 Corpses* and *The Devil's Rejects* act as the new, not necessarily improved, but equally hungry, murderers complete with southern charm.

## DEFINING SPACE: "THE HOME"

The concept of home in the horror genre embraces not just a physical structure, but ideas about privacy and the distinction between individual space and social space. Homes—whether they are houses, apartments, shacks, vans, or caves—are locations in which an individual is both solitary and part of a larger order (a family, collective, or group of roommates). It is reasonable to suggest, then, that horror films "can productively be seen as representations of the negotiation between the individual and the social."[5] Traditional ideologies associated with home and horror include comparisons of urban and rural areas and the social encounters within them. The groups of friends in both *The Texas Chainsaw Massacre* and Zombie's Firefly films intrude upon lifeways and social norms outside of their urban/suburban experiences on their visits to the rural South. These visits are purposefully presented as journeys to "a place where the rules of civilization do not obtain. . . . In horror, country dwellers are disproportionately represented by adult males with no ascertainable family attachments."[6] It is the lack of these attachments that is suggested as the reason for the bizarre and often homicidal tendencies of those living within the confines of deserted areas. On the topic of horror and "urbanoia," Carol Clover notes that in horror films

> country people live beyond the reaches of social law. They do not observe the civilized rules of hygiene or personal habit. . . . As with hygiene, so with manners . . . country people are often nameless or known by cognomina only. (Leatherface and Hitchhiker/Chop Top in *The Texas Chainsaw Massacre*)[7]

Lack of self-care, maternal leadership, and low economic class serve as a collective excuse for separation and otherness between rural clans and the home- and family-oriented city dwellers or suburbanites in horror. Without the picket-fence-straight teeth and clean hands of young city-goers, those left behind must fend for themselves, even if that means surviving on the leftovers of those visiting from afar.

The home acts as a secure setting in which the individual believes he is safe from the physical dangers and psychological judgments of the outside world. It may, however, also act as a source of claustrophobia in which the victim is not safe from the outside, but trapped within. Long before Zombie's remake, John Carpenter's *Halloween* explored the theme of home, and how it can be transformed from a refuge to a trap, by having Michael Myers—the original masked, knife-wielding killer—stalk babysitters in a suburban Illinois neighborhood. Carpenter's choice of babysitters as victims underscored the film's theme of safe spaces transformed into death traps. Babysitters—embodying the innocence and vulnerability traditionally associated with adolescent girls—had been archetypal characters in horror films and fiction dating back to the urban legends of the 1960s. Only slightly older and more worldly than their young charges, they are (unlike the children's temporarily absent parents) likely to be overmatched by *any* serious threat to the house and its occupants. As *Halloween* unfolds, the seemingly ordinary houses of the Haddonfield, Illinois, neighborhood in which it is set become mazelike pens for the young women who are too frightened to leave, but who (like the viewer) know that staying may lead to a violent death.

The central character in the film, Laurie Strode, is the *least* worldly of the three babysitters depicted—serious, bookish, and sexually inexperienced—and seemingly the least capable of fighting off a seemingly unstoppable killer. The home she is trapped in is the same one from which Michael was taken as a child, a labyrinth of hallways and crawl spaces that act as traps Laurie is unable to escape. Yet, it is Laurie who rises to the occasion and keeps Michael at bay until Dr. Loomis arrives to drive him away, thus becoming the archetypal example of what Carol Clover would later dub "the Final Girl."

The film opens on Halloween night, 1963, "with the first of a two-part temporal genetic structure in which a past event is enacted and then used to explain present day events."[8] The sins of the household—teenage "petting" and perhaps more intense sexual contact—are seen from the perspective of a masked stalker. The audience later discovers, after the stabbing of the young woman, that she was the older sister of Michael Myers, left at home to babysit him while their parents were away for the night. *Halloween*'s second "temporal segment" occurs fifteen years later as adult Michael Myers returns to Haddonfield to "take vengeance on the guilty parties or on their symbolic substitutes"—that is, Laurie and her fellow babysitters.[9]

The 2007 Rob Zombie remake makes the sex that is merely implied in the original film explicit: The audience not only hears the moaning of Judy Myers and her boyfriend Steve, but views their naked gyrating bodies, at first through a cracked door and then fully, as if the camera and the viewer have stepped into the room with them. The perilous sex act, now widely accepted by American horror movie buffs to be a guarantee of slasher-murder, should not have been witnessed at all. Intimacy, addiction, abuse, and obsession are often hidden behind the thick walls and doors of the home. But here, in the horror genre, those doors are flung open to expose our every imperfection.

Zombie's version of the now-classic tale explores the theme of home and its psychological effects, by elaborating the details of Michael Myers's family life. Straying from the original film's portrayal of him as an almost supernatural force of nature, Zombie adds more human qualities to the brutish giant on screen. In an interview with *TV Guide*, Zombie describes Myers's adult character as "losing himself behind [the mask he wears] until he has no actual personality of his own. He just is that mask . . . the classic white mask becomes his identity. . . . I didn't want Michael Myers to be supernatural."[10] Instead, Zombie injects images of a troubled family life: a mother who strips to pay bills, her abusive, deadbeat live-in boyfriend, a promiscuous older sister, and middle-school bullies whose harassment fuels the psychological storm within Michael. The Myers are a dysfunctional family of "white trash," teetering on the edge of poverty and—again—representing the socioeconomic role of "Other," even in suburban Illinois. To a younger generation of horror viewers, more aware of bullying than the original 1978 audience, this backstory is a key into the mind and home of a serial killer. On his barbarous evolution from hopeless child to murderer, Dr. Samuel Loomis, Michael's psychiatrist, notes:

> His eyes will deceive you; they will destroy you. They will take from you your innocence, your pride, and eventually your soul. These eyes do not see what you and I see. Behind these eyes one finds only blackness, the absence of light. These are the eyes of a psychopath.

Michael's actions are not, however, without purpose. His victims are those who—in the darkness of his twisted mind—represent the sins from his childhood home that continue to haunt his memories. The physical remains of the home also live on—still standing, though abandoned, on the outskirts of Haddonfield, and it is through this domicile that Laurie Strode is chased and, ultimately, imprisoned—cornered in its rotting crawl spaces, alongside the tombstone of Michael's mother. She is trapped physically within the structure, reduced to clawing at the walls of its nursery, just as Michael was once trapped there by his age and fatally dysfunctional family.

Just as Laurie and Michael exist within the claustrophobic walls of their home, the audience is also thrust into this feeling of tension "either because it [the shadow or danger] is just too distant to make out clearly."[11] This is not a new concept in horror; it is in such a negative space—a still and unfilled space—that Carpenter first "creat[ed] his terror out of an amalgam of imaginative projection on our part . . . and our perceptual vulnerability to ambush, which acts a kind of correlative to the bodily dangers depicted on screen."[12] Scenes that push Michael's masked face and stiff body to the very edge of the screen, a shadow that crosses Laurie's hand as she drops paperwork through a mail slot, make the viewing audience aware of the safety within their own home, and yet leads them to question this very safety when they are actively engaged in the stalking on the screen before them. Zombie reflects the original technique used by Carpenter: "[a] closed frame around his characters, in order to trap them in a space where their ability to see what was coming was greatly diminished, and there are occasions in which you can see the operation of this machinery with particular clarity."[13] This energy is observed not only in the home, but in theaters as well. The phenomenon of theatergoing does not simply relate to the watching of a film, but of participating in the film along with other viewers, whether two or two hundred. For moviegoers, there is safety in numbers, in the controlled confines of the theater and its "social space," and in the voluntary spending of money. That said, however:

Cinema's ability to make us look where it wants us to look always carries with it as a corollary the ability to prevent us looking at what it does not want us to see.... It's insinuating power and its literary sophistication depend on the fact that it can, when it wishes, narrow its line of sight to exclude elements of the worked it depicts.[14]

The space outside the frame, whether in a theater or home, is not merely an entrance or exit for something evil to pass through. It acts also as a transitional space "into which the unshowable (for whatever reason) can be secluded without entirely removing it from our imaginative grasp."[15]

## OUR HOMES, OUR SELVES

Rob Zombie's interpretation of *Halloween* reflects the corrosive effects of abuse and abandonment within the home, but one can also make a case, in reference to horror, for the power of social influence, and familial tradition and expectation. Just as the members of the Firefly family grow and evolve in the comfort of their ranch and surrounding property (cemetery, forest, barn, and shed), so does Michael Myers in his home and the surrounding parts of Haddonfield. We should not, however, immediately associate the terms "grow and evolve" with psychological growth; instead, the characters grow outwardly, in hunting "range" and victim count. Their identities also evolve, in that their roles are less forced and dynamically change based on circumstances. The Firefly family defends their rights to privacy, property, and gun ownership—traditional cornerstones of southern culture, particularly among the poor white residents of Appalachia, East Texas, and the Mississippi Valley. Similarly, Michael's choice of victims reflects his desire to kill those who rebel against the conservative morality of the Catholic Church. Women, particularly women who are sexually active and confident, are his prime targets—a point that Zombie underscores through the characters of babysitters Annie and Linda, both of whom stand up to authority and claim independence from stifling parental figures.

Nealon and Giroux note: "Like time, the spaces we occupy—geographic regions, nations, cities, hospitals, prisons, home, our bodies, not to mention those mental spaces and maps we sometimes inhabit—provide a framework for our experiences, as we learn who and what we are in society, our 'proper' place."[16] What we know of ourselves, the roles we play and the roles of others in respect to ourselves, is derived from the spaces we share with family, friends, coworkers, and neighbors. If this space is contaminated in any way, our perception of who we are is also contaminated. In a nature-versus-nurture situation, therefore, nurture may—under a broad spectrum of uncontrollable circumstances—amend or disable our ability to accept manners, politics, self-worth, and respect for life. Our "proper place" is not in a social atmosphere, working and abiding by the societal norms, but outside of them, lurking at the perimeter, watching for a lost victim. "Similarly, the designations of 'public' and 'private' are often conceived of in masculine and feminine terms . . . [as in] a woman's place, after all, is 'in the home,'"[17] where her socially defined role is to create the kind of stable childhood that Zombie's Michael was not privy to. Rather than remaining in the private space of their home and caring for him, his mother engages in a flagrantly public trade (stripping) in order to pay the bills, having chosen to live with a selfish, bullying drunk rather than a man who could enter the public sphere himself to support the family. Even today, such stereotypes remain powerful, and "working mothers are blamed for the transgressions committed by their children."[18] Michael's idea of private space (his home and those who inhabit it) is skewed, his perception of women now transformed from a private mother identity to a more public sexualized figure. It is the act of women having sex, then, that acts as a trigger for his later massacres.

This same modification of public and private space explains the dramatic change of Laurie Strode in Zombie's sequel, *Halloween II* (2009). After surviving Michael's attack in the first film, Laurie suffers from a growing list of physical and psychological wounds. The turning point, however, comes when she discovers her true identity: that she is Michael's baby sister Angel. At this point, the concepts of space and time lose their validity. Her understanding of who she is—the product of a perfect suburban home, complete with a loving set of parents and a group of semipopular friends (once again she is the bookish sexual innocent), is devastated. "I'm not me, do you understand what I'm saying?" she declares at one point "I'm Angel Myers, Michael Myers' sister." From then on, it is Angel who occupies the time and space previously occupied by Laurie Strode, complete with visions, memories and sensory reactions to the murder committed by her brother, one year to the night after the original event. Laurie ceases to identify herself as Laurie Strode; she is simply Angel from this point forward. She is, like Michael, finally home.

In surviving Michael's onslaughts (over and over again), Zombie's Laurie Strode functions, like Carpenter's, as the film's "Final Girl."[19] Carol Clover, describing the archetype for which she coined the term, might well have been speaking directly of Laurie:

> She is introduced at the beginning and is the only character to be developed in any psychological detail. . . . She is intelligent, watchful, level-headed; the first character to sense something amiss and the only one to deduce from the accumulating evidence the pattern and extent of the threat. . . . She is by any measure the slasher film's hero.[20]

Both Carpenter's and Zombie's versions of Laurie fit Clover's model, but the latter's re-visioning of *Halloween* creates a critical distinction between them. In Carpenter's version of the story, Laurie is, like the house she occupies and Haddonfield itself, an embodiment of pure innocence that Michael threatens. In Zombie's version, however, there *is* no pure innocence: Laurie/Angel is a product of the same irretrievably broken family, the same house of horrors, and the same fraught, imperfect town as Michael. If she is, ultimately, different than he is, it is because she escaped from all three before she could be scarred.

Films like *Psycho*, *Friday the 13th*, and *Scream* use the Final Girl to convince the audience that horrific violence could happen to even innocent and normal people in seemingly "safe" spaces—even their very own homes. Zombie's *Halloween* (like his Firefly films) goes further.

They suggest that, in the end, what we once sought to earn, buy, steal at the risk of social failure—the security supposedly guaranteed by house and home—may be nothing more than an illusion. The reality, Zombie suggests (in a message millennial audiences may find disquietingly resonant) is darker: It is within the home that we are most likely to discover the true location of evil: that of the Other or outsider, or that which hides within ourselves.

## NOTES

1. Thought to have originated with the graphic and explicit films of the late 1970s: *Last House on the Left*, *Friday the 13th*, and *The Hills Have Eyes*. Directors Wes Craven and Sean Cunningham celebrate ultraviolence, particularly acted upon young women at a historical moment in American history when "free love" and the civil rights were allegedly "changing" how we see the world and "the other."

2. Zombie pays obvious homage to Tobe Hooper's *The Texas Chainsaw Massacre* (1974). The chainsaw can be seen as a sort of "easter egg" and inspiration for Zombie's revamped slasher films.

3. Morris, "Justification of Torture-Horror," 51.
4. Roberts, "Slasher Films."
5. Krasniewicz, "Cinematic Gifts," 32.
6. Clover, *Men, Women and Chainsaws*, 124.
7. Ibid., 126.
8. Quoted in Krasniewicz, "Cinematic Gifts," 35.
9. Ibid.
10. Mitovitch, "Interview with a Zombie."
11. Sutcliffe, "The Unseen Offscreen," 122.
12. Ibid.
13. Ibid.
14. Ibid., 130.

15. Ibid., 131.
16. Ibid., 126.
17. Ibid., 127.
18. Ibid.
19. Clover, *Men, Women and Chainsaws*, 44.
20. Ibid., 44–45.

## BIBLIOGRAPHY

Clover, Carol J. *Men, Women and Chainsaws: Gender in the Modern Horror Film.* Princeton, NJ: Princeton University Press, 1992.

Krasniewicz, Louise. "Cinematic Gifts: The Moral and Social Exchange of Bodies in Horror Films." *Tattoos, Torture, Mutilation and Adornment*, edited by Frances E. Mascia-Lees and Patricia Sharpe, 30–47. Albany, NY: SUNY Press, 1992.

Mitovitch, Matt Webb. "Interview with a Zombie: An Inside Look at the New *Halloween*," *TV Guide*, August 2007. https://www.tvguide.com/news/rob-zombie-halloween-39734/

Morris, Jeremy. "The Justification of Torture-Horror: Retribution and Sadism in *Saw, Hostel*, and *The Devil's Rejects*." In *The Philosophy of Horror*, edited by Thomas Fahy, 42–56. Lexington: University Press of Kentucky, 2010.

Nealon, Jeffrey, and Susan Searls Giroux. "Space/Time." In *The Theory Toolbox: Critical Concepts for the Humanities, Arts, & Social Sciences*, 2nd ed., 126–128. Rowman & Littlefield Publishers, Inc. 2012.

Phillips, Kendall R. "Scream (Film, 1996)." *Pop Culture Universe: Icons, Idols, Ideas* (2017). https://popculture2.abc-clio.com/Search/Display/1505107

Roberts, Van. "Slasher Films." *Pop Culture Universe: Icons, Idols, Ideas.* 2017. https://popculture2.abc-clio.com/Search/Display/1505107

Sutcliffe, Thomas. "The Unseen Offscreen." *Watching: Reflections on the Movies.* Faber & Faber, 2000.

Zombie, Rob. *The Devil's Rejects.* 2005. Santa Monica, CA: Lions Gate Home Entertainment, 2005. DVD.

———. *Halloween.* 2007. New York: Weinstein Company Home Entertainment, 2007. DVD.

———. *Halloween II.* 2009. Culver City, CA: Sony Pictures Home Entertainment, 2010. DVD

———. *House of 1000 Corpses.* 2003. Santa Monica, CA: Lions Gate Home Entertainment, 2004. DVD.

*Chapter Seventeen*

# Coming Home to Horror
## Stephen King's Derry and Castle Rock
Alissa Burger

Small Maine towns appear frequently in the works of Stephen King: familiar-seeming places that belie the horror that lurks beneath their façade. These small towns may boast parks with lovely gazebos, welcoming libraries, and quaint downtowns, but they also have vampires (Jerusalem's Lot), a cyclically recurring evil that takes the form of Pennywise the Dancing Clown (Derry), and the devil himself (Castle Rock). The horror, however, often extends beyond the supernatural: Castle Rock may have been a temporary home for the devil with Leland Gaunt's coming in *Needful Things* (novel 1991; film 1993), but this is just one more evil in a long and dark history that has included a serial killer and a rabid dog, among other horrors. In many cases, the evil in these small towns poses a particularly significant threat to children, who are often its most vulnerable victims. In the film adaptations of King's *IT* (1990; 2017) and the Hulu original series *Castle Rock* (2018–present), adults return to the small towns in which they were children, and in so doing, return to not just the towns themselves, but to their own childhood memories, identities, and relationships. In each of these works, homecoming is a traumatic and gradual process, revealing truths about the individual characters, as well as about the small towns themselves, as each are shaped by dark secrets from both the past and present.

*IT* is one of King's most iconic and expansive novels, described by the author as his "final exam on Famous Monsters."[1] Following the lives of seven children—Bill Denbrough, Richie Tozier, Beverly Marsh, Mike Hanlon, Eddie Kaspbrak, Ben Hanscom, and Stan Uris—who battle a supernatural evil one adolescent summer in Derry, Maine, and who are drawn back twenty-seven years later by the discovery they did not destroy It, when the monster awakens from hibernation and begins to feed once more. The novel alternates between the characters' childhood summer of 1958, their adult return in 1985, and Mike Hanlon's diary segments, which chronicle the dark history of Derry, tracing the evil back hundreds of years. The monster appears to the members of the self-proclaimed Losers Club as Pennywise the Dancing Clown, the Wolfman, a leper, a giant bird, a gout of blood, and Bill Denbrough's murdered brother Georgie, among other guises, as "The monstrous face becomes in effect a screen on to which the perceiving subject unconsciously projects their fears."[2] These various manifestations make It's identity fluid and unfixed and, as a result, uncontainable. While this supernatural horror—and Derry's refusal to see or stop it—is challenge enough, these children also face horrors in their own respective homes, in their relationships with distant, overprotective, or abusive parents. King's decades-spanning epic has been adapted in two different formats: a two-night ABC miniseries event directed by Tommy Lee Wallace in 1990, and a two-part feature film, of which the first installment was Andy Muschietti's *IT* in 2017.[3] Each adaptation tackles King's source material in dynamically different ways as a result of (among other factors) the technology available at the time and the specific medium for which it was made,[4] but the themes of childhood, adult memories of that childhood, and the small town as a site and source of horror resonate throughout both.

In contrast, Hulu's *Castle Rock*, created by Dustin Thomason and Sam Shaw, takes King's canon as inspiration, rather than source material for a direct adaptation, using "one of the author's favorite creepy Maine burgs as a hub that connects all of his stories—the characters, the monsters, the legends—within a multiverse that serves as a backdrop for new prestige TV tales."[5] While there are a range of compelling characters driving the series, each with their own fascinating backstories and dark secrets, the small town of Castle Rock "feels like a frightful, ominous character in its own right."[6] In this unique approach, *Castle Rock* doesn't have an aim of adaptation, but rather seeks to "emulate the feelings evoked by the revered author's works—namely putting forth a story that unfurls in a surprising nature, weaving through multiple genres and ultimately even telling different tales."[7] Echoing the twenty-seven-years-later return of the Losers Club to Derry, Henry Deaver (played by André Holland) returns to Castle Rock at the report of a mysterious and nameless young man (played by Bill Skarsgård, who also plays Pennywise in Muschietti's *IT*) discovered in the depths of Shawshank State Prison. In addition to this current mystery, Henry finds himself drawn back to his own childhood, his adolescent relationships, his adoptive father's mysterious death, and his lost memories of the eleven days he went missing as a child in 1991 when he was eleven—the same age as the children of the Losers Club in *IT*. As with adaptations of *IT*, *Castle Rock* is shaped by the medium in which it is presented, in this case a Hulu original streaming series, and Jeremy Egner of *The New York Times* argues that the series serves as a "convergence of contemporary TV trends," combining the streaming medium with the formats of the anthology series and the "mystery-box show . . . a puzzle to be solved as much as a television series,"[8] with the suspense and gradually mounting horror an extended series can effectively provide.

## SMALL TOWN SECRETS

Derry and Castle Rock are both iconic landmarks in King's fictional landscape—small towns to which he returns time and again in both his short fiction and his novels. They are described in King's work in rich detail, to the point that "the reader knows more about [these towns] than he could know about his own hometown even,"[9] an act of creation which establishes Derry as "hyperreal."[10] In his description—and even more significantly in his exploration and interrogation—of each, King dismantles the idyllic nostalgia of the small town, digging beneath the surface to reveal dark secrets and horrors that are often unacknowledged or unspoken by the townspeople themselves. As Miles Orvell argues in *The Death and Life of Main Street: Small Towns in American Memory, Space, and Community*, "Americans dream of Main Street . . . as an ideal place; they have also dreamed it into being, created it and re-created it, as a physical place, the material embodiment of a dream."[11] This is the case in many of King's seemingly pleasant small towns, including Jerusalem's Lot and Haven, in addition to Derry and Castle Rock. As A. O. Scott notes of Derry in his review of Muschietti's film, "Derry, with its redbrick storefronts and its quirks and kinks, seems like a genuinely nice place to live in spite of the fact that its citizens, children in particular, turn up missing or maimed at an alarming rate."[12] While there are dark realities in each community, ranging from supernatural threats to the more prosaic but no less traumatic issues of poverty, addiction, racism, domestic violence, and child abuse, these are often ignored, with real world problems unaddressed, in favor of the dream of small town life described by Orvell. In this elision, the "glow of nostalgia . . . obscures some of the harsher realities of life on Main Street."[13] This dark historical bedrock upon which the towns are built also situates them in Martin Procházka's notion of "ghost town syndrome."[14] While Derry and Castle Rock are not abandoned, they are viscerally haunted by the atrocities which have gone before. The life of the town is dynamically engaged in "tales of the past, but it also haunts the present 'by the weight of history' . . . and the future, especially optimistic visions of the progress of civilization."[15] This complex temporal relationship results in "Ghost towns [which] perform this relationship of justice and temporality transforming conventional notions of memory, representation, or materiality and engendering alternative histories,"[16] in which personal memories of the past are unmoored and even the objective truth of what has gone before is uncertain. While few small towns would give much attention to their darkest secrets or actively commemorate the most horrific moments in their histories, in Derry and Castle Rock those horrors are frequent, pervasive, and aggressively ignored; the dark secrets are not just one unfortunate anomaly in the towns' histories, but ingrained into the very foundation of their identities, the construction of the small town memory, and the invested process of forgetting.

Bad things happen in Derry and Castle Rock. As Tony Magistrale argues in *Stephen King: The Second Decade*, with Derry, "a single city portrays evil's embrace of an entire community."[17] Much the same could be said of Castle Rock. Magistrale continues this analysis, noting that in *IT* "the physical geography of Derry, Maine, like that of Castle Rock, is meant to reflect the moral typography of the town and its history; it is a place where there is little that is kind or beautiful."[18] As Mike Hanlon recalls his father's words in King's novel: "In Derry people have a way of looking the other way."[19] They have turned their collective gaze aside from such horrors as the mysterious disappearance of Derry's first settlers, the collective massacre of the Bradley Gang, the racially motivated fire at the Black Spot, and the brutal murder of a gay man named Adrian Mellon at the most recent Derry Days celebration, among others. The entity preys on the most vulnerable members of the Derry community, as

> The various masks that Pennywise wears in luring children to their grisly deaths are symbolic of the masks that disguise and distort the true history of Derry itself . . . a history of persecution of outsiders—from blacks (as Hanlon's father reveals in his remembrance of the Black Spot), to the children who play in and around the town, to Adrian Mellon, who is murdered because he is a homosexual. Like the town's children, the gay and black communities of Derry exist outside the social mainstream. This puts them in the position to comprehend the workings of Derry more clearly than the rest of the town at the same time as they are the victims of its violent prejudices.[20]

What is most notable in these examples—and in understanding Derry itself—is that many of these acts of violence are not committed by It, whether in its Pennywise guise or another, but are rather acts of interpersonal violence committed by Derry residents on their fellow townspeople. As Joshua Rothman notes, writing about Muschietti's film: "All of these disparate evils would have existed anyway, but they are exacerbated by It—a creature that, in addition to eating children, 'feeds' by fanning the flames of violence, hatred, lawlessness, racism, misogyny, and sexual predation while disguised as a clown."[21] The violence reaches a crescendo once every twenty-seven years, with Its awakening and feeding cycles perhaps urging the residents of Derry on to greater violence than in the interim, but even in the lull between these cycles, Derry is a dangerous place.

Some of the most effective horror in the *IT* adaptations comes from the revelation—and subsequent dismissal by adults and longtime Derry residents—of this violence. In both versions of *IT* and in *Castle Rock*, there are characters who serve as amateur historians, narrating the towns' dark histories and drawing attention to sins the townspeople would rather have forgotten. In the 1990 miniseries version of *IT*, Mike Hanlon (Marlon Taylor) shares a scrapbook his father compiled of Derry's history with his class at school. Rather than this eliciting shock or sparking a conversation, the teacher thanks him for that "somewhat morbid history" and tells Mike to take his seat.[22] In Muschietti's 2017 film, the historian role passes to young Ben Hanscom (Jeremy Ray Taylor), a friendless new-kid-in-town who spends his time in the library learning about Derry. When he meets the others and becomes a member of the Losers Club, Ben finally has someone to share this information with, inviting them into his bedroom, the walls of which are papered with historical documents, newspaper stories, and posters of the missing children. Ben's map of old Derry is an essential piece in the children tracking the monster to Its lair, as they collapse the distance between past and present by projecting the old map over the schematic of the current sewer system filched from Bill's father's office.

In *Castle Rock*, the deceased Warden Lacy (Terry Quinn) serves as the town's unofficial historian for viewers, narrating in voiceover and flashbacks, as he raises the questions "Remember The Dog? The Strangler? Sure you do. . . . How about all the others that didn't make the headlines?"[23] With Castle Rock serving as the setting of *The Dead Zone* (1979), *Cujo* (1981), the novella *The Body* (featured in the 1982 collection *Different Seasons*),[24] *The Dark Half* (1985), and *Needful Things*, among others, the town has no shortage of boogeymen, running the gamut from supernatural to all too human. As Lacy's voiceover makes clear, these events are remembered, but not discussed, and acknowledged as rarely as possible. As Noel Murray argues, "It's like some kind of mental fog descended on Castle Rock long ago, preventing its residents from realizing how strange their daily lives are."[25] Just as with Derry, the link between the town and the actions of its residents is unsettling and inextricable: as Lacy continues his dark history of Castle Rock, he notes that "People say 'it wasn't me, it was this place.' . . . And the thing is, they're right."[26]

## HORROR AT HOME

In King's small towns, even home isn't safe. While the supernatural horrors and violent histories of Derry and Castle Rock are unsettling enough, the threat of abuse and violence the children face within their own homes creates a terror all its own. In *IT*, "Under the veneer of Pennywise's games and promises lurks the reality of deception and slaughter. The adult citizens of Derry mirror this very tendency in their behavior toward their children."[27] In the 1990 miniseries, "one way in which the seven children are brought together in this film is by virtue of parental neglect or cruelty. Ranging from dead or abusive fathers to hysterical and indifferent mothers, there is not a single positive portrait of a father or mother in this telefilm."[28] Muschietti's 2017 film explores these parent/child relationships in more detail than the 1990 miniseries, both in setting scenes within the children's houses and in their conversations about their homes and families. Bill's parents are distant and bereaved following Georgie's death, and Stan (Wyatt Oleff) faces the overwhelming pressure of preparing for his bar mitzvah and not disappointing his rabbi father. Eddie Kapsbrack's mother is overprotective and domineering, as she works to separate Eddie (Jack Dylan Grazer) from his friends and keep him solely dependent on her. Mike (Chosen Jacobs) is being raised by his tough-love grandfather after being orphaned when his parents were killed in a house fire, which may have been intentionally set. The most disturbing parent-child relationship in Muschietti's *IT*, however, is that between Beverly Marsh

*Home sweet horror: Bill Denbrough (Jaeden Lieberher) prepares to enter the house on Neibolt Street in* IT

(Sophia Lillis) and her father (Stephen Bogaert). King's novel and Wallace's 1990 miniseries describe this relationship as controlling and overbearingly paternalistic—underscored by Beverly's father's frequent imprecation that "I worry about you, Bevvie"[29]—with occasional physical violence and a "barely restrained incestuous urge."[30] In Muschietti's film, the tension and palpable threat in Beverly's relationship with her father much more directly implies sexual abuse, as he frequently touches her and repeatedly asks "Are you still my girl?" Almost anywhere is better—and safer—than home for the members of the Losers Club. As they prepare to enter the house on Neibolt Street—the epitome of the horrific domestic space—Bill (Jaeden Lieberher) tells his hesitating friends, "I go home and all I see is how Georgie isn't there.... Walking into this house, for me, is easier than walking into my own."[31]

Whether they are together in Derry or alone in their own homes, the children of the Losers Club are in constant danger: from It, the bullies who plague their daily existence, and even their own parents. They are always much safer when they are with their friends, since, as Carranza observes, "in a world where children are savagely murdered, and their parents are unable (or unwilling) to do anything about it, these children learn to rely on one another to protect themselves and future victims."[32] When the Losers Club encounters Pennywise in the house on Neibolt Street, It separates them before beginning to prey upon them, drawing them away from one another, but once they are all united and fighting against It together, they are able to drive the monster back into the sewers beneath Derry and escape with their lives. This taps into the story's "coming of age" narrative, as Louis Peitzman explains that "*IT* has always been a story about the loss of innocence, about the generational divide between children and the adults who don't listen to them, and about the shocking hatred that runs through even the most pleasant-seeming American towns."[33] Throughout the course of *IT*, the children of the Losers Club grow up, find strength in themselves and in one another, and go their separate ways; and with the exception of Mike, their paths take them far from Derry, until they are drawn back twenty-seven years later with Its return.

Isolation is similarly dangerous in *Castle Rock*, though the characters here seem to have less recourse and fewer opportunities to create bonds of friendship or community. The mystery that haunts Henry and colors the entire town's perception of him is in the lost memories of the eleven days he went missing as a child. He has no story, and without a clear narrative or publicly accepted identity, there is only suspicion and horror in the speculation that he is the one who killed his adoptive father. Similarly, the mysterious young man discovered in the depths of Shawshank State Prison has no story, no witnesses to what he has experienced or endured, and no name. He is referred

*The Kid (Bill Skarsgård) in* Castle Rock: *Cause or effect?*

to simply as "The Kid."[34] In *Castle Rock*, what happened to Henry and The Kid is the central mystery of the first season. Jennifer Ouelette reflects "Is the Kid truly evil? Is he a monster, a victim, or both? It's deliberately unclear; Skarsgård's performance of the Kid vacillates between vulnerability and ominous menace.... [The Kid is] a cipher."[35] Violence and disaster follow in his wake, and at times, he is demonstrably able to influence the actions of those around him, such as causing a shivving and jailhouse riot that frees him and Henry from a cell.[36] However, at other times, it is unclear whether The Kid is directly responsible for the violence that occurs nearby or whether he is simply a witness to the usual horrors of Castle Rock—one piece of a much larger picture.

In one instance, shortly after his release from Shawhank, The Kid wanders through Castle Rock and into the house of a seemingly happy family celebrating their child's birthday. Illustrating the horror that hides behind even the most everyday occurrences, the scene quickly devolves into one of violence and abuse.[37] While it is possible that The Kid's presence was a catalyst for this violence, a pattern of systemic, long-standing abuse is revealed in the family's screaming interaction, making it just as likely that this is their normal state of being, and The Kid is no more than a witness to the horrors that hide behind Castle Rock's closed doors and drawn curtains. This mystery of correlation and causation extends to Henry as well, as tragedy seems to follow him too, from his father's mysterious death to the carnage that ensues upon his return, underscoring the similarities rather than the differences between the two men, and drawing the question of influence into stark relief for both of them.

While Henry and The Kid are both shown in potential relationships with others, those connections are fragmentary and fleeting. Henry's relationship with his adoptive father was complicated and contentious, and when Henry returns to Castle Rock, his mother Ruth (Sissy Spacek) has advanced dementia, can't give him any answers, and at times doesn't even recognize him. Former Sheriff Alan Pangborn (Scott Glenn), now Ruth's lover and caretaker, is both the boy's childhood rescuer and a formidable opponent upon Henry's return. The most promising potential relationship, both in Henry's childhood and in his return as an adult, is with his former friend and neighbor Molly Strand (Melanie Lynskey), who has empathetic powers that allow her to hear Henry's thoughts and feel his emotions, an ability which turns out to be both a blessing and a curse. The Kid fares even worse, as nearly everyone who interacts with him does so with the intent of harming or killing him, including the new Shawshank warden (Ann Cusack), her corporate assistant (Josh Cooke), and a violent inmate with whom he is briefly housed.[38] The only people who seem to take a genuine and potentially protective interest in him are Henry and a young prison guard named Dennis Zalewski (Noel Fisher), who—deciding he has had enough of people looking the other way in Castle Rock—risks his job and ultimately loses his life while attempting to help The Kid.

Racism and the threat of violence runs through the myriad versions of *IT* in the story of the fire at the Black Spot and Mike and his family's experiences in Derry. It is also significant in *Castle Rock*, where Henry seems to be the only black man in town. He occupies an unbalanced liminal space between a returning son and an outsider, and "walks the streets like a man who knows he's not welcome in the place where he was raised, like someone who does not feel at all at home."[39] Henry's race and the town's assumption of his guilt in killing his adoptive father are inextricably intertwined. His childhood nickname was "The Black Death"[40] and as McFarland points out, "At no point do the people . . . make the presumption that this black adopted child might be innocent and as much a victim as his dead father." Firmly established as an outsider—despite the childhood he spent in Castle Rock—Henry can be excluded, denied, and abused without guilt or reprisal.

Like Derry, Castle Rock is populated with people whose sins are overlooked, ignored, or excused. Pangborn found Henry as a boy and returned him home, but he also allowed Warden Lacy to drive off with The Kid in the trunk of his car and maintained his silence for twenty-seven years. The cruelty and abuses of the guards at Shawshank continues unchecked until Zalewski makes his way through the prison, shooting fellow guards and employees who have mistreated prisoners, before being shot himself. Even Henry discovers himself capable of evils he never suspected, taking on the erstwhile warden's role and locking The Kid once more in a cage in the bowels of the now-abandoned Shawshank Prison. In the closing voiceover of the first season of *Castle Rock*, Henry supplants the repeated "people say" with "we," implicating himself in the violence and horror of his hometown as he reflects "'It wasn't me, it was this place.' That's what we say."[41]

## COMING HOME TO HORROR

As Andrew Barker notes, the story of *IT* is "a meditation on childhood, trauma, and forgetting,"[42] and in both versions of *IT* and *Castle Rock*, adult characters return to their childhood homes, realize how much of those years they have forgotten, and have to engage in the painful process of remembering to find their way not just back home, but back to themselves in order to understand and survive. The kids of the Losers Club come back as adults and find that being together again evokes memories they had forgotten, a remembering that is essential to their ability to once more stand against—and this time, beat—It. They remember collectively, so that as one recalls the details of a particular day or a specific horror, the others do as well and, in so doing, verify and validate their friends' memories.

In *Castle Rock*, the remembering process is more contested and fraught with fear and self-doubt. For much of the first season, Henry cannot remember what happened the day his adoptive father was mortally injured. Henry and The Kid's recovered memories at times blur and overlap with one another and, even at the season's conclusion, there is much about which Henry remains unsure, which is articulated by The Kid, who tells him, "I know you still have doubts."[43] The Kid's memories are similarly contested, particularly in Season One's penultimate episode "Henry Deaver," which posits an alternate dimension and reality in which The Kid himself is Henry Deaver, the son of Matthew and Ruth, with memories of an entire life lived before he left Castle Rock, returned, and found himself locked in a cage. As viewers, we are unsure of what Henry and The Kid each remember, what they have forgotten, what they are hiding or lying about, and what their actual stories may be. In both versions of *IT* and in *Castle Rock*, the contested process of returning and remembering brings each character back to themselves, back to their home, and back to the horror.

## NOTES

1. King, "Afterword," 1045.
2. Sears, *Stephen King's Gothic*, 193.
3. Muschetti directed the second chapter of *IT* (2019), which will be released in 2019.
4. In addition to the varying levels of special effects of each production, based on available technology and budget, the miniseries format is structured around the need for regular commercial breaks, the cliffhanger preceding the hiatus of a couple of days between the first and second installments, and Standards and Practices regulations that determine what can and cannot be shown, including representations of children in danger and levels of onscreen violence.
5. Egner, "'Castle Rock.'"
6. Conway, "'Castle Rock.'"
7. Wigler, "'Castle Rock.'"
8. Egner, "'Castle Rock.'"
9. Anderson, *Linguistics of Stephen King*, 122.
10. Ibid.
11. Orvell, *Death and Life of Main Street*, 7.
12. Scott, "Review: 'It' Brings Back Stephen King's Killer Clown."
13. Orvell, *Death and Life of Main Street*, 129.
14. Procházka, "American Ruins," 29.
15. Ibid., 30.
16. Ibid., 32.
17. Magistrale, *Stephen King: The Second Decade*, 101.
18. Ibid., 101–2.
19. King, *IT*, 461.
20. Magistrale, *Stephen King: The Second Decade*, 103–4.
21. Rothman, "What the New Movie Misses."
22. *IT*, directed by Tommy Lee Wallace, 1990.
23. *Castle Rock*, Episode 1.2, "Habeus Corpus," directed by Michael Uppendahl, aired July 25, 2018, on Hulu.
24. *The Body*'s Ray Brower is directly referenced in *Castle Rock* in Lacy's passing mention of "the fall after they found that boy's body out by the train tracks" ("Habeus Corpus"). Many critics have also noted similarities between *The Body*, Rob Reiner's film adaptation *Stand By Me* (1986), and both film versions of *IT*, including the collective group of child protagonists, the unreliability and hostility of home and parents,

the long shadow cast by the death of a protagonist's brother, and the search for a dead body (Barker; Peitzman; Robinson).

25. Murray, "'Castle Rock,' Season 1, Episode 8: Dangerous and Foolhardy."
26. *Castle Rock*, "Habeus Corpus." This narrative of reflection and justification is echoed through similar voiceovers in subsequent episodes by both Reverend Matthew Deaver (Adam Rothenberg; Episode 1.9, "Henry Deaver") and Henry (Episode 1.10, "Romans").
27. Magistrale, *Landscape of Fear*, 112.
28. Magistrale, *Hollywood's Stephen King*, 185.
29. King, *IT*, 572.
30. Magistrale, *Stephen King: The Second Decade*, 106.
31. *IT*, directed by Andy Muschietti, 2017.
32. Carranza, "Rebirth of King's Children," 10.
33. Pietzman, "'It' Is a Better Coming-of-Age Movie."
34. The notion of a single fixed story or definitive narrative is interrogated throughout *Castle Rock*, including in the possibility of parallel narratives and other worlds, the chance that the sound Henry and others hear may indicate the existence of a portal between these worlds in the woods (what is referred to as a "thinny" throughout King's Dark Tower metaverse), Henry and The Kid's memories of these competing worlds, and Ruth's engagement with multiple timelines and narrative repetitions as a result of her Alzheimer's disease.
35. Oulette, "Slow-Burn Psychological Horror."
36. *Castle Rock*, Episode 1.10, "Romans," directed by Nicole Kassell, aired 12 September 2018, on Hulu.
37. *Castle Rock*, Episode 1.5, "Harvest," directed by Andrew Bernstein, aired 8 August 2018, on Hulu.
38. *Castle Rock*, "Habeus Corpus."
39. McFarland, "'Castle Rock' and the Quiet Terror."
40. *Castle Rock*, Episode 1.8, "Past Perfect," directed by Ana Lily Amirpour, aired 29 August 2018, on Hulu.
41. *Castle Rock*, "Romans."
42. Barker, "Film Review: Stephen King's 'It.'"
43. *Castle Rock*, "Romans."

# BIBLIOGRAPHY

Anderson, James Arthur. *The Linguistics of Stephen King: Layered Language and Meaning in the Fiction*. Jefferson, NC: McFarland, 2017.

Barker, Andrew. "Film Review: Stephen King's 'It.'" *Variety*, September 5, 2017. https://variety.com/2017/film/reviews/it-review-stephen-king-1202547601/

Carranza, Ashley Jae. "The Rebirth of King's Children." In *Uncovering Stranger Things: Essays on Eighties Nostalgia, Cynicism and Innocence in the Series*, edited by Kevin J. Wetmore, Jr., 8–19. Jefferson, NC: McFarland, 2018.

*Castle Rock*. Hulu.com, Hulu Originals, 2018.

Conway, Lani. "'Castle Rock' Is the Stephen King-Inspired Horror I Didn't Know I Needed." *Zimbio,* August 12, 2018. http://www.zimbio.com/TV+News/articles/VjoxPIn1Zbr/Castle+Rock+Stephen+King+Inspired+Horror+Didn

Egner, Jeremy. "'Castle Rock' Is a Stephen King Story That Isn't Really a Stephen King Story." *New York Times,* June 19, 2018. https://www.nytimes.com/2018/07/19/arts/television/ castle-rock-stephen-king-hulu.html

*IT.* Directed by Andy Muschietti. Los Angeles: New Line, 2017.

*IT.* Directed by Tommy Lee Wallace. New York: ABC, 1990.

King, Stephen. "Afterword." In *IT,* 1043–46. Forest Hill, MD: Cemetery Dance, 2011.

———. *IT.* New York: Scribner, 1986.

McFarland, Melanie. "'Castle Rock' and the Quiet Terror of Being the Other." *Salon,* July 24, 2018. https://www.salon.com/2018/07/24/castle-rock-and-the-quiet-terror-of-being-the-other/

Magistrale, Tony. *Hollywood's Stephen King.* New York: Palgrave Macmillan, 2003.

———. *Landscape of Fear: Stephen King's American Gothic.* Bowling Green, OH: Popular Press, 1988.

———. *Stephen King: The Second Decade,* Danse Macabre *to* The Dark Half. (Twayne's United States Authors Series). Woodbridge, CT: Twayne, 1992.

Murray, Noel. "'Castle Rock,' Season 1, Episode 8: Dangerous and Foolhardy." *The New York Times,* August 29, 2018. https://www.nytimes.com/2018/08/29/arts/television/castle-rock-season-1-episode-8-recap.html

Orvell, Miles. *The Death and Life of Main Street: Small Towns in American Memory, Space, and Community.* Chapel Hill: University of North Carolina Press, 2012.

Oulette, Jennifer. "The Slow-Burn Psychological Horror of *Castle Rock* Makes for Must-See TV." *Arts Technica,* September 4, 2018. https://arstechnica.com/gaming/2018/09/the-slow-burn-psychological-horror-of-castle-rock-makes-for-must-see-tv/

Peitzman, Louis. "'It' Is a Better Coming-of-Age Movie Than a Horror Film." *Buzz Feed News,* September 8, 2017. https://www.buzzfeednews.com/article/louispeitzman/it-is-a-better-coming-of-age-movie-than-a-horror-film

Procházka, Martin. "American Ruins and Ghost Town Syndrome." *The Companion to American Gothic,* edited by Charles L. Crow, 29–40. Hoboken, NJ: John Wiley & Sons, 2013.

Robinson, Tasha. "Stephen King's IT Is the Rare Monster Movie with Too Much Monster." *The Verge,* September 6, 2017. https://www.theverge.com/2017/9/6/16257788/it-movie-review-stephen-king-andy-muschietti-pennywise-the-clown

Rothman, Joshua. "What the New Movie Misses about Stephen King's 'It.'" *The New Yorker.* September 10, 2017. https://www.newyorker.com/culture/culture-desk/what-the-new-movie-misses-about-stephen-kings-it

Scott, A. O. "Review: 'It' Bring Back Stephen King's Killer Clown." *New York Times,* September 6, 2017. https://www.nytimes.com/2017/09/06/movies/it-review-stephen-king.html

Sears, John. *Stephen King's Gothic* (Gothic Literary Studies). Cardiff: University of Wales Press, 2011.

Wigler, Josh. "'Castle Rock': How Hulu's Stephen King Anthology Series Was Born." *Hollywood Reporter*, July 25, 2018. https://www.hollywoodreporter.com/live-feed/castle-rock-series-premiere-stephen-king-hulu-series-explained-1129538

*Chapter Eighteen*

# It Follows and the Uncertainties of the Middle Class

Katherine Lizza

*It Follows*, a 2014 supernatural horror film written and directed by David Robert Mitchell, uses fear as a lens through which to explore sexuality within the context of middle-class, white, suburban America. The characters' movements through Detroit and its neighboring suburbs blur the line between affluence and poverty, and a variety of shots show the parallels between the two locations. *It Follows* presents a unique homage to the suburban-set slasher films of the past, using a relentless evil—willing to pursue its victims across boundaries—to represent the fears of the young adults growing up in American suburbs today.

The story of *It Follows* centers on nineteen-year-old Jay, played by Maika Monroe, and her experience with a supernatural, sexually transmitted, stalking entity. Jay and Jeff are in the early stages of their relationship when they have sex in the backseat of a vintage car outside an abandoned building in inner-city Detroit. Soon after, Jeff exits the car and fumbles with something in the trunk while Jay recounts what she expected of her life as a young adult, mentioning that she feels aimless despite her newfound autonomy. As she finishes her thoughts, asking "Now that we're old enough, where the hell do we go?" Jeff incapacitates her with a chloroform-soaked rag. She wakes up some time later inside the graffitied, dilapidated building, where Jeff reveals his true purpose for consummating their relationship: ridding himself of a curse by bestowing it on her.

He explains, "This thing ... it's gonna follow you. Somebody gave it to me and I passed it to you back in the car. It can look like someone you know, or a stranger in a crowd, whatever it can do to get close to you." If she does not "pass it along" to someone else through the same intimate means, the entity will kill her, and then him. Shortly thereafter, Jeff abandons Jay—still groggy from the anesthesia—at her suburban home and drives away. The remainder of the film surrounds Jay's desperate attempts to circumvent this curse and survive as long as possible while "it" stalks and terrorizes her and her friends.

## THE GEOGRAPHY OF RACE AND CLASS

At first glance, it appears that *It Follows* is a cautionary tale of unchecked sexuality and the danger of sexually transmitted diseases. In fact, however, the film explores the vulnerabilities of a population obsessed with maintaining middle-class whiteness. Specifically, the film is about young Americans growing up and failing to see the difference between the impoverished, allegedly dangerous city and their assumed-to-be-safe suburban homes. *It Follows* takes place in a significant narrative moment in these characters' lives, during which they have a considerable amount of freedom and a general lack of supervision. Their experiences in the "real world"—including the absence of parental guidance, few memories of how society is purportedly "supposed to be," and a lack of the financial security typically associated with suburban life—leaves these young adults feeling lost, and uncertain about what the future holds for them. Instead of inheriting, from their parents, a fear of the dangers lurking in the city of Detroit, they are entering into adulthood with larger fears about their own environment and what lies ahead.

Detroit was once a compact city at the center of America's industrial heartland. At the beginning of the twentieth century, the automobile industry brought it tremendous wealth, and transformed its landscape. The Packard Motor Car Company constructed the world's largest automobile factory on the city's east side, and other firms followed. The jobs on the assembly lines of seven major automobile companies needed to be filled, and—because they paid well and required little to no previous training or expertise—they attracted recent immigrants along with African Americans migrating from the Jim Crow South, transforming the city's workforce. The city offered opportunities for full-time employment at livable wages for blue-collar workers, about 22 percent of whom had only a high school education.[1] The Packard Plant alone employed upwards of 40,000 workers during peak production.[2] According to the Occupational Wage Survey of Detroit, in 1951, manufacturing employment then totaled 619,000 workers, of whom "half were employed in the motor vehicles and equipment industry." Among those surveyed, "about 95 percent of all factory workers in manufacturing establishments were employed in union plants" and these workers received "relatively high" factory wages, making on average about $2.01 per hour (the equivalent of about $20.95 in 2019).[3]

The rising growth and development of the city peaked after World War II. The Edsel Ford expressway and John C. Lodge freeway opened in the 1950s, creating avenues of escape to the suburbs. The construction of these highways displaced 17,000 residents and a disproportionate number of ethnic neighborhoods were completely destroyed.[4] The city experienced widespread "white flight," a term describing white residents' abandonment of the inner city for the suburbs, which drained the city of both demographic and economic diversity. In 1956, Packard went out of business, forcing thousands to search for employment elsewhere.[5] By the 1970s, the automobile industry as a whole had declined even further: General Motors laid off 38,000 and put another 48,000 workers on leave and, like many one-time residents of the city, American Motors had moved its headquarters out of Detroit to the suburb of Southfield.[6]

As mechanization has replaced human labor across the manufacturing industries in recent years, Detroit's automotive-sector employment has steadily diminished. After decades of population decline, local government mismanagement, and a number of national crises including the Great Recession in the late 2000s, Detroit filed for Chapter 9 bankruptcy on July 18, 2013, with an estimated $18 billion in debt, the largest municipal bankruptcy filing in U.S. history.[7] The disappearance of manufacturing jobs that once allowed young adults to aspire to a middle-class lifestyle affects Detroit to this day as the city grapples with losing the industrial identity that once defined it.

The main plot of *It Follows* unfolds within and around Detroit, which is especially poignant considering the intersections of sexuality, race, and class in America. It is no coincidence that Jay, a white teenager, contracts the sexually transmitted curse in the parking lot of the abandoned Packard Motor Car plant and that her first encounter with the entity takes place within the decaying factory building. Jay's dreams of freedom and escape from her adolescent life take the form of using her lover's car to travel "up north maybe," and so follow in the footsteps of countless white residents who abandoned the city before her.

The majority of the film revolves around Jay's pursuit for the arbitrary daydream of her adult life, which continues despite the presence of a horrifying supernatural creature. As Jay and her friends drive out from their neighboring suburban community into the city, Jay looks silently out of the passenger window at boarded up buildings that once sold "discounted auto parts," abandoned row houses defaced with graffiti, and cracked and empty sidewalks now overgrown with weeds. This juxtaposition of an impoverished and underresourced city with Jay's experience in the suburbs reinforces the viewer's understanding of the difference between a white, middle-class suburbanite's view of their own lifestyle and their view of the inner city.

Whiteness, as a marker of identity, is "a constantly shifting boundary separating those who are entitled to certain benefits from those whose exploitation and vulnerability to violence is justified by their not being white."[8] In order for whiteness to exist in American society, blackness must also exist for the white population to define itself against. This binary, rather than simply existing as a concern about skin pigmentation, is entirely dependent on the existence of an "othered" population. Strategies of identity-making and self-affirmation are unstable *because* they are entirely dependent on contrasting bodies.

The formulation of a middle-class identity, likewise, requires the existence of at least one contrasting population. The majority of Americans, regardless of race, are not members of the economic elite and so have experienced economic exploitation on some level, but race-based oppression depends on scapegoats to "divert our attention from those who have [...] power."[9] These sources of distraction have historically consisted of immigrants and people of color, and the diversionary rhetoric surrounding these populations exploits white Americans' frustrations and fears regarding their socioeconomic status. White, middle-class Americans' anecdotes about undeserving "welfare queens" (typically imagined as women of color), or about immigrants "taking jobs" from white Americans, support this worldview, affirming the idea that their economic plight is the fault of these others. Racism both enables and thrives off this fear-based society, which portrays specific nonwhite populations as blights on the country.

*It Follows* pulls back the curtain of certainty surrounding the cultivation of this type of white, middle-class self-image and exploits suburbanites' fear of the city—more specifically, of its association with crime, isolation, and blackness. In the film, the dividing lines between wealth and poverty are the streets which mark the border between the city of Detroit and the neighboring suburban communities. At one point, Jay's friend, Yara, reveals how tangible the divide appears as they travel into the city: "When I was a little girl my parents wouldn't allow me to go south of Eight Mile. And I didn't even know what that meant until I got a little older and I started realizing that that was where the city started, and the suburbs ended." Eight Mile Road exists as a physical dividing line between counties, and a cultural barrier that separates the predominantly African American urban core from the white, middle- to upper-class suburbs to the north.

David Robert Mitchell intentionally wrote this distinction between the city and suburbs into the film. He elaborated in an interview: "The idea of the separation between the suburbs and the city was an important thing to show. [. . .] As someone who grew up in the area, I'd say there are wonderful, beautiful places within the city. I'd hate for people to think that's the only thing there is in Detroit—I'd just like to say that up-front—but it's about that separation."[10] This separation is of note because it highlights a shared image that many Americans, particularly those who live anywhere *but* Detroit, have of the Michigan city—one defined by poverty and crime.

Yara's parents warn her not to travel into the city because they made a clear connection between Detroit and violence. In July 1967, Detroit notoriously became the site of eight days of rioting. Images of US Army tanks rolling down the streets of Detroit flooded homes across the nation on television screens and the front pages of newspapers. By the end of the week, forty-three people were dead, thousands more were hospitalized, and homes and businesses were damaged to the tune of $45 million.[11] Images of rioting and other forms of chaos created an impossible-to-shake impression that Detroit was an inherently violent place, while the predominantly white suburbs surrounding it were (like all suburbs) naturally safe spaces. That impression of the city, however, failed to take into account the years of economic decline and racial discrimination that led to despair, frustration, and finally violence. Perceptions of Detroit as violent and chaotic accelerated white flight, further emptying the city and further reinforcing perceptions of it as a dangerous wasteland.

Writer Jerry Herron elaborates, in his book *AfterCulture: Detroit and the Humiliation of History*, on the power of this kind of distorted imagery:

> It is impossible to convey the eerie effect of so much real property—houses, department stores, office towers, theaters, shops, schools, apartment buildings, hospitals, hotels, fire houses, mansions, streets, fountains, whole neighborhoods—having simply been left behind, as if the inhabitants were carried off by some terrible natural disaster. Detroit is a worse-case illustration that seemingly demands an explanatory caption, with everybody getting a chance to ward off his own special demons by abandoning them to speculation here.[12]

Herron goes on to explain that these types of images, which portray Detroit as a "city of the dead," are regurgitated as a way of accounting for the tremendous amounts of loss that the city has endured. He notes that "it's impossible not to take the loss personally, particularly if you are white and middle class and not bound to remain here, except in memory."[13] The protagonists of *It Follows* are white, middle-class teenagers with the ability to enter and leave the city as they choose. Whether or not they feel the loss personally is unclear—they are too young to remember, let alone have participated in, the city's vibrant industrial heyday—but they blur the lines of distinction between city and suburb by travelling between the two spaces in a vintage car that is both a product and an evocation of that era. Their travels thus call to mind a time when the young, white adults who occupied the city's now-deserted spaces and worked in its now-moribund automobile factories could look forward to a life worth daydreaming about.

*It Follows* further blurs the segregations of city and suburb in its depiction of the similarities between Jay's hometown and the neighboring city. Shot after shot blurs the lines between wealth and poverty: houses are framed from the same distance, forcing the viewer to acknowledge the similarities that unite them, regardless of geographic circumstances that divide them. Jay's backyard swimming pool, abandoned and then torn apart by a passing storm, is reminiscent of the dilapidated buildings of the inner city. Both Jeff and Greg drive vintage cars, not because of their rarity and the status it confers, but because the collapse of the industrial economy has reduced the production of newer models and left young people unable to find a job that would let them afford to buy one.

Through these shots, and the conspicuous absence of any characters of color, *It Follows* presents the viewer with a world whose inhabitants lack a body or population to define whiteness or middle-class status in opposition

Blurring the lines between the urban and the suburban in It Follows.

to. Even Yara's thoughts about traveling into the city reveal, as she continues her previous thought, the absurdity of the society needing to defend itself: "I used to think about how shitty and weird that was. I mean, I had to ask permission to go to the state fair with my best friend and her parents only because it was a few blocks past the border," to which Jay notes a shared experience with her mother. These young adults no longer see the borders that once shaped their parents' identities and experiences in the suburbs outside of Detroit because those boundaries no longer exist.

Jay and her friends are, of course, not the only ones able to transgress borders. One of the most horrifying aspects of the curse in the film is that "it" will follow its victims anywhere—even into the assumed bastions of safety for white young adults in suburban America. The entity appears throughout the film in places associated with security, wealth, and beyond that, whiteness. "It" appears at Jay's school, starkly out of place, as an old woman in a hospital gown; "it" emerges within her home as a disheveled, urinating woman and again as a freakishly tall man who ducks into a teenager's most sacred space: her bedroom; "it" stalks her from her neighbor's rooftop; "it" interrupts the protagonists' trip to a vacation home owned by Greg's family and ultimately follows Greg to *his* suburban home, appearing as his own mother. In all of these instances, "it" disrupts areas considered safe, secure, and white, bringing with it threats traditionally associated with the unsafe, chaotic, and black inner city.

Given these circumstances, Jay's question "Where the hell do we go?" seems even more bleak after Jeff passes the curse on to her within the city. There *is* no "where" to go to escape from the curse. Jay cannot leave the entity behind as she drives out of the city limits or travels to a distant lake house, emulating the pattern that many middle-class Americans followed in years past to escape from urban decay. The curse in *It Follows* will interrupt Jay's everyday life, appearing in places she and many other teenagers typically think of as safe. Despite the well-intentioned warnings the protagonist's parents gave about their safety, forbidding them to travel without permission into the city south of Eight Mile Road, they end up experiencing more terror and violence in familiar spaces than they ever did in Detroit itself. That two of the appearances of the entity involve looking like Jay and Greg's respective parents speaks to the teens' unpreparedness for violence from those closest to them. They have been led to believe that only strangers—those labeled as "others," living in poorer neighborhoods and attending segregated schools, plagued by disproportionate amounts of crime and pollution—are a threat to their well-being.

## "WHERE THE HELL DO WE GO?"

The horror of the entity is reinforced by its ability to stalk its victims relentlessly. The supernatural element in *It Follows* is able to keep tabs on its victims endlessly, and possesses a memory of the order in which its victims contract the curse. The dread in the film rises from these aspects of the entity, as the tagline for the film explains: "It doesn't think. It doesn't feel. It doesn't give up." These inhuman qualities enable the entity to haunt the characters at every waking moment, creating a sense of anxiety seen very clearly in Jeff's behavior and in his rented home, which resembles a paranoia-shrouded fortress. The irony of Jay's car monologue lies in the fact that, although she finally has the type of freedom she "used to daydream about," the entity that stalks her has infinitely more freedom, mobility, and power than she ever will, making her pursuit of the ideal adult life impossible. The existential crisis triggered by her newfound autonomy is supplanted by the realization that she is not invincible, not safe, and may soon die.

This reading of *It Follows* implies that the entity represents the passage of time and the inevitability of death. At one point near the conclusion of the film, Yara reads an excerpt from Fyodor Dostoyevsky's novel, *The Idiot* aloud:

> And the most terrible agony may not be in the wounds themselves but in knowing for certain that within an hour, then within 10 minutes, then within half a minute, now at this very instant—your soul will leave your body and you will no longer be a person, and that this is certain. The worst thing is that it is certain.[14]

The entity is slow-moving but will inevitably catch its victim. Even when it doesn't appear to be an immediate threat after characters pass it to one another, it can be seen watching and waiting in the distance. The feelings of horror and dread within the film largely come from the characters waiting for their inevitable fate. Fear of death is a universal human experience, and the integration of a plot involving a sexually transmitted monster is especially noteworthy in this light. Mitchell himself explained in an interview:

> We're all dealing with our mortality on some level. Sex and love are some of the ways that we're able to push it away or push it a little bit into the distance. It's how we cope. It's finding some peace through our relationships with other people. Sex is an important part of that. To me, that's what it comes down to—you're not going to get away from it, but you can still find some happiness in between.[15]

Relationships, both sexual and platonic, can function as a means of finding purpose or value in life, serving as a distraction from the inevitability of death. Moving beyond emotions, sexual relationships lead to procreation, which postpones the death of the species if not of the individual. In *It Follows,* however, having sex has the potential to shorten an individual's lifespan, bringing an end to population growth.

The entity that stalks Jay thus functions as an analog of what Michel Foucault dubbed "biopower," a tool with which the State seeks to enact its "biopolitics:" the control and management of certain populations. Biopower determines which lives are deemed (or forcibly made) expendable.[16] The curse within *It Follows* grants the cursed individual the power to determine which people he or she is willing to pass the curse on to, but most choose to exercise it within a culture of normative sexuality. Even though she is granted the option of choosing how to keep the curse from killing her, and deciding which individuals are expendable, Jay continues to subscribe to heteronormative standards when choosing which lives she is willing to risk, and only considers partners who are white and from her approximate social class.[17] The characters are constantly venturing to areas that should be inhabited by different populations, yet they rarely interact with anyone outside of their white, middle-class circle of friends. This lack of any "othered" populations for Jay to consider when "it" is passed on to her forces her to only kill off members of her peer group.

Considering this reading, the entity within *It Follows* would result in the ultimate demise of the heteronormative straight, white, middle-class identity. White, middle-class individuals only having sexual relationships with white, middle-class individuals of the opposite gender—the very behavior strictly enforced in a normalized suburban utopia in order to create ideal offspring—would, ironically, decimate the middle-class population once "it" was introduced into the community. In a sense, "it" can be read as the city of Detroit's horrifying revenge against the white residents who once abandoned it in droves. If the entity did not completely decimate the white, middle-class population, it would create a sense of paranoia that someday, "within an hour, then within 10 minutes, then within half a minute, now at this very instant," it could.

The film is driven by Jay's struggle, largely on her own, with her mortality. *It Follows* maintains a very clear separation between the protagonists and their parents or other guardian figures. Throughout the film, Jay's mother is physically only depicted in ways that foreground her emotional distance from her children. She is often seen in a separate room with her back turned away from her family, or in dissecting shots that show her hand gripping a cigarette or pouring alcohol into a cup. This lack of parental supervision leaves Jay and her friends searching for answers on their own, acutely aware of their isolation and unable to look to authority figures for help. The physical distance between Jay and her mother highlights their inability to communicate their concerns to one another. Moreover, even *if* this barrier of communication between parents and protagonists was erased, the anxieties that likely shaped the adults' perceptions of the world would remain radically different from those Jay and her friends are experiencing, and perhaps incomprehensible to them.

The sense of terror that the young protagonists' parents intended for them to accept was an anxiety surrounding a lack of distinction between their modest middle-class life and that of the lower classes. This reflects the fears of many Americans around the time of the film's release. According to a 2014 survey conducted by researchers at Chapman University, one of the top concerns of Americans was "running out of money in the future."[18] Such concerns about financial stability have continued to persist among the American public. According to the 2016 edition of the same survey, 39.9 percent of Americans reported they were "afraid" or "very afraid" of "not having enough money for the future" and 37.5 percent feared an "economic or financial collapse."[19] The 2018 version of the survey found higher levels of financial anxiety, with 57 percent of those surveyed reported to be "afraid or very afraid" of "not having enough money for the future."[20]

*It Follows* places these fears squarely in front of the viewer, suggesting that the financial stability that the suburbs appeared, decades ago, to represent is rapidly dissolving. Jay's question, "Where the hell do we go?" is a question many Americans—particularly those of the millennial generation—continue to ask as they contemplate economic uncertainty, the failure of many jobs to pay a living wage, and a cumulative national student debt of approximately $1.5 trillion.[21] Citizens of Detroit, in particular, have continued to ask "Where the hell do we go" in the years since the city filed for bankruptcy.

## CONCLUSION

The ambiguous end of the film relates to Detroit in this moment. Jay and her friends drive into the city one last time to confront the entity that has tormented her, going to the public pool that they had frequented in the past. Their plan to defeat the horror using electronic devices and a loaded pistol, although reckless, appears to work. After shooting "it" several times, the pool slowly fills with blood, something that only Jay appears to be able to see. Later that night, Jay has sex with her longtime friend, Paul, and the two are later shown walking, hand-in-hand, through their neighborhood. A figure follows behind them in the distance, however, leaving their true fate uncertain.

The figure walking behind the couple is ominous and hints that Jay and her friends did not triumph over the curse, but only have succeeded in delaying the inevitable for one more day. A more hopeful interpretation of the ending, however, is that Jay and Paul are walking toward their future together, unafraid and stronger after their ordeal. This relates to the very motto of Detroit: *"Speramus meliora; resurgent cineribus,"* which translates to: "We hope for better things; it shall arise from the ashes."[22] Relating to the film, the viewer is left to question where the protagonists will "go" from here and if they themselves will "arise from the ashes" after the traumatic events that led them to this moment. The only thing that is clear is that Jay has stopped running, instead choosing to simply move forward, free of her concerns about the uncertainties of adulthood.

## NOTES

1. Farley, Danziger, and Holzer, *Detroit Divided*, 71.
2. Arte Express, "Plant History."
3. "Occupational Wage Survey: Detroit, Michigan, December 1951."
4. Poremba, *Detroit,* 127.
5. Arte Express, "Plant History."
6. Poremba, *Detroit,* 137–138.
7. Davey and Walsh, "Billions in Debt, Detroit Tumbles into Insolvency."
8. Kivel, *Uprooting Racism,* 17.
9. Ibid., 78.
10. Lambie, "It Follows."
11. Poremba, *Detroit,* 133.
12. Herron, *AfterCulture,* 204.
13. Ibid., 206.
14. Dostoyevsky, *The Idiot.*
15. Meyers, "It Follows."
16. Stoler, *Race and the Education of Desire,* 80–81.
17. In a moment of desperation, it is implied Jay passes the curse to three men she sees partying on a boat. In this scene, Jay's actions can be read as an attempt to push beyond restrictive class barriers toward upward mobility through a relationship as a recreational private boat can be seen as an indicator of wealth.
18. Earl Babbie Research Center, "Survey of American Fears, Wave 1."
19. Earl Babbie Research Center, "Survey of American Fears, Wave 3."
20. Earl Babbie Research Center, "Survey of American Fears, Wave 5."
21. Friedman, "Student Loan Debt Statistics in 2018."
22. Lee, "What Does Detroit's Motto Mean, Anyway?"

## BIBLIOGRAPHY

Arte Express. "Plant History." *The Packard Plant Project.* 2019. http://packardplantproject.com /history/index.html

Davey, Monica, and Mary Williams Walsh. "Billions in Debt, Detroit Tumbles into Insolvency." *The New York Times*, July 18, 2013. https://www.nytimes.com/2013/07/19/us/detroit-files-for-bankruptcy.html?pagewanted=all&_r=0

Dostoyevsky, Fyodor. *The Idiot*. Urbana, IL: Project Gutenberg. https://www.gutenberg.org /files/2638/2638-h/2638-h.htm

Earl Babbie Research Center. *The Chapman University Survey of American Fears, Wave 1*. 2014. https://blogs.chapman.edu/press-room/2014/10/20/what-americans-fear-most-new-poll-

———. *The Chapman University Survey of American Fears, Wave 3*. 2016. https://blogs.chapman.edu/wilkinson/2016/10/11/americas-top-fears-2016/

———. *The Chapman University Survey of American Fears, Wave 5*. 2018. https://blogs.chapman.edu/wilkinson/2018/10/16/americas-top-fears-2018/

Farley, Reynolds, Sheldon Danziger, and Harry J. Holzer. *Detroit Divided*. New York: Russell Sage, 2000.

Friedman, Zack. "Student Loan Debt Statistics in 2018: A $1.5 Trillion Crisis." *Forbes*, June 13, 2018. https://www.forbes.com/sites/zackfriedman/2018/06/13/student-loan-debt-statistics-2018/#2ff59f817310

Herron, Jerry. *AfterCulture: Detroit and the Humiliation of History*. Detroit: Wayne State University Press, 1993.

*It Follows*. Directed by David Robert Mitchell. New York: RADiUS-TWC and Dimension Films, 2014. DVD.

Kivel, Paul. *Uprooting Racism: How White People Can Work for Racial Justice 3rd Edition*. Gabriola Island, BC: New Society Publishers, 2011.

Lambie, Ryan. "It Follows: David Robert Mitchell Discusses His Terrifying Horror Movie." Den of Geek. February 24, 2015. https://www.denofgeek.com/us/movies/it-follows/244006/it-follows-david-robert-mitchell-discusses-his-terrifying-horror-movie

Lee, Ardelia. "What Does Detroit's Motto Mean, Anyway? And Is It Still Relevant Today?" *Daily Detroit*, August 18, 2016. http://www.dailydetroit.com/2016/08/18/detroits-motto-mean-anyway-still-relevant-today/

Meyers, Jeff. "It Follows: An Interview with David Robert Mitchell on His Ingeniously Creepy Horror Film." *MovieMaker*, March 11, 2015. https://www.moviemaker.com/archives/moviemaking/directing/it-follows-an-interview-with-david-robert-mitchell-on-his-sexy-scary-horror-film/

Occupational Wage Survey: Detroit, Michigan, December 1951. Bulletin of the United States Bureau of Labor Statistics, No. 1086. https://fraser.stlouisfed.org/title/4510/item/495110

Poremba, David Lee. *Detroit: A Motor City History*. Charleston, SC: Arcadia Publishing, 2001.

Stoler, Ann Laura. *Race and the Education of Desire: Foucault's History of Sexuality and the Colonial Order of Things*. North Carolina: Duke University Press, 1995.

*Chapter Nineteen*

# "We're All in Our Private Traps"
## *Reconfiguring Suburbia's Protective Borders in* Psycho *(1960)*

Kevin Thomas McKenna

The bulk of cinema scholarship's discussion of mid-twentieth-century American suburbanization in the horror film has focused on Don Siegel's *Invasion of the Body Snatchers* (1956) or similar films, with Alfred Hitchcock's *Psycho* receiving little attention.[1] Suburban spatial ideology, however, plays a significant role in facilitating horror in Hitchcock's film. Both central characters, Marion Crane (Janet Leigh) and Norman Bates (Anthony Perkins), share a desire to distinguish the protective values of private space from the uncertain, ever-present threats of the public sphere, attempting to ward off threats that are more social than physical.[2] Marion seeks private protection in a marriage and suburban home with Sam, while Norman uses the Bates's antique residence to shield and protect his secrets. In their pursuit of what Marion calls a "private island," the two figures violate the spatial dichotomy between public and private that they venerate, ultimately revealing the private, domestic space of suburbia to be what Norman calls a "private trap."[3] Hitchcock's ambiguous characterizations and formal ruptures of private space's boundaries illuminate domestic privacy's inability to deliver the control, order, and protection it offers through suburbanization, a contradiction that casts suburban ideology as a monstrous force and suburbanites as its victims.

American suburbia, in the years immediately following World War II, was more than a place; it was a spirit, "a state of mind" that found its home in the undeveloped rural peripheries beyond urban metropolises and cities, growing with purchases of each newly constructed house.[4] Suburbia did not create monsters out of nothingness. Instead, suburbia's "physical distance, social distinction and a degree of cultural control" were an amalgamated reification of intensifying preexisting desires.[5] Political sponsorship supported the construction and purchases of homes in the suburbs that were merely "an outward expression" of the conceptual divisions suburban ideology perceived, desired, and socially enforced.[6] The expanding spaces and spreading ideology of postwar suburbanization harbored and empowered monstrosity.

*Psycho* critiques suburbanization in two ways. First, it uses the story of Marion and Norman to overtly challenge privacy's promises of security and control, which suburbanization places in rigidly enforced, presumably permanent, boundaries. Second, Marion and Norman transgress the revered social and material boundaries necessary to realize those promises, illustrating them as contradictory failures and illusions. Suburban ideology's recognizable tensions fuel the ambiguity Hitchcock masterfully wields to elicit horror in *Psycho*. Just as distinctions and associations between private and public space become blurred, so—for characters and spectators alike—do the dichotomies of victim and monster.

## THE HORROR OF THE SUBURBS

While markedly different from its predecessors, post-WWII suburbanization was not the first iteration of a large exodus from urban centers. In the nineteenth century, sharp divisions of public and private spheres taking hold in Victorian England were finding their way across the Atlantic.[7] The advent of "the steam ferry, the omnibus, the commuter railroad" and other modes of transportation enabled citizens of densely populated cities to retreat to the periphery by the middle of the century.[8] Once "the centrifugal movement of the middle class gathered force after 1865," many citizens no longer had to live in the densely populated cities where they worked.[9] The city—perceived as "dirty," "noisy," and ridden with crime, immorality, and unsavory communities—was sectioned off from the new center of virtuosity: the domestic home.[10] By 1870, privatization was built into the design of the detached home.[11] Early suburbanization's spatiality is symptomatic of its ideological associations with control, security, and order. Suburban ideology is a judgment, a dualistic value system equating suburban privacy with protection from the perceived evil city that was a threatening public space. While mid-twentieth-century suburbanization varies greatly in its scale from its nineteenth-century predecessor, its ideology is continuous, differing only in its greater intensity.

The massive relocation brought about by postwar suburbanization represented an emphatic shift from community found in public spaces to "privatization."[12] Following the Second World War, over 90 percent of the male and female population was marrying.[13] To accommodate the growth in domestic households created by people marrying at younger ages and having children at a higher rate, "the prefabricated suburban tract home" was offered as an alternative to urban living and relocated tens of millions of people.[14] Sociality was no longer confined to busy, crowded, public theaters, streets, and stadiums in the city, but relocated to the suburban home, the family yard, and the neighborhood street on a mass, hegemonic scale.[15]

Suburbia's domestication of the public social realm is illustrative of suburban ideology's construction of privatizing technologies and tools designed to offer mastery of the environment. The television was "the ultimate expression" of suburbanization's private consumption and mastery, and by 1960 a television could be found in 90 percent of all American homes.[16] The suburban television allowed families to extend out into the televisual world of the public, "to the global, to an infinity of reach" while maintaining the ability to control which images were brought back into the home through such masterful extension.[17] Television perfectly paired with suburban ideology's fixation on order and control; with the turn of the dial, families decided what type of world lay beyond their front door . . . and which parts would be permitted to enter.[18]

Yet, suburban privacy was not static—confined to the home and neighborhood—it was mobile, and masterful extension was paired with masterful exception.[19] Rapidly increasing car ownership in postwar years enabled suburbanization by providing a tool that offered accessibility to leisure and necessity still found in urban spheres or dispersed across suburban "low-density patterns."[20] The youth culture of suburbia valued the automobile's "mobility and privacy" for dates.[21] The newfound "drive-in culture" created by the intersection of these two developments exemplified suburban spatiality's contradictions and its problematic ideology.[22] While suburbia was designed to provide its residents with spatial and ideological distance from urban centers, the car provided necessary connection to the city, a masterful exception to its spatial separation, extending domestic privacy onto the public highway to go to public places.

The geographical boundaries between urban and suburban were less visible and less forcefully policed than the social barricades that existed to protect the perceived utopia of the suburbs. The language of "white flight" is so commonly associated with suburbanization that the two are almost synonymous,[23] and post-WWII suburbanization continued the process of "redlining" by which home appraisers and loan providers "undervalued neighborhoods that were dense, mixed, or aging," particularly in urban areas occupied by African American and marginalized ethnic communities.[24] Many suburbs instituted homeowners' associations that would ensure that "people of color were systematically excluded" in an attempt to maintain suburbia as an ideal exclusively for "white middle-class families."[25] The segregation of a privately controlled space by homeowners' associations reified the spatial separation of the public realm from the private community in a social form. In the context of suburbia, then, "privacy" is established through social barricades. Akin to the family's use of domestic walls as physical barriers against unwanted intrusion, suburban divisions and assumed mastery assigned the role of gatekeeper to entire suburban communities. While domestic gatekeeping represented mastery, its communal enforcement revealed its aim to construct order in social homogeneity, a "flattening out of . . . identities."[26] It recognizably materialized a social boundary of "us" and "them" by which order is contingent upon the identification and exclusion of the latter.[27]

Beyond its exclusive nature, suburban ideology also imposed rigid social control within suburbia via "domestic containment" and rigid gender roles.[28] Anxiety over the collapse of traditional private feminine spheres and masculine public space in the suburban home, the increasing frequency of wives joining the workforce, and the sexualization of youth culture reinvigorated policing of traditional gender spaces and roles.[29] In suburbia, the housewife's role was a passive one; she was expected to focus on caring for the children, home, and needs of her husband without complaint.[30] Deviation from suburban domesticity's culture of monogamy and heteronormativity—infidelity or homosexuality—would result in "ostracism," and ejection from the suburban social realm, and such intense pressures inflicted their own violence upon women.[31] Gender, not innate but socially constructed, was enforced by "rituals" designed to illustrate the woman's need for security and man's "ability to protect her," perpetuating suburban ideology's control over social behavior in its own backyard.[32] Women were stripped of any empowering independence and "voice."[33] Suburbia constructed privacy as a feminine need of security and masculinity's ability to offer control; mastery was unequally distributed.

Mid-twentieth-century suburbanization's privatization, and its monstrosity, was not merely a cultural phenomenon but a "government sanctioned ideal."[34] Suburbanization was made possible by the consumption of suburban goods and tools enabled by specific political actions. The government implemented legislation that facilitated the mass production of homes, financed the loans necessary to purchase such homes, and built the highways necessary to move into suburban homes without worry of accessibility to jobs in the city.[35] Thus, the government materialized and made suburban ideology readily available, supplying the private spaces and the means of masterful control and exception. Government sponsorship was a tacit endorsement of suburban ideology's social divisions and its values of control, order, and protection—an endorsement that further exculpated suburbia and suburbanites from its monstrous implementation of suburban values.

## HORRIFIC SUBURBAN IDEOLOGY IN *PSYCHO*

Alfred Hitchcock's desire to mark the "monster" of his horror film as an "internal/secular" threat to spectators, particularly suburban spectators, resulted in a film saturated with allusions to suburbia.[36] Marion's flight to Fairvale from Phoenix, using the highway and her private car to run away toward domestic bliss with her lover Sam Loomis (John Gavin), allegorizes flight from cities to the domestic suburb. The Bates Motel stands as a symbol of the sixty thousand motels that were operating at the time of the film's release—part of suburbia's drive-in culture.[37] Even Norman's explanation to Marion that they have vacancies because "[t]hey, uh, they moved away the highway" is a reference to the government's development of new highways to facilitate suburbanization.[38]

Can these allusions to suburbia be read, however, as a critique? The methods that Hitchcock uses to create a sense of horror in his work suggests that they can. The film establishes, through its two central characters, the same spatial and spiritual division of public and private that suburban ideology relies upon, then—almost immediately—shows it being transgressed and rendered ambiguous. *Psycho* thus simultaneously venerates and violates the core principle of suburbanization: that private space delivers the protection, control, and order it promises. Indeed, it renders claims of control and protection horrifyingly illusory.

Sigmund Freud, in his seminal text *Beyond the Pleasure Principle*, describes *angst* as "a particular state of expecting the danger or preparing for it, even though it may be an unknown one."[39] The latter element of the definition is central to Hitchcock's construction of spectatorial horror in *Psycho*, as the film challenges clear distinctions of victim and "monstrous other." Hitchcock's *oeuvre* and Bernard Herrmann's screeching score cue spectatorial anxiety, establishing the expectation of a threatening monster, but one that is never clearly controlled or defeated. Suburban ideology, which relies upon a clear spatial dichotomy of *private* and *public*, a social dichotomy of *us* and *them* . . . perceived to identify, control, and master monstrous threats, is the film's true monster.

When Marion and Norman dine together in the parlor, Hitchcock formally separates and juxtaposes the pair to seemingly erect the necessary boundaries for spectators to establish a clear monster-victim dichotomy. Hitchcock stages Marion in the back left of the room at the dining table and Norman in the front right corner of the room. He divides the room via shot-reverse-shots, framing each character in medium shots that alternate and push into close-ups, highlighting suburban divisions. Marion is sitting on a cushioned bench, behind the table set with a decorative sugar container and elegant white

*Domestic plates and private space in* Psycho.

*Public world and private control in* Psycho.

pitcher, next to curtained windows and an electric lamp—elements which visually assign her to a modern, domestic, interior space.

When Hitchcock cuts to the reverse-shot, it is just that, a reversal. Norman is sitting on a wooden chair, with a wooden chest behind him, upon which sits two stuffed birds surrounded by decorative shrubbery and a candle.

Unlike the windows over Marion's shoulder, the wall behind Norman holds hanging pictures. Norman is pictured in a *mise-en-scène* that equates him with an antiquated and obsolete external, natural world. Through a suburban lens, the editing and visual associations seem to imply a clear identification of suburban advancement and domesticity that might position Marion as the potential victim or heroine and Norman as the threatening monster from the public sphere.

However, while the shot-reverse-shot structure seems to dichotomize the two, the sequential back and forth of these shots actually relates and entangles them. Both Marion and Norman express suburban ideology in their masterful and controlling desires to clearly divide private and public space. Marion's encounter with Norman in the parlor at the motel illustrates her devotion to the suburban ideal. Marion explains that she is in search of a "private island," a domestic utopia with Sam where she can escape the unwanted advances, male gaze, and perceived judgment that she endures in the public sphere. She is positioned on the couch, surrounded by china, eating slowly and modestly—depicted as if she is already in the family dining room, a space that suburbia prescribes and for which she yearns. Marion seeks suburban domesticity's security.

For Norman, the parlor scene exemplifies his shared desire for suburban promises. Just as the kitchen utensils and interior domestic appliances highlight Marion's coveting of domestic security, the shots of Norman illustrate his coveting of the control of privacy. Suburbia's promised masterful and controlling extension is embodied in the birds found in the background. Norman tells Marion: "I enjoy stuffing birds because they are quite passive, to begin with." His hobby is not birds, as he clarifies before this line, but "stuffing things." Norman enjoys the assumption of an active role that follows the process of manipulating passive, deceased things from the outside world and integrating them into his private space. The birds hang not as exemplars of the threatening exterior world described earlier but are, instead, privatized totems reminding him of his authoritative and masterful masculine activity. To this end, both characters are connected to suburbanization's private ideals.

While the spectator sees Norman framed in medium shots gradually pushing in to close-ups, the camera dramatically shifts from a frontal position to a profile shot tilted at an upward angle. Because this cut first introduces the owl, the only bird of prey, at the mention of "Mother," the owl and its attacking posture which looms over Norman in the background can be read as "Mother." Norman desires to control "Mother," keeping her suppressed and the secret of her corpse domestically contained. After Norman expresses his hatred for the "illness" afflicting "Mother," Marion asks: "Wouldn't it be better if you put her . . . *someplace*?" As Norman leans forward, mimicking the owl's (therefore "Mother's") attacking posture, he asks: "You mean an institution? A madhouse?" He characterizes the institution's public nature as a violent opposition to domesticity. It is loud with "the laughing and the tears" and densely populated with "all the eyes studying you," much like the densely populated public spaces of urban cities. If institutionalized, "Mother" would lose her control, and so, too, Norman would lose his control over "Mother." Norman shares Marion's reverence for privacy because of its capacity for masterful control.

Both Marion and Norman wish to make real the promises of suburban ideology, but in order to do so, both must transgress the very boundaries that promise suburban privacy. After the film's establishing shot, when the camera moves through the window to interrupt the privacy of their afternoon tryst, Marion is lying on the bed in her bra and skirt while Sam stands shirtless above her. Marion expresses her disdain for having to engage in secretive, lurid, intolerable, and threatening (according to suburban ideology) romance: "Oh Sam, I hate having to be with you in a place like this." Marion sees herself from the ordered and controlled perspective of the domestic housewife: as a threatening, sexualized "other." She wants to eschew secret privacy for secure privacy, and with it, attain the self-exculpating exception to maintain these structures of judgment but direct them beyond herself. However, her determination to escape spaces sanctioned as "taboo" and shed her image of herself as suburban other forces her to violate suburban norms of feminine passivity.[40] Marion initiates the dinner date at home with her mother and sister, overbears Sam's initial apprehension to this idea, and steals $40,000 from Tom Cassidy (Frank Albertson) to make this domestic practice permanent, completely inverting suburbia's notion of masculinity and femininity.[41] Rather than relying on Sam to deliver security, she actively violates not only criminal law but the unwritten social contract of suburbia to obtain her own secure space.

Norman, similarly, must violate the very bounds of private space in his quest to assert a position of activity and control. When he stuffs birds, though they are already passive and perhaps already dead, he still must penetrate their feathers and skin, transgressing the most private of borders. Norman repeats this material intrusion of privacy with his gaze. His desire for control and order, and perhaps his emerging lust for Marion, causes him to peer through the hole he cut in the wall between the parlor and Room 1. His gaze extends into Marion's private space as she undresses and prepares to shower, then pulls her lurid image back into his private space of the parlor. His role as watcher, however, is hidden by the wall. He realizes suburban ideology's promised protective, self-exculpating mastery in his ability to reach out and penetrate private spaces, satisfying his epistemological control (the need to know what Marion is doing, how she looks in this moment), but he must puncture the firm boundary of the wall in order to exert this masterful extension. Norman occupies the role of gatekeeper, but he must pierce and weaken the gate to do so.

## HORRIFIC SPACE

Marion and Norman's reverence and transgression of suburban social and spatial ideals are best understood by Julia Kristeva's theory of *abjection*, which Barbara Creed applies to the horror film in *The Monstrous-Feminine*. In Creed's formulation: "That which crosses or threatens to cross the 'border' is abject. . . . Abject things are those that highlight the 'fragility of the law' and that exist on the other side of the border which separates out the living subject from that which threatens its extinction."[42] Stated more simply, abjection is a process by which a subject is confronted by a former piece of itself: a threat to the life of the subject, that underscores the porosity of borders and fractures their protective quality. Marion shifts from subject to abject subject by stealing money from her employer, exposing the "fragility of the [suburban social] law" because she recognizes its inability to limit activity to the masculine. Norman highlights the "fragility of the [suburban spatial] law" because his desire for control comes at the expense of privacy itself.[43]

The fragility of both laws is expressed through their incompatibility. For Marion to realize suburban promises of protective domesticity and marriage, she must violate the social parameters of domesticity (which would limit her to being a subservient and passive woman) in order to erect the same protective barriers Norman enjoys. Kristeva notes that "abjection is above all ambiguity. . . . It does not radically cut off the subject from what threatens it—on the contrary, abjection acknowledges it to be in perpetual danger."[44] Marion's premarital sexual relationship with Sam victimized her at the expense of constrictive, morally bound suburban ideals of celibacy; however, her inversion of suburban gender roles, her only means of transgression, solidifies her role as monstrous threat to suburban domesticity. Marion as monstrous threat can best be seen in her disruption of Norman's masterful control of the domestic container. Her presence disrupts Norman's attention and focus, drawing it to her, allowing "Mother" to seep out. Marion's mere presence posed a mortal threat to Norman's orderly world, which hastened his "ejection of the abject" and her suffering.[45] In this sense, Marion's presence in the film holds suburban institutions, and spectators, in perpetual *angst*, while Marion is both a victim and threat to suburban gender conventions.[46]

Norman, perceived as *Psycho*'s monster for obvious reasons, is also an abject subject victimized by his own monstrous transgressions. Returning to the owl as "Mother's" gaze, Norman is always under her watchful eye. Despite the material boundaries of the parlor wall and the Bates's house, he is always visible within the sight of "Mother," yet without the ability to always see or confine her. Norman is incapable of preventing "Mother" from overtaking his body, transgressing his most personal private boundary—he is the bird that is stuffed and "Mother" the taxidermist. In his attempt to exert mastery by domestically containing "Mother," he is permanently subjected to the domestic hierarchy—the subservient passivity of the dutiful son. Norman's masterful exception to move between material boundaries with ruptures and returns ultimately leads to his own downfall. As he realizes that Lila (Vera Miles) has penetrated the protective walls of his house, a point-of-view long shot from Lila's perspective out the window depicts Norman running back to restore order and control by resecuring his domestic privacy. However, it is the return—Norman's assumed mastery of returning to the role of controlling gatekeeper—that prompts Lila to run to the steps where she sees the cellar door. It is Norman's attempt to regain control that causes "Mother's" secrets to escape their domestic container, leading to its collapse and reversal. By the film's end, Norman is physically contained in jail and psychologically dominated by "Mother."

Marion and Norman share a reverence for suburban ideology and its promises of a private enclave, but in their attempts to achieve these goals both transgress the spirit of suburbia. The presented "fragility" of suburban boundaries ultimately results in the failures of their promises. The fracturing of private space unsettles the clear distinction of self and "other," victim and monster, that parallel—and are made more visible—by spatial segregation. Marion and Norman are each other's monsters, and in the course of the film each secures the demise of the other by attacking the suburban ideals the other valorizes.

Abjection's ambiguity and plurality is made most visible because the Bates Motel is a liminal and abject space. The parlor scene, and the majority of the remaining film, take place in inherently liminal settings. Geographically, the motel is an interstitial point between urban Phoenix and suburban Fairvale. Motels are, by nature, private businesses established along public highways that offer private spaces of rest and retreat open to public rental. The desolation of the Bates Motel makes public encounters unlikely but not impossible.

Norman's parlor is a private personal space, but one that adjoins the public guest-check-in desk. It is thus a hybrid, ambiguous space—quasi-private and quasi-public. Despite the Motel's ambiguity, Marion and Norman choose to treat the space as solely private, rendering them vulnerable to, and ultimately victims of, the threats arising from its public nature. Marion assumes that her room provides security, but it is, like her, penetrated and violated; Norman assumes that he can wield masterful control, but this assumption suffers the same death. The suburban boundaries that sustain these qualities are so rigid that they promote transgression, a process which exposes and further weakens their inherent fragility.

Liminality and spatial ambiguity render such hybrid spaces as abject, perpetually threatening to turn privacy's promises of mastery and control into falsehoods.[47] When Marion first arrives at the Bates Motel, Norman explains its desolation in relation to the postwar government-funded highway projects: "We have twelve vacancies. Twelve cabins. Twelve vacancies. They, uh, they moved away the highway." What was once a masterful extension of domestic privacy's security and protection has been pushed beyond new idealized suburban visions into the realm of public space and ideals. The motel has no occupants, the Bates have no income, and Marion has no witnesses as a result of the highway's relocation. The Bates Motel is thus a victim of suburbanization. Once an emblem of suburban necessity and innovation, the motel is now a threatening space in its isolation and inability to offer protection; its abject nature threatens domestic privacy. The Bates Motel is a "place" where privacy's "meaning collapse[s]," perpetually threatening the "extinction" of privacy.[48] Its abject space, the site of transgressive violence, serves as the catalyst that invites the transgression of the Bates's home's security and privacy, realizing the fragility of boundaries in their contradictory and impermanent nature.

## THE HORRIF(IED/YING) SUBURBANITE

Alfred Hitchcock extended the horrific ambiguity of the Bates Motel into the theatrical spaces in which the film was seen. In 1960, the novel circumstances under which *Psycho* was exhibited constructed the urban movie theater—at least for the suburban spectator—as an abject space, implicating it as a monster complicit in perpetuating suburban horrors and perpetual victims awakened to privacy's instability. Marion's trip in *Psycho*, allegorical of suburban migration, also self-reflexively allegorizes the historical suburban spectator's commute from private home to the public theater to see the film. The film industry was ill-prepared for the postwar expansion of the suburbs and the subsequent migration, so "first-run premieres" were still concentrated in "the downtown houses."[49] A major-studio release by a noted director—like *Psycho*—thus required the suburban spectator to commute, likely by private automobile, to a public downtown theater.

Hitchcock exerted command over the theaters that screened *Psycho* to what was, at the time, an unheard-of degree, forcing suburban spectators to willingly relinquish the perceived mastery and control they enjoyed at home.[50] Prior to *Psycho*'s release, American theaters were quasi-public places; they were privately owned but had open admission policies that allowed a person passing by on the street to purchase a ticket and enter the auditorium regardless of whether the film was about to begin or partway through.[51] Filmgoers could, if they chose, arrive midway through a film, watch the second half of the story, and then remain until the next screening to watch the beginning. Hitchcock, in order to keep the mid-story murder of the (apparent) heroine and "Mother's" true identity a surprise, imposed a no-late-admissions policy and required spectators to "stand patiently in ticket holder lines."[52] These policies transferred autonomy and control from the realm of spectator to that of director and theater manager, in effect, transforming the theater into a quasi-private space. Privacy was still associated with control, but neither was offered to the spectator, who now assumed a submissive role but retained the expectation—albeit undelivered—that complete control would be returned.[53]

This passage of authoritative control, however, is a transgression of suburban ideology's assigned roles and spatial values, cultivating an ambiguous space which opens up the spectator to ambiguous definitions of monster-victim. The *Psycho* theater was only quasi-private because the spectators' physical performances of shock—screams, jumps, and shakes—awakened them from individualized, docile viewing experiences to public performance.[54] The spectators, like Norman, could see the reactions of their fellow audience members across a "rich mix of allusions to gender, class, and nationality" but also recognize themselves as vulnerably visible, like Marion, to the gaze of others.[55] While perhaps shared by spectators of earlier horror films, this recognition is particularly troubling for the suburban spectator because it recognizably dissolved suburban social boundaries—offering proximity, and, perhaps, likeness to the suburbia's threatening "other"—in an ambiguous space which threatened the static singular distinction of private and public space. Additionally, the failed desires for security and control predicated on private boundaries that were being reflected on screen were part of the same ideology shared by suburban spectators.

The horrific ambiguity which undermines the certainty of privacy and mastery is left unresolved by the film's end. In the penultimate shot of the film, as Norman, subsumed by "Mother," sits in the jail cell and breaks the fourth wall by staring at the spectator with a grin as an image of a skull is momentarily superimposed atop his face, the scene giving way to the final shot of Marion's car being pulled from the swamp where Norman hid it. Formally, the boundaries between these frames are reconfigured as they collapse atop one another to form a single image. Norman's victimization by Mother and her violently threatening presence are no longer contained by the jail cell, but also extend into the private space of the car—the mobile, private space suburban spectators will now use to return to their private homes. The shot does not offer the spectator Creed's ejection of the abject subject, a separation of the threatening "other" that restructures boundaries in a new way. Instead, *Psycho*'s conclusion is, in Kristeva's words, "not purification but . . . [a] rebirth with and against abjection."[56] Negating purification and ejection, the film offers ambiguity in its conclusion. The film does not reestablish suburbia's spatial and social boundaries, but leaves them open, forcing the suburban spectators to redraw such bounds. Yet, the ease with which suburban spectators relinquished their masterful control and protection realizes that notions of mastery and order built into the foundation of suburban homes is merely an illusion. The film presents monsters as relational constructions of their potential victim; the boundaries that identify, barricade, or contain these monsters as fragile; and perpetual vulnerability as inescapable even in a private suburban home.

## CONCLUSION

Hitchcock's *Psycho* critiques the values of suburbanization in two distinct ways. First, allusions and references within the film signal suburbanization's alienating and exclusionary violences, reflecting the historical horrors of the suburbs. Second, *Psycho* uses Marion and Norman as figural reflections of suburbanization's private privileges and desires, only to have both characters violate the very ideological boundaries they wish to preserve. Marion and Norman's violation, and inability to rectify the stability, of such boundaries simultaneously presents a horrifying ambiguity to the spectator and an incommensurability that draws back upon the political critique of suburbanization in the film. The historical spectator is implicated as a monstrous consumer in suburbanization's alienating violence and victim to its inability to offer protection and stability in privacy. Norman/"Mother's" threatening fourth-wall breach in the final superimposition redirects Norman's proclamation from the parlor scene toward the suburban spectator: Their "private islands" are, in fact, "private traps."

## NOTES

1. Latham, "Subterranean Suburbia." To list all the references and myriad of ways suburbanization is studied in *Invasion of the Body Snatchers* would be too comprehensive for this note. The aforementioned reference, rather, is merely intended to be emblematic of the cultural commentary I wish to redirect toward *Psycho*.

2. It is important to note that from here, our discussion of the film will designate public space through two registers. The first level is geographical, in that the suburb is the place of the private community that offers individual households in an atomized privacy as opposed to spontaneity and business of the public urban environment. The second level is social, in that the material structure of the home separates internal private lives from external public lives outside of the home.

3. The quotes "private island" and "private trap" derive from Marion and Norman's conversation in his parlor office in the motel which will receive much further attention later in this analysis.

4. Silverstone, "Introduction," 13.

5. Ibid., 5.

6. Jackson, *Crabgrass Frontier*, 3.

7. Spigel, *Make Room for TV*, 12.

8. Jackson, *Crabgrass Frontier*, 20.

9. Ibid., 147.

10. Jackson, *Crabgrass Frontier*, 42, 149; Miller, "Family Togetherness and the Suburban Ideal," 398–399.

11. Jackson, *Crabgrass Frontier*, 56, 185; Miller, "Family Togetherness and the Suburban Ideal," 398. A "suburban style" began to emerge, with lawns and gardens that isolated the house and a hall and front parlor that divided social from familial spaces within the home.

12. Butsch, *The Making of American Audiences*, 247.

13. Ibid.

14. Butsch, *The Making of American Audiences*, 247–248. According Butsch, between 1946 and 1962, "23 million new homes were built in the United States, at least two-thirds in [the] suburbs . . . [and relocated] approximately 50 million people."

15. Beauregard, *When America Became Suburban*, 129.

16. Beauregard, *When America Became Suburban*, 113; Spiegel, *Make Room for TV*, 39, 102. Whether used for social viewing parties with neighbors or the locus of family togetherness, the television's "ability to bring 'another world' into the home . . . often figured as the ultimate expression . . . in utopian statements concerning 'man's' ability to conquer and to domesticate space."

17. Silverstone, "Introduction," 10.

18. Spiegel, *Make Room for TV*, 122.

19. Spiegel, "From Theatre to Space Ship," 225.

20. Car ownership remained fairly "stable" immediately before World War II, "at about 30 million vehicles" from 1930 to 1948, but then increased to 49 million vehicles in 1950 (Jackson, *Crabgrass Frontier,* 247); the rapid growth continued, reaching 74.4 million vehicles by 1960 (Dargay, "Vehicle Ownership and Income

Growth, Worldwide: 1960–2030," Table 1, 5). See also Beauregard, *When America Became Suburban*, 111, 128.

21. Bailey, *From Front Porch to Back Seat*, 19.
22. Jackson, *Crabgrass Frontier*, 246, 254–255.
23. Lassiter and Niedt, "Suburban Diversity in Postwar America," 4.
24. Jackson, *Crabgrass Frontier*, 197–198.
25. Spiegel, *Make Room for TV*, 6.
26. Ibid. The omitted word here signaled by the ellipsis is "religious." Spiegel here is making note of the ambiguity surrounding "white" referring to Catholic, Protestant, and Jewish people coming together in a suburban community. I diminished Spiegel's emphasis on religion here because I think that it can be more widely applied and compatible with Lassiter and Niedt's critique of suburbanization's racial misrepresentations to refer to the more important consequence of homogeneity and arbitrary binaries.
27. Tuan, *Space and Place*, 50.
28. Spiegel, *Make Room for TV*, 34.
29. Bailey, *From Front Porch to Back Seat*, 104, 108. Bailey notes: "In 1940, married women comprised only one-third of the total number of working women; within ten years the proportion of married women workers leaped to 52 percent."
30. Beauregard, *When America Became Suburban*, 126. Despite 52 percent of women entering the workforce after World War II, "[m]en, and many women, expected women to care for the children, maintain a home, and make the purchases that allowed her to be successful at both," and working in the public sphere was perceived to be a signal of lower class.
31. May, "'Family Values': The Uses and Abuses of American Family History," 10, 15. In the 1950s, as May states, there was "rampant alcohol and drug abuse among suburban housewives."
32. Ibid., 110. The "rituals," which Bailey notes were prescriptions, such as: men opening the car door for their female dates, paying for dates, and ordering the food for female dates.
33. Ibid. I intend this quote to echo its literal and figurative meaning in the same way Bailey uses it—by restricting women to speak to order their own meal and express an active role in romantic relationships and assert active roles in the world.
34. Spiegel, *Make Room for TV*, 33.
35. Spiegel, *Make Room for TV*, 33; Beauregard, *When America Became Suburban*, 84.
36. Tudor, *Monsters and Mad Scientists*, 49.
37. Jackson, *Crabgrass Frontier*, 254.
38. This exchange happens in the office of the Bates Motel. Marion asks if a room is available, and Norman references the highway to explain that nobody is staying at the motel at this time.
39. Freud, *Pleasure Principle*, 11, n.2.
40. Ibid.
41. Bailey, *From Front Porch to Back Seat*, 110, 21, 23. These actions reflect the control and dominance meant to be expressed by men in suburban dating rituals, but

just as striking here is the theft of the money itself. Bailey notes: "Money—men's money—was at the center of the dating system. . . . Money purchased obligation; money purchased inequality; money purchased control." Therefore, just providing the money for the home, regardless of the other actions, would be enough to violate the containment and impotence suburban ideology marks feminine.

42. Creed, *Monstrous-Feminine*, 10–11.
43. Ibid., 10.
44. Kristeva, *Powers of Horror*, 6.
45. Creed, *Monstrous-Feminine*, 10.
46. Marion's victimhood here is in reference to her victimization as an object for unwanted attention and gaze throughout the film: Cassidy, her boss Lowery, the policeman she encounters when fleeing from Phoenix, Norman, and the spectator.
47. This is a reference to Norman's line in the parlor that the colloquial aphorism "eats like a bird is actually a f— . . . fals— . . . falsity." So, too, as I am arguing, is suburbanization's privileging of domesticated private spaces.
48. Creed, *Monstrous-Feminine*, 10.
49. Gomery, "Coming of Television," 8; Nasaw, *Going Out*, 248; Pautz, "Decline," 3; Heffernan, *Ghouls, Gimmick, and Gold*, 66.
50. Williams, "Discipline and Fun," 362–364.
51. Ibid., 363.
52. Ibid.
53. Ibid.
54. Ibid., 364.
55. Ibid.
56. Creed, *Monstrous-Feminine*, 10; Kristeva, *Powers of Horror*, 31.

## BIBLIOGRAPHY

Bailey, Beth. *From Front Porch to Back Seat*. Baltimore: Johns Hopkins University Press, 1988.

Beauregard, Robert. *When America Became Suburban*. Minneapolis: University of Minnesota Press, 2006.

Blas, Elshiva. "The Dwight D. Eisenhower National System of Interstate and Defense Highways: The Road to Success?" *The History Teacher* 44, no. 1 (November 2010): 127–142.

Butsch, Richard. *The Making of American Audiences: From Stage to Television 1750–1990*. Cambridge, UK: Cambridge University Press, 2000.

Creed, Barbara. *The Monstrous-Feminine: Film, Feminism, Psychoanalysis*. London: Routledge, 1993.

Dargay, Joyce, Dermot Gately, and Martin Sommer. "Vehicle Ownership and Income Growth Worldwide: 1960–2030." *The Energy Journal* 28, no. 4 (2007): 140–173.

Freud, Sigmund. *Beyond the Pleasure Principle*, translated by James Strachey. New York: Norton, 1961.

Gomery, Douglas. "The Coming of Television and the 'Lost' Motion Picture Audience." *Journal of Film and Video* 37, no. 3 (Summer 1985): 5–11.

Heffernan, Kevin. *Ghouls, Gimmick, and Gold: Horror Films and the American Movie Business, 1953–1968*. Durham, NC: Duke University Press, 2004.

Hendershot, Cindy. "The Cold War Horror Film: Taboo and Transgression in *The Bad Seed*, *The Fly*, and *Psycho*." *Journal of Popular Film and Television* 29 (2001): 20–39.

Jackson, Kenneth. *Crabgrass Frontier: The Suburbanization of the United States*. Oxford, UK: Oxford University Press, 1985.

Kristeva, Julia. *Powers of Horror: An Essay on Abjection*. Trans. by Leon S. Roudiez, New York: Columbia University Press, 1982.

Lassiter, Matthew, and Christopher Niedt. "Suburban Diversity in Postwar America." *Journal of Urban History* 39 (2013): 3–14.

Latham, Rob. "Subterranean Suburbia: Underneath the Small-town Myth in the Two Versions of *Invaders from Mars*." *Science Fiction Studies* 66 (1995): 198–208.

May, Elaine Tyler. "'Family Values': The Uses and Abuses of American Family History." *Revue Francaise d'Etudes Americaines* 97 (September 2003): 7–22.

Miller, Laura. "Family Togetherness and the Suburban Ideal." *Sociological Forum* 10, no. 3 (September 1995): 393–418.

Nasaw, David. *Going Out: The Rise and Fall of Public Amusements*. Cambridge, MA: Harvard University Press, 1999.

Pautz, Michelle. "The Decline in Average Weekly Cinema Attendance: 1930–2000." *Issues in Political Economy* 11 (Summer 2002): 54–65.

Silverstone, Roger. "Introduction." In *Visions of Suburbia*, edited by Roger Silverstone, 1–25. New York: Routledge, 1997.

Spigel, Lynn. *Make Room for TV: Television and the Family Ideal in Postwar America*. Chicago: University of Chicago Press, 1992.

———. "From Theatre to Space Ship: Metaphors of Suburban Domesticity in Postwar America." In *Visions of Suburbia*, edited by Roger Silverstone, 217–239. New York: Routledge, 1997.

Tuan, Yi-Fu. *Space and Place: The Perspective of Experience*. Minneapolis: University of Minnesota Press, 1997.

Tudor, Andrew. *Monsters and Mad Scientists: A Cultural History of the Horror Movie*. Cambridge, MA: Basil Blackwell, 1989.

Williams, Linda. "Discipline and Fun: Psycho and Postmodern Cinema." In *Reinventing Film Studies*, edited by Christine Gledhill and Linda Williams, 351–378. Oxford: Oxford University Press, 2000.

# Index

9/11, 84, 103n25, 268, 271

abduction, 64, 248, 253, 256, 259–60
abjection, 86, 103, 105, 136, 163,
 170–75, 202, 207, 313–17
abuse, 127, 163–64, 166, 286, 288;
 family, 268, 273, 275, 291,
 284–85, 287
aesthetics, 20, 38, 116, 135, 166–69,
 190, 239, 311;
 montage, 8, 149, 211–22;
 reflection, use of, 189, 216
African Americans, 123, 296, 307;
 and poverty, 195–207;
 and commodification, 247–60
aging, 5, 170
Aguilar, Emiliano, 7, 147–61
ambiguity, 65–67, 82, 86, 306, 313–14,
 317, 319n26;
 spatial, 315–16
ambition, 23, 155–59, 174, 196
Amenábar, Alejandro, 7, 181–92
American dream, 79, 91, 131, 139, 143,
 247
Amit, Rea, 5, 15–31
*The Amityville Horror* (novel 1977, film
 1979), 6, 87
anarchy, 7, 109, 115–26
Anderson, Benedict, 55

*Angriff der Lederhosenzombies* [*Attack
 of the Lederhosen Zombies*], (2016),
 33–46
anxiety, 4–5, 65–66, 86, 91, 300, 308–9;
 about the future, 131–43, 150;
 about social class, 87, 248, 302;
 economic, 66, 79, 81–85, 90, 131–43;
 social, 22, 24, 27
architecture, 6, 87
Austria, 5, 33–51, 228

Banco, Lindsey Michael, 6, 79–97
Barker, Andrew, 288
Barker, Clive, 147, 196, 203
Baxter, John, 214–15, 222n2
Beal, Timothy, 1
Benjamin, Walter, 183–84
Bergland, Renée, 39
"biopower," 301
Bitel, Anton, 215, 220, 222, 223n16
*The Black Cat* (1934), 8, 227–45
Blake, Linnie, 56, 150
Blickle, Peter, 34
Bloody Mary (myth), 195, 197
*Blutgletscher* [*Blood Glacier*], (2013),
 33–51
bodies
 as property, 250–59;

exploitation of, 71–75, 249, 261nn8–9, 262n20
Botting, Fred, 207
bullying, 268, 274, 276
Burger, Alissa, 9, 279–92
*Burnt Offerings* (novel 1973, film 1976), 83, 85

*Candyman* (1992), 8, 195–209
cannibalism, 4, 101, 104, 267, 271
*Castle Rock* (2018), 9, 279–92
"category crisis," 5
Catholicism, 7, 72, 181–90, 191n21, 213, 258, 275
certainty, 2, 6, 8, 79–81, 86, 92n6, 190, 195–209, 213–14, 296, 302, 316
childhood, 1,3,46, 64, 85, 133–34, 258, 267–68, 276, 279–80, 287–88
city and danger, 136, 294, 297. *See also* crime; Detroit; decay, urban
class
  lower, 6, 86–87, 104, 106, 109, 148, 319n30;
  upper, 2, 64, 81, 87, 89, 123, 127n4, 156, 296;
  middle, 7, 9, 71, 83, 88, 104–11, 117, 125, *131*, 132–43, 156–57, 164, 270, 293–303, 307, 316;
  working, 2, 9, 63, 65–66, 72–73, 87, 93, 100, 103–4, 110–11, 150, 154, 156–57, 164, 198;
classism, 6, 99–113, 195–206;
  privilege, 2, 8, 80, 115, 122, 126, 202, 206–7, 317. *See also* economics
claustrophobia, 16, 187, 229, 232, 272, 274
climate change, 41–50
Clover, Carol, 170, 272–73, 276–77
Cohen, Jeffrey, 1, 4–5
Cold War, 103
Coleman, Robin Means, 203
Colonialism. *See* imperialism

community, 33, 40, 46, 55, 70, 105, 109, 198, 200–207, 281–82, 285, 295, 301, 306, 308, 318n2, 319n26
conflict, generational, 142, 285
conformity, 41, 71, 150–52
Confucianism, 22, 60
Conservatism, 7, 147–60, 275
control, 2–4, 60, 69, 71, 90–91, 101, 151, 159, 164, 171, 181, 183–84, 187–89, 238, 247, 250, 255, 285, 301, 305–20;
  loss of, 5, 44, 73, 105, 109, 117, 257, 275, 312, 316–17
counter-memory, 61
counterculture, 271
*Cradle Lake* (novel 2013), 84–92
Creed, Barbara, 313, 317
crime, 7, 23, 53, 58, 63, 68, 100–11, 115–27, 136, 141, 156, 200, 247, 296–97, 299, 306
Crowley, Aleister, 232, 241n15
Crutzen, Paul J., 44

Davinson, Rayna, 20
decay
  bodily, 155, 174, 200, 219, 295–96;
  social, 7, 66, 85, 93n20, 138;
  urban, 71, 131, 132, 138–39, 142–43
Dempsey, Michael, 214
*Deranged: Confessions of a Necrophile*, 6, 99, 106–11
Derrida, Jacques, 18, 35
Detroit, 7, 9, 131–43, 196, 293–303
*Devil's Rejects, The* (2005), 9, 267, 270–71
Diana, Princess of Wales, 154
Diaz, Eric, 73
difference, 2–4, 35, 65, 71–72, 105, 109, 125–26, 207
disability, 107, 140
Dissanayake, Wimal, 56, 61
Doctrine, 115, 147–48, 184–86, 190
"domestic containment," 308
domestic sphere. *See* space, domestic

domesticity, 79, 89, 104, 308, 311–13
*Don't Breathe* (2016), 7, 131–43
*Don't Look Now* (1973), 8, 211–26
doubling, 186, 255, 269
*Dream Demon* (1985), 7, 148–59
du Maurier, Daphne, 213, 217–19, 222, 223n9, 224n46
DVDs, 18, 127n3, 163
dystopia, 6–7, 46, 115–27

economics
 anxieties, 4, 6–7, 79–92, 116–25, 131–43;
 capitalism, 3, 41–46, 70, 73, 81, 86, 88–91, 99, 103, 139–41, 150;
 free market, 80, 139, 150;
 market forces, 6, 79–92, 99–111, 115–27, 131–43, 147–59;
 mobility, 147–59, 272, 274, 296–97;
 uncertainty, 6, 63, 66, 70, 72, 197.
 See also American dream; Great Recession
Eisenstein, Sergei, 214
entitlement, 121, 123, 126, 139, 143, 296
evil, 8–9, 53, 60–67, 84, 101, 103, 154–55, 202, 205, 270, 275, 277, 279–88, 303, 306

Falklands War, 151–52
family, dysfunctional, 99–111, 181–90, 267–77, 305–17
*The Family Plot* (novel 2016), 87, 89–91
"family values," 147, 150, 153–54
Farber, Stephen, 215
Fascism, 33–34, 230, 232
fear
 of technology, 5, 15–27, 87–90;
 of violence, 5, 63, 68, 70–72, 100–11, 115–27, 139–40, 142, 151–52, 197–200, 203, 248, 252–53, 260, 267–69, 277, 281–89, 296–97, 299, 308, 315–17;
 of globalization, 15, 35, 46, 70–71;
 of unrest, 5;
 of social change, 5;
 homophobia, 4, 155, 282, 308
Feineman, Neil, 212
femininity, 65, 151, 158, 312
"Final Girl," 37, 141, 273, 276–77
"The Forbidden," (short story) 196
Foucault, Michel, 301
Frankenstein, Victor [fictional character], 64–68
Freud, Sigmund, 2, 42, 80, 186, 309
Fuchs, Michael, 5, 33–51, 93n11

gatekeepers, 308, 313–14
gender, 1, 22–23, 40, 53–61, 64–74, 94n50, 149, 151, 195–96, 206, 301, 308, 316
gender roles, 58, 66, 71–73, 147, 150, 159, 313
Genette, Gérard, 35
"geography of evil," 8, 198
Gerow, Aaron, 18
*Get Out* (2017), 8, 247–63
ghosts. See haunting
Giroux, Susan Searls, 275
*The Golem* (1920), 228–30, 240n7
Gothic, 7, 63–66, 79–92, 140–53, 147–59, 217, 219, 223;
 American, 101–6;
 British, 36, 132, 181–83;
 Southern, 83, 89–90, 95, 132
Grant, Barry Keith, 71
Great Recession (2008), 7, 79–80, 131–32
grief, 60, 186, 213, 218, 220, 258

Hake, Sabine, 230
*Halloween* (1978), 267–68, 272–73, 277
*Halloween* (2007), 9, 102, 135, 275, 277
Halttunen, Karen, 107
*The Handyman* (novel 2017) 86–87, 91
Harrington, Michael, 103
*The Haunted* (novel 2012), 86–87

haunting, 6, *39*, 67, 79–92, 93n11, 93n20, 150, 182, 186–87, 190, 219, 269, 281
*The Haunting.* See *The Haunting of Hill House*
*The Haunting of Hill House* (novel 1959; film 1963, 1999), 80, 82, 91–92
Hayward, Susan, 55
*A Head Full of Ghosts* (novel 2015), 87–88, 91
*Heimat,* 5, 33–51
*Heimatfilm,* 34, 37–38, 45–46
*Hell House* (novel 1971, film 1973), 80, 82
*Hellraiser* (film 1987), 7, 147, 150, 153, 155–58
Herron, Jerry, 297
hillbillies, 4, 99–113. See also rednecks
Hills, Matt, 44
Hitchcock, Alfred, 9, 82, 212, 223n9, 267, 305–17
Hjorth, Larissa, 24
Hobbes, Thomas, 6, 115–29
Hobsbawm, Eric, 3
Hoeveler, Diane, 202
Hollywood
  and women, 7, 163–80
home invasion. *See* invasion, home
hometown, 281, 288, 298
Hooper, Tobe, 267, 269, 271, 277n2
horror
  Japanese, 5–6, 15–27, 28n3, 53–62, 184;
  Korean, 5–6, 15–27, 53–62;
  rural, 70, 99–111, 267–77.
  *See also* slasher film; Gothic
house
  as domestic space, 66–67, 150–52, 157, 186–90, 285, 305;
  as refuge, 67–68, 86–87, 183, 268–69, 272;
  as financial burden, 84–86, 91;
  as symbol of success, 85, 104, 157–59.
  *See also* haunting; space

*The House Next Door* (novel 1978, telefilm 2006), 83
*House of 1000 Corpses* (2003), 9, 267–82
*House of the Devil* (2009), 169
hypermasculinity, 6, 53–61
"hyperreal," 40, 287

identity, 5–8, 15–19, 33–34, 41, 54–61, 63–73, 87, 94, 122–24, 155–57, 199–207, 250–51, 273, 276, 280, 285, 296
ideology, 1, 3–4, 8, 33–34, 55, 60, 65–68, 74, 83, 122, 147–50, 196, 202, 231, 249, 257, 305–17
imperialism, 35, 56–57, 67–70
*In 3 Tagen bist du tot* [*Dead in 3 Days*], (2006), 33–49
independent film, 163–75
individualism, 101, 141, 150, 154–58
invasion
  home, 7, 59, 131, 138, 141, 148, 156, 182, 184, 187, 189–90;
  military, 229
*IT* (1990, 2017), 279–92
*It Follows* (2014), 7, 9, 131–43, 293–304

James, Benjamin, 7, 131–43
James, Wendy, 196, 201
Japan, 5–6, 15–31, 53–62, 184
Juvé, Juan, 7, 147–61

Kael, Pauline, 217, 219
Kaplan, E. Ann, 56
Kee, Jessica Baker, 203, 207
Kershner, Gregory, 204
Kim, Ji Young, 27
King, Stephen, 279–92
Kit, Borys, 44
Koenig, Frederick, 199
Koo, Luisa, 6, 53–62
Korea, 5–6, 15–31, 53–62
Kristeva, Julia, 313, 317

*Last House on the Left*, 101–2, 277n1
law, 115, 312–13;
  corruption, 271–72
Leffler, Yvonne, 44
liminality, 4, 9, 35, 64, 67, 74, 182–90, 287, 314–15
*Little Girls* (novel 2015), 84–86, 91
Lizza, Katherine, 9, 293–304
loss, 3, 33, 46–47, 66, 128n9, 133, 143, 157, 182–83, 201, 258, 285, 297
Lovecraft, H. P., 3–4

madness, 101, 105, 107, 182, 187, 229, 237, 239
Magistrale, Tony, 282
Mana, Davide, 79
Marino, Allyson, 6, 63–76
masculinity, 94n48, 104, 119, 121, 150–51, 202;
  domestic space and, 150–51, 308, 311–13;
  Korean, 6, 53–62
McKenna, Kevin Thomas, 9, 305–21
McNeill, John R., 44
Meeuf, Russell, 7, 131–43
memory, 38–39, 61, 86, 183, 202, 224n37, 229, 282, 297, 300
middle class, 9, 71, 156, 164, 306;
  as moral exemplars, 105–6, 110–11;
  economic decline of, 131–43, 293–304.
  *See also* American dream; class; suburbs
Mies, Maria, 73
millennial generation, 166, 268, 270–71, 277;
  economic anxieties of, 132, 134, 137, 142, 302
Miller, Cynthia J., 1–11, 195–209
Miramax Films, 163, 165
miscegenation, 203, 207
Mitchell, David Robert, 293, 295, 300
modernism, 229–31
modernity, 7, 23, 33, 45, 88, 104, 107–8
monstrosity, 65–66, 74, 88, 103–6, 108, 110, 186, 189–90, 202, 235, 306

the monstrous, 1–2, 64–65, 68–69, 71–73, 121, 150, 182, 201–202, 206, 280
monstrous feminine, 171
"monstrous other," 309
moral typography, 282
morality, 63–64, 81, 104, 107, 139–41, 183, 233, 275, 306
Moreno, Erika Tiburcio, 6, 99–113
Morrill, Jacqueline, 9, 267–78
Moser, Susanne, 45
Mosher, David L., 54
*Mother's Day*, 6, 99, 106, 108–11
Muir, John Kenneth, 222
Mumblecore, 7, 165–68, 170, 172, 174–75
Mumblegore, 7, 163, 166, 168–74
Murphy, Bernice, 90, 104
Muschietti, Andy, 280–85

national cinema, 19, 55–57
national myth, 53–56, 61
nationalism, 1, 3, 15, 33–34, 63.
  *See also* identity
Nealon, Jeffrey, 275
necrophilia, 107, 232, 234, 237
neoliberalism, 7, 81, 92, 137, 139–42, 147–61
Newman, Kim, 35, 64
Ng, Andrew Hock-Soon, 186
Ni Fhlainn, Sorcha, 198
Niezgoda, Brandon, 7, 163–80
*A Nightmare on Elm Street* (1984), 102, 151
normalcy, 84, 103, 105–8, 110
nostalgia, 33, 132, 142, 281, 290
Nye, Joseph, 36
Nyong'o, Lupita, 163, 174

Oliete-Aldea, Elena, 79
*One Missed Call* (2003), 16, 25–26
oppression, 7, 34, 57, 59–61, 106, 111, 175, 189, 247, 249, 296
Orvell, Miles, 281
Other, the, 57, 65, 67, 277

*The Others* (2001), 7, 181–92
Ouelette, Jennifer, 286

Pagnoni Berns, Fernando Gabriel, 7, 147–61
Pak, Hyeong-Jun, 27
paranoia, 37, 157, 172, 300–1
patriarchy, 6, 53, 57–58, 60, 65, 67–68, 72, 74, 141, 150, 169, 171, 188
patronization, 172
Peele, Jordan, 8, 247–49, 252–56, 258–60, 261nn8–10, 262n21
Peitzman, Louis, 285
*Penny Dreadful* (television series, 2014–2016), 6, 63–76
*Phone* (2002), 16
phones, 37, 54;
  cellular, 16, 21–25, 27, 90, 248;
  landline, 16–17, 19, 22, 134
Phu, Thy, 19
Pinedo, Isabel Cristina, 203
Pinker, Stephen, 3
place, role of in horror films, 4, 7–9, 33–35, 134, 140, 163, 186–89, 196–201, 247–63, 267–78, 279–92, 294–99, 305–21
plantation, 132, 249, 251–52, 254–56
Poelzig, Hans, 229–31
Poisa, María Gil, 7, 181–92
political economy, 1
politics, 3, 5, 9, 15, 27, 44, 55–56, 60, 83, 101, 102, 116, 118–19, 121–22, 124–27, 147, 150–52, 154, 170, 276, 301, 305, 308
POPfilms Collective, 163, 168, 178n48
possession, 41, 67, 83, 88, 172, 184
Poul, Alan, 203
poverty, 1, 9, 99–100, 102–3, 105, 109–11, 125, 131–32, 135–42, 198–99, 274, 281, 293, 296–98.
  *See also* class
power, 7, 35–36, 44, 70, 71, 94nn48–50, 108, 110, 111, 142, 163, 196, 296, 300–1;
  economic, 86, 89, 90, 99, 122–23;

feminine, 58, 60, 103;
patriarchal, 53, 65, 68;
political, 61, 63, 116, 124–27, 149, 152, 157;
social, 66, 202, 204, 206, 275
Prasch, Thomas, 8, 211–26
privacy, 9, 271, 275, 305–8, 311–17, 318n2
privatization, 147–48, 306–8, 311
Procházka, Martin, 281
*Psycho* (1960), 9, 82, 104, 267, 271, 277, 305–21
psychology, environmental, 9, 267–78
*The Purge* trilogy (2013, 2014, 2016), 6–7, 115–29

race, 1, 8, 65, 153, 195–96, 198, 206, 271, 287, 296
racism, 5, 102, 126, 200, 207, 249, 251, 255, 281, 283, 287, 296
Raphael, Raphael, 36
rednecks, 6, 99, 103–5, 111.
  *See also* hillbillies
Reiff, Michael C., 8, 247–63
religion, 1, 5, 88, 124, 126, 271.
  *See also* Catholicism
Rice, Charles, 184
*The Ring Virus* (1999), 16, 21–23, 25
*Ringu* (1998), 15, 17, 18–23, 25–27
Roeg, Nicolas, 8, 211–26
Rojas, Carlos, 18
Rose, Bernard, 8
Rothman, Joshua, 282

sacrifice, human, 123–24, 205, 207, 234
Sanderson, Mark, 212, 213, 218, 219, 223n9, 223n13
Satanism, 231–35, 236
"savage cinema," 267
Schneider, Steven Jay, 36, 82
Schwaab, Herbert, 230–31
Science, 5, 69
Scott, A.O., 281
*Scream* (1996), 9, 16, 277
Scruton, David, 3

security, 34, 109, 117, 121, 137–39, 156, 267–68, 270, 277, 294, 299, 306–8, 311–12, 315–16
*The Sentinel* (novel 1974, film 1977), 83
serial killers, 37, 99, 102, 105–7, 168, 199, 274, 279
sexual abuse, 27, 285;
 harassment, 126, 167, 285;
 predators, 132, 164–65, 173, 282–83;
 rape, 121, 142
sexuality, 25, 101, 107, 133, 140, 155, 158, 172, 257, 268, 301;
 teenage, 119, 133, 273, 276;
 transgressive, 153, 160n27, 232–33, 236–37, 242n29, 313;
 Victorian, 63–64
shock, 100, 141, 154, 213, 222, 237, 248, 256, 283, 316
Siddique, Sophia, 36
*Silver Bullets* (2011), 170–72
Sinyard, Neil, 212, 219
slasher film, 37–38, 40, 102, 106, 108, 131, 133, 135, 147, 252, 271, 273, 277, 293
slavery, 27, 41, 69, 71, 123, 132, 198, 249–59, 261n19
social upheaval, 2, 101
space, 16, 34, 46, 66, 85, 94n41, 183–84, 186–87, 198, 206, 212–13, 268;
 domestic, 66–67, 150–52, 157, 186, 188–90, 271–75, 285;
 liminal, 4, 185–86, 287, 314;
 private, 16, 22, 140, 276, 299, 305–6, 308–17;
 public, 67, 73, 150, 306, 308–9, 314–17
Stanfield, James, 252, 258
*Starry Eyes* (2013), 172–74
Steffen, Will, 44
stigma, rural, 136
subjectivity, 4, 53, 55, 57, 60–61, 184
suburbs, 3, 37, 101, 111, 272;
 as model of behavior, 104–6, 276;
 as refuge, 125, 303–21;

 as site of violence, 83–85, 117–18, 121, 125, 259, 267, 274;
 decay of, 9, 133–37, 293–304;
 racism in, 247–48.
 *See also* American dream; white flight

taboo, 72, 80, 100, 101, 141, 186, 312
technophobia, 15.
 *See also* fear
*The Tempest* (1611 play), 68–69
"terrible place," 163
*The Texas Chainsaw Massacre* (1974), 9, 267, 272, 277
Thatcher, Margaret, 7, 147–61
time, and terror, 215
Time's Up Movement, 163, 167–68, 173
Tipton, Elise, 23
Tomita, Hidenori, 24
Tomkins, Silvan S., 54
torture, 105, 111, 123, 173, 195, 230, 233, 237–40, 267, 269–71,
"torture porn," 271
towns, small, 38, 40, 280–82
traces, 39, 44
"traces of inhabitation," 183–84
transnationalism, 5, 15, 18, 20, 26–27, 34–37, 41–42, 46, 70
trauma, 86, 117, 141, 182–83, 187, 303;
 childhood, 268, 279, 288;
 national, 6, 53–62;
 past, 132, 140, 186, 235
Tsai, Peijen Beth, 19
Tudor, Andrew, 4–5

Ulmer, Edgar, G., 8, 227–32, 234, 236–37, 239–44
uncanny, 4, 34, 38–39, 181–82, 186–89, 231
United Kingdom, 147–61
urban legends, 195–97, 199, 204, 206, 208
urban decay, 117–19, 122, 124–29, 131–43, 293–304
"urbanoia," 272

*V/H/S* (2011), 168–69, 174–75
Van Riper, A. Bowdoin, 1–11, 115–29
violence, celebration of, 100–2, 127, 277n1

*The Wailing* (2016), 6, 53–62
war, and slaughter, 228–29
Ward, James J., 8, 227–45
Wee, Valerie, 20
Weinstein, Harvey, 163, 165, 170–71
Weirzbicki, James, 18, 20
werewolves, 64–65, 68, 103, 170–72
Westernization, 23
white flight, 295, 297, 307
white trash, 104, 106, 136, 271, 273
whiteness, 9, 136–37, 155, 294, 296, 298–99
Whitney, Allison, 16
Williams, Tony, 36
witches, 6, 64–65, 69–71, 73–74
Wittgenstein, Ludwig, 206
Wolfreys, Julian, 65–66
women, 6–7, 55, 58, 65–66, 89, 94, 101, 104, 108–11;
 ghosts of, 23, 53–54, 58–61, 170;
 social role of, 6, 22–23, 64, 69–70, 72–74, 103, 108, 140, 149, 152, 154, 157–59, 262n21, 272–76, 277n1, 296, 308, 313, 319n29;
 violence against, 27, 55, 58–59, 121, 156, 163–64, 169, 173, 197, 202, 249–52, 259–60, 251, 269, 273.
 *See also* witches
Wood, Robin, 34
World War I, 33, 183, 227–29, 232, 240n6
World War II, 15, 20, 39–40, 58, 181;
 postwar era, 20, 33–35, 247, 295, 305–6, 318n20, 319n30

xenophobia, 9, 26

Yoon, Kyong, 24
*You're Next* (2011), 170
youth culture, 7, 9, 24, 63, 117, 122–23, 131–43, 293–304, 307–8

Zombie, Rob, 267–69, 270–77
zombies, 4, 34, 41–43, 103, 121, 133, 239

# About the Editors

**Cynthia J. Miller** is a cultural anthropologist, specializing in popular culture and visual media. Her writing has appeared in a wide range of journals and anthologies across the disciplines. She is the editor of *Too Bold for the Box Office: The Mockumentary, From Big Screen to Small* (2012) and *Silence of the Lambs: Critical Essays on Clarice, a Cannibal, and a Nice Chianti* (2016), and co-editor of *Steaming into a Victorian Future* (2012, with Julie Anne Taddeo), *Border Visions: Identity and Diaspora in Film* (2013, with Jakub Kazecki and Karen A. Ritzenhoff), *Urban Noir: New York and Los Angeles in Shadow and Light* (2017, with James J. Ward), *The American Civil War on Film and TV: Blue and Gray in Black and White and Color* (2017, with Douglas Brode), and *Horrific Humor and the Moment of Droll Grimness: Sidesplitting sLaughter* (2017, with John A. Dowell). She is also series editor for Lexington's *Film and History* book series and serves on the editorial advisory boards for *The Journal of Popular Culture* and *The Journal of Popular Television*.

**A. Bowdoin Van Riper** is a historian who specializes in depictions of science and technology in popular culture. His publications include *Science in Popular Culture: A Reference Guide* (2002); *Imagining Flight: Aviation and the Popular Culture* (2003); *Rockets and Missiles: The Life Story of a Technology* (2004; rpt. 2007); *A Biographical Encyclopedia of Scientists and Inventors in American Film and Television* (2011), and *Teaching History with Science Fiction Films* (2017). He was guest editor, with Cynthia J. Miller, of a special two-issue themed volume (Spring/Fall 2010) of *Film & History* ("Images of Science and Technology in Film,") and the editor of *Learning from Mickey, Donald, and Walt: Essays on Disney's Edutainment Films* (2011). He is the editor of the *Martha's Vineyard Museum Quarterly*.

**Miller** and **Van Riper** are coeditors of *Undead in the West: Vampires, Zombies, Mummies, and Ghosts on the Cinematic Frontier* and its "sequel" *Undead in the West II: They Just Keep Coming* (2012, 2013), *1950s "Rocketman" TV Series and Their Fans: Cadets, Rangers, and Junior Space Men* (2012), *International Westerns: Re-Locating the Frontier* (2014), *Horrors of War: The Undead on the Battlefield* (2015), *The Laughing Dead: The Horror Comedy Film from* Bride of Frankenstein *to* Zombieland (2016), *What's Eating You?: Food and Horror on Screen* (2017), *Divine Horror: Essays on the Cinematic Battle between the Sacred and the Diabolical* (2017), *Terrifying Texts: Essays on Books of Good and Evil in Horror Cinema* (2018), *Elder Horror: Essays on Film's Frightening Images of Aging* (2019), and *Horror Comes Home: Essays on Hauntings, Possessions, and Other Domestic Terrors* (2019).

# About the Contributors

**Emiliano Aguilar** received his MA from the Universidad de Buenos Aires (UBA)—Facultad de Filosofía y Letras (Argentina). Among his publications are essays in *New Heart and New Spirit: Perspectives on the Modern Biblical Epic*, edited by Wickham Clayton; *Orphan Black and Philosophy*, edited by Richard Greene; *The Man in the High Castle and Philosophy*, edited by Bruce Krajewski; *Giant Creatures in Our World: Essays on Kaiju and American Popular Culture*, edited by Camille Mustachio and Jason Barr; and *American Horror Story and Philosophy*, edited by Richard Greene.

**Rea Amit** is visiting assistant professor of Asian Studies at Knox College, Illinois. He received an MA from Tokyo University of the Arts in aesthetics, and PhD from Yale University in film and media studies and East Asian languages and literatures. He has published on Asian media, aesthetics, and theory in journals such as *Philosophy East and West, Positions: Asia Critique, Participations: International Journal of Audience Research, New ideas in East Asian Studies*, as well as a chapter dealing with misrepresentations of Otherness in Japanese and Indian media for an edited volume on media culture in trans/national Asia.

**Lindsey Michael Banco** is an associate professor of American literature and culture at the University of Saskatchewan and has interests in gothic literature and nuclear culture. His articles and book reviews appear in *The French Review of American Studies, American Literary History, Journal of Popular Film and Television, Arizona Quarterly*, and *Gothic Studies*. He is the author of two books: *Travel and Drugs in Twentieth-Century Literature* (2009) and *The Meanings of J. Robert Oppenheimer* (2016).

**Fernando Gabriel Pagnoni Berns** is a doctoral student and works as a professor at the Universidad de Buenos Aires (UBA), Facultad de Filosofía y Letras (Argentina). He teaches courses on international horror films, and his work has been published in edited volumes such as *To See the Saw Movies: Essays on Torture Porn and Post 9/11 Horror*, edited by John Wallis, and *Critical Insights: Alfred Hitchcock*, edited by Douglas Cunningham. He is currently writing a book about the Spanish horror TV series *Historias para no Dormir* and editing an anthology celebrating the Frankenstein bicentennial.

**Alissa Burger** is an assistant professor of English and Director of Writing Across the Curriculum at Culver-Stockton College. She teaches courses in research, writing, and literature, including a single-author seminar on Stephen King. She is the author of *Teaching Stephen King: Horror, The Supernatural, and New Approaches to Literature* (2016) and *The Wizard of Oz as American Myth: A Critical Study of Six Versions of the Story, 1900–2007* (2012). She is currently at work on a book on Stephen King's *Dark Tower* series, its genre engagements, and its interconnections with King's larger canon.

**Michael Fuchs** is a fixed-term assistant professor in American studies at the University of Graz in Austria. He has coedited six collections, most recently *Intermedia Games—Games Inter Media: Video Games and Intermediality* (2019). In addition, he has authored and coauthored more than fifty journal articles and book chapters, which have appeared in venues such as *The Journal of Popular Culture*, *The Journal of Popular Television*, *The Cambridge History of Science Fiction* (2019), and *B-Movie Gothic: International Perspectives* (2018). For additional information on his past and ongoing research, check out his website, www.michael-fuchs.info.

**Benjamin James** teaches screenwriting, film history, and film production at the University of Idaho. His recent courses have focused on the history of US horror films and the cinematic legacy of Mary Shelley's *Frankenstein*. He has written two feature-length screenplays: *Captivity*—about his parents' kidnapping by Chechen terrorists; and *The Trail*—a horror-western set in the 1830s. He is currently developing the short psychological horror film: *Wake*.

**Juan Juvé** holds an MA degree in social sciences from the Universidad de Buenos Aires (UBA), Facultad de Ciencias Sociales. His publications include chapters in edited collections such as *Science Fiction and the Abolition of Man: Finding C. S. Lewis in Sci-Fi Film and Television*, edited by Mark J. Boone and Kevin C. Neece; *Bad Mothers: Regulations, Representations, and Resistance*, edited by Demeter Press; *Requiem for a Nation: Religion, Politics* and *Visual Cultures in Post-war Italy (1945-1975)*, edited by Roberto Cavallini; and *Twilight Zone and Philosophy*, edited by Heather Rivera.

**Luisa Hyojin Koo** is enrolled in the PhD program at the English department at the University of Wisconsin-Milwaukee. Her major area of interest includes Korean horror films, global and national cinema, trauma studies, and cultural representation. She received her Master of Arts in English from Yonsei University, and Bachelor of Arts in Comparative Literature and Culture from Underwood International College of Yonsei University. She is currently writing her dissertation on Korean national trauma and myth as portrayed by national films, as well as teaching composition and film classes in Milwaukee.

**Katherine Lizza** received her MA in American studies from Lehigh University and is an alumnus of Penn State University. She specializes in researching the historical influences of pop culture, specifically in American horror films. She previously taught a course at Penn State on the cultural history of horror and presented at the 2018 Film and History Conference. When she's not watching scary movies, Katherine enjoys spending time with her wife and cat in Pennsylvania. She can be found at thescholarinthewoods.wordpress.com.

**Allyson Marino**, PhD, is an assistant professor of English at Saint Leo University in Saint Leo, Florida, where she teaches courses on Love and Desire in Literature, Caribbean Literature, Critical Theory, and Literature and the Environment. Additionally, she is a cocreator of a new bachelor's degree program in medical humanities. Her research interests include women's literature, environmental studies, and US multiethnic literature and postcolonial studies.

**Kevin Thomas McKenna** is an adjunct instructor of humanities in the philosophy department at University of Central Florida. He earned a Master of Arts in film studies from the Humanities and Cultural Studies Department at University of South Florida. His research stands at the intersection of genre films, ecocriticism, and political economy, interrogating various spatiotemporal ontologies' role in shaping relationships of violence or care through American postwar suburban ideology to contemporary neoliberal globalization and privatization. Fusing ecocritical and spatial theoretical approaches to his investigations of political theory, he reveals privatization's displacements and pursues potential revisions in social and environmental contexts.

## About the Contributors

**Russell Meeuf** is an associate professor and director of the film & television studies program at the University of Idaho, where he researches issues of cultural diversity in popular media. He is the author of *Rebellious Bodies: Stardom, Citizenship and the New Body Politics* (2017), and *John Wayne's World: Transnational Masculinity in the Fifties* (2013). He is currently researching race and social class in contemporary, U.S. horror films.

**Erika Tiburcio Moreno** focused her PhD research on the serial killer in American horror movies from the 1960s to 1980s, analyzing the cultural and historical influence of this monster. She has published *Y nació el asesino en serie. El origen cultural del monstruo en el cine de terror estadounidense* (2019) and contributed to a chapter about the female monster in *Masters of Horror* for *Gender and Contemporary Horror Television*, edited by S. Gerrard, S. Holland, and R. Shail. Her interests include cultural studies, history, horror and popular culture.

**Jacqueline Morrill** holds an MFA in poetry from Sarah Lawrence College and has been performing poetry in and around New England for the last fifteen years. Though she has written two chapbooks and been published in numerous online and print journals, it is her love of horror that dominates her higher education curriculum at both Worcester State University and Clark University. Her fascination with cannibalism, psychopathy, and supernatural spiritualism serve as both poetic inspiration and educational prompts in her day-to-day life as an adjunct instructor. She currently lives on Lake Chargoggagoggmanchauggagoggchaubunagungamaugg with her partner and their barnyard of dogs and cats.

**Brandon Niezgoda** is a lecturer in communication studies at Drexel University, with writing having been published in *Fast Capitalism* and *First Monday*. His research focuses on the intersection of millennial culture, humanities, and the media industries, notably coediting *Global Perspectives on Health Communication in the Age of Social Media* (2018). Outside of academia, he works for the Public Health Management Corporation.

**Maria Gil Poisa** was born and raised in Galicia, Spain, and moved to the United States in 2010, where she earned her PhD in Hispanic studies from Texas A&M. She has taught Spanish language and culture, as well as film studies, at Texas A&M, Bates College, and College of the Holy Cross. Her research focuses on the fields of horror studies, film studies, and Hispanic studies.

## About the Contributors

**Thomas Prasch** is Professor and Chair of History at Washburn University. Recent publications include essays on F. W. Murnau's *Faust,* Robert Eggers's *The Witch,* noir-screwball fusions of the mid-1980s, Alfred Russel Wallace's spiritualism and evolutionary thought, and ethnicities in Henry Mayhew's *London Labour and the London Poor.*

**Michael C. Reiff** is a CollegeNow English instructor for Tompkins Cortland Community College at Ithaca High School, where he also teaches film studies. He curates and instructs the classics at the Carriage House film seminar through Cayuga Community College. He is also an English instructor at the Upward Bound summer program at Cornell University. Michael has been published in multiple books, including *Horror by the Book, Divine Horror,* and *Silence of the Lambs.* He will also be a guest lecturer at the upcoming 2019 Central New York Silent Film Festival. Michael lives in Auburn, NY, with his wife Anna and son Jack.

**James J. Ward** is a professor of history at Cedar Crest College where he teaches courses in European history, German history, Russian history, urban history, and film and history. He has published articles and reviews in *The Journal of Contemporary History, The Journal of Interdisciplinary History, Central European History, Slavic Review, The Journal of Popular Culture, The Historical Journal of Film, Radio, and Television,* and *Film & History,* among others. With Cynthia J. Miller, he coedited *Urban Noir: New York and Los Angeles in Shadow and Light* (2017).

www.ingramcontent.com/pod-product-compliance
Lightning Source LLC
Chambersburg PA
CBHW052056300426
44117CB00013B/2157